Strangers at Home

Jews in the Italian
Literary Imagination

Lynn M. Gunzberg

UNIVERSITY OF CALIFORNIA PRESS

Berkeley / Los Angeles / Oxford

University of California Press
Berkeley and Los Angeles, California

University of California Press
Oxford, England

Library of Congress Cataloging-in-Publication Data
Gunzberg, Lynn M.
    Strangers at home: Jews in the Italian literary imagination / by
Lynn M. Gunzberg.
        p.   cm.
    Includes bibliographical references and index.
    ISBN 0–520–07840–3
    1. Italian literature—History and criticism.   2. Jews in
literature.   3. Ethnic relations in literature.   I. Title.
PQ4055.J48G86   1992
850.9′35203924—dc20   91–46159
                                                                        CIP

Printed in the United States of America

1   2   3   4   5   6   7   8   9

For my father
Arthur S. Gunzberg
and in memory of my mother
Aline DuBin Gunzberg

Contents

Illustrations

Acknowledgments

This project was begun in the now distant 1975 as research on what seemed an obscure topic for a dissertation at the University of California, Berkeley and has evolved over the years as Italian and American interest in Italian Jews has developed and flourished. The research year in Florence, 1975–1976, would have been considerably shortened without the intervention of St. James's American Episcopal Church, which offered me their Katherine B. Child Estate Scholarship.

Brown University has likewise been generous by facilitating several research trips through its Faculty Travel Grants. Similarly, I am grateful to the Fulbright organization, specifically to the U.S. Department of Education and to the Committee for the International Exchange of Scholars for grants that allowed me the luxury of conducting extended research unhampered by other concerns in the summer of 1982 and during the academic year 1983–1984. Most particularly, I wish to thank Dean Sheila Blumstein and my colleagues, who assumed my duties in addition to their own, for the precious gift of leave time in the winter and spring of 1991; that, and a grant from the American Philosophical Society, made it possible for me to complete my research in the summer of 1991. Most of this work was done at the Biblioteca Nazionale Centrale of Florence, some at the Biblioteca Nazionale "Vittorio Emanuele" in Rome, institutions whose often difficult working conditions are more than compensated for by the richness of their collections.

Sincere thanks are due to Stanley Holwitz, Michelle Nordon, and

Diana Feinberg of the University of California Press for their efforts on my behalf.

Surely, I owe an enormous debt of gratitude to friends and associates who have helped me in so many ways over the years. I am immensely grateful to Dante Della Terza for his unstinting encouragement. From the time we met, over ten years ago, Sergio Romano has taken an active interest in the project, ferreting out books that could be of interest and discussing them with me. Marino Raicich, former director of the Gabinetto Vieusseux, opened the resources of his library to me and graciously put at my disposal his great knowledge of modern Italian culture. Several friends gave parts of the manuscript good tough readings and made valuable suggestions at various stages: Robert Dombroski, Samuel Cohn, Abbott Gleason, and the late David Herlihy. Gabriella Battista helped me wade through mountains of Fascist journals. With unfailing patience, Clare Durst guided me through the maze of computer techniques and, with cheerful accuracy, Cherrie Guerzon input revisions when I was unable to do it myself. Despite the pressures of their own work, two people read and re-read and helped me in other ways I shall never be able to repay. They are Jacqueline Gutwirth and, especially, my best critic and my best friend, my husband, Anthony Molho.

Introduction

The history of Italian Jews has been largely ignored by the English and American public. For years following World War II, any discussion of the Jews' tragic fate during the 1930s and early 1940s drew mostly on the experience of German and East European Jewry. Scholars and other commentators made occasional references to the experience of Jews in France, and sometimes, thanks to the moving account left us by Anne Frank, of Jews in Holland. But it was rare that these discussions took into account the suffering of Italy's Jewish population. Together with the Jewish settlements in Greece, Bulgaria, and Yugoslavia, the Jews of Italy seemed to have been forgotten, at least outside their homeland.

This lamentable situation has been gradually changing. Historians and literary critics—in England, the United States, and, of course, Italy—have written, with insistence and with moving eloquence, about the horrible experiences of the Italian-Jewish community during the years 1938–1945.[1] These accounts have struck a responsive chord with the public in English-speaking countries. Semipopular magazines such as the *New York Review of Books,* the *New Yorker,* and the *London Review of Books* have engaged distinguished scholars to contribute articles and sympathetic reviews of recent books devoted to Italy's Jews.[2] And

1. For a compelling and intimate account of the fate of Italian Jews, see A. Stille, *Benevolence and Betrayal: Five Italian Jewish Families Under Fascism* (New York: Summit Books, 1991).

2. See, for instance, A. Momigliano's account of Italian Jewish life in *New York Review of Books* 32, no. 16 (24 October 1985): 22–26, reprinted as "The Jews of Italy," in

American publishers have shown a commendable inclination to provide their readers with translations of works on the history and experiences of Italian Jews.

Several reasons might account for the revival of interest in the history of a Jewish community whose ancestry is rooted in Roman times. Perhaps most important, at least in the United States, has been the critical success of Primo Levi's memoir of Nazi captivity, *Se questo è un uomo* (*Survival in Auschwitz*) written in 1947, shortly after the author's return from Auschwitz.[3] An English translation followed in 1960.[4] Undoubtedly this translation added an Italian perspective to non-Italians' awareness of the history and fate of Italy's Jews. At first, the work did not attract the attention it merited, certainly not among American and English readers. But within the last ten years, English translations of nearly all of Levi's works have finally appeared. Although the wrenching fact of his captivity ultimately informs all his writings, Levi's austere and moving autobiographical works go well beyond the boundaries of the concentration-camp experience. He has delved into his family's more distant past and has assembled a collective portrait of some of his ancestors, creating in the process a picture of Italian-Jewish society in the generations immediately preceding the enactment of the Fascist racial laws.[5] Levi's works, together with those of Giorgio Bassani,[6] provide non-Italian readers with the most comprehensive literary portraits of modern Italian-Jewish life. Bassani in particular shows how many educated Italians supported fascism and espoused racial attitudes.

A. Momigliano, *On Pagans, Jews, and Christians* (Middletown: Wesleyan University Press, 1987), 238–253.

3. P. Levi, *Se questo è un uomo* (Turin: F. De Silva, 1947; Einaudi, 1958).

4. P. Levi, *Survival in Auschwitz* (London: Orion Press, 1960).

5. P. Levi, *Il sistema periodico* (Turin: Einaudi, 1975); English ed.: *The Periodic Chart* (New York: Shocken Books, 1984). Other notable works are: *La tregua* (Turin: Einaudi, 1963); English eds.: *The Truce* (Oxford: The Bodley Head, 1965), *The Reawakening* (Boston: Little, Brown, 1965); *Se non ora, quando?* (Turin: Einaudi, 1982); English ed.: *If Not Now, When?* (New York: Summit Books, 1985); *Ad ora incerta* (Milan: Garzanti, 1984); *I sommersi e i salvati* (Turin: Einaudi, 1987); English ed.: *The Drowned and the Saved* (New York: Summit Books, 1988), among others.

6. The best known of Giorgio Bassani's writings is *Il giardino dei Finzi-Contini* (Turin: Einaudi, 1962); English ed.: *The Garden of the Finzi-Continis* (New York: Athenaeum, 1965). Other works of Jewish interest include the stories "Una lapide in Via Mazzini," "La passeggiata prima di cena," "Gli ultimi anni di Clelia Trotti," "Lida Mantovani," in *Cinque storie ferraresi* (Turin: Einaudi, 1956); English ed.: *A Prospect of Ferrara* (London: Faber and Faber, 1962), and the short novel *Gli occhiali d' oro* (Turin: Einaudi, 1958), English ed.: *The Gold-Rimmed Spectacles* (London: Faber and Faber, 1960).

Bassani can be given major credit for having introduced the English-speaking public in the early 1960s to the subject of Italian Jews under fascism.

Other Italian Jews, themselves aging survivors of World War II, have rushed to record their own memoirs, evoking in their writings the horrors of the 1930s and 1940s as well as the peaceful and prosperous years preceding the imposition of the laws that systematically discriminated against them and their contemporaries simply because of their Jewishness.[7] Among these are depictions of Jewish family life such as Natalia Ginzburg's *Lessico famigliare* (*Family Sayings*), Augusto Segre's *Memorie di vita ebraica* (*Memories of Jewish Life*), Liliana Picciotto Fargion's *Lungo le acque tranquille* (*Along the Quiet Waters*), and Guido Artom's *I giorni del mondo* (*The Days of the World*). Others focus primarily on the Fascist period, such as Giancarlo Sacerdoti's *Ricordi di un ebreo bolognese: illusioni e delusioni 1929–1945* (*Memories of a Bolognese Jew: Illusions and Delusions 1929–1945*), Vittorio Segre's *Storia di un ebreo fortunato,* (*Memoirs of a Fortunate Jew*), and parts of Nobel-laureate Rita Levi Montalcini's charming autobiography, *Elogio dell'imperfezione* (*In Praise of Imperfection*). In categories perhaps by themselves are meditations on Jewish life and culture in Arnaldo Momigliano's *Pagine ebraiche* (*Jewish Papers*), Elsa Morante's novel *La storia* (*History*), and one of the first postwar renderings of the Italian-Jewish experience, Giuliana Tedeschi's searing Holocaust memoir, *Questo povero corpo* (*This Poor Body*). Alongside this spate of memoirs, a number of scholars have also explored the history of the Italian Jews, not only during the two decades of Fascist domination, but also during the last two centuries of Italian history.[8] And given the troubled racial climate in Italy today,

7. N. Ginzburg, *Lessico famigliare* (Turin: Einaudi, 1963), English ed.: *Family Sayings* (London: Hogarth Press, 1967); A. Segre, *Memorie di vita ebraica* (Rome: Bonacci, 1979); L. Picciotto Fargion, *Lungo le acque tranquille* (Milan: Pan, 1979), and *Il libro della memoria. Gli Ebrei deportati dall' Italia (1943–1945)* (Milan: Mursia, 1991); G. Artom, *I giorni del mondo* (Milan: Longanesi, 1981); G. Sacerdoti, *Ricordi di un ebreo bolognese: illusioni e delusioni 1929–1945* (Rome: Bonacci, 1983); V. Segre, *Storia di un ebreo fortunato* (Milan: Bompiani, 1985); English ed.: *Memoirs of a Fortunate Jew* (Bethesda: Adler & Adler, 1987); R. Levi Montalcini, *Elogio dell'imperfezione* (Milan: Garzanti, 1987); English ed.: *In Praise of Imperfection* (New York: Basic Books, 1988); A. Momigliano, *Pagine ebraiche* (Turin: Einaudi, 1987); E. Morante, *La storia* (Turin: Einaudi, 1974); English ed.: *History: A Novel* (New York: Knopf, 1977); G. Tedeschi, *Questo povero corpo* (Milan: Editrice italiana, 1946).

8. A very partial listing must include these fundamental works on the Fascist period: R. De Felice, *Storia degli ebrei italiani sotto il fascismo* (Turin: Einaudi, 1961, 1972); M. Michaelis, *Mussolini and the Jews* (Oxford: The Clarendon Press, 1978); G. Mayda,

exemplified in part by a newspaper poll about anti-Semitism in 1988 and most poignantly by the death of a young boy in the bombing of the Rome synagogue on 9 October 1982, the subject of Italian Jews has become a subject of pressing interest. Scholars and members of the wider public seem to share this judgment.

However diverse the works recently published on Italian-Jewish history and however different the intentions of their authors, one finds in them a widely shared opinion, a view that appears as a refrain: that the Italian-Jewish experience until the imposition of the Fascist racial laws was special and different from that of other European Jewish communities. It is argued that when compared to the discrimination and persecution encountered by Jews in Russia, Poland, and Germany, the Jews of Italy enjoyed freedoms and a tolerance among their Christian compatriots which were remarkable for the times. But Italian Jews were better off even in comparison to their French coreligionists. During the very years when France was being torn apart by the Dreyfus case, Italian Jews could boast among their members a prime minister, a mayor of Rome, a sundry collection of generals and admirals, and a host of other officials. This remarkable success could only be the expression of a society in which racial discrimination simply did not exist, where Jews and Christians saw each other as compatriots, men and women who shared the same culture and the same values, and who, during the last years of the *ventennio fascista,* confronted as best they could the same alien enemy.

This is not a new viewpoint. It is a common opinion that surfaces periodically in discussions about Italian Jews and about their history. Benedetto Croce and Antonio Gramsci voiced it. Benito Mussolini repeated it: anti-Semitism does not exist in Italy. It is not part of the Italian tradition. Susan Zuccotti's recent book on the Holocaust in Italy[9] underscores this judgment. By focusing on the willingness of common Italian people to expose themselves even to mortal danger in order to assist Jews threatened with deportation to the death camps, Zuccotti highlighted the differences between Italians on the one hand

---

Ebrei sotto Salò: La persecuzione antisemita 1943–1945 (Milan: Feltrinelli, 1978). The two principal general histories of Italian Jewry are: C. Roth, *History of the Jews of Italy* (Philadelphia: Jewish Publication Society, 1946); A. Milano, *Storia degli ebrei in Italia* (Turin: Einaudi, 1963). See also, A. M. Canepa, "Cattolici ed ebrei nell'Italia liberale (1870–1913)," *Comunità* 32, no. 179 (1978): 43–109.

9. S. Zuccotti, *The Italians and the Holocaust: Persecution, Rescue, Survival* (New York: Basic Books, 1987).

and Poles, Germans, and Austrians on the other. Precisely because Italy had not long been plagued by the scourge of anti-Semitism, Italians saw Jews as members of their own culture, as friends, neighbors, compatriots. People of the other nations, carrying with them the baggage of centuries'-old anti-Semitism, perceived the Jews as aliens living in their midst. At the very best they remained indifferent to the Jews' plight. At worst they helped the Germans and their minions carry out their barbaric mission to exterminate the local Jews.

Yet in these waning years of a century scarred by wars and marked by the emergence of ethnic voices insistently demanding to be heard, one wonders how appropriate it is to accept categorical statements about the relations between national majorities and racial and religious minorities. In the case of Italy's Jews, Arnaldo Momigliano and Furio Colombo, two of the most astute contemporary observers of that country's recent history and culture, have raised the possibility that the widely held view regarding the absence of traditional anti-Semitism in Italy may be somewhat optimistic, based as it is on only a partial examination of the available evidence.[10] If those who are content to accept this prevalent view were only to look into some dark, and often neglected, corners of the Italian past, they would discover there a host of disconcerting evidence that is difficult to dismiss. It is precisely this evidence that helps to redefine the problem of the relations between Italy's Jews and Christians.

Perhaps the most telling of all these pieces of evidence, at once an indicator of a troubled past and symbol of a culture's values, was the existence of ghettos for nearly three hundred years, until the Jewish emancipation in the years 1848–1870. Of course, streets had been reserved for Jews in Italian cities and towns since the Middle Ages—Cecil Roth notes that the oldest specific reference in medieval history to a Jewish quarter, the *judaica* of Salerno, dates from the year 1004[11]—though they were not like the closed ghettos of the sixteenth century. It is important to note, however, that from 1555 on, municipal and other local regulations of the ghettos were enforced even in cases where the Jews to be segregated filled only one street or just a few houses. Indeed, the Jewish population in modern times never exceeded one-tenth of one percent of the total population. True, the ghetto period

10. This view was expressed in reviews of Zuccotti's book, by F. Colombo in *La Stampa* 121 (7 June 1987): 3, and A. Momigliano in *New York Review of Books* 34, no. 15 (1987): 7.

11. C. Roth, *Jews of Italy,* 79.

was followed by years of assimilation and by the emergence of the Jews as prominent members of Italian society. This era of assimilation and apparent nondiscrimination were precisely the decades that Croce and Gramsci had in mind when they referred to the absence of anti-Semitism in Italy. Yet this period of less than a century (in some regions closer to half a century) was followed in 1938 by the sharp blow of the Fascist racial laws. This legalistic "reghettoization" of Italian Jews is a reminder of the fact that even years of assimilation had not completely eradicated long-standing traditions.

The racial laws imposed by Mussolini and his advisors are often dismissed as mere imitations of the German model, Il Duce's aping of his Teutonic ally and supporter. On occasion they are also seen as German impositions upon a reticent Italy, a price that Mussolini reluctantly paid in order to solidify Fascist Italy's alliance with Nazi Germany. However true these contentions may be, one may observe that these regulations did not just descend fully formed into Italy from Nuremberg. An equally strong case can be made that these laws resurrected local, indigenous traditions rooted in more than three centuries of Italian history, that furthermore they were an expression of an established pattern of thinking—an Italian pattern of thinking—about Jews and about the appropriate and acceptable relationships between them and their Christian hosts.

Throughout the 1930s, well before the declaration of the racial laws, that relationship showed what we can now perceive as unmistakable signs of crumbling. The prolific author, Mario Soldati, recounts the near-impossibility of publishing in 1935 one of his now best-known works, *America, primo amore*. Though publication had been arranged, the agreement was suddenly terminated without explanation, largely because in one chapter Soldati, a non-Jew, had declared his philo-Semitism. Only the Jewish publisher, Bemporad, was willing to risk it. A limited edition of five hundred copies appeared, sold out instantly, and was subsequently banned.[12] In addition, for several years the Italian popular press, including an entrenched, clearly anti-Semitic press, had featured increasing numbers of anti-Semitic articles, but these were often dismissed as the work of fanatics. Between 1938 and 1939 three retrospective anthologies on the Jewish question were published by

12. The reluctant publisher was Bompiani. After World War II, the book went through many editions. (From an interview with Mario Soldati.) D. Lajolo, *Conversazione in una stanza chiusa con Mario Soldati* (Milan: Frassinelli, 1983), reported in *La Stampa* 125, no. 132 (16 June 1991): 21.

Roberto Mazzetti.[13] Had these books appeared earlier, their prevalently anti-Semitic nature might have given Jewish readers pause to wonder what was in store for them. But their circulation was too limited and they were published too late to be of use in forecasting the approaching storm. And, in any case, Italy was a country where Jews felt safe. For awhile it was even a haven for Jews fleeing other nations, especially some 5,000 recently arrived Germans, Poles, Austrians, and others out of a total of 10,713 of foreign birth.[14]

Then on 14 July 1938, Mussolini published the *Manifesto of Racist Scientists,* a document largely written by Il Duce himself[15] declaring the existence of a pure Italian race to which Jews did not and could not belong:

Article 9
Of the Semites who over the centuries have set foot on the sacred soil of the *Patria,* nothing remains. The same can be said of the Arab occupation of Sicily; there is no trace of it except for a few names. This is because the process of assimilation has always been accomplished quickly in Italy. The Jews [on the other hand] represent the only population which has never been assimilated in Italy because it is made up of non-European racial elements which differ in every way from the [racial] elements which gave birth to the Italians.[16]

On 7 September, a new law gave foreign-born Jews who had entered Italy after 1 January 1919 six months to leave the country.[17] Some six thousand Jews were forced to emigrate.[18]

13. R. Mazzetti, *La questione ebraica in un secolo di cultura italiana dal 1800 al 1915* (Modena: Società tipografica, 1938); *L'antiebraismo nella cultura italiana dal 1700 al 1900* (Modena: Società tipografica, 1938); and *Orientamenti antiebraici della vita e della cultura italiana: saggi di storia religiosa, politica e letteraria* (Modena: Società tipografica, 1939).

14. R. De Felice, *Ebrei sotto fascismo* (1972), 6–9. De Felice cautions that these figures, gathered in the "secret" census of 22 August 1938 by the Interior Ministry's Office of Demography and Race, are not scientifically precise, based as they are in many cases on "Jewish-sounding" last names. They do not include some 28,000 "Italian" Jews residing in the colonies of Libya, Tripolitania, Cirenaica, Eritrea, and the Aegean islands.

15. A. Spinosa, "Le persecuzioni razziali," in *Il Ponte* 9 (1953): 1079; R. De Felice, *Ebrei sotto fascismo* (1972), 276. De Felice attributes this assertion to Mussolini's son-in-law, Galeazzo Ciano, in Ciano's *Diario, 1937–1938* (Milan: Rizzoli, 1938), entry for 4 July 1938, p. 209.

16. The *Manifesto* is reprinted in its entirety in R. De Felice, *Ebrei sotto fascismo* (1972), 541–542.

17. For the text of this and other racial legislation dating from 19 April 1937 to 9 February 1939, see T. Staderini, *Legislazione per la difesa della razza* (Rome: Tipografia della Camera dei Deputati, 1939).

18. A. Spinosa, "Le persecuzioni razziali," 955.

On 6 October, the Grand Council of Fascism openly acknowledged its anti-Semitic campaign, declaring the "Jewish problem" to be the "major component" of Italian racism.[19] At the same time, Jews were barred from further membership in the *Partito Nazionale Fascista,* the Fascist party, without which membership it was difficult, if not impossible, to find and hold most jobs. And as of 15 November, Jews could no longer send their children to public school or be employed in any capacity in any public school, from kindergarten to university, nor might "Aryan" students use textbooks written by Jews.[20] Thus, of the approximately 1,200 university professors with chairs, 98 were forced to vacate their positions,[21] "liberating" their chairs and 84 other teaching posts for "Italians" who had been precluded from them by the "Jewish invasion."[22]

And yet, the announcement of *R. decreto legge* #1728, the first of four major "Provisions for the Defense of the Italian Race" on 17 November 1938 stunned most Italian Jews, many of whom identified wholeheartedly with the Fascist movement and were convinced that the regime prized their loyalty. After the decree became law on 5 January 1939, civil marriages between Jews and "Aryans" would no longer be permitted.[23] In addition, Jews would no longer be allowed to perform military service, even in time of war, and any Jew currently under arms would be sent home. Jews were henceforth barred from any state employment and from owning or managing any business with more than one hundred employees or which received defense contracts. Similarly, Jews could no longer own more than fifty hectares of farm land or any land worth more than 5,000 lire or urban buildings worth more than 20,000 lire. Racial legislation even breached the walls of Jewish households. As of 17 November, Jews could not employ Christian servants and, perhaps the most grotesque of all, they lost legal parental control over children who did not share their Jewish faith or whose political ideas differed from those of their parents.[24]

19. T. Staderini, *Legislazione,* 112; R. De Felice, *Ebrei sotto fascismo* (1972), 296–299, 556.

20. T. Staderini, *Legislazione,* 22–27.

21. E. Tannenbaum, *The Fascist Experience: Italian Society and Culture, 1922–1945* (New York: Basic Books, 1972), 291.

22. *Il Popolo d' Italia* (13 October 1938), cited in A. Spinosa, "Le persecuzioni razziali," 960–961.

23. If the mixed couple could find a priest ("Ministro del Culto cattolico") or any other clergy willing to perform such a marriage, the State could not prohibit the religious wedding. The marriage would not be officially registered, however, thus preventing its legal validity. (See T. Staderini, *Legislazione,* 28.)

24. Ibid., 28–58; R. De Felice, *Ebrei sotto fascismo* (1972), 562–566.

Though clearly opposed to the violence against and deportations of the Jews in 1943,[25] in 1938 Italians, especially the voices of culture, were silent: "No intellectuals, writers, journalists, opinion-makers or *maitres-à-penser* were willing to protest the racial laws. Few demonstrated their approval openly and many just pretended to approve. But there was no real opposition, not even on the part of those who later became the leaders and heroes of the Resistance."[26] One of the most stunning examples was the lack of protest as prestigious university chairs held by Jews were vacated in response to the racial legislation.[27]

Now, over fifty years later, one is tempted to ask: could Italian Jews have seen it coming? Or might there at least be evidence to suggest that assimilation bred Jewish complacency rather than Jewish equality? Might the Italian experience offer support to claims made by some that integration—not only in the case of Italian Jews, but also in that of other religious and ethnic minorities in Europe and elsewhere—does not necessarily eliminate discrimination, but that, perversely, it reinforces it?[28]

There were, in addition to decrees and newspaper articles, other clues to deep-seated feelings which could have alerted contemporaries to the possibility of a chilling of public opinion about Jews. What is more, these clues were close to home, abundant and accessible, on thousands of bookshelves, between the covers of the latest popular novels or even in the books people had read as children.[29]

In this book I analyze the iconography of Italian Jews contained in works of popular literature written by non-Jews from the beginnings of the Risorgimento movement in the early 1800s to the enactment of the Fascist racial laws in 1938. I begin my study with the movements

25. This opposition and the positive action it engendered have been thoroughly and eloquently documented by S. Zuccotti, *The Italians and the Holocaust*.

26. F. Colombo, preface to S. Zuccotti, *L'Olocausto in Italia* (Milan: Mondadori, 1988) cited in "Il silenzio della cultura genera mostri antisemiti," *La Stampa* 125, no. 118 (1 June 1991): 18.

27. See, for instance, N. Caracciolo, *Gli ebrei e l'Italia durante la guerra 1940–1945* (Rome: Bonacci, 1986), 20–21. This is a reworking in print of the two-part television documentary, "Il coraggio e la pietà," produced in Italy under the auspices of the RAI and as such contains many interviews with eyewitnesses to and participants in the events of those times.

28. See, for example, H. Arendt, *Antisemitism*, vol. 1 of *The Origins of Totalitarianism* (New York: Harcourt, Brace & World, 1968), especially chap. 3, "The Jews and Society," passim. For Italy, see A. Canepa, "Cattolici ed ebrei," 44; and A. Canepa, "Reflections on Antisemitism in Liberal Italy," *The Wiener Library Bulletin* 30 (1978): 105.

29. On the contents of those shelves and general literary tastes of the 1930s, see G. Cattaneo, *Biblioteca domestica* (Milan: Longanesi, 1983).

for emancipation from the physical, historical ghetto and end with the "reghettoization"—de jure if not de facto—of the Jews. My contention is that Momigliano's and Colombo's insightful questions focus our attention in very much the right direction and that, as a consequence, categorical statements about the absence of Italian anti-Semitism must be reformulated. Croce's and Gramsci's pronouncements surely must be considered as valid if by "anti-Semitism" one refers to the vision of the programmatic elimination of Jews and if one compares modern Italy to Poland or Germany from 1933 to 1945. But the popular tradition in Italy which gave expression to the novels and poetry discussed in the following pages suggests a more complex reality, in which Jews were assigned a prescribed social role that they could abandon only by surrendering their Jewishness. Momigliano expressed his dismay that Croce, whom he remembered as having been so supportive of Jews during the Holocaust, after the war could only advise Jews to integrate themselves into society by shedding once and for all what he called their *peculiarità,* by which he meant their Jewishness.[30] Throughout the period covered in this study, a well-defined staple of *topoi* and metaphors intended to codify the separateness of Jews and their alienness from traditional Italian values and institutions was used by generations of Italian popular and semipopular writers. It was imagined, for instance, that as Jews overcame their limited ghetto horizons and assimilated into the middle and upper middle classes, they simply evolved from pariahs into parvenus,[31] changing their disguises, perhaps, but never quite shedding their spots.

One might be inclined to question the value of "popular," mass-market literature as an index of Italian cultural values. Giuseppe Petronio argues that *all* literature serves as such an index and he attempts to establish the exact meanings of *letteratura di massa* ("literature for the masses" or mass-market literature). He concludes that letteratura di massa is a historical and sociological term and should imply no judgment of literary quality. Indeed, he designates all modern literature from the French Revolution onward as letteratura di massa, an assertion that is highly debatable.[32] For the sake of clarity in this study I

30. A. Momigliano, *Pagine ebraiche,* 142.

31. On this terminology and the lack of substantive evolution in the thinking about Jews, see H. Arendt, *The Jew as Pariah: Jewish Identity and Politics in the Modern Age,* ed. R. Feldman (New York: Grove Press, 1978), 19 and passim. See also S. Gilman, *Jewish Self Hatred: Anti-Semitism and the Hidden Language of the Jews* (Baltimore: Johns Hopkins University Press, 1986).

32. G. Petronio, *Letteratura di massa. Letteratura di consumo. Guida storica e critica* (Bari: Laterza, 1979), xxxv.

prefer to maintain some distinction between "high art" and "letteratura di massa." It is, however, all too easy to relegate literary representations of the past to the realm of quaint curiosities and to dismiss contemporary portraits of social problems as mere fiction, idiosyncratic products of the artistic temperament. Literature, especially mass-market literature, was a medium of entertainment and might seem an odd place to turn for answering such vital questions as, in this case, the presence or absence of anti-Semitism in Italian culture.

Yet, as several recent critics have observed, popular literature can provide a precious storehouse of accepted and abiding opinion, precisely because such literature is written with an eye toward satisfying its consumers.[33] Literary sociologist, Lucien Goldmann, for instance, argues that the popular novel itself is nothing less than the "literary transformation of daily life . . . which has its origins in production for the marketplace,"[34] whereas Umberto Eco describes the interdependence between "ideological questions, the logic of narrative structure and the . . . marketplace." Eco goes on to state that "the demands of the marketplace . . . create textual situations which in turn demand to be 'filled' with ideological constructs."[35] In other words, authors of popular literary works achieve their success by continually giving the public what it wants to read: the characters, the plots, the political viewpoints that reflect the standards of the mass of readers. Max Nordau captured a crucial aspect of mass-market literature's appeal in his study on Zola. Zola's success, he reasoned, was derived from the fact that "the masses persist in habits, once adopted, much longer than the leaders and creators do. The success of [Zola's] last novels is explained, moreover, on quite other than artistic grounds. His *flair* for what is occupying public opinion is, perhaps, the most essential part of his talent. He chooses from the outset subjects of favour of which he is assured of the positive interest of a numerous public, . . ."[36] And Gramsci predicted that unless literature were to develop so that "high art" would treat matters of current popular concern—what he called "low cul-

33. U. Eco, *Il superuomo di massa: retorica e ideologia nel romanzo popolare* (Milan: Bompiani, 1978), vi, 30; see also "La letteratura di massa," in *Letteratura italiana,* ed. A. Asor Rosa (Turin: Einaudi, 1989), *Storia e geografia:* vol. 3, "L'età contemporanea," 969–1306, passim; G. Petronio, *Letteratura di massa,* especially ix–lxxxvi; B. Brunetti, *Romanzo e forme letterarie di massa: Dai "misteri" alla fantascienza* (Bari: Edizioni Dedalo, 1989), 13–27.

34. L. Goldmann, *Per una sociologia del romanzo* (Milan: Bompiani, 1967), 20.

35. U. Eco, *Superuomo di massa,* vi, 30.

36. M. Nordau, *Degeneration,* trans. from 2d German ed. (New York: D. Appleton and Co., 1895), 474.

ture"—"artistic" literature would lose favor to popular literature, "which . . . is an integral part of today's culture . . . and passionately felt."[37] Such literature also conveniently serves as a "vehicle for the [moral] ideology of the ruling class"[38] even when its ideological baggage is not openly displayed. The situational topoi, the presence and fate of certain characters, plot elements, and denouements in novel after novel, effectively transmit society's dominant cultural constructs.

Seldom, if ever, do authors of popular fiction propose alternative social models to those that already shape the lives of their readers. Rarely do they set out to jar the sensibilities of their readers, always preferring to return to familiar themes, reinforcing values and ideals readily and unquestioningly accepted by their public. Eco's formulation is that

the popular novel does not invent original narrative situations, but rather reshuffles a repertory of topical situations which have already been recognized and accepted, even loved, by its audience. . . . Readers, for their part, do not want formalistic experiments or problematic upheavals of their current system of values; on the contrary, they require that the novel confirm their own cultural expectations.[39]

Two examples from best-selling, early twentieth-century Italian writers will serve to illustrate Eco's assertions. In the figure of Clarissa,[40] the servant raised and virtually enslaved by her tyrannical mistress, we find a mixture of the stereotypical attitudes that combine in the class of servants as it is portrayed in popular literature: the gratitude of the penniless orphan saved from certain death by starvation, and dedication popularized in the nineteenth century by Manzoni's character, Perpetua. Clarissa belongs to that species of servant raised in her employer's home known as the "creata," who is instructed and molded by her mistress and from whom absolute loyalty is demanded. Out of her sense of duty and desire to fulfill her allotted role by rendering nearly superhuman service, Clarissa refuses liberation through a young man's love. The outlines of the plot are those of thousands of servants who

37. "La letteratura deve essere nello stesso tempo elemento attuale di civiltà e opera d'arte, altrimenti alla letteratura d'arte viene preferita la letteratura d'appendice che, a modo suo, è un elemento attuale di cultura, di una cultura degradata quanto si vuole ma sentita vivamente," in A. Gramsci, *Quaderni del carcere* (QI, 64–64 bis) (Turin: Einaudi, 1975), vol. 3: 2113.

38. F. Iesi, *Cultura di destra* (Milan: Garzanti, 1979), 109.

39. U. Eco, *Superuomo di massa,* 66–67.

40. A. Negri, "Clarissa," in *Finestre alte* (Milan: Mondadori, 1923), reprinted in *Novelle d' autrice tra Ottocento e Novecento,* ed. P. Zambon (Padova: Nuova Vita, 1987), 87–95.

grow old in the houses in which they work. What makes Clarissa's vicissitudes into a story is the extreme nature of her servility: her morbid attachment to the ungrateful hag who has humiliated and beaten her all her life.

At the other pole of society is the beautiful Ottavia, a wealthy married woman who for two years has met her young lover, Dino, in a luxurious apartment of yellow silk, crystal, and Persian rugs. Early in the story[41] we learn that Ottavia is separated from her "ignobly reprehensible" husband, as if his immorality were sufficient justification for Ottavia's two years of happiness. But fate will not excuse Ottavia for breaking her marriage vows. Betrayed already by her husband, she listens as her lover announces his forthcoming marriage and slips away. Though in both cases Ottavia is wronged, the women dreaming of romance as they read the story firmly know—and believe—that it was up to her to display faithfulness and fortitude in the face of temptation and to resist the illicit liaison.

Both women portrayed in these examples are expected to embody the values of their readers whose lives, as servants perhaps, or bored wives, differed from many of the lives depicted in popular literature only in the intensity of their hardship or luxury, strength or illness, hatred or jealousy. The course of these fictional lives is determined largely by the degree to which they stray from the norms practiced by the readers for whom they were created.

If one accepts the potential of popular literature as an informative window on a society and its values, one must conclude that an important element of Italian history of the past several generations is the existence of an undercurrent of cultural values—for our purposes, opinions—more or less acknowledged, about the place of Jews in Italian society. This undercurrent is a more or less constant stream of ideas and of time-honored judgments expressed in the fiction, broadsides, and other media of popular culture. In turn, it is precisely the strength and resilience of that culture which continuously nourish and give form to that literature. In the case of Italy from the time of the Risorgimento—when "Italy" was still just a "geographic expression,"[42] a peninsula divided into regions with individual rulers (many of them foreign), histories, and interests, and with Italian nationalism still a

41. A. Guglielminetti, "Il ritratto a pastello," in *Le ore inutili* (Milan: Treves, 1919), 1–13.

42. This description is attributed to Metternich. See D. Mack Smith, *Italy: A Modern History* (Ann Arbor: University of Michigan Press, 1959), 1.

vague notion—through the Fascist period with its pervasive nationalism and strident glorification of the imperial Third Rome, popular
literature manifests an intensive, self-reflective search for national identity. It portrays a society constantly redefining itself, forever on the
brink of change, yet, paradoxically perhaps, saddled with a self-image
that was molded over centuries by unchanging regional and religious
notions.

The enactment of the Fascist racial laws poses some important questions that hinge on this problem of national identity and shared values.
After all the regime's strategies to create consensus through education
and propaganda,[43] was there concern that the racial laws would destroy
the social fabric, thereby seriously undermining the laboriously constructed consensus of the previous decade and a half? Or did Mussolini
count on his ability to manipulate the enduring undercurrent of commonly held opinion about Jews which, through lack of protest, once
again silently endorsed their isolation?

This study attempts to lay the groundwork for answering these questions by probing this undercurrent of opinion about Jews. Chapter 1
provides the necessary background to the late eighteenth- and nineteenth-century Italian debate on the Jewish question. In chapter 2, I
analyze a novel growing directly out of that debate: Father Bresciani's
commercially successful *The Jew of Verona,* an excellent example of
popular attitudes toward Jews inspired by the religious Right in direct
reaction to the political upheavals of 1848. In chapter 3 I examine the
satire of G. G. Belli, one of Italy's major dialect poets, with close readings of his numerous sonnets devoted to Jewish themes. Chapter 4 is
an analysis of three popular novels written over the span of the nineteenth century, by Carlo Varese, G. A. Giustina, and Italy's most prolific novelist, Carolina Invernizio. Finally, in chapter 5 I focus my attention on the early twentieth century, particularly the fateful decade of
the 1930s, when writers such as Papini and Puccini, Carli and Callegari
returned to the traditional themes about Jews and to images used as
much as a century before by Varese and Bresciani.

In a study such as this, in which analysis of an endless string of works
containing Jewish characters was not desirable, selection of authors was
especially important. My choices depended upon two basic criteria:
writers had to be non-Jews, since the representation of Jews in works

43. On Fascist attempts to homogenize the culture and create consensus, see M. Isnenghi, *L'educazione dell'Italiano: il fascismo e l'organizzazione della cultura* (Bologna: Cappelli, 1979).

written by Jews raises special, additional questions of self-image, important problems that merit more thorough treatment than could be given
here;[44] writers had to produce popular literature, either written for the
mass market or, in the case of G. G. Belli's poetry, reproducing popular
opinions, since "high art" during the period under investigation was
unlikely to afford the necessary effective, direct insight into mass culture. Finally, all translations are my own unless otherwise noted.

I begin my study with the movement to emancipate Jews from the
miseries of centuries of ghetto life. I leave my study in 1938, to be precise on 17 November when *R. decreto legge* #1728 was officially announced and a juridical "ghetto" was reinstated. By the evening of that
day, a new phase in Italian-Jewish relations had begun.

44. For an introductory discussion of this important topic, see H. Stuart Hughes,
Prisoners of Hope: Italian Jewry in the Silver Age (Cambridge: Harvard University Press,
1983).

1

Jewish Emancipation

---

*Love Italy with all your heart, with all your soul and with all
your might. Let Italy be your one great love, unsurpassed,
unto your last heartbeat, your last thought, your last drop of
blood. After God, cherish Italy above every earthly sentiment.*

Elia Benamozegh 1847

*Apostolic Roman Catholicism will always be the only State
religion; it will never be permitted to practice any other
religion.*

Neapolitan Statutes 1848

The long history of the Jewish presence in Italy includes
four events of great importance. The first was the arrival of large numbers of Spanish Jews expelled from the Iberian peninsula in the 1490s
and their addition to a community that had been stable in Italy since
Roman times. The second was the establishment of ghettos throughout
the Papal State following Pope Paul IV's bull *Cum nimis absurdum* of
1555.[1] Although not strictly obliged to do so, rulers of areas outside
the pope's domain[2] also enclosed their Jewish populations in ghettos

1. For the text of *Cum nimis absurdum*, see K. Stow, *Catholic Thought and Papal Jewry
Policy* (New York: Jewish Theological Seminary of America, 1975).
2. Jewish residence was generally limited to the northern half of the peninsula. Few
Jews had lived in the south since the Middle Ages, with the exception of the period im-

16

thus regulating to a greater extent the civic lives of their former neighbors. The third major event in Italian-Jewish history was the emancipation of the Jews of Rome and elsewhere in Northern and Central Italy from the ghettos by Pope Pius IX in 1848. The Roman Jews did not enjoy their emancipation for long. In 1850, upon Pius IX's return from his self-imposed exile in Gaeta, the Roman ghetto was reinstated and endured as a Jewish enclosure until 1870. The fourth was the declaration, less than a century later, of the Fascist racial laws of 1938 which resulted, in effect, in a new period of Jewish isolation from an active role in Italian society.

Two complementary keys might help us to understand this reversal in the relations between Jews and non-Jews in Italy: the traditional, centuries-old philosophical stance of churchmen, writers, and politicians toward the Jewish presence and the contradictory notions of separateness and brotherhood accepted by the majority of the population. Yet beyond such traditional assumptions, toward the end of the eighteenth and throughout much of the nineteenth century, more specific discussions took place in Italy regarding the coexistence of the two populations.

The process and debate on emancipation within the context of the Risorgimento are the subjects of the following pages. This historical and philosophical background is central to evaluating the literary portrayal of Jews which, in times of political challenge to established values, was in large measure inspired by the conflict between orthodox and heterodox notions of society. With one eye toward the establishment and duration of the ghetto and one looking forward to the recent phenomenon of Fascist racism, we will confront and evaluate opinion that emerged from the controversy over the position of Jews in Italian society. One such emblematic statement was Benedetto Croce's pronouncement on anti-Semitism:

Fortunately [in Italy] there was no trace of that folly called anti-Semitism which consists of reinforcing the separation of the Jews, and [therefore] their solidarity against other peoples, by persecuting them and then expecting to overcome the consequences of persecution with additional persecution, that is, by reproducing the causes of evil instead of trusting in those gradual but reliable equalizers, intelligence and civilization.[3]

---

mediately following the onset of the Inquisition in 1492 when Jews flocked to Naples from Spain and Portugal.

3. B. Croce, *Storia d'Italia dal 1871 al 1915* (Bari: Laterza, 1943), 97–98.

Croce was writing about the period 1871–1887, the years immediately following Italian unification and Jewish emancipation. Yet, one wonders, how could old biases have died so very quickly? For, as we will see, stereotypical prejudices about the Jews were frequently expressed in literature preceding the Risorgimento.

The Ghetto

A logical and convenient focal point of much anti-Jewish literature was the ghetto in which Jews had lived isolated from the rest of the population since the mid-sixteenth century, so it is here that we begin our discussion of Jewish life in Italy prior to Emancipation in 1848 (1870 in Rome). Though the Rome ghetto, in the "foulest and ugliest part of Rome,"[4] was far and away the most severe of the Jewish enclosures in the peninsula, ghettos in general were unhealthy areas of considerable poverty, "where thousands of Jews are crowded within a narrow compass, and lead a close, unclean, and multitudinous life, resembling that of maggots, when they overpopulate a decaying cheese."[5] At the same time, however, forced to rely on its own human resources, the ghetto was a socially active organism. Within its walls it bustled with activity with about three-quarters of its working population scrambling to survive as merchants and peddlers, another fifth as artisans, and a small percentage in some kind of service, generally clerking.[6] But for the great number of inhabitants who had no work and depended entirely on the overburdened community for their livelihood, existence was a steady grind of demeaning indigence.

The impoverishment of these people in the Rome ghetto, compelled to live in sub-standard conditions, remained essentially unchanged through most of the nineteenth century. When Massimo d'Azeglio visited the ghetto in 1847, he came face to face with this enduring metaphor for inhumanity:

There is a district which extends along the Tiber near the Quattro Capi bridge. Or rather it is a shapeless agglomeration of badly kept houses and hovels, in

4. The Rome Ghetto was visited by Nathaniel Hawthorne in 1858. This description is to be found in his *The Marble Faun* (Columbus: The Ohio State University Press, 1968), 387.

5. Ibid., 388.

6. L. Livi, *Gli ebrei alla luce della statistica: Evoluzione demografica, economica, sociale* (Florence: Libreria della Voce, 1920), vol. 3: 138–140.

absolute disrepair and half-crumbling. . . . A population of 3,900 persons is squeezed into these huts where there's barely room for half that number. The narrow, garbage-strewn streets, the lack of fresh air and the filth, which are the natural results of such forced crowding of people most of whom are poor, makes this [area a] gloomy, stinking and unhealthy slum. These wretched families live piled on top of each other with no regard for age or sex, health or circumstance with often more than one [family] in each room. [And this] on each floor, in the attics and underground in holes which in happier households are used as cellars.

This is not a [full] description of the Ghetto, nor does it even reflect a thousandth part of the grievous conditions, the silence and neglect of poverty unknown [on the outside], which can be found inside its walls. Rather this is just a rough sketch because to do justice to it would require too much of me.[7]

Despite the human toll from such harsh living conditions, at the end of the eighteenth century the ecclesiastical authorities underscored their policy of spiritual and physical separation of Jews and Christians by insisting on continued confinement of Jews in the ghetto. Indeed, within a few months of his coronation in 1775, Pope Pius VI issued the *Edict Concerning the Jews*. It reinforced all of the age-old restrictions on Jewish life, some of which had fallen into disuse during the more humane reign of Pius' predecessor, Clement XIV. Designed to regulate all aspects of Jewish life as it related to the world surrounding the ghetto, the edict threatened physical violence for most transgressions. Thus, it was forbidden to pass the night outside the ghetto walls; to employ Christian servants, nurses, midwives, or even neighbors to light the Sabbath fires; to enter the parlors of convents or convent schools or churches, oratories, and hospitals, all under penalty of public flogging. Jewish women who attempted to impede the conversion of children, their own or others', would also be flogged, even though such conversion often included kidnapping and placement in the House of Catechumens resulting in permanent estrangement from the family. And any Jew who came within thirty "rods" of a House of Catechumens was to be punished with three "twists of the cord."

In addition it was forbidden for any Jew to possess, buy, copy, translate, or sell any codex or book of the Talmud or any such work containing statements against the Christian mystery. Indeed rabbis were to see to it that the men in their congregations became acquainted with Christianity by attending the obligatory, periodic Saturday conversionist lec-

7. M. d'Azeglio, *Dell'Emancipazione civile degli Israeliti* (Florence: Le Monnier, 1848), 24–25.

tures.[8] Jews must not display any aspect of their religious rites publicly. They might, for example, celebrate funeral services and light candles for the dead in synagogues, but any sepulchral inscriptions or corteges were prohibited.

Strict cultural separation meant that there was to be no familiarity between Jews and Christians, whether at home or in public. This interdiction also extended to business dealings: thus Jews were prohibited from owning shops or lodgings outside the ghetto either in their own names or by proxy. They could not sell meat, bread, or milk to Christians and Christian artisans could not make Jewish ritual objects. To avoid confusion in the population, the *sciamanno* or Jewish badge (generally yellow, sometimes red) was to be worn at all times, even inside the ghetto, by both men and women. But the most restrictive interdiction, and the one that caused the greatest general hardship throughout the Jewish communities of the Papal State, forbade Jews to work at any profession except that of *robevecchi*, rag-and-bone collector or old clothes peddler.[9] These interdictions were valid only for the Papal State, though the requirement that Jews not leave the ghetto after nightfall and the limitation of permissible occupations were generally applied throughout the north and center of the peninsula.[10]

Though the example of the Papal State set the tone, each region varied in the regulation of its Jewish population depending on the influence wielded by the local clergy and the degree of its submission to Rome; where ties to Rome were strong, the Jewish community often suffered. Jews in Piedmont, for example, were closely regulated, prohibited from owning property and from practicing most professions. In addition they were heavily taxed as in the Papal State—a justification being that since they were actively engaged in usury, even though they

8. Important research is currently being conducted on the conversionist mission of the Church, though with specific reference to the sixteenth and seventeenth centuries. See R. Martano, "La missione inutile: la predicazione obbligatoria agli ebrei di Roma nella seconda metà del cinquecento," in *Itinerari ebraico-cristiani. Società, cultura, mito* (Fasano: Schena editore, 1987), 93–110; F. Satta, "Predicatori agli ebrei, catecumeni e neofiti a Roma nella prima metà del seicento," in ibid., 111–127.

9. The edict of forty-four clauses is rendered in full in A. Milano, "L'Editto sopra gli ebrei di Pio VI e le mene ricattatorie di un letterato," *Rassegna mensile di Israel* 19 (1953): 65–80, 118–126.

10. For a detailed account of the legal position of Italian Jewry in the second half of the eighteenth century, V. Colorni, *Legge ebraica e leggi locali* (Milan: Giuffré, 1945). For the Napoleonic era through fascism, G. Fubini, *La condizione giuridica dell'ebraismo italiano dal periodo napoleonico alla Repubblica* (Florence: La Nuova Italia, 1974). See also G. Disegni, *Ebraismo e libertà religiosa in Italia: Dal diritto all'uguaglianza al diritto alla diversità* (Turin: Einaudi, 1983).

were required to charge lower interest than Christian lenders, their ill-gotten capital should find its way back to the government.

Where Jews found better living conditions was in regions with major ports. Even in the Papal State, the economic benefits to be derived from the commercial abilities and the international contacts of the Levantine Jews of Ancona was recognized in the sixteenth century and numerous concessions were granted them in an effort to develop the port. Except for brief periods of persecution similar to those that occurred regularly in the rest of the Papal State, the Jews of Ancona enjoyed a relatively privileged position throughout the eighteenth century.

Life for Jews in the port cities outside the Papal State, however, was considerably more rewarding. In the Republic of Genoa, for example, there were no ghettos. Jews were permitted to live among Christians and dress like them with no distinguishing badge. They could engage in manufacturing and employ Christian workers as well as own real estate. There were, of course, some restrictions: Jewish shops might be established only in the area of the free port and though Jews enjoyed free access to synagogue and cemetery, their funeral rites could not be held in public. Tuscany was a similar case in point. Although the Jews of Florence and Siena were ghettoed together with their coreligionists gathered from the countryside,[11] the port city of Livorno had a Jewish quarter known as "The Ghetto" but no organized enclosure as such. Indeed Jews were actively welcomed to the city to develop commerce and manufacturing. Thus they were involved especially in printing, textile manufacturing, and the coral industry as well as international export of these goods. Although the Livornese Jews thought of their city as "Little Jerusalem," the most important center of Jewish culture in the Mediterranean diaspora,[12] the lack of major restrictions also allowed Jews a standard of living considerably higher than that of their other Tuscan brethren to the point where they could enjoy cultural life that transcended the limits of their Jewish community.[13]

11. An excellent description of the Florentine ghetto in the nineteenth century can be found in G. Conti, *Firenze vecchia. Storia, cronica, aneddotica, costumi 1799–1859* (Florence: Bemporad, 1900), 429–438.

12. A. Milano, *Storia degli ebrei in Italia,* (Turin: Einaudi, 1963), 373.

13. Giuseppe Athias, a Jew who founded the first Masonic lodge in Leghorn in 1738, corresponded with G. B. Vico and L. A. Muratori, among others; see G. B. Vico, *Opere* (Milan-Naples: Ricciardi, 1953), 66n–67, 120; *Dizionario biografico degli italiani* 4 (1962): 525–526; the Jewish poet, Salamone Fiorentino, was admitted into Arcadia in 1791. An important study of Jewish intellectual life in this period, especially for Livorno, is A. Toaff, "Vita artistica e letteraria degli ebrei a Livorno nel 1700," *Rassegna mensile di Israel* 7 (1933): 335–355.

The most thoroughly studied of all the Italian-Jewish port communities is Venice,[14] so that here it may simply function as a point of reference. Though the Republic of Venice was independent of the Holy See, the ghetto there had existed since 1516 and was later expanded to include three contiguous ghettos. The Jews were taxed for the upkeep of the area, but were not obliged to live in it. Rather they could integrate themselves into the fabric of the city and surrounding areas and were primarily involved in export in Venice and silk manufacturing in Padua[15] as well as the more humble occupations, chiefly money lending, as everywhere. This position of privilege was not a stable one, however, and Jews were not really free to do as they pleased. Rather Jewish well-being depended almost entirely on the commercial success of the city as a whole. When the republic was threatened with economic difficulties, the Jews were among the first to suffer. Just such a situation occurred in the 1770s and in 1777 the Jews were presented with a *Ricondotta,* the Venetian version of the Papal *Edict of 1775,* which effectively limited Jewish commercial competition (with the exception of international export, which was not disturbed) by banning Jews from several professions and set Jewish living standards back centuries.[16]

The physical separation of the Jews from the rest of Italian society found expression in many notions about Jews which were so ingrained as to have become part of the culture. In much popular literature, some of it directly inspired by the Church, to mention a Jew was to conjure up an image of a moneylender, rapacious and never satisfied, in whose life love of money had replaced human affection and greed had banished morality. Usurers preyed on non-Jews, for so they were commanded by the Talmud. They isolated themselves from Christians, for so it befitted the "chosen people" to live. They were more content to dwell apart, for given their laws and customs, they envisioned different concerns and different goals for their people. They lived in the heart of every city and yet did not participate in city life, as if a nation within the nation. Nor did they have any ties to the land or to the solid values it represented. Thus, they had no stake in their place of birth; shifty

14. See C. Roth, *A History of the Jews of Venice* (Philadelphia: Jewish Publication Society, 1930) and B. Pullan, *The Jews of Europe and the Inquisition of Venice 1550–1670* (Oxford: Blackwell, 1983).

15. See, for example, A. Ciscato, *Gli ebrei in Padova* (Bologna: Forni, 1967).

16. See R. Calimani, *Storia del Ghetto di Venezia* (Milan: Rusconi, 1985). For an inspired, if somewhat impressionistic, account of the rise and fall of the Jewish position in Venice see M. McCarthy, "A Pound of Flesh" in *Venice Observed* (New York: Harcourt, Brace and World, 1963), 36–57.

and rootless, where their money was, there was home. Nonetheless their Christian brothers would welcome them if only they would admit to their error and convert. Instead their overweening pride kept them from salvation in Christ, and they were justly punished with interdiction designed to bring them eventually to the True Faith.

Ideas such as these were traditional to those familiar with Church-inspired literature. A favorite topic of such writings was the Jew and his money. The legendary avarice of the Jew and the usury he practiced to support it were persistent themes throughout the period in question, especially in times of economic crisis. Some accusations were made in essays and sermons, others were masked in poetry designed to entertain as well as instruct. One such "opera vaga e dilettevole" ("charming and delightful work") which enjoyed considerable success was a heroicomic poem *"Il pasto degli ebrei"* ("The Jews' Repast") from 1731 by the Abbot Antonio Veccei. In it, in what was to become a familiar pattern, the Jewish character hoards as much money as he can grasp and is still not content. Privy to the occult arts, this Jew-magus experiments in alchemy, attempting to transmute the limitless desert sands into gold, but, as every schoolboy knows, he is doomed to failure. Such foolishness is part and parcel of the customs of these "perverse," "lazy," and wicked Jews, the price of their stubborn refusal to free themselves from their "immoral" religion. The rewards of such a faith are at best worldly and ephemeral compared to the heavenly and eternal treasures promised to Christians. Accordingly Jews thrive on obscene pleasures, no better than "whores . . . fit only for the gallows."[17] Writings such as these were sometimes inspired more by visions of hush money than by actual conviction. Authors occasionally attempted to extort payment from the Jewish community in return for removal of their works from the market.[18]

Calculated to incite the populace against those recalcitrants who persisted in their refusal of Christianity, these simplistic works couched their accusations in everyday language and provided examples with which one could easily identify. Often woven into quotidian situations, in which the reader could recognize basic concerns of his own existence,

17. The popularity of this sort of literature was such that Veccei's *Il pasto degli ebrei* went through five editions before being revised and expanded in 1793.

18. For a full account of such writings up through the eighteenth century, see M. Steinschneider, "Letteratura antigiudaica in lingua italiana," *Vessillo israelitico* 29–31 (1881–1883), 1881: 165–167, 201–203, 229–232, 269–271; 1882: 206–208, 244–246, 371–373; 1883: 246–248, 275–277, 313–315, 380–381. See also A. Milano, *Storia,* 687.

were blood-curdling stories of ritual homicide for purposes of the vam-
piristic consumption of Christian blood, works such as G. P. Vitti's
Memoria su varj bambini martirizzati dagli ebrei (*Memoir Concerning
Several Children Martyred by the Jews*) (Venice: 1791) and the anony-
mous *Vita e martirio di s. Simoncino* (*The Life and Martyrdom of Blessed
Simon of Trent*) (Rome: 1775).[19]

What made it possible for literature reifying popular fears about the
Jews to engage its readership and perpetuate those same notions was
the paradoxical fact that this people lived in the midst of Christian society and yet was far removed from it. The Jewish situation throughout Northern and Central Italy was a living reminder of the refusal of
Italian society to absorb a population whose religious life it could not
control and whose political allegiance was, therefore, deemed suspect.

Enlightenment

In Italy, as in the rest of Europe, the "Jewish question"
attracted the attention of numerous thinkers during the eighteenth century. There were among them anti-Semites who were churchmen like
Paolo Medici, and laymen, such as Giuseppe Sessa, who had closer contacts with Jews. In his influential *Riti e costumi degli ebrei confutati*
(*Disputation on the Rites and Customs of the Jews*), Medici maintained
that Jewish resistance to Christianity was clear proof of blindness and
error. If Jews would not come freely to conversion, they should be
coerced.[20] Giuseppe Sessa, non-Jewish administrator of the pre-eman-
cipation organizational wing of the Jewish community, the so-called
Università israelitica, of Turin, focused his attack on the sins of the
Jews, particularly usury against non-Jews commonly believed to be

19. In 1759, Cardinal Lorenzo Ganganelli (the future Clement XIV) compiled a report refuting the claims by Polish priests of ritual murder among the Jews of Warsaw.
See C. Roth, *The Ritual Murder Libel and the Jew. The Report by Cardinal Lorenzo Ganganelli* (Pope Clement XIV) (London: The Woburn Press, 1934). In Italy one such sup-
posedly martyred child was venerated in the cult of Blessed Simon of Trent. Literature
based on ritual homicide surfaced from time to time, for instance the novel by Rocca
d'Adria (pseudonym of Cesare Algranati), *Nella tribù di Giuda* (Bologna: Garagnani,
1903). On the subject of ritual murder in general, see V. Manzini, *L'omicidio rituale e i
sacrifici umani con particolare riguardo alle accuse contro gli ebrei: ricerche storiche-sociologiche*
(Turin: Bocca, 1925).

20. P. Medici, *Riti e costumi degli ebrei confutati* (Florence: Viviani, 1736). This work
went through several editions and translations well into the nineteenth century.

prescribed in the Talmud,[21] and thus represented a traditional line of criticism based, for the most part, on questionable interpretations of Hebraic texts.

Yet there was also an important current of thought which tended to regard Jews more favorably while, at the same time, patiently insisting on their "otherness," indeed "alienness," in spite of their ancient roots in Italian culture. Even those thinkers who were most tolerant could not envision a solution to the "problem" which did not ultimately involve the absorption of the religious minority into Christian society. One would have to wait until nearly the middle of the nineteenth century for writers such as d'Azeglio and Belli to discuss and portray the Jews with their Judaism intact. In the eighteenth century, the *philosophes,* Jansenists, and *illuministi* ("Enlightened" thinkers), however obliquely they may have addressed the Jewish question, continued to write in the expectation that, as a result of more sympathetic treatment, the Jews could be induced to recognize their error.

The Jansenists, a group of Catholics often at odds with the Church hierarchy, regarded fairness as the only effective means to bring Jews to their faith. Echoing the leader, Henri Grégoire,[22] the abbot Gaetano Giudici maintained that tolerance was required by philosophy and religion itself:

Once removed from [a situation of] disgrace, once raised up from oppression, once brought to the usual status of men in society, the Jews should be more likely to embrace the universal brotherhood and join with Christians, their neighbors and brothers, and to create with them one big family, thus leaving behind them the [traditional] rejection on the part of every nation.[23]

The Jansenists held that their insistence on the purity and genuineness of the early Church, together with their historic aversion to "gentiles" or "degenerate" Christians, were motives for cordiality between themselves and the Jews. Additional ballast for this position were other opinions from French Jansenists. Pascal called Judaism the repository of the "true religion," a faith "divine in its authority, in its morality,

21. G. Sessa, *Tractatus de Judaeis* (Milan: 1717).

22. Henri Grégoire (1750–1801), bishop of Metz, was the most outspoken Jansenist proponent of Jewish emancipation in the France of the Ancien Régime. He wrote three works on the subject: *Essai sur la régénération physique, morale et politique des Juifs* (Metz: 1789); a revolutionary abridgement, *Motion en faveur des Juifs* (Metz: 1789); and later, *Mémoires sur l'état des Israélites* (Paris: 1819).

23. G. Giudici, *Discorso sopra l'articolo 355 della costituzione cisalpina riguardante il culto* (Milan: 1791), 31–32.

in its rites, in its doctrine and in its influence."[24] Along the same lines
G. M. Pujati attacked "the prejudice against Jews which is unfortunately the rule among Christians." Jews, he said, deserve better treatment because

among all the peoples of the world [Jews] alone enjoy God's particular blessing. . . . [and] these special blessings hold great promise because Christ was a
Jew. . . . [our religion] is built on Judaism. . . . and, finally, the Jews have been
shielded and preserved for so many centuries as proof of [God's] merciful plan
to watch over them always.[25]

It was inconceivable, however, that Jews be permitted to retain their
distinct religion and customs; "embracing the universal brotherhood,"
to borrow Giudici's phrase, meant conversion. Conversion of the Jews
was always the ultimate goal. But for the Jansenists conversion was to
be more than just a means to bring about the end of Judaism as a rival
religion and a visible reminder of the failure of evangelism. The providential "return of the Jews"[26] would signal both the renewal of the
Church, restoring it to its former splendor,[27] and the rebuilding of
Jerusalem.[28] Unfortunately the message of Jansenism appealed mainly
to those high-minded intellectuals who were predisposed to tolerance.
The conviction of the official Church, that through their misery Jews
were paying a just price for their sins, held far more sway.

Just as French thinkers Grégoire, Pascal, and others had offered direction and leadership in the development of Italian Jansenist thought,
Italian illuministi were inspired by the French philosophes. Among the
French, Montesquieu and Voltaire had formulated important and influential ideas about society using the treatment of the Jews to sym-

24. B. Pascal, "Pensées," in *Oeuvres de Blaise Pascal,* ed. L. Brunschvicq (Paris: Hachette, 1904–1921), vol. 3: 196–197.

25. G. M. Pujati, *Esame della opinione de' moderni millenari cattolici riprodotta a difesa del regno visibile in terra di Gesù Cristo* (Venice, 1814), reprinted in R. Mazzetti, *La questione ebraica in un secolo di cultura italiana dal 1800 al 1915* (Modena: Società tipografica, 1938).

26. For a detailed exposition of this Jansenist concept, see F. Ruffini, *La vita religiosa di Alessandro Manzoni* (Bari: Laterza, 1931), vol. 2. The expression "return of the Jews" was coined by the Abbot Duguet in a conversation with Bossuet. See also, M. Caffiero, "'Il ritorno di Israele.' Millenarismo e mito della conversione degli ebrei nell'età della Rivoluzione francese," in AA.VV., *Itinerari ebraico-cristiani. Società, cultura, mito,* 161–229.

27. E. Degola, *Saggio di Osservazioni sulla chiave dell'Apocalisse esposta da Francesco Ricciardi,* Cod. Vat. lat. 13136, f. 11, cited in F. Ruffini, *La vita religiosa,* vol. 2: 375.

28. See R. H. Charles, *Eschatology: The Doctrine of a Future Life in Israel, Judaism and Christianity* (New York: Schocken, 1963).

bolize urgently needed change. Yet their attention to the way societies dealt with their Jewish populations was prompted more by concern for the well-being of those larger societies than for that of the Jews. Thus the Jewish situation served as a sort of bellwether for the progressiveness or backwardness of the particular society and the philosophes persisted in their notion of the Jews as a marginal people.

Montesquieu is a case in point. In his *Esprit des lois* (*Spirit of the Laws*)[29] he pointed out the inability of the Church to keep pace with the times and become enlightened, to banish the superstition that had caused it to burn a Jewish child at the stake. The times conceived of the world in broader terms, encompassing an almost infinite diversity of customs and beliefs, and the truly enlightened mind understood the need for universal tolerance. Tolerance, however, does not signify acceptance and even Montesquieu was not impervious to stereotype. He praised the Jews for their tenacity in the face of "continuous destruction"[30] while he took them to task for their "love of money" and their sanctimonious arrogance about their religion.[31] Indeed, it was this tenacity, manifested in their adherence to tradition, which kept them from enjoying complete tolerance and acceptance.

Tradition was also the stumbling block in Voltaire's thought on the Jews.[32] Voltaire exemplified the philosophical struggle against the power of organized religion coupled with rejection of those who retained their particularism and would not be made over in an "enlightened" image. Voltaire criticized Judaism throughout his works,[33] but offered contemporary Jews a solution: they need only shed their alienating identity and assimilate to the new concept of the world.[34]

One current of enlightened thinking, however, was ultimately to influence beneficial change in Jewish life. The relativism of Montesquieu with its general message of tolerance in the face of social diversity

29. Montesquieu, *L'Esprit des lois*, XXV, 13, in *Oeuvres complètes* (Paris: Editions du Seuil, 1964), 709.

30. Montesquieu, *Lettres persanes*, letter 119, in *Oeuvres complètes*, 125.

31. Ibid., 93.

32. See H. Graetz, "Voltaire und die Juden," *Monatschrift für die Geschichte und Wissenschaft des Judentums* 17 (1868): 161–174, 200–223.

33. Herbert Solow points out that these attacks were part of a lifelong struggle to discard a heritage of Christianity and the Bible. See "Voltaire and Some Jews," *Menorah Journal* 13 (1927): 186–197, and Peter Gay adds that the aspersions addressed to Jews were ultimately aimed at Christians, in *The Party of Humanity: Essays in the French Enlightenment* (New York: Knopf, 1964), 97–108.

34. P. Aubery, "Voltaire et les Juifs," *Studies on Voltaire and the Eighteenth Century* 24 (1963): 67–69.

sowed the seed that was to grow into the first emancipation in France and Italy.[35]

In Italy where religious dissent was at a minimum, the overwhelming majority of its population adhered to a standard, orthodox Roman Catholicism. The illuministi attended to problems they deemed more pressing than the question of religious freedom. When the subject did arise their approach to the Jews was ambiguous. G. B. G. d'Arco, for instance, was in favor of emancipation, but in stating his case he declared the Jews intolerant and antisocial, forced by their religion to be "by its very nature a group disassociated from the State in which it lives and against whom it has [both] the duty and the desire to fight."[36] Pietro Regis, a professor of theology at the University of Turin, was in favor of according citizenship to the Jews, but slowly because they were not yet ready for it. They should enjoy more civil rights and access to certain professions and the arts, but at the same time be induced to abandon their uniquely Jewish traditions.[37] Giovanni Antonio Ranza, a Piedmontese Jacobin, took a more balanced approach and assigned responsibility to both Jews and Christians while adding an openly political dimension to the debate. In order to assimilate the Jews and keep the peace in the Cisalpine Republic, both Jewish and Catholic religious leaders should swear an oath of "eternal defiance to kings and aristocrats and oligarchies." To the same end, churchmen should abjure their loyalty to the pope, and rabbis should abjure Moses' commandment on usury,[38] by which all Gentiles are considered foreigners and therefore fair game for fraud.

35. For an absorbing study of French Jews vis-à-vis the Church, the *philosophes,* and each other, see A. Hertzberg, *The French Enlightenment and the Jews* (Philadelphia: Jewish Publication Society, 1968).

36. G. B. G. d'Arco, *Della influenza del ghetto nello Stato* (Venice: G. Storti, 1782), cited in F. Della Peruta, "Le 'interdizioni' israelitiche e l'emancipazione degli ebrei nel Risorgimento," *Società e storia* 19 (1983): 77–107.

37. P. Regis, *De judaeo cive* (1795), cited in Della Peruta, "Interdizioni," 89.

38. The "commandment on usury" is Deuteronomy XXIII, 19. Ranza's article "Giuramento preceduto da abiura" appeared in his revolutionary newspaper *L'Amico del popolo. Giornale istruttivo del repubblicano Gio. Antonio Ranza,* 31 December 1797, cited in *I giornali giacobini italiani,* ed. R. De Felice (Milan: Feltrinelli, 1962), 217–218. Usury was and would remain the inevitable stumbling block, an indelible mark against the Jews. In a poor country in which the public had depended for centuries upon the *monti di pietà,* the authorized loan institutions, as well as clandestine banks (the majority of which were owned by Jews), the subject of money lending invariably prodded an exposed nerve and found an audience eager to berate its practitioners. Only in 1745 did the subject of loans find disinterested discussion by Scipione Maffei. "Why should we consider usury a sin," he reasoned, "when no pawn is asked, so that the transaction is

Of all the illuministi who favored emancipation, the only writer who appeared to accept the Jews *as Jews* was Giuseppe Compagnoni, a prolific journalist, political historian, revolutionary, poet, novelist. In his *Saggio sugli ebrei e sui greci* (1792) (*Essay Concerning Jews and Greeks*) he analyzed the history of the ancient Jews and projected his admiration for their "strength in adversity," their devotion to tradition, and their learning onto modern Jewry. The turning point in Jewish history was the conquest by Titus and the beginning of the Diaspora. From that time on, the Jews were the children of disgrace

without land to support them, detested, cursed by all, divided like herds though more by fate than human intention, without citizenship, without property, languishing in abject slavery in Asia and Africa.

This was because both the Christian and Moslem religions held the Jews as common enemies in a superstitious zeal that through the ages has repeatedly been stained with Jewish blood.[39] In spite of this it was the Jews who brought the rebirth of culture and the arts, and this in Europe where they were "treated worse than in other places." If Jews had not been tormented for seventeen centuries, Europe could have benefited sooner from Jewish commercial acumen and such useful inventions as the letter of credit. Indeed much of Jewish culture was ignored just because it was Jewish and that was a grievous error. If more people knew Hebrew there would be less slander against the Jews. A prime example is the way in which people regard the Talmud. Those who cannot read it will believe anything about it and hold it against the Jews instead of recognizing its importance as a "remarkable collection" of laws. If one knew the Jews better, instead of criticizing their traditions one would admire their course of history and the unity and tenacity with which they maintain their culture. But as everyone knows,

---

actually less damaging . . . to our fellow man?" Despite Maffei's efforts, however, the shadow of usury continued to cloud relations between Jews and Christians, ultimately justifying the emargination of the smaller group. See S. Maffei, *Dell'impiego del denaro* (Rome: Stamperia Vaticana, 1745). The actual interest charged by the Jews was often the same or less than that of the Church-established *monti di pietà*. Jewish loan institutions were abolished in Rome in 1682. By the end of the century, potential borrowers petitioned the authorities to reopen them because without competition, the *monti di pietà* were gouging the public. See R. De Felice, "Per una storia del problema ebraico in Italia alla fine del XVIII secolo e all'inizio del XIX," *Movimento operaio* 7, no. 5 (1955): 681–727.

39. G. Compagnoni, *Saggio sugli ebrei e sui greci* (Milan: Agnello Nobile, 1806), 29–30.

this has not been the case and when reading that history one inevitably feels one's blood run cold

with horror at the story of all the calamities the Jews have endured through the centuries. [At the same time] one is transported by sublime admiration in seeing how this wretched band not only survived nearly total destruction, but, reunited (even now) under its traditional laws and faithful to its principles, its customs [and above all] its ancient Religion, remains the unique example in all the earth of determination and constancy. [All this was accomplished] without ever disturbing the peace of the governments under which they live in any way. And now they are silently regaining their ancient glory.[40]

Although Compagnoni's approach to Jewish history and the Jews of his time went well beyond the familiar tolerance of the illuministi, the portrait he painted contained various points that just narrowly avoided reproducing the familiar stereotypes. Thus, he described Jews as the bearers of a curse, a wretched band doggedly faithful to its particularist traditions, a unique example in all of history of determination and constancy, a group silently but surely on the ascendancy once again. To be sure, Compagnoni attributed positive characteristics to the Jews, but these were qualities that served to categorize them, setting them even further apart from the rest of the population. Compagnoni's musings on the Jews did not go unnoticed. Indeed there were some who stood to benefit politically from Jewish alienness, whether freely adopted or imposed, as demonstrated by an incident regarding the publication of the *Saggio*.[41] Compagnoni's interpretation of Jewish history was phrased in such a way that his intentions could be easily distorted and his text bowdlerized.

In 1791, Compagnoni submitted his text to the scrutiny of one Count Fabrizi, censor in service to the Duke of Este, who rewrote it. The result was a philosophical "letter" to Francesco Capacelli bearing Compagnoni's name and published in Modena, a version of the *Saggio* jarringly woven through with anti-Jewish commonplaces, what Compagnoni was later to call "just the opposite of what I had written . . . a mishmash of absurdities."[42] Fabrizi deleted Compagnoni's allegations of Jewish constancy, cultural purity, and sense of history and, instead, defined Judaism as "real superstition . . . the root of serious disorders"

40. Ibid., 18–19.

41. V. Colorni, "La polemica intorno al *Saggio sugli ebrei e sui greci* di Giuseppe Compagnoni," in *Studi sull'ebraismo italiano* (Rome: Barulli, 1974), 73–76.

42. G. Compagnoni, *Memorie autobiografiche,* ed. A. Ottolini (Milan: Treves, 1927), 127.

and Jews as "inexorable enemies of Christianity" waiting for the Messiah, whose coming will give them "the right to cheat and swindle." He ended with the grave warning that "were [the Jews] to gain *Emancipation,* to throw off the yoke of *foreign domination,*" Catholic nations would do well to keep them under surveillance and "treat them strictly" ("usino un qualche rigore").[43]

The political opportunity afforded by Compagnoni's discussion of the place of Jews in Italian society was one Fabrizi could not ignore. In the face of increasing French dominion over northern Italy, Fabrizi was shifting his loyalty away from the Estensi. Whereas Este rule had been relatively enlightened where Jews were concerned,[44] Fabrizi thought he could ingratiate himself with the conquerors through a tough stand on the Jewish question. What is significant about Fabrizi's attempt to discredit both the Jews and the Duke of Este was, first, his own perception that tolerance toward the Jews was somehow a demonstrable weakness on the part of the Estensi and would surely be recognized as such by the French, and, second, on a greater scale, the enduring timeliness of the whole question of Jewish alienness.

Many Jews reflected the negative representations of them in their own lives by adhering to the isolating concept known as *galut* ("exile"). *Galut* functioned as a self-fulfilling prophecy: Jews were ghettoed, taxed, and persecuted in their own birthplace because, to a certain extent, they were perceived by others in the same way they perceived themselves: "different," "a nation apart." Galut was the logical result of the accusation of nonparticipation, the Jews' destiny imposed by those very people who denied their participation.

The notion of galut was particularly strong in those cities in which the ghetto encompassed a greater portion of Jewish daily life, isolating them still further from the events of the wider world. One result was that often Italian Jews were largely unaware of political movements elsewhere on their behalf. Most, for instance, had heard of the French revolution, but many did not realize that Jews had anything to gain by it. A contemporary French traveler to Rome described a visit to the ghetto in which he informed a group of its inhabitants about the progress made in France by members of "their nation":

They believed that France was turned upside down to the benefit of no one. . . . but as soon as I told them that the goal of the revolution was to assure

43. Fabrizi's counterfeit edition was published as: G. Compagnoni, *Lettere piacevoli se piaceranno* (Modena: Società tipografica, 1791), 167–194, in particular 190–191.
44. A. Milano, *Ebrei in Italia,* 301–303.

all men of their absolute equality and to impose on all men equal duties . . . regardless of their religion or their nation, and that the Jews were specifically accorded all the same advantages, these unfortunate people were so astonished it was hard to believe. They did not dare believe it; they were afraid to believe me lest I deceive them. "You mean," they said, "that we are also called men and have the same rights as others, that we can progress by dint of our talent and virtue!"[45]

Smaller, wealthier segments of some Jewish communities, however, had become familiar with the enlightened European concept of man and his role in society. Enlightened Jews adhered to *haskalàh* (the Hebrew term for enlightenment), a European movement whose goal was to prepare Jews for assimilation by educating them away from galut. Haskalàh attempted to replace isolationism by promoting Jewish patriotism in their place of birth and residence.

Jewish enlightenment resulted in impatience for change which manifested itself in Jewish participation in Masonic lodges and in the publication of such theoretical works as Isacco Levi's treatise *Il difensore degli Ebrei o sia lettera di Isacco Levi al Signor du Fresne mercante di Smirne (The Defender of the Jews, or Isaac Levi's Letter to M. du Fresne, Merchant of Smyrna).*[46] Here Levi identified the root of the "Jewish problem" to be the political power of the Church, that is the union of Church and State, which made conversionist writings and other attacks on Jews more dangerous than in other countries. Jews also stood their ground answering their detractors in works such as *Difesa contro gli attacchi fatti alla nazione ebrea intitolato "Dell'influenza del Ghetto nello Stato" (Defense Against the Attacks on the Jewish Nation in the Book Entitled "On the Influence of the Ghetto in the State")* (1784), a rebuttal to G. B. G. d'Arco, and looked to the future in *Considerazioni di un israelita sulla sorte dei suoi confratelli nel Piemonte nei secoli scorsi, sul loro stato presente e sui mezzi più propri a migliorarne l'avvenire (A Jew's Thoughts on the Fate of His Brothers in the Past Centuries in Piedmont, on Their Present State and on the Best Means to Provide Them a Better Future),* a self-help book from 1790. As their titles indicate, these works were acts of self-defense and were written from positions of weakness, but they also indicate growing strength and awareness.

45. J. Gorani, *Mémoires secrets et critiques des cours, des gouvernements, et des moeurs des principaus états de l'Italie. Par Joseph Gorani, Citoyen Français* (Paris: Buisson, 1793) vol. 2, "Des Juifs," 378–379.

46. *Il difensore degli Ebrei o sia lettera di Isacco Levi al Signor du Fresne mercanti di Smirne* (London: 1784; Turin: 1785).

At the end of the eighteenth century the sermons of *haskalàh* were put to the test. In the face of a history of Jewish persecution and the threat of a French takeover, the question arose: where lie the sympathies of the Jews? It was not an idle query for the French revolution had stirred Italian Jews, although their pro-French sentiments were by and large limited to hope of liberation. Realizing what the French could do for the Jews, Alessandro Verri hit the mark when he reported: "In their servitude [the Jews] listened with delight to promises of liberty [made by] the French Republic, that seductress of a world oppressed by tyrants and priests."[47]

In the 1790s, the Roman Jews were repeatedly accused of sedition and placed under surveillance for working for the "downfall of ecclesiastical government through the French."[48] Eventually they expressed their sympathy for the invaders, a position that met with the predictable storming of the ghetto. The priests and municipal authorities had easily awakened the dormant anti-Semitism of the mob: if the French were the enemies of God and children of the Devil, then Jews and other French sympathizers were the natural allies of the Antichrist.[49] Fears of Jewish connivance with the French were quickly translated into poetry that was popularized on handbills. One such poem, a sonnet of 1793, defines Italian Jewry as "scroundrelly rabble" and "inspirers of the Jacobins."[50]

The expected arrival of the French in any city with a Jewish population was an opportunity for a riot directed against the ghetto as a "last ditch" protest. During one such incident in February of 1798, the Roman *sanfedisti* ("Fighters for the Holy Faith"), armed bands of rural and urban masses, attacked French supporters in the name of their ancestral faith and ancient customs.[51] They were led by three crucifix-wielding priests, who pursued the "Jacobin" Jews and whatever French they could ferret out, shouting "Viva Maria!" and "Viva Gesù!"[52]

47. Cited in R. De Felice, "Problema ebraico," 705.

48. Ibid., 706.

49. Ibid.

50. This sonnet is found in the collections of the Museo Centrale del Risorgimento in Rome.

51. The term *sanfedista* has had a varied history. In 1815 the reactionaries of the Papal States were known as *sanfedisti*. During the Restoration, the term was used by the liberals throughout the peninsula to derogate the conservative defenders of throne and altar by referring to the slaughter in the Neapolitan revolution of 1799. After 1815 sanfedista indicated the political government of priests in the Papal State and the masses of people whom they co-opted.

52. R. De Felice, "Problema ebraico," 713.

These so-called "Viva Maria!" riots were generally answered with military intervention to restore order. But such measures could only insure a brief peace, for the mechanisms of change had been put in motion and upheaval was on its way.[53]

Napoleonic Interludes

Twice in the span of a few years, the Napoleonic invasions of Italy, like a deus ex machina, brought about the emancipation of Italian Jews—at least those not under Austrian domination. In both instances the reforms introduced by the French were short-lived, being imposed from the top by an alien and conquering power. Even if some intellectuals and urban residents might applaud such measures, the Italian masses often resented them. The history of Italian Jews from 1797 to 1815 reflects these two basic problems: the far-reaching but fragile and ephemeral nature of this "first" emancipation and popular reactions against the French policies.

One can identify several motives in the French approach toward the Italian Jews: (1) a concern to secure allies in a country where they found themselves unwelcome among the traditionally conservative masses; (2) an intent, demonstrated also in other conquered territories, to develop a local middle class and to achieve this by drawing on the centuries-long experience of Jews in banking and commercial affairs; (3) an ideological commitment to civil equality, regardless of nationality, religion, or social class; and (4) a desire to identify new sources of income which they obtained, in part, from religious minorities such as the Jews, in exchange for emancipation, both physical and political.

As the French advanced, increasing numbers of Jews were freed from the ghettos and declared to be equal to the rest of the population. Liberation was complete by 1798 and proclaimed by Antonio Pacifici representing the Roman Republic on 18 February of that year. In a

53. Intervention on behalf of the Jews was not limited to military confrontations with their persecutors in the piazza. With the French menace always in the background, a vigorous debate ensued in the press when the pamphlet *L'Amico della Ragione* (*The Friend of Reason*) an "enlightened" work favoring emancipation appeared in 1796 in Ferrara, a major Jewish center. The conservatives reacted immediately by publishing *L'Araldo Cattolico* (*The Catholic Herald*), which prompted the liberals to counter quickly with *L'Amatore della Verità Risorta* (*The Admirer of Resurrected Truth*), a publication that had the blessing of the French command.

speech replete with Romantic overtones and utilizing, at that early date, all the militant rhetoric of the Risorgimento, he addressed the

oppressed sons of Abraham, [you] who are a goodly part of the generous people of Rome, the usurpers of the throne segregated you from us in order to humiliate you and rob you more easily. They have made you hateful to Christians who are supposed to embrace everyone and hate no one. [But now] you shall also be free. Hurrah for the God of Abraham and Jacob! who by the invincible hand of the immortal Berthier[54] has redeemed you from years of slavery under the tyranny of a modern Pharaoh. From now on, if you are good citizens, you shall be our Brothers, our equals: one law shall prevail for us and for you.[55]

The Jews reaped enormous economic benefits from the presence of Napoleon's troops in Italy. At last permitted to practice every profession and engage in any commercial activity, they established businesses outside the ghetto walls, extending even beyond urban areas into major agricultural centers. But in some regions this return to a more normal way of life was interrupted almost as soon as it began.

This fragile respite depended upon the presence of French troops to hold the reactionaries at bay, and in 1799 the French were pushed out of Italy by the combined forces of the Austrians, Russians, English, and sanfedisti. The French evacuation occasioned new attacks on the Jews; the mob joined the anti-French troops and sacked the ghettos and Jewish quarters of Sinigaglia, Livorno, Ancona, Ferrara, and Rome, where police intervention was necessary to quell the riots. The Roman authorities even went so far as to promise the soldiers carte blanche if they could conquer the city.[56] This interval of repression and reprisals proved to be a bloody one for the Jews. Bonamini of Pesaro witnessed one such event and recorded it in his diary:

The Jews suffered enormous damage, and in the space of a few hours they repaid [society] for all the usury, the larceny, their filthy monopoly of every type of business, especially financial . . . Imbeciles! and they were convinced that liberty was theirs, that they had been freed from their ancient bondage which those deicides so richly deserved![57]

But almost as quickly the wheels of fortune turned again: the worst fears of the reactionaries were realized with the return of Napoleon and this time the Jews were guaranteed liberty until 1815.[58]

54. General Berthier headed the French invasionary forces and occupied Rome in February 1798.
55. R. De Felice, "Problema ebraico," 709.
56. G. A. Sala, *Diario romano degli anni 1798–1799* (Rome: 1888).
57. R. De Felice, "Problema ebraico," 716–717.
58. Liberation was gradual as the troops moved through the peninsula, but in any

The emancipation restored the Jews to free and open dealings with their Christian countrymen. What it did not do was release them from the institutionalized doubts about their loyalty or the numerical threat they might pose to their country once a higher standard of living strengthened the "Jewish nation." Therefore when the Assembly of Jewish Notables and the Great Sanhedrin met in Paris (in 1806 and 1807 respectively), these issues were foremost among their deliberations. The task of these two bodies was to enact reforming legislation that would render the Jews assimilable by correcting their errors, such as usury, which "make them odious or despicable in the eyes of their fellow citizens." Jews would also assimilate better if there were fewer of them, and to achieve this the Sanhedrin required each consistory, or geographical administrative unit for Jews, to see to it that every third marriage was contracted between a Jew and a Christian. In this way "Jewish blood would one day lose its 'special nature'."[59]

Such social planning based on a forced numerical decline of Jewish families and this attempt to alter the "special nature" of Jewish blood is the true underbelly of the rhetorical references to "regeneration of an ancient people." The goal of total Jewish assimilation with France and the Regno d'Italia was to be reached by several means. The abolition of usury and the secondhand trade would settle the problem on a commercial level: forced to operate within Christian society, Jewish business activity would also bolster the imperial economy and encourage the Jews to consider themselves nationals of the country of their birth. But in "liberating" Jews from their demeaning former trade, the deliberations of both august bodies of Jewish notables resulted in the imposition of more regulations on Jewish economic life; after 17 March 1808, when Napoleon issued his version of the regulations emanating from the work of the Assembly and the Sanhedrin, in order to be licensed to engage in commerce Jews would have to prove themselves innocent of usury. Feeling that through "emancipation" they had traded one set of restrictions for another, Italian and French Jews quickly dubbed Napoleon's decree "Décret Infame."[60]

The "Infamous Decree" also limited Jewish mobility and residence.

---

case in most of Italy the enactment of the Edict in 1799 had not been quite as harsh as in 1775.

59. For a complete record of the proceedings of the Great Sanhedrin, see D. Tama, *Raccolta degli atti dell'Assemblea degli Israeliti di Francia e del Regno d'Italia convocata a Parigi* (Livorno: Meucci, 1807). See also, R. De Felice, "Problema ebraico," 720–726.

60. C. Roth, *A Short History of the Jewish People* (London: East and West Library, 1948), 345.

A property requirement was imposed for settlement in the Empire. Since Jews had previously been forbidden to own land, this restriction was presented as a great opportunity; for some, undoubtably, it was. It afforded them an opportunity to rid themselves of the popular stigma of the shiftiness and instability of the "Wandering Jew." However, it was a clear attempt to modify the nature of Jewish life in Europe, which was essentially concentrated and urban. And the resulting infringement on historically Christian landholding traditions fostered additional resentment against the Jews.

Indeed this reaction had been building within conservative and popular elements of the population since the first Napoleonic emancipation and came to the surface at the time of the partial restoration of 1799. Popular anger at the Jewish response to the French and the freedoms granted to the Jews by the invaders was expressed in numerous broadsides that became more violent in tone as the threat of successful French rule increased. In an anonymous poem someone warned the Jews unequivocally against any further republican actions. Set to the *Dies irae,* this *"Canzonetta nuova sopra gli Ebrei"* ("A New Song About the Jews") offers grim testimony to the situation. A poem in twenty-two verses, it is one long list of accusations:

> *Dies irae, dies illa*
> Listen to the people scream
> Vendetta against the Jews . . .
> The Day of Wrath has come.
> It is useless to flee
> Invoking the Messiah.
> Let him [rather] kill them in the street.
> *Dies illa lacrimosa*
> On gibbets they repose
> Either hung or impaled, [who cares?]
> As long as they breathe no more.[61]

The "Canzonetta" sounds the alarm of a people cornered, lashing out at those who stood to gain by the fearsome and inevitable French victory. In the poem the Last Judgment is at hand; the "people," thirsty for vengeance, will execute the punishment ordained by God. The Jews must stop running; their cowardly appeals to the Messiah are in vain. They have incurred divine wrath by their persistent refusal to stay in their place. They removed the *sciamanno,* sported instead the revo-

61. *Canzonetta nuova sopra gli Ebrei* published in Rome in 1799, cited in De Felice, "Problema ebraico," 716–718.

lutionary cockade, and sought military service. They have despoiled churches, trafficked in holy goods, and trampled over religious scruples. The pernicious cowards cannot hide from the waiting gibbet: neither their craven leaders, who foul their beds in terror invoking the patriarchs, nor their whores who consort with the enemy, nor even their shameless maidens who pretty themselves for the French. They are entirely without feeling and they thirst for blood. But now the tables are turned: whether they be shot, impaled, or hanged, they are certain to burn in Hell everlasting.

In this attack the anonymous voice demonstrated its own lack of faith in the durability of traditional barriers erected against a minority that was being schooled in the notion of rights. The Jews' "place," as defined by those who perpetuated that confinement, was no longer adequate to contain them. Thus the emphasis on possible sexual contact between Jews and the enemy reveals fears about the mongrelization of society, whereas the concern for Church property was an attempt to demonstrate, in the name of cultural values, that Jews deserved the fate that awaited them.

Even after 1800, an active current of anti-Semitic literature continued to enjoy popular dissemination. This category extended to theatre as well, that is, literature to be consumed in public. One such example is sufficient: 1810 brought the revival of *Il matrimonio ebraico, ovvero la Sinagoga* (*The Jewish Wedding, or the Synagogue*), a vicious comedy that had been banned from 1797 to 1798. Little more than a parody of Jewish religious practices, the play portrayed rabbis in priestly vestments performing lewd acts. Its reappearance precipitated riots in many cities so that it was proscribed anew.[62]

Although such police action as outlawing a public spectacle that was demeaning to Jews was prompted more by a desire to keep the peace than by concern for Jewish sensibilities, nonetheless it meant that for a while Jews in several cities would have to endure one less form of ridicule. But to those writers who argued the merits of Jewish separateness, this modest respite bespoke troublesome French interference. Jewish "progress" and the legislation that both occasioned and protected it gave reactionary theorists of the "Jewish question" much to respond to.

One of the most obvious points of attack was the French regulation

---

62. R. De Felice, "Problema ebraico," 725. See ahead, chap. 3, for a discussion of this kind of satirical theatre.

that permitted Jewish ownership of land. It appeared to Francesco Gambini, the Piedmontese political economist, that the French had betrayed fellow Christians by giving away that last bastion of privilege from which Jews should be excluded at all costs. In his pamphlet on the subject,[63] in addition to the usual assertions of Jewish separateness, rapacity, and unsuitability for citizenship—all of which should preclude legal title to land—Gambini warned that a Jewish presence in the countryside would destroy the sound homogeneity of the peasant world. Peasants had to be protected because they constituted "the most precious of all classes," "the true native race of every country," those who

support the militia and the useful arts and who continually breathe new life into the urban population which, for its part, is constantly being corrupted and is decaying due to its familiarity with luxury, soft living and sedentary professions.

Conceding land to the Jews and allowing their usury and fraud to spread beyond the already-contaminated city would result in dangerous "denationalization." But

as long as the nation has a solid base in those who own land and work the soil, it will always endure because the dominant [national] spirit and the instruments of public safety will always be the same.[64]

This notion of Jewish decadence appeared in many guises. Seven years before Gambini's treatise, G. B. Giovio had delivered a paper in which he explored the reasons for the fall of the chosen people after Biblical times. He concluded that there was no logical reason for it, but that it could be due to their concept of a vengeful God "a terrible warrior . . . who will have them place a victorious and insulting foot on the necks of the conquered nations." As a result, the Jews, former bearers of light and knowledge, now owe their continued existence to Christian charity and are often mistreated by those who forget that Christ died for all men.[65]

63. F. Gambini, *Dell'ebreo possidente* (Turin: Stamperia Pane, 1815).

64. Ibid., cited in Della Peruta, "Le 'interdizioni,'" 80–83. Gambini wrote another pamphlet attacking the notion of Jewish citizenship and giving the countryside as an excuse: *Della cittadinanza giudaica* in 1834. Monaldo Leopardi, the poet's father, echoed similar attitudes such as "the sanctity of the soil" in his *Axioms*. Preference for rural (to the exclusion of urban) populations and values would return in the twentieth century in the nativist rhetoric of *Strapaese* in publications such as *Il Selvaggio* (see chap. 5).

65. Entitled "Sublimità e decadenza degli ebrei somma, inesplicabile," reprinted in *Memorie di religione, di morale e di letteratura* (Modena: 1823), vol. 4: 33–34.

By idealizing the Jews of the Bible and establishing them as a standard of comparison, writers such as Giovio, and perhaps also Compagnoni, assigned modern Jews an impossible goal and, at the same time, created an ideal climate for ready criticism when the ideal could not be fulfilled. The charismatic days of the patriarchs, obscured in the shadows of antiquity, were veiled in mysticism and symbolism. Their remoteness made it impossible to visualize or evaluate them. What remained of them were their wraggle-taggle descendents in the ghetto. And yet Christianity had sprung from Old Testament Judaism, and it was this fact that provided theorists with their most potent argument about the Jews: insisting that the Christian religion was an improvement on its parent, they were convinced that the Jews had precipitated their own eclipse by their stubborn refusal to move with the times and accept Christianity.

Emancipation

Events after the fall of Napoleon demonstrated the fragility and superficiality of the first Jewish emancipation in Italy. The Restoration brought Jews almost full circle along the path to their prerevolutionary status of 1775. In some areas, such as Tuscany, where ghettos had been abolished, Jews were still allowed to dwell where they wished. In others, however, notably Piedmont and the Papal State, the Restoration marked a return to the degrading conditions outlined in the 1775 edict, with the exception of the sciamanno. Worse, the provisions from 1775 were enforced more stringently than ever in the backlash of this rigidly reactionary period. Gone was the relative leniency of the eighteenth century which Cecil Roth has termed "tolerant inefficiency."[66] Jewish property owners who had acquired their holdings under Napoleon were now compelled to sell, often at ridiculously low prices. Educational facilities were again closed to them, and they were forced to abandon all dignified and lucrative professions and return to menial and degrading occupations. The years of freedom during the Napoleonic period, however, had awakened large numbers of Jews to intellectual citizenship alongside Christians for the first time in nearly

66. C. Roth, *History of the Jews of Italy* (Philadelphia: Jewish Publication Society, 1946), 48.

two hundred and fifty years, provoking a change in outlook which made the journey backward all the more bitter.

The French interlude that promised so much growth and vitality had been all too brief, for in many ways the restoration of the old rulers meant the return of the old philosophies. The Restoration saw the conflict between the Church trying desperately to maintain its grip on the Jewish minority and those thinkers and activists promoting the radical changes of the Risorgimento. Their opinions on the nature of the Jewish presence in Italy came to symbolize the much larger power struggle. And their analysis of Jewish religion and behavior revealed their deep-seated political and social aspirations.

Among the several voices raised to debate the Jewish question in Restoration Italy, the most formidable belonged to Fr. F. F. Jabalot, pro-procurator general of the Order of Preachers (Dominicans). Spokesman for the sanfedista element, Jabalot came into his own at this time and could well serve as a symbol of the Restoration ethic. His pamphlet, *Degli ebrei nel suo rapporto colle nazioni cristiane* (1825) (*On the Jews in Their Relationship with Christian Nations*) is a "classic" of religiously and politically inspired, nonracial, anti-Semitic philosophy.

Jabalot begins his study by attacking those Christian philosophers and churchmen who wrote on behalf of Jewish emancipation. These philosophes, he argues, overvalue the Jews and exaggerate the social benefits of their rehabilitation while constantly harping on the rights of man.[67] The churchmen who defend the Jews, above all the Jansenists, especially Grégoire,[68] betray the moral imperative of Catholic solidarity and have allowed Rome to become a "spiritual Babel."[69] Among those who preach compassion and benevolence are some who belong to a secret society whose goal is to destroy what it calls bigotry and intolerance and substitute preferential treatment for Jews. They do not realize the danger to the social order which would ensue as a result:

67. Jabalot's special bugbear in this regard was Cav. Bail who, in reaction to the setback for Jews after the fall of Napoleon, had written *Juifs au dix-neuvième siècle* (1816) and in 1823 *État des Juifs en France, en Espagne et en Italie depuis le commencement du cinquième siècle de l' ere volgaire jusqu' à la fin du seizième,* the latter for a contest on Jewish life during that period with regard to civil rights, commerce, and literature. Jabalot need not have worried: Bail lost to a contestant representing the point of view of the official Church.

68. In his *Mémoire sur l'état des Israélites.*

69. F. F. Jabalot, "Degli Ebrei nel suo rapporto colle Nazioni Cristiane," *Giornale ecclesiastico* 3 (1825); reprinted in R. Mazzetti, *L'antiebraismo nella cultura italiana dal 1700 al 1900* (Modena: Società tipografica, 1938), 124.

Do they [honestly] believe that a people whose religious duty it is to curse
Christians on a daily basis; who is forever waiting for a Messiah to rise within
it and free it from slavery and then by force of arms terrorize and conquer the
earth to its dominion; a people who considers all other peoples its enemies, its
oppressors, and all the kings [of the earth] as tyrants over it and who, therefore,
is looking for the right moment to break its chains and take its place among
the free and sovereign peoples; do they [really] believe that such a people can
ever submit to be obedient citizens, peaceful and devoted to the land of their
birth and to their fellow citizens? If they believe that then they haven't got an
ounce of sense [between them].

The Jews in Italy claim that they wish to participate fully in politics
on behalf of their country, not against it. The wish to serve unselfishly
and hold office. But the wise man pauses to ask: does not "my country,"
to a Jew, mean "my own interests, and those of other Jews, my people?"
Jabalot recalls Herder's *Adrastea,* which envisions the Jews as a parasitic
organism that, once it has permeated its Christian host, will systematically multiply until it takes over. Christians must, therefore, remain
ever vigilant for the day when the Jews within their midst may over-
whelm them and repay them in kind for centuries of subjugation. The
unrelenting example of history is proof that retribution is imminent.
The Jews are as a blood-crazed beast for centuries held in check because
of ancient transgressions. It is better that the "wise and venerable restrictions" remain in place for the "good of society and of the Jews
themselves." The very existence of the Jews is a sort of miracle, an example of God's mercy, for though they are foreigners in the land of their
birth, they are everywhere, and everywhere they turn their backs to the
whip. Everyone has seen them with horror for they are set apart from
others by a mark worse than that of Cain himself: on their foreheads
they bear the inscription "Deicide." [70]

A nation within the nation: the enduring accusation. During the
Restoration the concepts of political affiliation and loyalty were part
and parcel of faith in God. Nation had been fused to Religion and Jews
being deicides and Jacobins at heart were thought to have tried to kill
God in their native land by helping to lead Italy into the ignominy of
French, republican domination.

One Giovanni Vicini heard Jabalot preach a vitriolic Lenten sermon

---

70. Here Jabalot was quoting from Lamennais, *Essai sur l'indifférence en matière de
religion* (1823), vol. 3, chap. 23. He considered Lamennais in his ultramontane period,
"perhaps the most eloquent metaphysician of our day." See Jabalot, "Degli Ebrei," in
Mazzetti, *Antiebraismo,* 124.

at San Petronio in Bologna in 1826. Vicini, a well-known lawyer and doctrinaire republican,[71] was working on a case that hinged on a Jew's right to inherit from a Christian father who had died intestate.[72] He took the opportunity presented by the facts in the case to answer Jabalot, expanding his legal remarks into a treatise, *Voto di Verità: degli Ebrei* (1827), on the genuine Catholic approach to the presence of a Jewish sect in Italy.[73] Although Jabalot and other reactionaries before and after him conceived of Jews as natural enemies of the Church, Vicini, a liberal Catholic, argued that the Church actually needed the Jews. At the same time, he determined the origin of the undeniable friction between the two groups: the ultimate responsibility, he said, lay with the Church. This was because having been restored to excessive power, the Church considered any aberration from its self-defined orthodoxy as heresy and it was wasting its energies in demonstrating its superiority and administering punishments. In so doing it damaged itself as well as its victims. Jews could not be considered heretics having never been Christians. Indeed, such anti-Jewish legislation could lead to wholesale baptisms and feigned conversions that would only serve to weaken the Church. If instead it represented peace and love as it was enjoined to do by its founder, the Church could attract Jews and heretics back into the fold.

The Church had failed in part of its religious mission and it had failed politically. What should have been a unifying force throughout the peninsula had instead alienated people and set Italian against Italian: the Church,

not powerful enough to conquer this beautiful country nor virtuous enough to renounce temporal matters even though they are forbidden by heaven and detested by mankind, adhered instead to that cunning strategy . . . *Divide and*

71. Vicini had been president of the provisional government of the Cispadane Republic in 1796 and later Secretary General of the Cisalpine government. See G. Vicini, *Memorie biografiche del giure consulto G.V. da Cento* (Aquila: Forcella, 1882).

72. In this case the father, G. Levi, had converted to Christianity and died leaving one Christian son and two Jewish sons. General opinion held that the Christian son had a right to the entire inheritance. Vicini argued that this belief reduced Jews to the level of heretics against whom such legislation was common. See G. Vicini, "Gli ebrei nel diritto romano e nel diritto canonico," reprinted in R. Mazzetti, *Questione ebraica,* 143–158.

73. Vicini was known for his legal tracts (*Voto di Verità*) in defense of noteworthy clients. Owing to its more philosophical nature, this treatise has the subtitle *degli Ebrei* (of the Jews) in place of the client's name. It was reprinted as an appendix to G. Vicini, *Giovanni Vicini: memorie biografiche e storiche* (Bologna: Zanichelli, 1897).

Rule. So now we owe a debt to the Court of Rome: that we have witnessed the weakening of religious feeling among the faithful and that *Italy is still unable to unite under one standard!*[74]

Unification or even a full measure of Christian expression was impossible in Italy while certain groups, born and raised there, were legislated out of the social fabric. For this, too, the Church was responsible and ultimately suffered the consequences. The real problem as Vicini saw it was that unless Jews were willing to convert and thus take their place in society, the Church would never attain the predominance it sought. The Christian religion had within itself the necessary elements to persuade any skeptic, and all it needed to do was to apply the gentle persuasion that came from heartfelt faith. This would be possible only if bigots such as Jabalot remembered the teachings of the Gospels. If more churchmen lived by the Gospels, much ecclesiastical anti-Semitism could be eliminated.

The *Voto di Verità* was well received by a significant number of people,[75] for in Vicini's work lay the common-sense resolution to the conflict between religion and liberty, Church and Risorgimento. But successful achievement of one was rendered impossible by an imbalance in the other. Whereas Religion, defined as Nation, was used against the Jews in the accusations of Jabalot and others, the inverse concept had a positive application. From Vicini's *Voto di Verità* onward, liberal Catholicism, Neo-Guelphism, and Mazzinism placed the religious problem at the center of the Italian patriotic cause and considered unification of the peninsula into a sound nation unattainable while some Italians were walled-up within its cities.

What was especially significant and ultimately positive about Vicini's treatise was that the denial of Jewish civil rights before 1848 came to symbolize the plight of Italy under authoritarian rule and foreign domination, and Jewish aspirations to integration were identified with the Italian desire for unity. Emancipation of what amounted to a very small percentage of the population played a definite role in the creation of the Italian constitutional state. As the proponents of a secular Italy

74. Ibid., 211.
75. The publication of *Voto di Verità* was quite an event. Vicini's audacity was applauded by the liberal intelligentsia, but he was bitterly attacked by the clerics and government officials who depended on the Court of Rome. He was asked to retract his ideas and refused. The Curia accused him and his printer of slander, fined them, and condemned them to spend a week in a convent. See G. Vicini, *Memorie biografiche del giure consulto G.V.,* 24.

matched themselves against the conservative forces in favor of Italy under the pope, the Jewish captivity in the ghetto—like that of the ancient Hebrews in Verdi's *Nabucco*—and the exclusion of Jews from the civil and social life of their compatriots became a symbol of Church misrule and backwardness. It was clear that political unity could not be achieved while the Church retained the power to repress one segment of the population and that Italian liberation would be incomplete without the liberation of the Jews.

But there was one stumbling block in the theory. For all Vicini's concern for the Jews, nowhere in his essay did he suggest that they be tolerated, respected, and allowed to live freely *as Jews*. In his eyes, fellow citizens who persisted in their distinctly Jewish identity would, to a certain extent, remain foreigners. He was not alone in his point of view; liberal Catholics generally assumed that, some time in the near future, it was inevitable that Jews would become Catholics like themselves. Indeed, in order for emancipation to function positively in the creation of the new nation, most people believed that the recently freed Jews would have to change significantly and adapt to the life and expectations of the dominant majority. These obstacles to Jewish assimilation were discussed by numerous proponents of emancipation and Risorgimento—chief among whom were Cattaneo, Mazzini, and Gioberti— each according to his special interest.

The pragmatic approach to the Jewish question by a nonreligious thinker is best exemplified by Carlo Cattaneo in his pamphlet *Ricerche economiche sulle interdizioni imposte dalle leggi civili agli israeliti (An Economic Investigation into the Civil Restrictions Imposed on the Jews).*[76] Cattaneo insisted on the necessity for reforming the Jews by economic means. Traditional aversion to Jews was of religious origin and began in the fourth century, but financial considerations were soon to contribute the most durable of all foundations for anti-Semitism. The usual excuses for relegating money lending to the Jews—the Aristotelian theory that money is infertile and as such should not be handled— served as a psychological balm to those beset by creditors. Excluded from common law and not subject to religious sanctions, Jews assumed the task of keeping capital in circulation. What was needed, though, was cash flow on a much larger scale than the small number of Jews could provide: agriculture and commerce were all but choked without

76. Cattaneo's work was written in 1835, but publication was delayed by the Milanese and Viennese censors until 1837. It was first published in the *Annali di Giurisprudenza pratica* (Milan, 1837), vol. 23, bearing the date 1836.

a pervasive capitalistic system of loans and interest. As the Jewish monopoly on money grew, general poverty also grew and the lines at the moneylenders' doors lengthened. Cattaneo describes the violent, anti-Jewish outbreaks from the Middle Ages onward in terms of historical materialism, that is, as the rebellion of those who owned little or nothing against the only possessors of wealth, to whom they owed no allegiance and were not bound in any way. Chased, as a result, from land to land, Jews were left with only "l'amor del lucro" ("love of money")[77] as a focus for their lives, a fixation that emboldened them and helped them endure. There was no secret charm known only to the Jews for amassing huge fortunes. Actually, Cattaneo reasons, the interdictions against them, although morally depressing, kept them from wasting time in study and self-improvement, time that was better spent making money. A similar evaluation could be made of the dress code and laws against construction of new housing! They ultimately saved Jews money and it is well known that money begets money.

Cattaneo seems never to have looked beyond the cliché of "l'amor del lucro" in his estimation of the Jews. Significantly, he ignored the reality of the masses of Jews, who existed in utter poverty, and concentrated on those with money. However, he argued that the all-consuming Jewish fixation on money as well as their furtive cleverness, human insensitivity, and lowliness were the result of historical circumstances rather than racial or biological factors. Thus the "problem of capitalism" should not be expressed in terms of birth, race, or blood but solely in terms of education. What the Jews needed, therefore, was redirection to lead them away from egotism and hostility toward social cooperation. The only way to bring this about was abolition of the interdictions. Human nature, their love of luxury, of humanistic study, of honors would bring Jews back into the mainstream of civil life. Contrary to popular belief, Judaism posed no threat to Christianity. And the greatest benefit of all was that the Jew would bring with him his hoarded wealth and release it back into the economy.

Cattaneo's pamphlet on the interdictions is perhaps more famous among the pro-Jewish essays than is warranted. Its progressive stance is easily exaggerated by comparison with the writings of Jabalot, for instance, since on the most basic level it *does* argue for removal of harsh and unfair laws. But Cattaneo does not attempt to debunk any of the

77. C. Cattaneo, *Sulle interdizioni israelitiche* (Rome: Sestante, 1946), 69. This is a critical edition of the original pamphlet.

myths about Jews. On the contrary, he works within the framework of accepted ideas, especially in his treatment of Jews and moneylenders, which actually reinforces the stereotype, making the concept of "redirection" seem a vain hope and the Jew seem unassimilable.

Both the republican Mazzini and Neo-Guelph Gioberti envisioned reform on a purely religious level. For Giuseppe Mazzini, the inspiration of Risorgimento patriots, political progress was inexorably linked to religious renewal;[78] indeed the answer to most questions, political or existential, was to be found in God. Imagining himself a sort of latter-day Moses ("Moses wanted first and foremost to create the Nation"),[79] Mazzini assigns Judaism (which he calls "Mosaism") a definite role in the birth of united Italy. Judaism is the living incarnation of the prophecies of the past and has a mission for the future. But in order to contribute effectively to the "new light, the new life in God,"[80] Judaism would have to be transformed and Jews rise above their

pile of symbolic rituals and pull themselves up from materialism, [that is] the model [for living now] that is condemned to die in the face of the Idea which has been granted immortal life.[81]

The newly emancipated Jews had a job to do: to go beyond the "hedge" of dogma ("[they must] break through the hedge") and ritual, and the particularism of a single religion, in order to attain the infinite, the realm of pure Religion. For it was Religion that was to become the moral base of the new Nation.[82]

This concept of mission also found ample expression in Vincenzo Gioberti and his concept of Italian moral hegemony as defined in his seminal work, *Del primato morale e civile degli Italiani* (*On the Moral and Civil Primacy of the Italians*). His Neo-Guelphism was derived in part from the myth of the mission of the Italian people to enlighten civilization with their Catholic culture through the papacy. Guelphs had done that once before. The Neo-Guelphs, under the leadership of a new pope, would advance the Italian cause once again. One example

---

78. In G. Tramarollo, "A cento anni dalla morte di Giuseppe Mazzini," *Rassegna mensile di Israel* 38 (1972): 327.

79. G. Mazzini, letter to the prominent Jewish philosopher, Elia Benamozegh, *Epistolario*, 20 January 1870, in *Scritti editi e inediti*, national ed. (Imola: P. Galeati, 1906–1943), vol. 89, appendix, 348.

80. Ibid., 349.

81. Ibid.

82. Ibid.

Italy should give to the world would be a successful movement for national unity, a rapprochement of all its diverse factions. Italians should work to mold local political sentiments into national political consciousness. Since for Gioberti patriotic sentiment and religion were so closely knit, such an effort would bring about the salvation of the Church as well.

The rapprochement could not possibly occur in a country that permitted the persecution of religious minorities, for such practices were harmful to victim and victimizer alike. For this reason, Gioberti, "founder and spiritual father of democratic nationalism," fought anti-Semitism in the Kingdom of Sardinia.[83] Persistence in the kind of blind bigotry which the Catholic Church had manifested over the years would leave the Church empty of its enlightened adherents without whose support it could not ultimately survive. Failure of either half of the organic unity, Nation-Religion, would leave the other half bereft and unviable.

Gioberti, like his liberal colleagues, looked back to the Jews as the inspiration of Christianity. Echoing the Jansenists, he argued that the Jewish people had presented the world with the biblical basis for civilization: creation and redemption, Genesis and the Gospels, fundamental Christian doctrine. Thus Jews were essentially strays from the Christian fold and, in an oblique way, participants in that Christian community that they had prepared for the world in ancient times. As such they must be shielded from persecution:

The best way to lead Israel gone astray back to the sheepfold is to treat [the Jews] with that precious and magnanimous charity which is the hallmark of our religion. Whoever does the opposite, even if he call himself a Christian and Catholic, is in fact a Gentile.[84]

Once rehabilitated after centuries of mistreatment, Jews would have to be lured out of their particularism by the Catholic religion. The Catholicism of some, which had not developed beyond formalistic and extrinsic ritual that imposes and depends upon moral enslavement, would have to give way to the Catholic Christianity of the Romantics, *de profunda anima,* which liberates and redeems the spirit.

Gioberti's gospel of brotherhood was echoed in the liberal press, in two Tuscan newspapers, *La Patria* and *L'Italia,* as an integral part of

83. So wrote the jurist Scipio Sighele in his attack on the proceedings against Alfred Dreyfus. See E. Landolfi, *Scipio Sighele: Un giobertiano tra democrazia nazionale e socialismo tricolore* (Rome: Volpe, 1981), 186.

84. V. Gioberti, *Del Primato morale e civile degli Italiani* (Turin: 1926), vol. 2: 84–85.

their debate on Risorgimento. *La Patria*[85] became a standard-bearer for the cause of tolerance. Its Catholic editor, Raffaello Lambruschini, emphasized that promoting civil rights for Jews was the duty of liberal Catholics in liberal regions such as Tuscany. Parity in opportunity, amelioration of living conditions, and preparation for citizenship were rights for which Jews were eligible from birth according to the dictates of God and religion. Any treatment of Jews which did not attain these minimum standards would leave a pathetic legacy to posterity.[86]

La Patria also discussed the place of Jews in Italy directly through the series of letters on emancipation from the Ferrarese Jewish philanthropist, Salvatore Anau. One of the thorniest problems tainting the image of the Jews as they awaited liberation by Risorgimento was the question of patriotism, an issue repeatedly dusted off and applied against them in times of crisis. Anau demonstrated the emptiness of that traditional stigma by stating the case for Risorgimento and emancipation simply and decisively:

There is no redemption beyond civil liberty. [Similarly] you have no country beyond the one which witnessed your birth.[87]

What about religion? It was not, he admonished, such a burning issue. Indeed, time would adjust all religious matters:

For me it is sufficient if man can be free to believe as he chooses. It is sufficient that a religion, which is guilty of nothing more than being created somewhat different from the dominant one, not be segregated by law, and I [will] leave it to time to decide whether or not these different religions will one day be transformed and absorbed by the principal faith or will continue to exist. The important point is that the religion of social morality be applied equally for everyone.[88]

To the Jews of the 1848 Emancipation in regions such as Tuscany who had attained the right to regulate their civic activities and allegiances, Anau advised that they assume responsibility for their own social welfare:

85. *La Patria* began publication in Florence on 2 July 1847 and ceased 30 November 1848.

86. For his religious and disinterested sentiments, Gioberti called Lambruschini "the master of the liberal Catholics." See S. Anau, *Dell'emancipazione degli Ebrei*, pamphlet (Florence: 1847), 3–4.

87. Ibid., 14.

88. S. Anau, *Schiarimenti di Salvatore Anau nelle sue lettere per la emancipazione degli Ebrei* (Florence: 1848), 13–14.

Be free, know your Christian neighbors and spend your lives for the good of your country and your fellow [citizens], both Christian and Jew.[89]

The editor of *L'Italia*,[90] G. B. Giorgini, was considerably more militant when it came to advocating Jewish emancipation. His newspaper bore the motto: *Riforme Nazionalità* ("Reforms, Nationality") and Giorgini's pro-Jewish rhetoric lived up to the program implicit in the slogan. On 17 July 1847 Giorgini began a series of articles with an editorial entitled "La causa israelitica" ("The Jewish Cause"). Here he proclaimed that the issue of Jewish civil rights was a banner behind which all those dedicated to progress in Italy were gathering, that this cause would be furthered in the pages of the newspaper, and that persons of like mind were invited to lend their support.

From 24 July to 6 November 1847 Giorgini attempted to debunk the various stigmas attached to the Jewish population and problems of cohabitation arising from them. First he wrote about "shiftless," "rootless" Jews who for nearly two thousand years had been "rejected, tormented, exploited like animals and worse than animals . . . their name is called shame and their touch profanation." Rootlessness was an especially pernicious charge during a time of budding patriotism. To this stereotype was added the Jewish reputation for clannishness and isolation which was bolstered by the enforced claustration of the ghetto. Giorgini described this stigma that, at the time, appeared almost impossible to reverse because of the constant historical need for protection and flight. Wherever there is a Jewish community, he pointed out, the memory of Judas remains very much alive "in everybody's hopes." With these words he pinpointed the key to the bewilderment of the outsider who confronted the orthodox, "exotic" ritual of the "small, obscure band" of Jews. Excluded from participation in the outside world, the Jews turned inward, shoring up those attributes that made them unique and, apparently, unassimilable. Denied their rights historically and held at bay socially, Jews fulfilled the grievous role allotted them.

Judaism is as unchanging as its defamation, Giorgini continued, and this has led to a paradoxical situation. Whereas ghetto Jews resembled nothing so much as "exotic plants which, having been welcomed into our garden, stand out in the midst of the surrounding vegetation," once emancipated they would become indistinguishable from the rest of the population. In reality, therefore, their ethnic characteristics had little

89. Ibid., 25.
90. *L'Italia* was founded in Pisa in 1847 and ceased publication in 1848.

to do with the (fictitious) desire for isolation, with the "nation within the nation," and everything to do with the laws of proscription.

There were only two avenues open to legislators regarding religion: tolerance or intolerance. Those who favored repression justified themselves in part by complaining that given the example of Jewish clannishness, Jews would not pull their weight in what should be a common effort toward historical progress, that is, Risorgimento. This was not an illogical argument: why contribute to a complicated and risky process from which one was unlikely to derive a reasonable benefit? Anyone who believed that the Jews would or should sacrifice themselves for the good of the majority from which they were excluded was foolishly presumptuous. However, those proponents of the Risorgimento who were in a position to help the Jews had to understand that assisting the Jews to win their freedom was a step toward achieving that Risorgimento, and that unification and the continued existence of Jewish ghettos were mutually exclusive phenomena. Historical progress could not be realized while in every major city and several smaller ones, throughout Northern and Central Italy, such symbols of backwardness, of prejudice and exclusion, in short, of disunity, remained in place.

Deliverance

In 1846 the Jews and the writers and politicians who pleaded their cause looked to the new pope, Pius IX, for help and were not disappointed.[91] Giorgini, his fellow Neo-Guelphs, and other Catholic liberals correctly interpreted the pope's mind in their approach to the plight of the Jews. Although Pius's fear of the Risorgimento was eventually to disillusion his liberal supporters, early in his reign his sincere desire to help the Jews gratified those who had faith in him.

Of all the progressive writers, the one who heralded Pius IX's arrival with the greatest enthusiasm was Massimo d'Azeglio. Indeed the aristocratic Piedmontese novelist, painter, essayist, and political activist proved to be one of the greatest champions of the Jewish cause in the nineteenth century. Struck by the bitter sight of the Roman ghetto and

---

91. For background information on the reign of Pius IX see A. Monti, *Pio IX nel Risorgimento italiano* (Bari: Laterza, 1928); R. De Cesare, *Roma e lo stato del papa dal ritorno di Pio IX al 20 settembre,* 2 vols. (Milan: Longanesi, 1970); A. M. Ghisalberti, "Pio IX, papa," *Enciclopedia italiana* 27: 321 (Rome: Treccani, 1950).

with a mind unclouded by prejudice and free from visions of Jewish conversion, d'Azeglio investigated the reality of ghetto life and published his findings. Beyond the description reproduced at the outset of this chapter, d'Azeglio meditated on the causes of unchristian behavior toward Jews. Political malaise was one sure source of anti-Semitic violence after the experience of the French Revolution, the Napoleonic Wars, and the despotism of the Restoration. Massive ignorance in religious matters was another and this was exploited continually by priests and lower-echelon officials of the Papal State. It manifested itself in the repeated riots and sackings of the ghetto at times of political crisis. Misunderstanding of the Jewish religious nature was evidenced by the requirement that Jews attend conversionist sermons. But the worst of all the burdens on Jews, second only to the ghetto itself, was the system of taxation which, together with the prohibition of profession and trade, were designed to keep the Jews in a perpetual state of penury. These taxes, which d'Azeglio lists in his book,[92] appear to have been conceived in nightmare, products of a paranoid obsession with *contrapasso* ("just punishment") for usury, deicide, and thirty pieces of silver. Surely this treatment produced a state of constant anxiety in those who had to provide for their families. In his emphatic recreation of one such ghetto dweller, as in the earlier account of the ghetto environment, d'Azeglio the painter described and d'Azeglio the humanist suffered for his fellow man:

Let us imagine that poor Jew who has to be a father to his family and provide for it. . . . We see him return to his miserable hovel after a day of running up and down the streets of the city in search of filthy rags to peddle. He brings with him nothing or, at best, only negligible fruits of his labors. Let us try to enter his heart while he meditates in vain some vendetta against those who deny his family not luxury, not the diversions of the rich, but bread and air—fresh, healthful air—light and sunshine: those invaluable treasures which God lavished on the weak as well as the strong, on the rich as well as beggars! Imagine the anger, the desperate hate that gnaws at the heart of that wretched man.[93]

This state of affairs more than any other was an indication of the damage that intolerance, backwardness, and greed had done to Italy. Other civilizations had abandoned such practices long before and d'Azeglio believed the upper classes to have outgrown them. Intolerance was still rife among the masses, however, and it was up to the cultured levels of society to educate their inferiors.

92. M. d'Azeglio, *Dell'Emancipazione*, 26–27.
93. Ibid., 33.

A fine example was being set by Pius IX who demonstrated his concern for the Jews early on in his reign. He abolished the conversionist lectures and certain tributes and ameliorated some of the crowding in the ghetto by allowing some Jews to move out. D'Azeglio was opportunistically generous in his praise of the pope. He pointed out that Pius IX understood how to interpret the signs of the times when major political newspapers such as *La Patria* and *L'Italia* had pleaded the cause of Jewish emancipation from the very first issue. Principal among the needed changes was that the Church disentangle itself from politics, thereby assuring its renewal. A Church that derived its strength from spirituality rather than repression would aid Italy in the struggle against foreign domination. Religion and Risorgimento would unite for the common good.

D'Azeglio's words, coupled with the example of the pro-Jewish demonstration led by the popular rabble-rouser, "Ciceruacchio" (Angelo Brunetti), were most effective in prompting Pius IX to order the doors of the Ghetto opened and its walls pulled down forever. D'Azeglio's pamphlet was published in January 1848. On 26 March of that year, from the pulpit of S. Maria in Trastevere, padre Ambrosoli preached unconditional tolerance toward Jews. Finally, on 17 April 1848 Pius IX gave the order to dismantle the gates and part of the walls of the Rome ghetto and of the other ghettos in the Papal State. The next day was the first day of Passover, the annual commemoration of the liberation from Egyptian slavery, and that year the holiday was celebrated as never before during the preceding three hundred years of captivity.

Largely through the good offices of Massimo d'Azeglio's brother, Roberto, liberation was declared in mid-June in most-Catholic Piedmont, a region long synonymous with reaction.[94] Soon, since Jewish emancipation had been won throughout so much of the peninsula, it became an expected corollary to general political liberation. This is not to say that resistance to the emergence of Jews in Italian life had miraculously disappeared, but that opposition took the form of individual and isolated incidents and that the reactionaries could no longer draw on the authorities for support.

Except in Rome: emancipation in that stronghold of intense reaction was a good deal more complicated than in the rest of Italy. The removal of the Ghetto doors did not signify the cessation of prejudice nor of opportunism for those who profited financially from the precarious

94. See B. Terracini, "L'emancipazione degli ebrei piemontesi," *Rassegna mensile di Israel* 27 (1961): 301.

status of the Jewish community. Within a year-and-a-half from that Passover eve, the Jewish community experienced repeated sackings under various pretexts: once to find great sums of money that had mysteriously disappeared from circulation; once in an attempt to locate Christian religious objects, or simply as part of general uprisings. During this period Pius IX renounced the Risorgimento and withdrew from the politics of liberation. He fled to Gaeta in November of 1848 and on 9 February 1849 the Roman Republic was proclaimed. To the Jews came freedom and the right to participate in civil government, just as during the Napoleonic era. And like that earlier interlude, the republic soon fell, the Pope returned, and many of the old interdictions seesawed back into place.

The Church had no intention of abandoning its mission of conversion so that the Jews continued to finance the House of Catechumens and the Convent for Converted Females. In addition Jewish families continued to endure the tragedy of kidnap and forced baptism of their children, such as in the infamous Mortara case.[95] Public education was forbidden as was travel without special permits. Nor was the financial burden lightened in any significant way. Since investments were severely limited and ownership of property expressly forbidden even after 1849, the Roman Jews were virtually imprisoned in an open ghetto.

But despite the severity of interdiction, the physical barrier of the ghetto had been destroyed and contact with the Christian community was possible. On 13 October 1870 all remaining limitations to Jewish civil and political freedom were abrogated by Victor Emmanuel II. The forces for emancipation of the Jews and for unification of the peninsula ultimately converged on Rome. Unification became a reality; the emancipation of the Jews of Italy was complete.

As each ghetto gate opened and as the walls came down, Jews rushed en masse to overthrow cultural barriers that had kept them from living as full-fledged Italians. Along with legal parity Jews prepared for assimilation with extensive efforts at "self-improvement," attempting to rid themselves of their off-putting Jewishness and, in its place, affirming their *italianità*. They strove for and attained economic and political positions in the mainstream of Italian life. Those who could often bought

95. The six-year-old Mortara was kidnapped in 1858 and raised in a House of Catechumens. His case brought intervention from Napoleon III and Sir Moses Montefiore, but the boy was never restored to his family. He took holy orders and became a professor of theology. See *Encyclopedia Judaica* 12: 354–355 (Jerusalem: 1971); G. Volli, "Il caso Mortara nel primo centenario," *Rassegna mensile di Israel* 26 (1960): 29–39, 108–112, 149–157, 214–221, 274–279.

land—visible evidence of their stake in the destiny of their *patria*. Little by little, Jews and former Jews began to enjoy the good life.

The fact that Jews were able to achieve this goal in a relatively short time might appear to point to a certain superficiality of anti-Semitic feelings underlying the phenomena of ghettoization and hundreds of years of anti-Jewish legislation. Indeed, Antonio Gramsci, like Croce before him though in different terms, asserted that because of assimilation "there is no anti-Semitism in Italy." This was because traditional Jewish separatism had been overcome by the process of Risorgimento. Moreover, he stated categorically, this was a spontaneous occurrence. Jews did not ally themselves artificially with an already flourishing movement; rather

the formation of the Jewish national consciousness parallels the formation of Italian national sentiment among the Piedmontese or the Neapolitans or the Sicilians. It is merely one moment of the same process and could well symbolize it. Thus at the same time Jews residing in Italy became Italians.[96]

Whatever distinct characteristics Jews might retain, these would in no way detract from their Italianness, at least to no greater extent than did the regional peculiarisms of their fellow Italians. Once Jews saw themselves as Italians, Gramsci stressed, those changes demanded by Cattaneo, Mazzini, and Gioberti would be unnecessary. Jewish attitude, then, would overcome anti-Semitism. Together with this major development in Jewish world view—the assimilation that Gramsci welcomed—two other cultural stumbling blocks would crumble: municipal particularism and Catholic claims to universal spiritual hegemony. Mirroring the Jewish movement away from the notion of galut toward assimilation, Gramsci observed the large-scale transformation of self-image from municipal and regional *integralismo* to national allegiance. Thus in both camps, Jewish and Christian, he noted the tendency to abandon "medieval" cultural homogeneity and aspire to heterogeneity, thereby creating an environment in which anti-Semitism could not exist. Gramsci's mistake was to assume that assimilation could, by its very nature, eliminate anti-Semitism. Instead, as events in Jewish history proved time and again, assimilation had little if any effect on anti-Semitism.[97]

96. A. Gramsci, "Ebraismo e antisemitismo," (Notebooks 2 and 10), reprinted in *Il Risorgimento* (Turin: Einaudi, 1966), 166–169.

97. A. Canepa, "Reflections on Antisemitism in Liberal Italy," *The Wiener Library Bulletin* 30 (1978): 105. Canepa cites the Dreyfus affair and the adoption of *völkisch* ideology by assimilated German Jews as cases in point.

Both Croce and Gramsci presented the elimination of anti-Semitism as one of the achievements of Unification, using reaction to the Jewish minority, its segregation or integration as a yardstick to measure the effects of Risorgimento. If, however, the Risorgimento left such a profound legacy, then the popular literature of the period should have reflected these aspirations, much like the high-minded Romanticism of Manzoni or Nievo or Leopardi. But the inspiration behind most popular literature—especially those works in which Jews figured as prominent characters—was diametrically opposed to Risorgimento ideals. Instead of the vision of the d'Azeglios or even the religious-political goals of the Giobertis one reads the ultramontane echoes of the Jabalots. Indeed it was largely in popular literature that one encountered those elements, such as Catholic universality (*cosmopolitismo*), which Gramsci labeled "feudal vestiges." At this level of literature, the pluralism of those who sought a place in society was portrayed as a social spoiler, a potential generator of unrest. The conflict between orthodox and heterodox visions of the society was rendered in themes of external religious difference and internal religious struggle and resolved in favor of conversion to the dominant religion in the works of authors who considered the Jews worth saving. In those authors who did not, Jews were portrayed as objects of ridicule—too conniving yet foolish, spineless, or avaricious to be redeemed. In the novels discussed in chapters 2 and 4, we shall see what Croce and Gramsci failed to take into account: that in most religiously motivated popular literature Risorgimento was a distant thunder and anti-Semitism was very much alive.

2

Altar and Throne: Bresciani's *Jew of Verona*

Religion is the paladin of liberty.
Rosmini

If there was one lesson to be learned from the centuries of isolation in the ghetto, from the literature for and against emancipation, and from the difficulties faced during those first years on the outside, it was that Jews had to convert in order to take their rightful places in society.

This was the prevalent attitude among churchmen and lay thinkers alike, among those who viewed the ghetto experience as a necessary tribulation to bring Jews to embrace Christianity as well as those who promoted equal rights for this special group of Italians. Certainly some Jews were able to earn rank and respect while retaining their Jewish identity. Yet even among such champions of Jewish integration as d'Azeglio and Tommaseo, the concept of regeneration ultimately implied assimilation through conversion to Catholicism. Anything less than the definitive end to Jewish particularism was inconceivable.[1]

1. Exceptions to the rule were very rare. A. M. Canepa reports on the Milanese cleric, Ambrogio Ambrosoli, who, on 26 March 1848, shortly after the proclamation of the Roman Republic, preached a sermon in Santa Maria in Trastevere in which he invoked the concept of universal religious tolerance and argued for "unconditional" emancipation of the Jews. Canepa calls him the only Catholic cleric to propose integration without conversion, in "Emancipazione, integrazione e antisemitismo liberale in Italia: il caso Pasqualigo," *Comunità* 29 (1975): n. 174, 182.

Quite apart from the Church's coercive efforts in this regard—among these, the programs of conversionist sermons, the Houses of Catechumens, and the forced baptisms—conversion was "in the air," a product of the revival of popular religious sentiments which swept Europe in the early nineteenth century. Though it is Jewish conversion that concerns us here, conversion at this time was just as likely to involve Protestants and lapsed Catholics as Jews.

There were as many approaches to conversion as there were special interest groups who saw themselves in a position to gain or lose by it. Of these, two groups are of particular interest. The first was made up of artists and activists who adhered to the cause of the Risorgimento, subscribing to and expressing themselves according to the spiritual and artistic aesthetics of Romanticism. The second group consisted of those who represented the authoritarian Church in its campaign to retain its hold on both the religious and political life of the peninsula.

The Romantic movement distinguished itself in part through its philosophical stance in religious matters, its notion of tolerance, and, with regard to minorities, its impassioned yet steadfast political activity in their behalf. At the same time religious ecstasy was a great source of inspiration to its artists. Chateaubriand, among the many Christian apologists, was the most successful at translating this passionate faith into terms that appealed to the Romantics: "Of all the religions which have ever existed, Christianity is the most poetic, the most humane, the most propitious for liberty, for the arts, for literature."[2] For him and others, poetic beauty was a celebration of their faith in God who is the source of harmony and imagery for the poet. Christianity, he said, is in its very essence poetic.[3]

It was the poetic nature of Christianity which particularly suited the religious temperament of the Romantics, who often expressed religious ecstasy following a moment of illumination. Sometimes religiosity took the form of total mystical absorption that transformed the natural into the supernatural, as in Chateaubriand's encounter with primeval nature and the infinity of the Cosmos.[4] More often, in conversion narratives,

2. F. R. de Chateaubriand, *Génie du Christianisme* (Paris: Gallimard, 1978), pt. 1, bk. 1, chap. 1, 469–470.
3. Ibid., pt. 2, bk. 3, chap. 8, 708.
4. "Venture into the American forests which are as old as the earth. If you are still, all is quiet; as you move, the forest sighs. With the approach of night, the shadows lengthen and you hear herds of wild animals pass in the darkness . . . the forest grows restless, trees fall, an unseen river flows before you . . . The traveler sits on the stump of an oak tree to await the dawn. He gazes about him at the starry night . . . He feels uneasy,

profound faith followed the moment of realization of divine intervention, the sign from God after a dark period of spiritual anguish. Probably the most famous of these was the great Romantic novelist Manzoni's description in *I promessi sposi* (*The Betrothed*) of the villainous Innominato's night of torment and the sudden peace and newfound strength he feels as he accepts his victim Lucia's certainty of God's pardon. Stories of conversion, including Manzoni's own religious crisis in the church of San Rocco, were common during this period. Some accounts, such as those of the Jews Alphonse Ratisbonne and Davide Norsa, were published and, in turn, inspired others to convert. Manzoni wrote an impassioned letter on the subject to Marco Coen.[5]

Religion, then, and particularly conversion, was conventionally described in emotional terms. Conversion was no less than a rebirth of conviction and dedication to which Romantic sensibilities were especially receptive. But there were some, converts and their catechists, who considered the question of conversion in quite a different light. Whereas Manzoni promoted conversion of the Jews and of lapsed Catholics such as himself for purely spiritual reasons, in the literature of the Catholic Right, conversion was also expressed in terms of political urgency; and the political crisis of the day was the Risorgimento.

In 1844 after a year of intense study, the Jewish writer Giacomo

---

excited, as if waiting for some unknown thing. His heart starts to pound with extraordinary fear and incredible pleasure as if he were about to be admitted to some secret of the godhead." (Ibid., pt. 2, bk. 4, chap. 1, 720.)

5. Coen had informed Manzoni of his intention to convert and Manzoni replied on 7 September 1842 affirming the existence of divine intercession and the sign from God: "Pray to Her, the holy, blessed, glorious, merciful Daughter of David, for her powerful intervention, for recently she has given us a clear and consoling sign [of her powers]." See A Manzoni, *Lettere,* 3 vols., ed. C. Arieti, vol. 2: 244–246, in *Tutte le opere,* ed. A. Chiari, F. Ghisalberti (Milan: Mondadori, 1970), vol. 7. The allusion to a recent conversion refers to Ratisbonne's famous, sudden conversion in Rome in 1842. See *Narrazione storica della prodigiosa apparizione dell'ebreo Maria Alfonso Ratisbonne, avventata in Roma il 20 gennaio 1842, nella chiesa parrocchiale di Sant'Andrea delle Fratte, de' PP minori di San Francesco di Paolo* (Rome: n.p. 1892), 87; see also, "La conversione miracolosa di Alfonso Ratisbonne nel cinquantesimo anniversario," in *Civiltà Cattolica* 43 (1892): 513–533. Norsa gives Manzoni credit for guiding him to Christianity and recounts Manzoni's religious experience: "An illustrious Catholic worked with pious zeal for my well-being. I learned from him that in his youth he had been skeptical: he was living in Paris among free thinkers. But he wasn't at peace with himself and his spirit was increasingly troubled. Tormented by doubt, one day he went into the Church of San Rocco and said 'Oh God, if you're there, let me recognize you and end my suffering!' From that moment on he was a believer, and in the True Faith he found genuine peace." See D. Norsa, *Pensieri di un cattolico* (Prato: Guasti, 1850); 2d ed. rev. (Florence: Cooperativa, 1874), 29ff.

Lombroso converted. Lombroso's catechist was a disciple of the fiery father Jabalot and, with the increasingly severe climate of repression in Milan in the 1840s,[6] Lombroso's writings began to reflect the vitriolic message of that ecclesiastical defender of Austrian domination and religious orthodoxy.[7] Jews, he declared, "will be free from now on to adopt or refuse the Catholic religion." The Jews, however, "tend to try to upset the order of things"; were they to continue to adhere to their faith, one day they might well be accused of "conspiring, at least indirectly, against the governments under whose tutelage they now live." One day, he warned, the criminal codes could be invoked to quell "this new kind of rebellion against the established order."[8] On the surface Lombroso's observations on the Jews and his advice that they convert to avoid the political consequences of their behavior appear to be no more than the usual expressions of hostility from a Jew who is also an anti-Semite. But underneath there lies the tacit acknowledgment of vulnerability: [the Jews] "pray openly every day for a *risorgimento,* which, were it to take place, would smash all the altars and overturn all the thrones." This is the key to the central, nonreligious dimension of the portrayal of Jews in the literature of the Catholic Right. It was focused on all Jews, but especially on those in larger communities where there was greater circulation of liberal ideas and a population that was increasingly adhering to the cause of the Risorgimento. Therefore, although Lombroso and others exaggerated Jewish political influence and the threat posed by such a small number of people with minimal resources, their fears were not altogether groundless.

Both the Church and the Risorgimento activists considered the Jews their property: one as a source of new converts and added strength for the Church, the other as a captive population to liberate and co-opt into their efforts to unify the peninsula and create a secular nation. Father Antonio Bresciani's *L'Ebreo di Verona* (*The Jew of Verona*), written at the height of Risorgimento unrest, typifies the bitter conflict

6. These were the years of Radetsky's military government of Milan and Lombardy-Venetia. See *Storia di Milano* (Milan: Treccani, 1963–1966), vols. 14–15, passim.

7. G. Lombroso, *Degli ostacoli che le consuetudini oppongono alla evangelica rigenerazione degli ebrei e come superarli. Corrispondenza epistolare tra il canonico professore Taddeo dei Consoni e Giacomo Lombroso letterato israelita. Opera pubblicata in occasione della solenne professione di fede di quest'ultimo al cattolicesimo* (Milan: 1844). This exchange of letters was published in honor of Lombroso's baptism to serve as a guide to conversion of the Jews and refutation of their messianic expectations. The volume is dedicated to His Imperial Highness representing the August Monarchy in Lombardy.

8. G. Lombroso, *Dei perfezionamenti che l'Evangelo ha apportati alla legge Mosaica* (Milan: 1845).

between these two groups as the Church tried to stem the tide of revolution. The novel is a historical fantasy in which the conversion of a Jew strikes a blow to the heart of rebellion and scores a small triumph for the forces of reaction. Within the general scheme of oppositions—evil versus good, sectarian violence versus ecclesiastical repression, Romanticism/Risorgimento versus Jesuitism—lies the religious and political drama of the Jew of Verona. The author's approach to the conversion and politics of his protagonist, though necessarily slanted to bring grist to his own mill, provides in spite of itself a remarkable portrait of a Romantic hero, and in particular, a Risorgimento activist.

As the cause of the Jews became interwoven with the almost religious cause of the Risorgimento[9] there developed an apposite iconography of the politicized Jew. The Jew, open to politics after the twenty-year respite from life in the ghetto, was pictured, in certain circles, as an aggressive political figure to be reckoned with. Had this been the work of liberals, they might have minimized the "radical" element in Jewish Risorgimental sympathies while emphasizing the economic misery of the Jews and their lack of civil rights. But this was a portrait painted by ultraconservative Catholics who feared for the stability of the established order. For a time this new conception of the Jew succeeded in supplanting the traditional stereotype of the cowardly, money-grubbing, hook-nosed miser.

The dichotomy between the grim reality of the Jewish situation before the final emancipation and the overestimation of their political power was the product of the fear of imminent and cataclysmic changes on the part of arch-conservatives who saw themselves as probable victims. Therefore this phenomenon was not due so much to the actions of the Jews themselves as to their connection with the Risorgimento, the most visible political expression of Italian Romanticism. The outspoken critics of the authoritarian world of the Catholic Right were often the most vociferous supporters of Jewish emancipation. They were the great Romantics such as Mazzini, Manzoni, and d'Azeglio, themselves targets of reaction to the strong political component of their writings and to their charismatic leadership.

The Romantic movement, with its strident pronouncement of new ideas, its youthful political energies, and its component of popular, egalitarian religiosity, threatened to obviate the possibility of establish-

9. The Risorgimento was considered by many a sort of religious crusade and the fervor of liberation and unification was often expressed in religious terms in literature. See M. Sticco, *La poesia religiosa del Risorgimento* (Milan: Vita e Pensiero, 1961).

ing religious uniformity because it kept alive the menacing reality of heterodoxy.[10] Due to the very nature of Romanticism, this bane of misbelief was bound to enjoy wide currency, for the Romantic "poetic" impinged heavily on Italian artistic and political life. Thus, in their reaction to it, both the adherents and the critics of Romanticism merged religion, art, and politics.

A prime example of the intermingling of art and politics is found in the writings of Mazzini. His many articles on the emotional and political aims of art influenced scores of engaged artists of the day and generated widespread reaction in conservative circles. For Mazzini, in poetry there was the society of the "people" on a grand scale:

Poetry moves with the centuries and with events. Poetry is life, movement, the flame of action, the star which lights the path of the future . . . *Popular* poetry has spread everywhere, an epic poem of revolution, riot and satire . . . Creation does not rest on thrones or monastic altars. Poetry has abandoned the Europe of the past [and has gone] to inspire the new, young beautiful Europe of the people . . . Would you compare the petty, dismal, bloodless poetry of individuals, poetry of empty form which lives and dies within the gloomy confines of a palace, a chapel, an old castle, with the great, solemn, tranquil, confident *social* poetry which acknowledges only God in heaven and the *people* on earth?[11]

Interwoven with Mazzini's theory of "popular" literature was the idea of religion to be achieved on a literary as well as a political level among long-oppressed peoples who, in a newfound "youth," were just beginning to construct their own history. Here the points of conflict with anti-Romantic literature are clear. Such an approach to national culture would seem to deny the historical role of the Church as a national unifying institution and, from the Church's perspective, eternal repository of a people's history. So said Father Bresciani in a letter to the General of the Jesuit Order: Romanticism, he wrote, "is an *irreligious and anti-monarchical* literary faction. Christian topics are always on its lips, but that's just to make it easier to eat away at the most holy institutions of the Catholic Church . . . Every Italian man of letters who calls himself a Romantic is also a Liberal."[12] Perhaps the best-known

10. On the subject of Italian heterodoxy, see G. Salvemini, *Stato e Chiesa in Italia*, vol. 3 of *Opere* (Milan: Feltrinelli, 1969), chap. 4, "La religione del popolo italiano," especially 113–116.

11. G. Mazzini, "Ai poeti del secolo XIX." This article was first published in Fasc. III of *Giovine Italia* (1832). Reprinted in *Scritti editi e inediti*, nat. ed. (Imola: P. Galeati, 1906–1943), vol. 1: 349–374.

12. The letter is dated 29 December 1831 and cited in F. Iannace, *Il conservatorismo cattolico in Antonio Bresciani* (Rome: Trevi, 1973), 113–114.

reply from the Right to Mazzini's articles, as well as to the many Romantic artists influenced by them, are the four essays by Bresciani united under the title *Del romanticismo italiano* (1839). Bresciani argued that Romanticism

is not natural in itself, nor is it natural for the *Italians* or [the people of] other *cultured Nations*. Furthermore it is *harmful* to *Religion,* to worthy *politics* and to *Morality.* Thus [will one be] increasingly attracted to the school of our classic, major writers.[13]

The Catholic Right fought Romantic literature on as large a scale as it could muster with its own weapon: the printed word.[14] Early on it created its own press supported by the Church and by various religious societies. The early nineteenth century in Italy witnessed the flowering of many special groups each rallying around a religious or a political ideal. Turin, as d'Azeglio wrote in his memoirs,[15] was a particularly good example of this given the prominence of some of the members of the religious societies, but the general picture varied only slightly in the other major Italian cities.[16] The best known of these groups in Turin was the Society of Christian Fellowship ("Amicizia cristiana").[17] In

13. A. Bresciani, *Del romanticismo italiano* (Parma: P. Piaccadori, 1853), 36. Not one to be undone by the presence of an anomaly in his theory on Romanticism, Bresciani explains the adherence of the religious and moral Manzoni to the ranks of the Romantics with the statement that the great author joined the "school" for the glory of religion as a "dike" to prevent Romanticism from inflicting further damage on the minds of Italian youth! (p. 35) See also G. Faldella, "La beretta del Padre Bresciani e la testa di Giuseppe Mazzini," *Gazzetta del Popolo della Domenica* 14 (1896): n. 25.

14. ". . . by means of the press . . . we managed to create that illusion and that ruinous prestige which caused [the public] to formulate so many foolhardy and insane hopes. By means of the press we can also correct the consequences of this, at least in part. In order to lead [people's] minds back to the straight path, we must employ the same means which were used to lead them astray." [Comment on the publication of the *Lettera pastorale di monsignor Garzilli vescovo di Bovino, Enciclopedia ecclesiastica* 1 (30 July 1821): 249–250.]

15. "After the restoration of 1815 . . . there was a fresh recrudescence of [religious] zeal so that I found Turin full of Catholic societies, where one paid only a trifle, but which served to attract the public and keep a tight rein on the Jesuits." M. d'Azeglio, *I miei ricordi* (Turin: Einaudi, 1949), 417.

16. See G. De Rosa, *Storia del movimento cattolico in Italia* (Bari: Laterza, 1966), vol. 1, chaps. 1 and 2, passim.

17. The "Amicizia cristiana" network had roots in the eighteenth century. The first was founded in Bern in 1782 by Nicolaus Diessbach as a secret society after the disbanding of the Jesuit order in 1773 by Pope Clement XIV. See De Rosa, *Storia del movimento,* vol. 1: 27ff. One of these groups was organized in Florence under the auspices of Baron Ricasoli and counted among its members the young priest, Antonio Bresciani.

1817 it was opened to the public and renamed "Amicizia cattolica,"[18] with the declared purpose to promulgate *buona stampa* ("the good press").

The vague term buona stampa was concretely represented by a number of periodicals well before the founding of *Civiltà Cattolica* in 1850. It was in these pages that Catholic anti-Romanticism found frequent expression. Chief among these periodicals were the *Enciclopedia Ecclesiastica e morale* in Naples (1821–1822); the *Giornale Ecclesiastico* in Rome under the direction of Jabalot (1825–1826); and *L'Amico d'Italia* founded in Turin by Cesare Taparelli d'Azeglio (1822–1829).[19] Though these publications were short-lived, there were many of them, all propounding more or less the same principles.

The goal of these periodicals was to restore and defend both the Church and monarchical authority. Altar and throne were cooperative institutions, each shoring up the other by preaching absolute faith in papal government or by intervening in political matters. The reactionary press played a definite role in this. It had a clear message to impart and that was an urgent one: that it was of utmost importance to "[re]arrange the religious attitudes of the society."[20] That is, as the individual owed allegiance to God, since his personal salvation was at stake, so society as a whole owed the same allegiance in order to secure its salvation. This compenetration of religion and society[21] was also reflected in the absolute authority of the monarchy. Religion and monarchy could only be restored together since they shared common interests and goals. The origins of the Church's current despair lay in the aberrations of eighteenth-century encyclopedism, the Enlightenment, and the revolution of 1789. There were some who would deny the age-old doctrine whereby all temporal power derived from God. In addition, unity of religion was perceived to be the key to harmony in the governing of the state, for the concept of obedience of the subject was of religious origin and given divine sanction in the person of the monarch. There was clearly no room in this system for religious minorities or political

18. The group was composed of lay persons, chief among these Cesare Taparelli d'Azeglio—father to Massimo and to the Jesuit Luigi, one of the founders of *Civiltà Cattolica*.

19. Of note were also *Memorie di religione, di morale e di letteratura* in Modena, first published in 1822, and *Giornale degli apologisti della religione cattolica* in Florence (1825–1827), *inter alia*.

20. "Riordinamento," *L'amico d'Italia* 2, t. 4 (1823): fasc. IV, 104.

21. G. Verucci, "Per una storia del cattolicesimo intransigente in Italia dal 1815 al 1848," *Rassegna storica toscana* 4 (1958): fasc. 1, 251–285.

fringes, for it was they who were tampering with tradition: they who were attempting to waken the docile, somnolent masses to the reality of the Church's centuries-old exploitation of their credulity, their poverty, and their ignorance. It was up to buona stampa, and its cohort, the *Azione Cattolica* (Catholic Action Organization), a lay movement created to counterbalance nascent political parties, to close the floodgates.

With the revolutions of 1848, attacks on the Jesuits, and Pius IX's flight to Gaeta, the question of religion and society became particularly compelling. F. G. Ventura's manichaean world view outlined in the *Giornale ecclesiastico* of 1825 seemed even more appropriate in 1850:

Today as at the beginning of time society seems split into two great peoples who make up the city of God and the city of Darkness. By now there appear to be only Catholics and Atheists . . . that is to say men who believe everything there is to believe and men who no longer believe anything.[22]

Stunned into marshaling his defenses, Pius IX accepted the proposal of Bresciani and other prominent Jesuits to found a journal that could combat the secular press. In 1850 *Civiltà Cattolica*, the most successful of all Italian Catholic publications, saw the light.[23] The staff was handpicked by Pius IX for this enterprise.[24] He instructed the staff on the character the journal should assume and his wishes were outlined in the editorial of the first issue. The goal of this formidable bulwark against the twin conspiracies of secular philosophy and liberal politics was to

lead the philosophy and the course of civilization back to that concept of Catholicism from which it seems to have departed three centuries ago . . . We urgently need this beneficial conspiracy or holy crusade, if you will, against the invasion of heterodoxy; for once it rises among us, it will only strengthen the deviant path of social ideas so that we may never hope to straighten them out again . . . Our program, like our title, our standard, our vestments, our solemn vow of faith: *Civiltà Cattolica*.

Militant and ready for battle, *Civiltà Cattolica* chose its weapons. In order to stand its ground in this duel of words and ideologies, the

22. F. G. Ventura, "Della disposizione attuale degli spiriti in Europa rispetto alla Religione, e della necessità di propagare i buoni principi per mezzo della stampa," *Giornale ecclesiastico* 3 (1825): 27.

23. For an excellent account of the creation of *Civiltà Cattolica* and the first few troubled years of its history, see the introduction by G. De Rosa to *Civiltà Cattolica 1850–1945*, 3 vols. (S. Giovanni Valdarno: Landi, 1971), vol. 1: 9–101.

24. Among them were Matteo Liberatore, Isaia Carminati, Luigi Taparelli d'Azeglio, and Carlo Maria Curci, editor-in-chief.

editors opted for a style of writing which would be both accessible and attractive to the average reader. To be sure, the great majority of people was conservative and Catholic and either indifferent or hostile to the Risorgimento. Still, operating as it did from a position of repression under which pressure was mounting slowly but steadily, the Right could not ignore the need to bring its cause to the people in terms they could understand and accept. Thus *Civiltà Cattolica* discarded the traditional, abstruse language of papal documents and learned theological discussions and confronted current problems in an unpretentious but intense manner.

Father Antonio Bresciani[25] assumed the literary editorship of *Civiltà Cattolica* with the understanding that the works published therein would serve to propagandize the moral content of the rest of the journal. He undertook to "lead civilization back to the concept of Catholicism" partly through his own novels. Thus one finds in *L'Ebreo di Verona*, for instance, an all-out tribute to papal authority: the strong arm at the service of kings to quell riots and discipline the populace, as well as the defender of the rights of the poor, of widows and children.[26] For Bresciani, in return, *Civiltà Cattolica* served as a ready-made publisher for his novels. Indeed, given his acerbic attacks on the "terrible days of the Mazzinian Republic," one could consider these novels a compendium of antirevolutionary spirit[27] as for Catholic readers Bresciani became a symbol of anti-Mazzinism.[28] Readers responded to his apocalyptic visions of revolution, responsible as it was for

ruthless secret homicides . . . horrible vows and diabolic rituals, for daggers against the Cross and profanation of the Holy Eucharist, for the cult of two-faced Janus on the Campidoglio and of Eleusinian mysteries.[29]

Bresciani was apprehensive about his literary assignment, but was told he need only reproduce what he had actually observed during the Roman Republic. Adopting Diessbach's advice on the importance of

25. For an excellent account of Bresciani's life, the reader is referred to the entry in *Dizionario biografico degli italiani* (Rome: Treccani, 1972), 179–184. Valuable references are also given in the appendix to F. Iannacce, *Il conservatorismo cattolico.*

26. A. Bresciani, *L'Ebreo di Verona*, in *Civiltà Cattolica* (Rome: Civiltà Cattolica, 1850–1851), vol. 1: 207. Citations from the novel refer to this edition and are included in the text.

27. G. Spadolini, "L'intransigentismo cattolico dalla 'Civiltà Cattolica' al 'Sillabo'," *Rassegna storica toscana* 4 (1958): fasc. 1, 309–332.

28. See *Commentario della vita e delle opere del P. Bresciani*, appendix to *Opere* (Rome-Turin: Ufficio della Civiltà Cattolica, 1865–1869).

29. Ibid., xcviii, cited in Spadolini, *L'intransigentismo,* 309–310, n. 2.

good books "excellently written in terms of style, elegant and pleasing" but also capable of combating error and inculcating "the dogmatic and moral truths of our sacred Religion,"[30] he overcame his fear of writing novels and filled the pages of *Civiltà Cattolica* with nine of them. *L'Ebreo di Verona* appeared in the first issue and continued to be serialized through the journal's first six volumes (1850–1851). In a sense it "grew" with the periodical and as the first literary work in a new publication, faithfully reflected the developing editorial policy.

L'Ebreo di Verona served as the medium through which *Civiltà Cattolica* first broached the Jewish question. Over the years *Civiltà Cattolica* took a contradictory stance toward the Jews. It attempted to apologize for anti-Semitism by emphasizing that throughout Church history Jews were responsible for all the calamities they endured and that anti-Semites were justified in their retaliations. *Civiltà Cattolica* featured several articles on Jews during the early years. These were mostly diatribes against the Talmud and the specifically Jewish crimes it inspired, attacks that were so common by this time that they had become formulaic.[31] At the same time the journal condemned the use of violence and injustice (a concept subject to infinite interpretations) against Jews. By attacking world Jewry, however, *Civiltà Cattolica* could discredit the staunchest enemies of Church influence: liberals, freethinkers, anticlericals, Jansenists, freemasons.[32] These were the fomenters of revolution. But of all of these the most pernicious were "the silent machinations of the Jews" ("li sordi raggiri degli Ebrei").[33] Jews were all the more dangerous because they worked in secret.

30. From a memorandum to Father Lanteri, 1841, Archivio "Civiltà Cattolica," in Bresciani, *Opere*, VI, vol. 6: 1.

31. A sampling from the first three years of *Civiltà Cattolica* reveals entries under "Giudei" in which Jews are accused of "cruelly and obstinately persecuting Christianity" (VI, 659), of "praying to God to exterminate Christianity [together] with its kings and its ministers" (Ibid.), of searching the Talmud for ways to deny Christ (VII, 203). See *Indice delle materie contenute negli undici volumi che formano la prima serie della Civiltà Cattolica* (Rome: Civiltà Cattolica, 1853), 96. Similar material, although more biblical in nature, is included under the heading "Israeliti." See p. 113.

32. A. M. Canepa speculates that "perhaps the Masons, though clearly responsible for much of the agitation against the Church, were too respectable among the middle classes to be attacked directly, without first tainting them with collaboration with an accursed race." In "La *Civiltà Cattolica* and Clerical Antisemitism in Italy 1800–1900." Unpublished manuscript.

33. *Memorabili avvenimenti successi sotto i tristi auspici della repubblica Francese* (Venice: F. Andreola, 1799), p. 6. The Jewish conspiracies ("from which to foment changes which would place them on the level of other citizens" [p. 6]) are grouped under the heading of the "storm of popular revolutions" (p. 5). Pamphlet cited in *I giornali giacobini italiani*, ed. R. De Felice (Milan: Feltrinelli, 1962), xx–xxi.

Bresciani's historical novel deals with the period immediately prior to its writing, a radical departure from the conventions of the historical novel. The main characters conspire, murder, and sometimes love against the backdrop of the wars of independence and the assault on the Quirinal, 1846–1849. These characters are made to exemplify specific sectors of Risorgimento society; they have almost no emotional depth, in fact, no life at all, apart from their limited, didactic roles. As such the novel is instructive in the manner befitting *Civiltà Cattolica*.

The plot is a standard blend of intrigue, violence, and religion. Aser, the Jew of Verona, is a young artist in Rome. He saves the pious, virginal heroine, Alisa, from a menacing crowd and though he is Jewish, for both it is love at first sight. He belongs to a secret society, however, and his political engagement soon carries him away from Alisa to the wars of 1848 and later to pursue radical politics in Switzerland. After many adventures of war and espionage, Aser suffers a bad fall. He recovers and thankfully converts only to be murdered by his former allies in the secret societies.

The novel is certainly more anti-Risorgimental than it is openly anti-Semitic. Except for some gratuitous insults to stereotyped ghetto dwellers, such as

"You trust the Jews, this dirty, ignorant, stingy and cowardly people who for two cents would outperform Judas? . . ."

"You can't compare foreign Jews with the filthy, stinking, ragged Jews of our Italian ghettos." (I, 324)

Jews are generally treated in a political context. Or rather, one Jew is and he stands for all the rest as the personification of Judaism. The protagonist, Aser the Jew of Verona, is made to embody many of the author's fears. Sensing the inevitable downfall of his religious power base, Bresciani fills page after page with attacks on the new wave of Risorgimento liberalism through the adventures of his protagonist, while his other characters and episodes function in verification of *Civiltà Cattolica*'s doctrines on revolution. The Risorgimento is the bane of modern life and the Jew of Verona, a Romantic hero, is the epitome of Risorgimento.

The supporting characters in the novel fall into one or the other of two categories: some are peaceful, law-abiding decent folk; the others are outlaws, seditionists, anarchists. The first group is fairly passive, the second is aggressive, always plotting against the common good.

The first group is represented by the virtuous heroine, Alisa Capegli, and by her father, Bartolo. He is a well-to-do and sometimes befuddled Roman gentleman, a conservative idealist who dreams of a prestigious united Italy firmly guided by those principles that inspired Gioberti's *Del primato morale e civile degli Italiani*. He is the enemy of the secret societies, but numbers their members among his friends. Despite his revolutionary associates, Bartolo is a thoroughly peaceful man who argues that uprisings are not the only way to unite Italy, for revolutionaries are always caught and imprisoned. Better to imitate the mice of Venice. While the lion of San Marco slept, the little mice nibbled at him taking care not to wake him. All the while they soothed his wounds with their honeyed tongues and little by little gnawed through to his heart and killed him. On the one hand this is a nightmarish vision of the developments that were about to engulf Bresciani's Italy. On the other, it seems Bresciani's wish that this certain disaster should be as painless as possible.

Alisa is an emotional innocent who divides her life between her home and the confessional. She is a model of virtue, steadfast, unworldly and entirely passive. Her opposite, Polissena, is militant and so engaged in revolution that there is not "a hair on her head that is not dedicated to *Giovine Italia*." Highly intelligent and sophisticated, she can acquit herself in any situation. Polissena is a messenger for the revolutionary groups and travels the length and breadth of Italy, alone, in their behalf. The messages she delivers are written on white silk and carried "between the ribs of her whalebone corset or even between her breasts because silk does not rustle like paper. If a rather immodest police officer were to search her, the rascal would be fooled" (II, 90). Bresciani demonstrates his lack of respect for Polissena by describing her work in terms of her underwear. That she is buxom is suggested by his vulgar choice of the word "cogni" or "wine barrels" to describe the bosom of her corset and the use of "sollazzare" denoting "enjoyment" to indicate that these "cover" the breasts. He also insinuates that Polissena is practiced in enduring sexually compromising situations, in this case bodily search by some "rather immodest" police officer or other. Though well-born and educated, she has been ruined by her political opinions. Compared to the heroine, the politically active woman is a tart.

Still, for the purpose of a convenient contrast between good and evil, Alisa and Polissena are constant companions. When Alisa asks her friend to accompany her to confession to an old Jesuit priest, Polissena tries to talk her out of it:

Confessing to a Jesuit is like climbing into your own tomb. Don't you know that the Jesuits are the most defiant enemies of virtue; that they subtly bewitch innocent minds? . . . all your wrongdoings would be put on a list and sent every Saturday to the General of the Order, who meditates once a week on the sins of young women. When you want to marry, your fiance asks the General confidentially for that list. You see, the Jesuits are cunning, fraudulent, mean and cruel—all cloaked in the hypocritical guise of piety. Don't trust them if you want to save your soul. (I, 91)

Bresciani, on the defensive, has put anti-Jesuit canards in the mouth of the villainous Polissena. These were almost as pervasive as anti-Semitic commonplaces. One senses Bresciani's perverse delight in making up such tales about the order as a passive attack on the order's detractors. Predictably the heroine of his story will hear nothing against the priests and stands firm in her unquestioning faith.

Polissena tries a new strategy: she substitutes Alisa's religious books with liberal political novels. In Bresciani's universe dedication to Risorgimento can not exist in the same organism with religious devotion. The two are born enemies. Polissena gives Alisa the books that affirm a symbiosis between religion and patriotism: *Marco Visconti* by Grossi, *Margherita Pusterla* by Cantù, and *Niccolò de' Lapi* by d'Azeglio. Unable to rouse Alisa to the political needs of the moment, Polissena leaves for the war, having composed a letter to the girl she had tried so hard to instruct in Giobertian "civil Christianity." The letter codifies those elements in Bresciani's system which separate the virtuous from the patriotic, and once again the author's doctrine is couched in an attack on those same beliefs:

Civil Christianity, which keeps pace with the progress of nations, is not a religion for petty hearts and narrow minds. . . . the nuns instilled in you a medieval sort of piety, vulgar, plebian piety which feeds on rosaries, novenas, masses and communions. Yours is the Christianity of the Jesuits. You can not rise to the noble, sublime, divine Christianity of Gioberti. Too bad for you. (II, 311)

Polissena's Romantic sentiments are those of Mazzini (whom Bresciani had accused of corrupting youth)[34] in "Ai poeti del secolo XIX" even to the language used and to the notion that Christianity, like the popular poetry he referred to, must progress with the times.

<hr>

34. A. Bresciani, *Del romanticismo italiano,* 35.

In the struggle between good and evil, the feminine quality of virtue and the masculine quality of patriotism, Alisa's maidenly purity can not be shaken. There is a certain propaganda value in this strength of character, but it is a limited statement quickly made and Bresciani makes it relatively early in his story. Virtue is instructive only when contrasted with evil and Bresciani provides a portrait of evil several volumes long. This was a time-honored technique and an effective one given the audience of *Civiltà Cattolica*: a mass of convinced Catholics, many as yet ignorant of lay government, who were, at the same time, targeted to be the beneficiaries of revolution. Readers had to be acquainted with the villains—in this case the secret societies under the general heading of *Carboneria*[35]—in every grisly aspect of their inhuman criminality, so that they would be moved to condemn them in an effort to prevent the oncoming storm of change. It was more or less an article of faith that most devout Catholics were against revolution, so in describing the secret societies in nearly hyperbolic terms, Bresciani would be merely reinforcing currently held opinions. For those who were not aware of subversion in their midst, Bresciani's exposition would be a revelation.

The secret societies were as insidious as they were deceitful, for, like Polissena, not daring to speak plainly, they cloaked their degenerative poison in noble sentiments. They were also violent, like another perverted female, the assassin Barberina d'Interlaken, the "Great Virgin of Helvetian Communism." Babette traveled throughout Europe intercepting diplomatic messages, forging checks and passports, dispatching her enemies with poison or stiletto. At only twenty-three years of age, obeying the orders of the band of cutthroats, she had already taken many lives. A virago who tore out the eyes and organs of Swiss Catholics and paraded them through the streets,[36] she was a hideous distortion of Christian womanhood, but a typical revolutionary. Such women were to be found in Rome as well:

35. "Carbonarism," a term now used loosely to indicate revolutionary secret societies, provided a focus for political opposition, first in Napoleonic and then in Restoration Italy. It was especially influential in the Neapolitan revolution of 1820 and in the 1831 insurrections in Bologna, Parma, and Modena. See R. Soriga, *Le società segrete, l'emigrazione politica e i primi moti per l'indipendenza* (Modena: Società tipografica modenese, 1942).

36. Here Bresciani is probably referring to the attacks on the Jesuits and the defeat in 1847 of the Sonderbund, the league of seven Swiss Roman Catholic cantons, suppressed after a month of civil war.

One could often hear them singing in the taverns "long live Hell and those who go there! Death to Saint Peter!" And together with Garibaldi's bandits quite a few of them committed robbery, sacrilege and ghastly murders. Where these furies come from, who knows? Probably some murky den of conspiracy. (I, 670–671)

Compared to Alisa and Bartolo, clearly the most interesting characters are members of the secret societies. Bresciani describes them as if they were all one person: egomaniacal, duplicitous, brave, irresponsible, and stingy toward family, but devoted and generous to itself, tenacious and invincible. Like hydras, the more they are trampled the more they flourish; as each cell is suppressed another springs to life elsewhere. As if acknowledging this ability, they have chosen a serpent for a symbol. Pleased with this device, Bresciani lists the snaky qualities shared by the *carbonari*: snakes slither through the undergrowth, in and out of cracks in decaying walls; they nest under rocks and trees, under towers and even under God's altars; they hide at the bottom of wells, in empty tombs, and in dark caves in poisonous solitude. In their shadowy underworld they plot the demise of their prey and bide their time. Exposed to the light, they coil and hiss, and with head erect transfix their horrified victims with a bloody stare. Then they strike and kill. Everyone has been warned of the danger of snakes and yet no one is prepared to fight them.

The author's fear of the secret societies is clearly expressed in the sentence structure of his frantic description of their machinations. One is struck by the breathless quality of the verbal phrases in the present tense:

Italy should have no illusions, she should not believe herself at peace. Right now [the secret societies] are angrier and more vicious than ever: now they are gathering, many of them, all at once, and they are closing ranks to plot together in the most secret hideouts in [many] cities; they sharpen their guard; they plan new strategy; they strengthen their deceit; they incite the lazy; they encourage the timid; they restrain the reckless; they are always on the lookout for their advantage; they seize opportunities; they catch governments in error and they twist and turn them until the mistakes become crises. Hypocrisy and simulation have given them access to the confidence of Princes, to cabinet secrets, to the deliberations of ministries, to the Chiefs of Police . . . Work by day, keep watch by night: they never tire. (I, 217–218)

A sample of the Italian reads:

Assottigliano gli avvisi, apparecchiano nuovi intendimenti, rafforzano gl'inganni, sollecitano i pigri, dànno baldanza ai timidi, ritengono gli avventati; . . . colgono gli sbagli de' governi, gli aggirano, gli attraversano . . .

Their meetings resemble the witches' covens that so gripped the religious imagination in ages past. There the devil is worshiped at his altar. Satan is the God of the secret societies. In order to obtain the Host so that they can hold services that will mirror the Mass but as a perversion of it, the women of the group go to Church in the morning and take Communion, but without swallowing the wafers. These they use at night to worship Satan. One of the members presides at the altar and leads his comrades in a prayer to the devil:

Our God and our Lord, receive in homage the blood and body of your capital enemy. Here is Christ at your feet, do with him what you will. You have already had the Jews crucify him and he deserved it: this scoundrel wanted to usurp your kingdom and you gave him his just rewards . . . This vile and timid God fled to the top of the skies, but through his priests we pull him back down to earth and we have our hands on him. Now let him pay us the penalty for having preached poverty, obedience and pardon for our enemies. Death to priests, death to Christ! (I, 410–411)

The revolutionaries are continuing the crucifixion of Christ begun by the Jews. By bringing down the Church, by terrorizing the priests, the secret societies are continually recrucifying Christ. They are the henchmen of the devil in his war against God.

One of the devil's finest disciples is the Jew of Verona. Of all the characters in the novel, Aser is the only one who develops. Early on he functions mainly as a symbol of Mazzinian revolution and the Jewish involvement in it. Like Aser, Mazzini's hero is a poet and a patriot:

The poet . . . is the chosen one of the people, a son of the people, and the joy, pain and affections of millions echo in his spirit.[37]

Poets! brother of the eagle! Favored by nature![38]

We young people need you! . . . We need to hear your voice, your anthem in the midst of the struggle which surrounds us.[39]

The poet/hero soars like an eagle, but is the son of the people. A saintly figure, he takes upon himself the people's joy and sorrows, and in return inspires his people through his art and his deeds. He is the voice of the people.[40]

37. G. Mazzini, "Letteratura poetica della Boemia," in *Scritti editi e inediti,* vol. 1: 378.

38. G. Mazzini, "Ai poeti del secolo XIX," 369.

39. Ibid., 370.

40. Such a figure materialized in the 1840s: the poet Goffredo Mameli with his "choral" poetry in which he intended to interpret the sentiments and aspirations of the political movement. The poem *Ai fratelli Bandiera* amply demonstrates Mazzini's influ-

In many respects Bresciani's protagonist resembles Mazzini's Risorgimento hero quite closely. He is an artist, in this case a painter. Like Mazzini's selfless poet/patriot who assumes the burdens of others, Aser is the essence of unselfish dedication to a cause. He gives freely of himself. Mazzini's hero is "favored by nature" with the lyric gift, able to dispense beautiful verses with which he gives a voice to the collective poetry that "quivers in the spirit" of the people. Aser is favored by fortune, blessed with the resources with which to finance both the secret societies and artists who express and interpret the times in which they live. But in this novel the similarity exists to make a negative point. As was the case with his presentation of the characters at the outset of his story, Bresciani has also construed Aser's nature and his allegiances in terms of good versus evil. In this case the opposition is between Aser and a religious and political ideal. Thus in the struggle between the Church and the devil Aser is working for the wrong side. In delineating Aser, Bresciani has taken a portrait of artistic magnanimity and political perfection and turned it inside out to reveal a hideous and dangerous underside.

Being a Jew, however, Aser does not live up to Mazzini's ideal of the artist as the "son of the people." As a Jew, he is neither strictly bound by societal norms nor identifiable in terms of them. Indeed, except for his politics he remains a mystery even to his closest allies. They acknowledge that he is fearless and intelligent, the most valuable member of the "corte sacra" (sacred band). He has a special knack for recruiting soldiers from among the rabble. Drunks, wife-beaters, and deadbeats respond to Aser and willingly become cannon fodder for the cause. His loyalty to Carbonarism is absolute, but his comrades can only speculate about his true identity:

Most people say that he is the illegitimate son of some great northern prince and he *did* come to Rome with a passport from Hamburg. He carried letters of introduction from the leading bankers of Hanseatic cities; he was recommended to several consuls; he was always together with Lord Minto.[41] He spends a lot and never lacks for money. He dresses elegantly and his home is

---

ence and the urgency of the political situation. See G. Pirodda, *Mazzini e gli scrittori democratici* (Bari: Laterza, 1976), par. 77, pp. 66–71.

41. Bresciani is probably referring to Gilbert Elliott-Murray-Kynymond, second earl of Minto (1782–1859), prominent member of the famous Scots family and an influential Whig. He was ambassador to Berlin, first Lord of the Admiralty, and Lord Privy Seal. In 1847 he was sent by Palmerston on a much-publicized official visit to Rome and Turin in support of the national sentiments of the liberal opposition. Bresciani's use of such a remote yet known figure is meant to lend historical veracity to his tale.

fit for a prince. He lends money to the greatest Prussian, Hannoverian, Swedish, Danish and Norwegian artists. He speaks many languages well, especially French, English, and Italian, and in Italian he has such a soft and delicate accent as was never heard in a German mouth. He plays the harp and the piano, he sings sweetly, he paints masterfully, he rides horses with style . . . You know he is a great friend of Mazzini and Ruffini . . . and is in continual correspondence with the heads of the Young Germany movement. Not to mention the Swiss: he is well-known to all the revolutionaries of Lausanne, Bern, Geneva, Zurich and other cantons. In fact, for us he is a delight . . . (I, 326–327)

Aser is a person of unknown origin with a bottomless purse, international connections, perfect knowledge of many languages; he is talented and always on the move. Bresciani's description is overloaded, but all the details he furnishes contribute to an almost classic portrayal of the legendary Wandering Jew. Where Aser differs from the folk hero is that he is not an old man with a long white beard dressed in rags, as pictured in the engravings of Gustave Doré. Moreover Aser's constant travels under an assumed identity result from political choice rather than the expiation of a curse. The legend of the Wandering Jew is an ancient one and very widespread—factors that permit considerable latitude in delineation of the figure.[42] But throughout the existence of the legend, chroniclers sometimes embellished "eyewitness" accounts with the descriptive elements befitting well-known contemporaries. Bresciani seems to have followed this tradition. Given the popularity of the legend it was natural for him to have grasped at these folk stereotypes in his search for the Jewish characteristics to create his protagonist. His insistence on certain elements of the legend, however, reveal an additional source of inspiration. Aser's international associations are with people of the highest rank. Much of his youth was spent in Germany and Northern Europe. He is a patron of the arts and, as the author reveals later, he comes from a banking family. In the person of the Jew of Verona, Bresciani appears to have combined two traditions: the venerable legend of the Wandering Jew and the legend-in-the-making of the contemporary, international, dynamic, and very rich Rothschild family.[43] The two elements that both sources have in common are the international nature of Jews' lives and their perennial re-

42. For a comprehensive treatment of the origin, incidence, protagonist, and development of the legend of the Wandering Jew, see G. K. Anderson's exhaustive study *The Legend of the Wandering Jew* (Providence: Brown University Press, 1965).

43. It is important to note, however, that Bresciani modeled his character on the famous family only insofar as it served as living evidence for certain stereotypical characteristics he wished to stress: the Rothschilds took no part in liberal politics and Aser's political allegiance is not meant to reflect theirs.

source of large quantities of liquid capital. And these are the elements that reappear most frequently as Bresciani continually adds to and reworks his portrayal of the Jew of Verona.

Revolutionary politics functioned in a network that embraced much of Europe, though reactionaries who, like Bresciani, lived in fear of revolution overestimated the interaction of groups across national borders as a giant web, finely meshed, ready to suffocate those who remained loyal to the traditional partnership of altar and throne. Thus Bresciani contemplates a Europe that is totally and irrevocably mobilized, with Austria, Switzerland, Germany, France, Piedmont, Tuscany, and the rest of the Italian peninsula ready to explode.

One by one Aser acts out all these fears. Calling himself a silk merchant from Danzig, he travels rapidly between revolutionary meetings to confer with leaders. His contribution to the revolution is characteristic of that of the rest of European Jewry:

Italian, German, Polish, Bohemian, and Hungarian Jews help us in all sorts of ways. They give us money, printing equipment, books and newspapers from all over. But what is even more important, Jews of all ages and walks of life, calling themselves salesmen, travel on missions for us. They couldn't be more faithful and dependable. They manage to be everywhere, they spy through every crack and slip through every hole [in the wall]. You could say they're our electro-magnetic telegraph. (I, 324)

Simple observation would reveal that Italian Jews would not generally have such resources, but, the author cautions, one must not measure all Jews with an Italian yardstick. The Jews of whom he speaks come from places where Jews are

free, cultured and rich; where they go to universities; they're friendly with [the right] groups; they have business in every port, banks in every major city. They work in all levels of government stopping just short of being gentlemen of the bedchamber in the royal palaces. (I, 324)

Being so dedicated and held in such esteem is usually no less than what one could normally expect from a dynamic protagonist of a Risorgimento novel. Not so in this case. Regardless of his level of culture or his personal fortune, Aser's Judaism precludes any positive assessment of his actions. Bresciani stresses that Jewish loyalty to the cause is no manifestation of humanitarianism, but rather the result of their overriding hatred of Christianity:

It's neither greatness of mind nor generosity nor kindness which binds them so closely together, it's the rage of Judas. They would give their lives to assure that the resurrection of Europe recrucify and rebury Christ. (I, 324)[44]

For much of the story Aser participates as well in this collective wrath. In his role as a Risorgimento hero, or latter-day Judas, and in light of his hatred of Christ, he makes the inevitable anti-Jesuit statements and credits Gioberti's book, *Il Gesuita moderno* (*The Modern Jesuit*) with having opened his eyes and induced him to fight retrograde churchmen. Gioberti's exposé of the character and state of Jesuitism in the mid-1840s is the work of a Catholic who feels betrayed on religious grounds by members of his own faith. His attack, some of it directed against Bresciani himself, reads, not surprisingly, like Bresciani's diatribes against the secret societies. So in Gioberti one reads that a Jesuit prefers to attack his enemy from the rear. If he does meet his adversary face to face, he will embrace him for all to see while furtively planting a dagger in his heart: another version of the kiss of Judas. The nineteenth century is an era in which Jesuitism finds itself with many enemies for in reality it is nothing more than

a secret society, a permanent conspiracy, a perennial ambush against those states which harbor it as long as they refuse to become its absolute and perpetual vassals.[45]

Having learned his lesson well, Aser concludes:

Because we wish to regenerate Italy we cannot tolerate this scum in our midst . . . Call them retrograde, enemies of every new freedom granted by the Pope to his dominions, brigands feeding on the people in order to keep them ignorant, bound with doubly thick chains to Austria, traitors to their homeland . . . (I, 674–675)

By this point in the novel Bresciani has made his politics clear and the battle lines are drawn. Were it not for the convention in nineteenth-century novels that the protagonist not be a wholly negative character,

44. These outraged sentiments appear in Joseph De Maistre: "Without a doubt there has always been vice and some of it wicked. But up until the eighteenth century, within the very bosom of Christianity, there had never been a rebellion against God. And especially there had never been a sacrilegious conspiracy of so many intelligent minds against their maker. This is what we have witnessed in these times. The men of this century have prostituted their genius to irreligiousness. They have made war on God with His own gifts." Cited in F. Leoni, *Il pensiero controrivoluzionario nella storia d'Italia* (Rome: Mediterraneo, 1976), 24.

45. V. Gioberti, *Il Gesuita moderno* (Milan: Bocca, 1940), vol. 2: 111–112.

what little action there is in this story would come to a standstill. The plot is saved by the imperative that the author reform his protagonist and in so doing deliver a religious message as well as a political one. Bresciani's protagonist is guilty of several sins among which are factionalism, duplicity, and undercover activities against the established order which lead to murder. The most serious of all his faults, however, is his Judaism for which mere repentance is not sufficient to gain him the road to salvation. Aser must set about to atone for his political and religious shortcomings, and the rest of the novel deals with the process of his redemption.

As the story progresses, Aser's artistic sensibilities begin to affect his view of the political and moral situation of his troubled times. And with Aser's each new realization the reader is predisposed to react to him as an increasingly positive character. Here one must bear in mind the devout nature of the first audience for *L'Ebreo di Verona,* the readers of *Civiltà Cattolica.* For them it was most instructive to observe Aser's gentleness at the outset when he rescued Alisa from a militant crowd, kindness that was stifled and nearly extinguished by his devotion to revolution.

The first of these moral awakenings takes place in Genoa where he witnesses the plight of twenty Jesuit priests imprisoned in a ship's dark, unventilated hold on a charge of infanticide.[46] Upon seeing the priests in their marine prison, Aser becomes morally indignant with himself. Not even Eugène Sue in *Le Juif errant*[47] or Gioberti in *Il Gesuita moderno* had advocated such harsh treatment of the Jesuits, he reasons, and he rues the day he ever followed Mazzini's orders to hunt them down. The young Jewish revolutionary is astounded when the Jesuit superior turns the other cheek, pardoning his tormentors. He is impressed by this discovery and leaves "with a brand new feeling in his heart" (II, 66). Exercising that generosity that had originally moved him to work for the unification and regeneration of Italy and which will ultimately bring him to conversion, he feels genuine pity for the priests.

Aser's values continue to undergo profound change. He begins to

---

46. In Bresciani's account, the Jesuits are accused of having encouraged ritual murder. Since the Jesuits had a history of spreading the ritual murder libel against the Jews, it is not surprising that sooner or later the charge would reflect on them. See the report commissioned by Cardinal Ganganelli, the future Pope Clement XIV, on the role of the Jesuits in the ritual murder libel in Poland, in C. Roth, *The Ritual Murder Libel and the Jew. The Report by Cardinal Lorenzo Ganganelli* (London: The Woburn Press, 1934).

47. Sue's novel had been translated into Italian in 1846 by F. D. Guerrazzi.

appreciate the stability inherent in traditional Catholicism and its importance for the well-being of Italy. Feeling betrayed by the secret societies, whose actions do not reflect their humanitarian rhetoric, Aser begins to see through their philosophical pretenses. All they create is bloodshed while political problems remain the same: nobility still retains its power enslaving the people. The more he sees of the dreadful conditions in Europe, the more he is convinced that revolutionary politics are the work of Satan, created to destroy peace, and that the resultant state of the world is God's punishment:

Plague, damnation and the scourge of God chastize our century, a punishment so universal and so severe that no century in history has suffered God's wrath more than we. (V, 676)

He deserts his comrades in Vienna and resolves to break off all contact with the secret societies.

The terrain is now prepared for his conversion. Little by little, throughout the story, Aser has become acquainted with various aspects of Catholicism. From the imprisoned Jesuits he learned Christian charity. Other lessons come his way somewhat more obliquely, but as he becomes familiar with the new religion, he will recognize what he should have understood long before. Fearing for Aser's life on the eve of his departure for the wars of 1848, the pious Alisa gives him a gold medallion of the Immaculate Conception of the Blessed Virgin. She hopes that the Madonna will protect him and move his heart to repentance and desire for salvation. And on the battlefield of Curtatone a dying girl gives him a crucifix. He wears both of these gifts around his neck vaguely intuiting their protective powers.

In Switzerland Aser falls from a precipice and is miraculously saved. He is found by a hermit, a priest in hiding from the fury of the secret societies. The priest sees the crucifix and Alisa's medal around his neck and tells him to attribute his salvation to the protection of the Madonna. Later, stupefied by what he has learned, Aser will inform him that he did not know the meaning of these Christian symbols:

I, a Jew and a wicked man, without realizing it, wore around my neck the symbols of my eternal salvation. (VI, 290)

The priest, Father Cornelius—an obvious attempt by Bresciani to recreate Manzoni's Fra Cristoforo figure—celebrates Mass occasionally in a nearby cottage and he takes Aser there to recuperate. A Jew mindful of the past sufferings of his people at the hands of priests, Aser can hardly believe this holy old man is carrying him to safety at considerable risk to himself. Not only is the man a priest, but also a stranger, and Aser—following what is by now a familiar pattern in this novel—thinks back to his association with the secret societies. These so-called philanthropists bore their unnatural hate even against their own family and friends. How their insatiable passion for blood and lucre contrasted with this gentle yet powerful example of Christian charity! Asking no questions and expecting no retribution, this venerable priest succored him for the sake of the pure joy that comes from compassion.

The cottage in which Aser recovers from his fall belongs to a family of devout Catholics. The oldest daughter instructs her younger siblings in cathechism and in this way Aser learns her Christian doctrine and absorbs the message of faith, hope, and charity. Little by little he comes to doubt his Jewish beliefs and the process of conversion begins. Struggling with himself and with considerable pain, he renounces his hatred of Christ and finally achieves a state of peace and indescribable joy.

There remain two enormous barriers to overcome which separate Aser from the world of those whom he respects and loves: his Judaism and his past in the secret societies. He fears that the family will find out that they have extended hospitality to a Jew, and here Bresciani uses the disparaging word *giudeo*. As long as he worked for the carbonari, he bore his religion and his politics with pride, even arrogance. Now he is tormented by shame for both of these moral sins:

"Father, I am not a Christian."

"You mean to say . . . that you gave yourself over to the radicals who proclaim their Christianity and then deny Christ by committing sacrilege, who make war on the Christian religion and its ministers."

"I am surely [one of the] wicked, but as if that weren't enough, I am also a Jew." (VI, 285)

Aser's problems are not insurmountable. He must exorcize his demons, answer blasphemy with praise to God, and the curses that lodge in his heart with a blessing. Taking a cue from Manzoni's character, the Innominato's, religious awakening that "God pardons so many things for one act of charity,"[48] Aser swears to fight the secret societies with the same fervor as he will overcome the demons who strive to banish Christ from his heart and imprison him in his Judaism.

48. A. Manzoni, *I promessi sposi* in *Tutte le opere,* vol. 2, bk. 1: 357.

As a Christian, Aser has the desire and the duty to forge a new life for himself and partake of the sacraments. Able once again to hold his head up high, he writes a stirring letter to Alisa confessing his related sins of Judaism and revolution and describing his former life in the light of his salvation:

Until now my life was beleaguered by remorse, confusion, hatred, envy and anger. All of which I hid behind a polite and genteel exterior while inwardly I despised heaven and earth, mankind and the God I did not know. Now I am at peace with myself and I see everything from a different perspective. Especially other people for whom I feel true brotherhood and whom the secret societies, which pretend to promote brotherly love, secretly detest. . . . Without your help I could not have risen from that stench and reached such an exalted condition. (VI, 297)

As a Jew and a radical Aser knew not God, or at best he knew the wrong God, for his life was mired in filth and undone by confusion and wrath. But the letter reassures Alisa that this erstwhile sinner has cast off error and finally conforms to her own high standards and she begins to plan for a future that includes Aser. One would think that all problems were solved for the former Jew of Verona, that Aser has fulfilled his usefulness in Bresciani's diatribe, but the author has one more job for his hero, one that will deal a final moral blow to the secret societies and serve as a warning for the adherents of the Risorgimento.

When Aser is fully recovered from his fall and fully baptized, he goes to look up the local carbonari. His reputation is known to them, and they reproach him bitterly for deserting the cause. He in turn defends the Christian feelings that promoted his change of heart. Perceiving him a liability to the movement, Aser's former comrades in that violent fraternity murder him forthwith. Meanwhile Alisa and Bartolo are on their way to join him. The happy family, expecting to forge an engagement, is confronted with the death, and the novel ends on a note of mourning and martyrdom.

L'Ebreo di Verona was very popular with readers, widely translated and reprinted in numerous editions. The critics, however, did not treat Bresciani kindly. His contemporary, Francesco De Sanctis, berated him for his poor style and long-windedness and, in a bitterly ironic tone, for being a coward. The fault lay in his lack of true faith and his reliance on the perpetual motion of formalistic ritual.[49] Indeed, Bresciani and the other authors of buona stampa perceived their world in such narrow

49. F. De Sanctis, *Saggi critici* (Bari: Laterza, 1952), 44–70.

terms that in their writings they were forced to rely on such unrealistic premises as the struggle between absolute good and absolute evil. This gave rise to what Gramsci was later to call "Brescianism": propagandistic literature that is "shabby, dismal, often vulgar and disgusting like *L'Ebreo di Verona*."[50] Gaetano Salvemini agreed with De Sanctis's and Gramsci's assessments of what the novel represents. Taking their lead from the Church hierarchy, which, he said, has always feared changing times, conservative Catholics confused faith with regime. They filled their readers with descriptions of a totally Catholic Italy that had been corrupted during the Risorgimento and conquered by the secret machinations of the masons. Even Pius IX himself was convinced by the novel, Salvemini concludes, though there was very little truth in it.[51]

As if in anticipation of attack from all his detractors, Bresciani defended his position with a postscript to *L'Ebreo di Verona*. He insists that the events of 1846–1849 included in his novel were not the workings of his imagination. They all happened as he said they did. He was there. He changed the names but not the situations. Thus the infamous Babette was a real person he says, and with her the amazon Polissena. And Aser, the Jew of the title? He was also real: "The events concerning poor Aser are true."[52]

The question still remains: what about Aser? Not as a specific, historical personality, but as a type and, especially, as a Jew of the Risorgimento. Those critics who wrote about *L'Ebreo di Verona* considered the real protagonist to be the secret societies in their assault on established religious and political values. No one, however, has considered the Jew of the title who assumes more and more importance as the story progresses. Indeed, in the novel's postscriptural "dialogue," which contains Bresciani's self-defense, his imaginary interlocutor objects first to the author's choice of a Jew as protagonist: "Oh no! A Jew! What nonsense! You can practically smell the stench of the ghetto. Is this any way to go about things? Just a fatuous, miserable whim! A Jew!"[53] Yet, throughout the novel it is the description and activities of Aser which, up to the moment of his conversion, argue an ultra-Catholic view of the nature of the Risorgimento.

To begin with the secret societies, Bresciani hysterically identifies

50. A. Gramsci, *Quaderni*, notebook 6, 5, reprinted in A. Gramsci, *Letteratura e vita nazionale* (Turin: Einaudi, 1972), 21.

51. G. Salvemini, *Stato e chiesa in Italia*, 113. The use of the word "Masons" probably represents all the secret societies of which the Masons were only one faction.

52. In a preface to the 1860 edition addressing Padre Carlo Maria Curci. A. Bresciani, *L'Ebreo di Verona* (Rome: Civiltà Cattolica, 1866), a reprint of the 1860 edition.

53. A. Bresciani, "Ai lettori dell'Ebreo di Verona," in *Ebreo di Verona*, vol. 6: 539.

them with repugnant creatures: hydras, witches, serpents. They are the criminal outgrowth of the Jewish sin of deicide. The devil works within them as they profane the Eucharist in the same way that the devil worked through the Jews to profane Christ's corporal body with the crucifixion. This deadly assemblage insinuates itself into society, sometimes striking and killing outright with lightning speed, like the adder, sometimes strangling slowly, constraining it to accept godlessness or die.

Aser, one of the most dedicated of revolutionaries, is like quicksilver. Born outside established society, he cannot be held within certain norms, which means that his behavior is unpredictable. He can quite literally get away with murder. Yet with typical Jewish deviousness, he has created a perfect facade of conformity and respectability. Given his engaging appearance, he is received everywhere, in Italy and abroad, as part of the international conspiracy against the Italian Catholic power structure. In traditional anti-Semitic superstition this would be a specific network of Jews plotting to overthrow Christian society by squeezing it dry in an economic vice. Among Catholics during the Risorgimento, the stereotype was broadened to encompass the various liberal groups who, on the model of the Jews, had been French sympathizers at the end of the preceding century.

Bresciani's insistence on the international nature of the Risorgimento movement is not without foundation. The major revolutionary groups such as the *Veri Italiani* were made up in large part of Italian exiles living in London, Brussels, France, Corsica, and North Africa, and those foreign nationals whom they were able to recruit, as well as Italians from all over the peninsula.[54] The poet-warrior Alessandro Poerio learned modern Greek in order to converse with his Greek companions in the movement.[55] The Jewish protagonist fits conveniently into a double stereotype based on the parochial fear of the international and having at its core the notion of danger to the thrones of Italy, beginning with that of St. Peter.

Aser is an emblematic Jew at the same time as he is a symbol of Mazzinian revolution. How closely does he reflect the standard iconography of the Risorgimento hero? Giulio Cesare Abba[56] describes the men who ventured to Sicily with him as part of Garibaldi's *Mille* as men

54. See C. Francovich, "Filippo Buonarroti e la società dei 'Veri Italiani,'" in *Albori socialisti del Risorgimento. Contributo allo studio delle società segrete (1776–1835)* (Florence: Le Monnier, 1963), 132, 134.

55. R. Barbiera, *Immortali e dimenticati* (Milan: Cogliali, 1901), 283.

56. G. C. Abba, "Da Quarto al Volturno—Noterelle d'uno dei Mille," in *Memorialisti dell' Ottocento* (Milan-Naples: Ricciardi, 1953), vol. 1: 754–894.

from many parts of Italy, though preponderantly from Lombardy. They dressed elegantly, but were energetic, enthusiastic, and anxious to go to war. They seemed on the whole cultured and politically aware. Poerio, for instance, knew seven languages.[57] One older man, Francesco Bartolomeo Savi, was a professor of literature. A friend of Mazzini, he had been imprisoned for revolutionary activities. Most of these political adventurers, however, were young like Goffredo Mameli, who died for the cause at age twenty-one.

Fictional heroes of the novels written during the Risorgimento present an idealized but valid portrait of the same phenomenon. Thus d'Azeglio's Ettore Fieramosca is a good-natured young man, courteous, valorous, beloved, and esteemed. He is generous and noble of heart, but also coldly rational when necessary. In short, he has all the good qualities of an Italian warrior.[58] Add to this Mazzini's idealized portrait of the artist who "lights the path of the future,"[59] and it is evident, ironically, that in Aser Bresciani has portrayed the epitome of the Risorgimento hero.

After 1848 Jews throughout Italy, with the major exception of Rome, enjoyed the kind of freedom they had not known for nearly three hundred years. They adhered to the movement for Unification with great enthusiasm. In the more liberal areas of the peninsula where restrictions had been somewhat relaxed after the first ("Napoleonic") emancipation, Jews participated in Risorgimento activities from the earliest days. Jews enrolled in the *Carboneria* from its inception in 1815 in such numbers that in Livorno, known as *il cantiere della rivoluzione* ("the shipyard of revolution"),[60] the police in 1817 listed the names of forty-four Jewish carbonari involved in the struggle against the restoration of the Lorena granddukes.[61] Similarly, Jews were involved in the 1831 uprisings at Modena and Reggio Emilia, and in the work of *Giovine Italia* in Vercelli in 1833. Two Jews of Livorno, Montefiore and Ottolenghi, headed the society of the Veri Italiani and were arrested for their activities. It is said that Mazzini's expedition in Savoy

57. Barbiera, *Immortali e dimenticati*, 283.

58. M. d'Azeglio, *Ettore Fieramosca* in *Tutte le opere letterarie* (Milan: Mursia, 1966), 24–25. Mazzini is said to have declared: "He combined the two extremes so admired by Byron and rarely found in one person: an almost childish sweetness and leonine energy which he revealed in moments of exceptional difficulty."

59. G. Mazzini, "Ai poeti del secolo XIX."

60. The phrase is attributed to Metternich. See G. Bedarida, "Gli ebrei e il Risorgimento italiano," *Rassegna mensile di Israel* 27 (1961): fasc. 7–8, 301.

61. Ibid.

was financed by a certain Todros, one of the wealthiest Jews of Turin.[62] Finally, Jews also participated physically in the war for independence with several Jews listed among Garibaldi's 1,077 volunteers, the Mille.[63]

Propaganda went hand in hand with battle in the struggle for Risorgimento. When the concept of buona stampa found fruition in the various Catholic journals published in the 1820s and later in *Civiltà Cattolica,* and as its proponents then proceeded to fulfill their charge to combat the flourishing lay press, the most obvious enemies were the liberal newspapers, some of which (notably, *Antologia*) were attacked as seditious and suppressed for advocating revolution. Jews were especially active in this aspect of the movement. Given their life at the margins of society, Jews were relatively free to participate in what appeared to be their daily business. Outside the Papal States and especially in Tuscany where Jewish commercial activity was encouraged, Jews were printers, publishers, and booksellers. Those at work in trade had commercial contacts in other Italian states and foreign countries; together with the merchandise that was being continually shipped throughout this network, prohibited materials found fairly secure passage. Within the Papal States and particularly in Rome where Jews dealt for the most part in scrap and secondhand merchandise, it was precisely their miserable economic state that was so valuable to the movement. Many who were unable to establish proper shops hawked their wares from pushcarts. Their mobility and, sometimes, anonymity made them ideal peddlers of outlawed goods. This activity was so common in Rome that the police were able to define the Jew as "a great disseminator of perverse books."[64] Where they could, educated Jews collaborated on literary and scientific journals. Among these, two Jewish journals were of particular importance: *Rivista Israelitica,* founded in 1846 and printed in Parma, was prohibited in the Papal States; *Educatore Israelita,* the better known of the two, founded in Vercelli in 1856, reminded emancipated Jews of their patriotic duty.

How accurately does Aser represent the Jew of the Risorgimento? If one makes allowances for certain authorial exaggeration such as the assertions that all Jews who support the movement are wealthy, that

62. See S. Foa's detailed entry "Israeliti" in *Dizionario del Risorgimento nazionale* (Rome: Vallardi, 1931), vol. 1, "I fatti," 523–536. This article contains many valuable bibliographical references concerning Jewish participation in the Risorgimento.

63. This list will be found in M. Rosi, "Spedizione dei Mille," in *Dizionario del Risorgimento nazionale,* 681–691.

64. Bedarida, *Gli ebrei,* 301.

they hobnob with the high and mighty, that they are people of mysterious origin—irrational stereotypes generated by fear—then Bresciani's portrait of the Risorgimento Jew has some grounding in fact. In its basic outline, therefore, a character such as Aser is not impossible. Add to this those traditionally "Jewish" traits of wealth, extraordinary mobility, exoticism, and intrigue, and the character may well have been plausible to the devout, conservative Catholic audience for which Bresciani's story was intended. The popularity of the novel at the time and its numerous editions and translations indicate in part that the reading public found the protagonist attractive and his adventures diverting.

But the characters and the plot in themselves do not account entirely for the popularity of *L'Ebreo di Verona* with the public or for its poor reception among critics. One must seek these ultimately in the ideological foundations of the work which are revealed in the denouement. The hero successfully completes his appointed task, in this case conversion, and in a nineteenth-century novel one would expect him to be rewarded for it, especially since the author gives us to believe that Aser intends to renounce his "Jewish" attributes (except, probably, his wealth) when he claims Alisa as his prize. This leaves him the sin of revolution to expiate. Bresciani appears to resolve this dilemma as simplistically as he did the religious one. As Aser realizes the religious error that has ruled his life, so, at the moment of conversion, does he abjure radical politics, which are antithetical to Christian life. Up to this point the story seems straightforward and predictable, but it is here that the author surprises his readers. After his conversion, Aser not only renounces his former comrades but also turns on them. Bresciani makes his hero a sort of exterminating angel sent to unearth revolutionaries and destroy them. But the ultimate sinners, diabolical radical politicians, cannot tolerate a soul won over to the Church and in the end the hero dies a martyr: a most Christian death.

In his postscript Bresciani imagined himself under attack for this unorthodox ending. Indeed it seemed that in his about-face Aser had found the key to happiness. When he abandons Judaism and politics he turns one hundred and eighty degrees from a state of aggression to passivity and from bad to good. Similarly, it cannot be pure coincidence that, following this pattern, by reversing the letters of his name, Aser, one obtains Resa, or "surrender." As it stands, all this is an ideological statement, but Bresciani's ideology is profoundly pessimistic and his mission is to issue a strong warning. Thus this handsome, talented, intelligent, and, most of all, repentant convert must be killed off to warn readers of the coming triumph of evil over good. In the logic of *L'Ebreo di Verona* the death of Aser, had he not converted, may have been justified and, probably, expected, but the death of a new Christian, as he prepares to partake of the sacrament of marriage, is tragic.

To return to a basic query that was alluded to earlier, why should Bresciani have chosen a Jew for his protagonist? Though Jews figured prominently among Risorgimento activists, the percentage of their participation was high relative only to their small population, so this is, at best, only a partial explanation. Bresciani had been ordered to report on the years 1846–1849 in novel form. These were the years of attacks on the Jesuits, most notably by Gioberti who, among others, was promoting the cause of Jewish emancipation and linking it with the hated Risorgimento. But *Civiltà Cattolica* had more direct ways to rebut Gioberti and his cohort. There are two possible answers to this question. The Jew was convenient because those stereotypes that could be so helpful in delineating the character were already in place, predating Bresciani's effort by far. These were not acceptable to everyone, but the mass of Bresciani's readers were likely to assume them to be true. This made Bresciani's task of "reportage" on the crimes of secret societies that much easier and that much more credible. But by 1850 such canards could be applied to radicals *tout court* thus obviating the need for a Jewish protagonist.

The only possible situation in which a Jewish protagonist was absolutely necessary was in the matter of conversion through which the Jews would return to the bosom of established religion and strengthen it. All the elements are there for Aser's to be considered a classic account of conversion. He is surely sinful and his life has been one of intense error from the very beginning. Despite his Judaism and his politics, however, there is something likeable about this man. He has strong convictions and a rich emotional life. His struggle against the forces of Darkness begins from the moment he accepts the medal of the Madonna from Alisa, although until the episode with the Jesuit prisoners it appears the devil is going to retain custody of his soul. He wrestles painfully with his emotions, with his life history, as well as with centuries of traditional Jewish *empietà* ("wickedness") (VI, 285).

In spite of his famed pronouncements against Romanticism, by opting for a Jewish protagonist who was exotic by definition, and by endowing him with so many positive qualities, chief among these being bravery and the willingness to convert, Bresciani gave in to the reigning literary convention and created a Romantic hero. Even the conversion

sequence contains distinctly Romantic elements as Aser fights to overcome his misplaced sense of honor and commitment to the cause. Indeed, a distinctive element of Italian Romanticism was precisely this
political engagement. Bresciani attempts to set Aser straight, however,
as he conjures up a situation in which to deliver a final lesson on the
dangers of the Risorgimento. But here, too, Romanticism wins out
over anti-Romanticism. Aser renounces politics and dies for it. The superficial message is that the secret societies are a perversion of Christian values and deadly to those religious souls whom they consider
their enemies. The brutal finale imparts another lesson, however, a
more pragmatic one and one that anti-Romantic Catholics may not
have suspected: it is useless, indeed immoral, to abandon one's political
commitments. One could live as a Catholic and at the same time be
a committed activist as the most respected Risorgimento figures did.
If, however, the act of conversion impelled one to betray one's former
comrades, then there was no point in exchanging one identity for another which could only lead to death.

Conversion of the Jews, however, was the Church's absolute goal.
This compulsion goes hand in hand with the unwritten dictum that in
nineteenth-century Italian literature conversion was the only possible
path for a Jew. It was inconceivable that a protagonist not conform,
in the end, to the dominant ethos. In Bresciani, however, during that
bitter time of troubles for the Church, conversion took on a whole new
aspect. Assuming that Manzoni's humanitarian efforts to convert the
Jews and Gioberti's insistence on charity of method and intentions in
"leading Israel gone astray back to the sheepfold"[65] were emblematic
of the desires of liberal Catholics in this regard, one realizes how sharply
they differed from the ambitions of reactionary Catholics such as Bresciani and the convert, Lombroso. In the writings of this latter group,
ideology appeared to supersede religion and immediate self-defense to
replace long-range philosophical objectives. Here in part is the origin
of De Sanctis's Romantic assertion of Bresciani's lack of faith. The authoritarian Church was under attack from the liberals and Jews were
identified with radical politics. Indeed Bresciani, with remarkable originality, reworked the iconography of the Jew to include the dynamic
attributes of the Risorgimento activist. Conversion of the Jews, normally a solemn religious process, when discussed in the literature of the
Catholic Right became, first and foremost, a political goal.

65. V. Gioberti, *Primato* 2: 84–85.

L'Ebreo di Verona has come to stand for all that was wrong with religiously inspired popular literature of the nineteenth century and Bresciani for the most reactionary right-wing politics. Yet in its day, the novel went through at least seventeen editions from ten publishers in five cities and was translated into English, French, German, and Portuguese. Bresciani's novel created the standard for fiction in *Civiltà Cattolica* and his assessment of his Jewish character set the tone for nearly all subsequent discussion about Jews in the journal's frequent articles up through the Fascist period. In the 1930s, Gramsci defined writers of empty, reactionary literature as "grandchildren of Father Bresciani," and, nearly a century after the novel's publication, Croce, too, had cause to refer to it. Alarmed by what he perceived to be Fascist efforts to rehabilitate Bresciani's reputation, he wrote:

For Bresciani to be considered honorable at this time, Italy would have to have sunk to a level of stupidity and moral degradation which is still far off and from which let us hope merciful Heaven will always protect us. We must be on our guard against those who urge us with their prayers to allow this to happen.[66]

Croce need not have worried. As the upheavals which fostered the writing of *L'Ebreo di Verona* in 1849 and their recrudescence during the *ventennio fascista* fade into history, the novel has been relegated to the pages of scholarly studies. The fundamentalist sentiments it embodies, however, in today's world are translated into political action and are very much alive.

66. B. Croce, *La Critica* 40, fasc. 5 (20 September 1942), 287.

3

Belli's Roman Jews

Só ttutti lupi de l'istessa pelle:
Ammazz, ammazza só ttutti una razza.

(They are all wolves under the skin. Scratch 'em and see:
it's all one race.)

Belli

The satire of G. G. Belli descends from a long, quintes-
sentially Roman tradition. The hub of its vast empire, ancient Rome
attracted crowds of adventurers, thieves, pedants, courtesans, and philosophers who were regularly lampooned in verse. Throughout the centuries, the daily life of the bustling neighborhoods and the doings of
the high and mighty, often scandalous and corrupt, furnished rich material for satire. In Belli's day (1791–1863) the metropolis continued
to provide every imaginable activity: religious, commercial, intellectual,
illicit. It was a picturesque city of ceremonial splendor and habitual
squalor, teeming with people from the most varied backgrounds.

The largest ethnic group in the city was the Jewish community. The
Jews had always been distinct from the Romans, even more so after
1555, but since their history had been interwoven with that of ancient
Rome, they considered themselves Romans. Still, their self-image did
not always correspond to that held by Church authorities and the
Christian masses. Ethnic distinction, "foreignness," was often made
painfully clear through satire on occasions such as Carnival which per-

mitted popular expression. There were two types of satire which later fed into Belli's portrayal of the Jews of Rome: one popular in origin—the *giudìata* (a farce about Jews) designed for the entertainment of the masses; one learned and pseudoliterary—the *Pasquinata* involving those close to the centers of power. Though arising at different ends of the social spectrum, both satirical genres shared a fundamental premise: the conviction that Jews were assigned a specific role and status from birth and that as long as they refused conversion, their behavior should reflect their assigned place.

Central to this notion of status was the topographical locus of the ghetto, its walls and gates circumscribing the area in which to perform permitted activities. Should the inhabitants of Christian Rome desire the services of Jews, they knew where to find them; it was, however, preferable that the majority of Jewish vendors not venture out to mingle with the general populace.

Coupled with the restrictions on Jewish occupation and religious observance, and largely derived from them, were objectified fears that were translated into stereotypes. These, in turn, quickly found their way into satire. The Jewish presence offered all the stimulus necessary for satirical derision. The need to mock fed on the oddity of Jewish ritual; on the strange Judeo-Roman dialect that was Roman, yet not entirely recognizable as Roman; on the *sciamanno* that set Jews apart from their fellow Romans.

Belli inherited this entrenched code, which he both enlisted and transformed in his poetry. His sonnets reveal a desire to "humanize" the Jews, to recoup individual types from an undifferentiated mass, to uncover and familiarize the complexity of their reality. But given the antiquity and the pervasiveness of the satiric tradition in Roman literature, especially the codified ways of thinking about Jews, to what extent was Belli able to dissociate Jews from the clichés about the typical ghetto dweller? How original and personal is his portrayal of the apparently unassimilable Jewish population that dwelled in the midst of the Roman community?

Tradition

Popular anti-Jewish satire, the giudìata, had a theatrical form of its own which developed in the Middle Ages from pre-Lenten festivities. Before evolving into a farcical play it was a type of public entertainment involving cruel treatment of a Jew. D'Azeglio notes "from ancient times the poor Jews themselves were used as diversions for Christians."[1] Tradition has it that an early form was the Carnival "game" in which an elderly Jew, closed in a barrel, would be rolled down the Testaccio hill, often resulting in his death.[2] Since it culminated in death, this medieval practice has been identified as a vestige of the ancient rites of exorcising evil during the spring festivals.[3] It was accompanied by singing and dancing, which included the spectators thus involving them as a sort of chorus in the giudìata.[4] The Jew here figured as a scapegoat, sacrificed as the Carnival "King." Perhaps, too, this commemorated the Passion, the sufferings of Christ, "King of the Jews."[5] Eventually Jews were able to substitute payment for this ritual, thus financing the Carnival games. They were, however, forced to participate in a race, the *palio* or *corso degli ebrei* (Jews' race).[6]

With the demise of the barrel roll, the giudìata took the form of a satirical play. As with other popular plays of the epoch, it was performed on a cart, a device that allowed it to be seen in many areas of the city on the same day. It was to prove one of the most welcome of all the Carnival festivities, from which it transcended the limitations of

1. M. d'Azeglio, *I miei ricordi* (Turin: Einaudi, 1949), 362.

2. D'Azeglio's account of the barrel roll names the Capitoline hill instead of the Testaccio. (Ibid.) Belli, in his notes to sonnet 532 of the *Sonetti romaneschi*, describes the Testaccio as a place where "the city of Rome used to hold often cruel and bloody public spectacles." See G. G. Belli, *I sonetti*, ed. Giorgio Vigolo (Milan: Mondadori, 1952), vol. 1: 751. All examples of Belli's poetry are taken from this edition.

3. P. Toschi, *Le origini del teatro italiano* (Turin: Boringhieri, 1976), 326. In his fascinating discussion of *giudìata* and its allied form, *barabbata*, Toschi links these festivities with the common medieval and Renaissance Carnival practice enacting the abuse and death of the Carnival "King." Originally the Carnival King was a divinity and portrayed as Saturn, the god of agriculture. Later he was secularized to symbolize the old year.

4. Toschi goes so far as to regard the sentiments behind this practice as one of the building blocks of theatrical representation: "Evil dies at the hands of the chorus which, delirious, sings and dances. Death resolves itself in an orgy. There is something ineluctably savage, not just prehistoric but nearly pre-human at the base of these ritual and dramatic customs out of which our theatre will develop." (Ibid.)

5. See F. Clementi, *Il Carnevale Romano* (Città di Castello: Edizioni R.O.R.E.—Niruf, 1938–1939), vol. 1, chap. 1, "Le origini," which traces the Roman Carnival from its origins through the nineteenth century and contains many references to the role of Jews in the pre-Lenten festivities. For a more general discussion of medieval and Renaissance Carnival practices, see M. Bakhtin, *Rabelais and His World* (Cambridge: M.I.T. Press, 1968), 198 and passim.

6. The Carnival games were financed principally by the Jews. The *Codex Vat. Lat.* 6792, f. 76 indicates that the tribute was imposed upon the Jews as payment "for being permitted to practice their rites and ceremonies." This so-called Agone and Testaccio tribute was collected regularly until 1847. See A. Milano, *Storia degli ebrei in Italia* (Turin: Einaudi, 1963), 600.

the Carnival context and became a prominent aspect of contemporary popular comic theatre.[7]

The Jew as object of derision was nothing new in literary tradition; Jews had been portrayed satirically in Italian literature for centuries. With the occasional exception of a quick-witted character, the Jew was generally a victim, a cowardly object of mockery and cruel jesting and no match for his oppressor. This tractable character became the popular stock type. In Franco Sacchetti's fourteenth-century *novelle,* for instance, Jews are locked in a privy[8] or surrounded by excrement in their synagogue.[9] The scatological nature of the stories and Sacchetti's pictorial style suggest that such episodes, so similar to the ubiquitous *lazzi* ("buffoonery," generally obscene), were easily translated into the popular theatre of the piazza.

The giudìata also contributed farcical elements to the established theatre. Pietro Aretino (1492–1556), for instance, features a Jewish robbivecchi in *La Cortigiana* (*The Courtesan*) and a peddler in *Il Marescalco* (*The Smith*). These characters, placed in ridiculous situations, make such stereotypical statements as: "I'm happy as long as you spend your money"[10] and are similarly stylized with sallow skin and huge noses, a physiognomy reproduced in the masks of Renaissance popular theatre.[11] The *entr'acte* quality of these episodes which have little to do with Aretino's dramatic flow, points to their derivation from popular farce.[12]

By the early seventeenth century, the giudìata had become a fixture

7. "Whenever they [giudìate] are performed, a vast multitude draws near and listens with great enjoyment and ceremony." See G. Crescimbeni, *Istoria della volgar poesia* (Rome: 1702), vol. 1, chap. 4: 198ff.

8. In *Novella* 190 of Sacchetti's *Trecento novelle* the trickster, Gian Sega di Ravenna, clears his way to a young Jewish girl by locking up her traveling companions; see F. Sacchetti, *Opere* (Milan: Rizzoli, 1957), 636–642.

9. *Novella* 24 in Ibid., 106–108.

10. P. Aretino, *La Cortigiana,* in *Teatro* (Lanciano: Carabba, 1914), vol. 1: 157.

11. Aretino's Jewish characters were not, as Klein suggests, the predecessors of all those Jews who populate Italian comedy since Aretino did not invent the characters. He did, however, "legitimize" them by including them in his scripts, which figure prominently among early sixteenth-century comedies. See J. L. Klein, *Geschichte des italienischen Drama's,* vol. 4 of *Geschichte des Drama's* (Leipzig: Weigel, 1866–1869), 513.

12. The giudìata absorbed theatrical models for content and character, as well as the custom of utilizing the written plot summary or *canovaccio.* An early detailed canovaccio (1588) from Pesaro reads: "Discussion Between Two Jews with One Stanza of Argument, One Sicilian Song and Serafino's *Strambotto.* All Honest Things and Worthy of Every Noble Spirit. Recently Brought to Light by Zan Frittada and the Son of Fortunato." It was published in its entirety by L. Bonfigli, "La letteratura popolaresca marchigiana," *Rivista marchigiana illustrata* 4 (1907): 7–10, 51–54. See also, G. Caprin, "La 'commedia ridicolosa'," *Rivista teatrale italiana* 13 (1908): 215–221.

in the spectrum of the Roman comic theatre and was known throughout Northern and Central Italy. Jewish characters differed little from one farce to another with only individual situations to add some variety. The most common stock character was the argumentative Jew. Two or more outlandishly dressed and masked characters becoming increasingly upset with each other was the very stuff of popular theatre.[13] The most common *lazzo* because of the evident possibility for obscenity was circumcision, derived from the lazzo of castration in the *Commedia dell'Arte*.[14] The dialects of Italian Jews furnished still another pretext to portray Jewish characters and, indeed, people whose speech seemed garbled, who yelled or babbled incomprehensibly were often the elements of farce.[15]

The giudìate have been called "good-humored popular farces," examples of the natural Roman tendency to satirize everything rather than manifestations of real anti-Jewish sentiment of the type that forced Jews into the ghetto and usurped their livelihoods. When Jewish characters were portrayed as poor, it was because the giudìate gave Christian Romans the opportunity to momentarily forget their own poverty. When the satirized Jewish characters were rich, it was the result of "understandable" envy stemming from Roman admiration for Jewish business acumen and inventiveness in adversity.[16] Regardless of their inspiration, however, at times these giudìate went well beyond mere comic intent and were used to mock the Jews and, sometimes, to provoke the populace against them.

The most infamous giudìata in this respect was the well-known *'Gnora Luna* (*Lady Luna*) (1752)[17] consisting of four *canzonette* (songs).

---

13. Two giudìate involving such characters were published by Giulio Cesare Croce in the 1620s: *The Tremendous Argument between Mardocai and Badanai with a Party, Dinner and Music Given by Them as a Sign of Peace* in which two Jews argue for one hundred and ten verses over a duck; and *The Noisy Battle Between Two Jews of Ancona over a Goose in which Between the Dead and the Wounded One is Blinded and One Loses His Nose*.

14. The Jew, often a rabbi, would brandish a large knife before the terrified stock character, Zanni. See, for example, the scenario *Il finto principe* in A. Bartoli, *Scenari inediti* (Florence: Sansoni, 1880) and the plays *La Mula* of Basilio Locatelli and *Il Pedante* of Flaminio Scala.

15. In *The Man from Aquila Who Became a Jew* Abruzzese dialect is distorted to resemble Judeo-Roman. Judeo-Roman is called "the speech of Trastevere" in *The Jew Who Became a Count or The Mad Tognino* and in *Gli Strappazati* ("The Harassed") it is Italianized. The Jews in Orazio Vecchi's madrigal comedy, *Amphiparnaso*, argue among themselves in stunning cacophony.

16. A. Bragaglia, *Le maschere romane* (Rome: Colombo, 1947), 227.

17. A. Milano gives this date of publication and states that it remained in print until

Grotesquely satirizing Jewish marriage customs, greed, dishonesty, and love of money, it plays on all the stereotypes, all of the common insults. The full title summarizes the work: "The Story of Baruccabà, Wherein Is Recounted His Wedding to 'Gnora Luna—Her Death—His Second Marriage to Diana Stimisciò—His Desperation over the Escape of His Bride—The Death of Baruccabà—And How the Rabbi Was Thrown in the River."[18] The language is a jumble of Hebrew (often misunderstood and distorted), slang, Venetian, Lombard, and the dialect of the Marches, but other dialects were introduced as the work spread throughout Italy.

And spread it did. All over Northern and Central Italy the songs, set to the very popular tune *Minuet of the King of Sardinia,* were sung at the gates of the ghetto, into open windows, at passing Jews, often leading to street fights or near riots. Major disturbances erupted in Ferrara and Alessandria. Then the giudìata became a successful play performed in established theatres which drew large crowds. During the period of Revolution and the Napoleonic rights of man such performances disappeared from the theatre, but when the Jacobins took flight and Austrian rule was restored, *'Gnora Luna* was revived. Repeatedly banned as inflammatory and dangerous to public safety, it reappeared in city after city, in dialect after dialect, until at last, on the eve of the Jewish emancipation, no longer mere satire, it was made to transmit a threat to Jewish society at the hands of the forces of reaction.[19]

The learned tradition in Roman satire on the Jews was represented by the *Pasquinata,* an anonymous poem or epigram affixed to the marble remains of a Hellenistic statue known as Pasquino. Unearthed in 1501, the statue was mounted on a pedestal in what is now Piazza Pasquino. Any facet of Roman life was deemed fit target for these writings

1910; see *Ebrei in Italia,* p. 88. E. Levi writing in 1916 states that "it is still in print today for the benefit of peasants and the 'people'." See "La Signora Luna," *Giornale Storico della Letteratura Italiana* 67 (1916): 98–104.

18. For the complete text, see *Lo Sposalizio di Baruccabà e 'Gnora Luna* (Florence: Salani, 1878).

19. E. Levi mentions specifically a three-act play entitled *'Gnora Luna: scene di vita ebraica fiorentina.* The action takes place between December 1847 and March 1848. The songs were sung in "Judeo-Florentine" at the doors of the ghetto in a seemingly last-ditch effort to harass its population. This text has been reprinted in *Rassegna mensile di Israel* 6 (1932): 546–579. Levi's article includes a bibliography of the many Italian editions of *'Gnora Luna.* This giudìata also made its way to Germany in 1819 with the poet Wilhelm Müller who included it in his *Egeria:Sammlung Italienischer Volkslieder* (Leipzig, 1829). It was translated into German in 1838 by August Kipisch and rendered as *Das Fräulein Luna.*

which took their name from Pasquino or its surrounding walls where they were posted for all to read. Since the *Pasquinate* were written, more is known today about this form of satire than about those related to Carnival festivities.[20]

In a city as prone to ecclesiastical and political corruption as Rome, Pasquino served almost as a chronicler, keeping a running tally of popular sentiment concerning current events. The *Pasquinata*, as Cattaneo suggested, was a "soul searching by the whole society, a reaction to the principle of evil, and sometimes the only available weapon against triumphant vice [just] as salt staves off decay."[21] The key word here is "reaction"; it is the one concept that unifies all the *Pasquinate*, no matter whom they are directed against, no matter how gentle or ferocious the satire. The *Pasquinate* involving Jews do not differ from this general description.

After the establishment of the ghetto, Jews were, in a sense, more visible, not only because of the yellow hat or veil they were supposed to wear, but also because they were concentrated in the very heart of Rome. That the popes kept the Jews in the ghetto for three hundred years was, for many Romans, a satisfactory arrangement. Every so often a pretext was found to permit ruffians to assault the ghetto and for the violent elements in the society this was a satisfactory arrangement. What was looked upon with disfavor was the propensity of some popes to have friendly relations and, worse, financial dealings with Jews.

The apparent ease with which prominent Jews could become part of the Pope's circle—or so it must have appeared to the have-nots—disturbed Pasquino considerably. One such case was the association between Pope Clement XIV and his financial advisor, the banker Ezechiele Ambron.[22] Clement XIV had disgruntled some of the faithful

20. Most of the scholarship about the *Pasquinata* dates from the last century when the debate centered more on the origin of the statue's name than on the nature of the literary institution. Most notable for his interest in Pasquino in the satiric tradition is V. Cian, who in "Gioviana," *Giornale Storico della Letteratura Italiana* 18 (1891): 277–357 points out that Pasquino was a focus for varied types of satire which changed constantly with the political and cultural situation. The statue was sort of an instant publisher of new examples of poetic genres, mostly political and anticlerical. More recently scholars have tackled a myriad of specimens trying to isolate "genuine" sixteenth-century *Pasquinate* in order to define the genre. See *Pasquinate romane del Cinquecento* (Rome: Salerno, 1983).

21. C. Cattaneo, *Opere edite e inedite* (Florence: Le Monnier, 1881), 147.

22. Ambron was descended from a distinguished, scholarly family that had lived in Rome since the expulsion from Spain in 1492. He was also a literary patron. See H. Vogelstein–P. Rieger, *Geschichte der Juden in Rom* (Berlin: Mayer & Muller, 1895–

by disbanding the Jesuit order in 1774 and now he added "insult" to injury by associating closely with a Jew. Upon Clement's death, Pasquino was covered with satirical assessments of the pope's reign. In 1775 some of those were directed at Ezechiele Ambron. One, in verse, tells how that "typical" Jew had insinuated himself into the Pope's confidence, possibly by pretending to admire Christianity and allowing Clement to hope in his future conversion. He held the Pope's trust by advising him on delicate financial matters while at the same time he mercilously deceived him with outrageous usury.[23]

Another *Pasquinata* on the death of Clement XIV concentrates entirely on Ambron as he learns of the death of his friend and protector. Since it is set in the pattern of the *Dies irae* of the Requiem Mass, this *Pasquinata*,[24] was probably meant to sound like a death knell for the Pope's Jew:

> *Dies irae, dies illa,*
>   Vedo Ambron che sbuffa e strilla . . .
> Adirossi Iddio medesimo
>   Nel mirar tra il Cristianesimo
>   Un nemico del battesimo, . . .
>   Amen[25]

(*Dies irae, dies illa,* I see Ambron scream and bluster, . . . God himself flew into a rage when he saw an enemy of baptism hobnobbing with a Christian.)

In its entirety this doggerel celebrates God's wrath against "perfida Sionne" ("perfidious Zion") and the "reo popolo circonciso" ("guilty, circumcised people"). But this is standard fare. More important, it preaches eternal separation of Christians and "Israel, immondo gregge" ("Jews, the unclean herd") as the only way to prevent such clever enemies of Christianity as Ambron from finding a haven in the highest offices of the Church and corrupting it from the inside. Lest the bold Jew continue to "confuse Talmud and Breviary," the new pope "who

---

1896), vol. 2: 273–281, and A. Milano, *Il ghetto di Roma* (Rome: Staderini, 1964), 392–393 and passim.

23. See P. Romano, *Pasquino e la satira in Roma* (Rome: V. Ferri, 1932), 111, for text of the poem.

24. E. Del Cerro, *Roma che ride: settant'anni di satira (1801–1870)* (Turin-Rome: Roux e Viarengo, 1904), 100–101; S. Foà, "Pasquino e gli Ebrei," *Vessillo Israelitico* 57 (1910): 441–445.

25. S. Foà, "Pasquino," 441–443; P. Romano, *Pasquino,* 111–113.

will be an agent of good/will hand Ambron over to the executioner."
Enforcement of the ghetto laws, such as the sciamanno, is the only way
to prevent the Jews from "trampling a Christian country." In the mean-
time the only safe place for Ambron is the hands of the executioner.[26]

Just about twenty years later Pasquino was again provoked to express his hostility toward the Jews. The cause this time was a most disturbing political situation: the arrival of the French. In contrast to other
Italian cities during the second half of the eighteenth century, Rome
held firm against the ideas of the Enlightenment. By and large the society remained static preferring to bend itself, as it had for centuries,
to the papacy from which it received economic and political structures
by which to live. Those revolutionary ideas that managed to penetrate
this carapace found little sustenance among the general populace. The
Jews, however, received the message of the rights of man with hopeful
enthusiasm, thus becoming in fact potential subverters of Rome's carefully developed hierarchical system.

The French seized on this fraction of the population to gain a foothold in the city. By freeing the Jews in 1798 General Berthier co-opted
a weak minority element of the society and pitted it against the dominant group. The mob, incited by priests, had already expressed its opposition to the French and to Jewish emancipation with the famous
"Viva Maria!" riots. Given all this upheaval, Pasquino, a "codino"
("reactionary") to the end, unleashed a torrent of satirical and tragic
sonnets against the French, the Jews, and their Jacobin supporters.

In some cases the verses against the Jews were even more ferocious
than those against the invaders. One reason for this was that Jews
formed a precise group and a fairly known quantity. Another explanation for this poetic vituperation was the nagging question that recurred
at times of political stress and was to plague Italian Jews well until the
end of fascism: just how Roman (later, Italian) were the Jews? During
normal, daily life Jews could be kept at arm's length in the anomalous
position of less-than-fully-Roman Romans. Under pressure from the
outside, however, they were expected to forget their recent history and
resist the French. But the Jews remained

Ribelli sempre ad ogni potestà
Vivendo in Roma dissero: Monsù.[27]

26. Pasquino even devised an "epitaph" for Ambron who disappeared soon after the
death of Clement XIV. The verses recommended the gallows for all the Jews of Rome.
But Ambron had not been put to death; rather, aware of the hostility against him, he
fled the Papal State for Florence.

27. E. Del Cerro, *Roma che ride*, 98.

(As always rebellious against all authority, though they lived in Rome they said: *Monsieur*.)

What was worse, they aided the French financially and politically. In recompense for their traitorous actions, Pasquino predicted that the Jewish people itself would be betrayed. Since it was well known that the Jews were waiting for the Messiah, and since the French presence in Rome had proven beneficial to the Jews but had also caused tremendous unrest, Pasquino equated the Roman Republic (1798–1799) with the Age of the Messiah. In this example the messianic-republican experience sours and the rabbi abandons his flock to the French peril and takes refuge in the synagogue:

> Finirà non v'ha dubbio, il nostro scorno.
>   Verrà il Messia da noi sì sospirato,
>   Liberi noi sarem, e il Franco armato
> Farà sì che godrem lieto soggiorno.
> Quand'ecco *mordivoi*, che il suo sermone
>   Troncò da lungi un strepito, un bisbiglio,
>   Fuoco, gridando, a questa rea nazione.
> Pallido in volto allor senza consiglio
>   Nelle Scole si chiude il bacchettone
>   E il popolo abbandona al gran periglio.[28]

(Our disgrace will surely end when the Messiah, for whom we have waited so long, finally comes. We will be free and the French with their arms will assure us a happy time of it. But then, *mordivoi,* his sermon was cut short by a distant rumble, a whisper, and he yelled "Fire!" to his wicked people. Pale-faced and frantic, the hypocrite locked himself in the synagogue and abandoned his congregation to grave danger.)

The satire in this poem is of a more subtle vintage than the usual *Pasquinata*. The ridiculous figure of the bombastic and cowardly rabbi is obvious; the stylistic play, less so. At the moment in the story when reality imposes itself on the rosy vision of a republican future and the rabbi's prediction is subverted, the poet interrupts the learned hendecasyllable of the sonnet with the ethnic intercalation *mordivoi,* a common Judeo-Roman exclamation that is totally out of place in the poem. The rabbi's prophecy of messianic glory is empty rhetoric. He reveals himself to be as defenseless as all his coreligionists, for all it takes is a distant "whisper" of disorder to reveal his inglorious timidity. Perhaps, the poem implies, the Jews can't make it on the outside and the ghetto is the best place for them after all.

28. S. Foà, "Pasquino," 443.

With the restoration of Pius VII and the reign of the stern Leo XII, Jews were returned to the ghetto. The popes reinstated stiff taxes, the curfew, and the conversionist sermons at Sant'Angelo in Pescheria adjacent to the ghetto and ordered the Inquisition to watch and report to them. It appeared that the Jews had stepped backward in time to 1775; of the earlier regulations, only the sciamanno was omitted.

But not for long. Since the wearing of the sciamanno was the only way Jews could be distinguished from the rest of the population outside the ghetto, Pasquino reminded the Pope of the

> . . . legge antica più der Culiseo,
> Che porti lo sciamanno ogni Giudio,
> E strilli sempre per le strade: aèo.[29]

> (. . . law older than the Colisseum: that Jews should wear a badge and when in the street shout as their peddlers do: aèo.)

Leo XII did not need much coaxing and the sciamanno was reinstated forthwith. Pasquino also had a message for the Jews regarding the identifying mark: the Lord had marked Cain's forehead and sent him to wander through the world. The sign was to serve both as a mark of shame and as a message that he should not be killed. Ignoring the tragic aspect of Cain's eternal life, in a vicious sonnet addressing Cain as a catch-all reference to the Jews, Pasquino reminded Jews of the need to separate them from "i romuli nipoti" ("the descendants of Romulus") and advised them to be grateful for the sciamanno's protection:

> Bacia quel segno, anima vile, e taci.[30]

> (Kiss that badge, lowly creature, and be silent.)

G. G. Belli

Not all the *Pasquinate* were so violent in nature. Though rare, verses suggesting at least a superficial tolerance were also left on the statue. These point to a more measured satire of the kind that inspired Belli. Whereas Pasquino had threatened to burn down the ghetto as revenge against those who refused to submit to wearing the badge[31]

29. Ibid., 444.
30. E. Del Cerro, *Roma che ride,* 99.
31. "Che se mai nun lo portin per dispetto, /abbasta che voi dite: date foco/Che noi faremo er focaraccio in Ghetto." See S. Foà, "Pasquino," 444.

he also advised a more level-headed approach to the Jews in the name of the True Faith:

Pe difenne la Santa Religione
   Tutto se deve fà, de fà se deve; . . .
Ma se pijalla poi con antra gente,
   Senza perché, per semprice sospetto,
   Dio nun lo vone, e er Papa nun consente.
Lassate, dunque, d'insurtarne er ghetto,
   E tali quali che ve stanno in mente
   Che ce rimedierà Dio Benedetto.[32]

(To defend the True Faith one must do whatever is needed. But when it comes to attacking other people for no better reason than some mere suspicion, God doesn't want it [that way] and the pope prohibits it. So stop picking on the ghetto. [And anyway] God will see to carrying out whatever you have in mind.)

Although far from preaching actual acceptance of the Jews, such *Pasquinate* promoted a truce based on faith in ultimate retribution.

As religion lay at the heart of many of Pasquino's sayings, it was also the complex matrix of a large number of Giuseppe Gioachino Belli's *Sonetti romaneschi* (*Sonnets in Roman Dialect*) and other writings.[33] Though Belli far outdistanced Pasquino in his range of interests, much of his work is a commentary on the activities of religious figures. Although Pasquino concentrated mainly on the upper echelons, Belli spared none of the clergy, targeting monks and parish priests all the way up to the pope.

Beyond subject matter, Belli also perpetuated certain stylistic features of the *Pasquinata*. After Aretino, the favorite model for *Pasquinate* was the sonnet, and with few exceptions Belli employed the sonnet for the corpus of his poems.[34] He also developed some of the formal devices popularized by Pasquino: the anagram[35] and the pun. In the case of Pius VII, for instance, Pasquino, mindful of the nepotism of preceding

32. Ibid., 443-444.
33. With reference to Belli's troubled religiosity as it informed his poetry, see G. P. Samonà, *G. G. Belli: La commedia romana e la commedia celeste* (Florence: La Nuova Italia, 1969).
34. Of the impressive output of 2,279 poems in Roman dialect presented as "complete" by the great Belli scholar Giorgio Vigolo, only 24 are not sonnets.
35. Pasquino often anagrammatized the letters of his satirical target's name to prove a point and Belli maintained the tradition. But whereas Pasquino merely scrambled *C-a-r-d-i-n-a-l-i* to obtain *Ladri-cani* ("Thieving dogs"), Belli composed sonnet 1136 "*Er nome de li cardinali*" arriving in line eleven at *Ladri-cani* and then proceeding to instruct the reader on the effect of "thieving dogs" on religion.

popes, admonished in a pseudocommandment: "Settimo, non rubare" ("VIIth, thou shalt not steal"). Belli used this device in his rendering of the Commandments.

Belli also surpassed his satirical predecessor in his approach to the city of Rome and its inhabitants. Pasquino and other satirists concentrated mainly on protest, most of it motivated by specific problems. Whereas occasionally they may have hit upon some basic truths, unlike Belli they did not generally aspire to the universal. Belli's goal was to immortalize the Roman people, especially the lower classes, allowing him to transcend the particularistic and make more general statements on the human condition.[36] So he informed his friend, Francesco Spada, of his intention to

set forth normal Roman speech as it is spoken by the Roman mouth, that is, absolutely unaltered and without any embellishment. . . . I don't want to transcribe popular poetry, but rather discuss popular matters in my poetry. . . . And if with such a palette of local colors I manage to portray the civil, moral and religious existence of our Roman people, I believe I will have created a reasonably valuable picture of everyday life, since I do not view my subjects through the lens of prejudice.[37]

Aided by his remarkable ear, his sensitivity to shades of meaning, and his acute powers of observation, Belli left an outstanding portrait of

36. In this regard Muscetta mentions Belli's reading of *La Nouvelle Héloïse* in which Rousseau confronts the obligation of the modern writer to understand contemporary society in its entirety and to incorporate it in his works: "Playwrights today," he warns, "[merely] copy their conversation from one hundred [select] homes in Paris. Beyond that one learns nothing of French mores. In this great city there are five or six thousand souls [of the type] who will never be represented in the theatre. . . . today's Authors . . . would feel dishonored to know what goes on over a Merchant's counter or in a laborer's workshop. They are capable only of portraying illustrious personages." See J-J. Rousseau, *La Nouvelle Héloïse* (Paris, Hachette, 1925), vol. 2, letter 17, pp. 340–341. Earlier he states plainly: "My goal is to know mankind and my method is to study it by means of its myriad relationships" (Ibid., letter 16, p. 325). Belli mentions reading Rousseau in *Journal du Voyage de 1827*; see G. G. Belli, *Lettere, Giornali, Zibaldone* (Turin: Einaudi, 1962), 53, 80. See also, C. Muscetta, *Cultura e poesia di G. G. Belli* (Milan: Feltrinelli, 1961), 256–257.

37. Letter to Francesco Spada (5 October 1831). Belli repeated these words in his *Introduzione* to the *Sonetti romaneschi* in December of the same year. His decision to break with the poetic style of the Roman academies in the manner outlined in the letter to Spada and in the preface to the *Sonetti* dates approximately from 1828 after his reading of the Milanese poet, Carlo Porta. The definitive version of the *Introduzione* was not completed until 1847. The letter to Spada, which could serve as a sketch for the preface, demonstrates Belli's commitment to his original program. See G. G. Belli, *Le lettere* (Milan: Cino del Duca, 1961), vol. 1: 239; and G. G. Belli, *Lettere, Giornali, Zibaldone*, 374.

his city at all levels of society, earning himself the enduring critical appreciation that makes it possible to call him "the plebian Shakespeare of Italian literature . . . On the level of expression [he is] Dante's only rival."[38] Approximately 10 percent of his Roman mosaic was devoted to some aspect of Jewish life and its effect on non-Jewish citizens. Ironically, although Belli claimed to be unbiased, a realistic portrayal of the Jews required the poet's Christian interlocutors to voice pervasive common prejudice. Thus Belli's portrayal of the Jews is a far more complex one than that revealed by the *Pasquinate*; his is a learned eye, which, while it observed and recorded the popular image, could see beyond it.

But perhaps one of the greatest differences between Belli and Pasquino is the aim of their writings and their consequent effect on the people satirized. As secretary to Pope Gregory XVI, Belli had assumed the role of Pasquino, the "chastizer of vice," with one important difference. Whereas Pasquino existed so that dissent could be instantly rendered public, Belli, ever prudent, eschewed publication, preferring to recite his poetry to his friends.[39] This is an important point. Whereas Pasquino's brutal satire of the Jews was "published" soon after it was written and may have had adverse effects on Jews, (e.g., the issue of the sciamanno), Belli's sonnets were not public and not intended to engender negative reaction against the Jews. Belli's superlative portrait of the Jews of Rome had no polemical basis beyond pointing to the fruits of injustice: moral humiliation and economic misery.

Giuseppe Gioachino Belli (1791–1863) was a highly cultured, philosophically and politically complex, and often ambiguous individual. He is commonly remembered as a liberal[40] and yet he founded the Accademia Tiberina, one of the many antiquated and reactionary cultural

38. F. Ferrucci, "Il mito," in *Letteratura italiana,* ed. A. Asor Rosa (Turin: Einaudi, 1986), vol. 5, *Le questioni,* 543.

39. Indeed, the common, probably mistaken, assumption about the future of the sonnets is that at least at one point Belli wished them destroyed "some day." In a letter to G. Neroni Cancelli, dated September 1838, he says: "In your letter of 18 June you spoke of my 300 unpublished sonnets. . . . There are two thousand of them, but they should be kept hidden and then, one day, burned." See E. Colombi, *Catologo-mostra di manoscritti e lettere autografe di G. G. Belli nel 150° anniversario della sua nascita* (Rome: Cuggiani, 1941), §219, 37. But if this were really his intention, why elaborate an introduction over sixteen years? Alberto Bacelli logically points out that if he had wanted his poetry destroyed, he could have done it himself. See A. Baccelli, "G. Gioacchino Belli e l'abate Tizzani," *Il giornale d'Italia,* 30 August 1939. More likely, Belli wanted to withhold his work from publication and gave it to Tizzani for safekeeping.

40. But Giacinto Spagnoletti maintains that Belli never had a liberal period and was "clearly" a product of the Restoration. Belli's liberalism, he maintains, is really a miscalculation by what he calls "positivist" criticism from the first important Belli scholar, Luigi

institutions in Rome with deep roots in Arcadia[41] and in the Restoration. Belli scholars have long sought to reconcile the conservatism of his early life and his later reactionary writings with his adoption of Enlightenment philosophy and the powerful critique of Roman institutions expressed in his *Sonetti romaneschi*. That he was deeply attached to the principles of the Church is evidenced by the wounded bitterness of his anticlerical stance. At the same time he admired Voltaire[42] and was clearly influenced by him. Even his literary style reveals contradictions.[43] He was simultaneously given to pedantry, as demonstrated by his personal writings in the *Zibaldone,* yet he wrote almost freewheeling dialect poetry.[44] Given these contradictions, it is of crucial importance to look at Belli's cultural formation,[45] if one is to understand his position on the Jews, the group that so stimulated his imagination and peoples so many of his sonnets.

It has been suggested that the poet's family situation was at the root of this apparent conflict between philosophy and political reality. Belli belonged to a class that lived at the social margin of the gentry. Though his family was cultured and comfortable, it was dependent on government employment and unlikely to achieve any significant measure of economic independence. During the Roman Republic the family was forced to flee and lost everything. This, Belli states unequivocally, was the start of all his hardships.[46] Belli and his family had learned some bitter truths: that proclamations of liberty for some could lead to pro-

---

Morandi, onward. Presumably he includes Vigolo and Muscetta in this group. See G. Spagnoletti, introduction to G. G. Belli, *Le lettere,* 27.

41. In 1818 Belli was "received into Arcadia" with the poetic name Linarco Dirceo.

42. Belli provides us with a clue as to why in a passage from Voltaire (*Lettres d'Amabed,* 14) which he copied out into the sixth book of his *Zibaldone* (3312): "I swear to you there was never such an enormous contradiction on earth as that between the government of Rome and its religion." See G. G. Belli, *Zibaldone,* MS in nine volumes and two volumes of indices, Biblioteca Nazionale "Vittorio Emanuele" di Roma.

43. Vigolo, in an attempt to define the poet through his sonnets, seems to have misinterpreted the following passage from the *Introduzione*: "Io non vo' già presentar nelle mie carte la poesia popolare, ma i popolari discorsi svolti nella mia poesia" ("I don't want to transcribe popular poetry, but rather discuss popular matters in my poetry"). In the article "La poesia di G. G. Belli," *Il Mondo,* 1 February 1924, Vigolo writes: "This man's identity disappears and is disseminated to the people all around him, as if he were immersed in the river Lethe or a baptismal font, in which the old, Arcadian personality died and a new man was reborn with all five senses reawakened to life and reality."

44. See G. Almansi, "I sonetti dell'insignificanza di G. G. Belli," in *Tre sondaggi sul Belli* (Turin: Einaudi, 1978), 5–46.

45. For an ample analysis of Belli's cultural background supported by an admirable reading of his works, see C. Muscetta, *Cultura e poesia di G. G. Belli.*

46. "Perhaps, dear friend, you think I dwell too much on these political matters, but

scription and impoverishment for others and that liberty and equality were anything but synonymous.[47]

Disillusioned by social inequality and desirous of greater opportunity for himself and his family, the young Belli concentrated on the causes of inequality and its solution. In 1824 he began to assemble his *Zibaldone*,[48] a compendium of readings and commentary, into which he copied out sizable tracts from Montesquieu (*Lettres persanes*), Voltaire (*Histoire de Jenni, Lettres d'Amabed*), d'Herbigny (*Des destinées futures d'Europe*), and Volney (*Les Ruines*). From d'Herbigny Belli learned to distrust theocracy, from Montesquieu to value pluralism, and from Volney a passion for social justice. These themes are made amply explicit in the *Sonetti romaneschi*. It was especially Volney's dictum "Live for the benefit of your fellows so that they will live for you"[49] which seized his moral imagination. The theme of doing justly unto others recurs continually throughout the corpus of 2,279 sonnets. Belli, however, goes beyond "live and let live" to "live and provide for others to live." In sonnet 21 *"Campa, e lassa campà"* ("Live and Let Live") (19 February 1830) he writes:

> S'ha da vede, per dio, la bbuggiarata
> Ch'er cristiano ha d'annà ssenza carzoni,
> Manco si cquelli poveri cojjoni
> Nun fussino de carne bbattezzata!
> Stassi a sto fusto a ccommannà le feste, . . .
> . . . chiamerebbe bbonziggnor Maggnelli,[50]
> Pe ddijje du' parole leste leste
> "Sor E', ffamo campà li poverelli."

(By God it's a dirty trick that a man has to go without pants as if his poor balls weren't baptized flesh. If I were pope and running the show, I would

---

I need to describe to you the origin of all my subsequent misfortunes." "Mia Vita," autobiographical letter to Filippo Ricci (1811) in G. G. Belli, *Lettere, Giornale, Zibaldone,* 5–22.

47. "Once the violence stopped . . . a general amnesty in the miserable name of liberty was solemnly proclaimed far and wide. But it was belied daily as new blood was shed. . . . Public opinion was solidly against this fanatical and deceptive egalitarianism and it would soon topple that fragile colossus with feet of clay." (Ibid., 11.)

48. G. G. Belli, *Zibaldone.* Henceforth passages from the *Zibaldone* will be identified in the text by *Zib,* followed by a Roman numeral to indicate the volume and a page or entry number.

49. Count Volney, *La loi naturel* (Paris: Librairie de la Bibliothèque Nationale, 1898), vol. 2: 106; Belli, *Zibaldone* III, 1918.

50. President of the Annona e Grascia, the authority that oversaw the price and distribution of food.

call on Monsignor Magnelli and tell him simply: "Mister Whoever-you-are, let's provide for the poor.")

If this is a gentle complaint, 1169 *"Li du' ggener' umani"* ("Rich and Poor") (7 April 1834) is genuinely indignant and even blasphemous. It expresses the poet's frustration at living in a triangular society with the wealthy few on top and the wretched masses at its base:

> Noi, se sa, ar monno semo ussciti fori
> Impastati de mmerda e dde monnezza.
> Er merito, er decoro e la grannezza
> Sò ttutta marcanzia de li siggnori.
>   A ssu' Eccellenza, a ssu' Maestà, a ssu' Artezza
> Fumi, patacche, titoli e sprennori;
> E a nnoantri artiggiani e sservitori
> Er bastone, l'imbasto e la capezza.
>   Cristo creò le case e li palazzi
> P'er prencipe, er marchese e 'r cavajjere,
> E la terra pe' nnoi facce de cazzi.
>   E cquanno morze in crosce, ebbe er penziere
> De sparge, bbontà ssua, fra ttanti strazzi,
> Pe cquelli er zangue e ppe nnoantri er ziere.

(It's well known that we [common folk] are born covered with shit and garbage. Worthiness, manners and nobility all belong to the wealthy. For His Excellency, for His Highness: incense, money, titles and luxury; for us artisans and servants: thrashing, pack saddles and the hangman's rope. Christ created houses and palaces for the princes, marquises and knights, and he gave us prick-faces the [bare] earth. And when he died on the cross, in his agony he had the goodness to shed his blood, for them. What did we get? The serum.)

The meek in Belli's world have indeed inherited the earth, the bare earth, and little else except for harsh treatment and poverty. Is all humankind created in the image of God? Belli seems to have some doubts, for why, then, is there such radical inequality in the world? And what kind of God is he? If the pope, who sits at the top of the social heap pulling the strings that make his subjects obey like so many marionettes, is God's viceroy, then mustn't God be even more brutal and capricious? Perhaps religion and the optimism it implies is all a *bbuggiarata,* a cruel joke. Christ's death on the cross was meant to redeem and unify mankind, but it failed to do so because society was already irrevocably divided. And so it has remained from that day forward. The theme of the unjust distribution of goods and opportunity was a constant one in Belli. In 981 *"Er monno"* ("The World"), instead of Christ shedding his blood from the cross, a watermelon sheds its seeds. But the common man may only taste, not eat, the seeds: the rich and powerful want them back.

By 1847, Belli appears to have thrown up his hands in despair while jokingly suggesting a way to end class problems once and for all. In sonnet 2169, known as *"Privilegi di classi"* ("Class Privilege"),[51] the poet opts for a solution that comes from the established top of society:

Eh, Ppapa io, nun me faria confonne!
Voria ridusce er monno a ppoc' a ppoco
Tutto quanto in du' crasse: *ommini e ddonne.*

(If I were Pope, I would see it all clearly! Little by little I would want to divide the whole world into two classes: *men* and *women.*)

Frustration ultimately gives way to resignation or rebellion. Belli opted for the latter, "rebelling" against the social injustice that pervaded his society by abstracting episodes from the Bible and creating, in Roman dialect, his own "Abbibbia" ("Bible"). One of his preferred themes is the story of Cain inasmuch as it is symbolic of a universal social discourse. The poet is sympathetic toward Cain because he was a simple man ("un omo com' e nnoi de carne e dd'osso"—"a man like us [made] of flesh and bone") who could not comprehend or bear the Lord's favor toward his brother. In sonnet 180 *"Caino"* ("Cain") (6 October 1831) he writes:

Nun difenno Caino io, sor dottore,
Ché lo so ppiù dde voi chi ffu Ccaino: . . .
    Ma quer vede ch'Iddio sempre ar zu mèle
E a le su' rape je sputava addosso,
E nnò ar latte e a le pecore d'Abbele,
    A un omo com' e nnoi de carne e dd'oso
Aveva assai de inascidijje er fele:
E allora, amico mio, tajja ch'è rrosso.

(I'm not defending Cain, no sir, because I know more about him than you do: . . . But to see God always spit at his honey and his turnips but not at Abel's milk and sheep, [well] for a man made of flesh and bone like us, that was enough to poison his bile. So my friend, cut it, it's ripe.)

---

51. This poem has no title, but Vigolo reports that on the back of the manuscript Belli wrote "Privilegi di classi" (G. G. Belli, *Sonetti,* vol. 2: 2900, n. 10.)

"Tajja ch'è rrosso" ("cut it, it's ripe") is a metaphor taken from the language of watermelon vendors. The proper time to cut a watermelon is when it's "red" or ripe, so "tajja ch'è rrosso" means that it's time to act. Cain acts: he rebels when he can no longer stand his situation. He takes advantage of the Lord's momentary inattention and kills his brother. In Belli's Bible, Cain's revolt against injustice becomes the original sin superseding the Judeo-Christian tradition of Adam, Eve, and the apple. In punishment, the Lord sends Cain out to wander the earth.

This sonnet ventures far beyond the Bible story in its exploration of the human condition. A close reading of Belli's subtle hendecasyllable reveals a masterful poetic technique. Belli utilizes the Cain legend for its familiarity and drama as a point of departure, but then crafts the line in such a way as to establish an eternal power relationship between God, the learned or leisure class, and the common man leading his life of denial and frustration. The dramatis personae are aligned one below the other in the crucial sixth position in each line (or fifth and sixth in the case of "Caino" and "Iddio"). Thus from Caino (line 1) we go up the social ladder to *voi* ("you," formal plural, in line 2), that is, the learned man (*sor dottore*), and up one more step to God (*Iddio*, line 9). From there God spits down at Cain's labors (*je* = to, or at, him, line 10). Cain is then subsumed under the universal *nnoi* ("us"), humanity made out of flesh and bone. By dint of experiencing a similar life of hardship, the common man (*io, nnoi*) knows more about Cain's troubles than the "doctor" will ever be able to learn, so for the time being the narrator assumes a tone of superiority, calling his social better *amico mio* ("my friend") in the last line and advising him, and everyone, to do his part against the injustice of his situation, "tajja ch'è rrosso." Finally the universal is personalized and the relationship between Cain in the first line and the narrator ([*m*]*io*) in the last line is sealed with each sharing the sixth metric position as they share social misfortune.

Together with the earlier protests of *Campa e llassa campà* and the bitterness of the later *Li du' ggener' umani*, "tajja ch'è rrosso" has all the trappings of incitement to civil strife. And yet, since for the most part the sonnets were circulated only among a few friends during Belli's lifetime,[52] his poetry is more an observation of man's fate than a call

---

52. An exception to this general rule must be made for 2076 "*Lo scaricabbarilli der Governo*" ("The Government Buck-passer") (17 January 1845). It circulated by word of mouth with the title " *'N odore dde rrivoluzzione*" ("In the Odor of Revolution"):

Ce penzeranno lòro: ecco sti santi
Cos' hanno sempre in bocca, per dio d'oro!

to action. Similarly, Belli's career was circumscribed within specific limits. Except for the questionable liberal interlude, which coincided with his period of greatest poetic creativity, Belli appears to have been quite conservative. Although some of his work and, therefore, his politics were known to papal authorities, in order to maintain his modest bureaucratic job for the popes and at their pleasure, he was forced to disguise his role as in-house "censor." This put a considerable strain on his liberalism. If he trod softly, if his satire remained humorous, if his criticism seemed good-natured, he could go on with it unimpeded. And as late as 1847 he was able to write the (chronologically) penultimate sonnet of the corpus, 2244 "*Le cariche nove*" ("New Jobs") in which he mocks those same authorities as they trample each other in the struggle to obtain or maintain their jobs. As in the early poetry, they are priests and thugs, cardinals and spies, lawyers and secretaries—all part of Belli's daily reality.

It is, therefore, nearly impossible to categorize Belli's philosophy with airtight certainty. As he aged his vacillation between old and new, conservative and liberal, gave way increasingly to Catholic dogmatism and in the end the retrograde tendencies won out. As his attachment to the Church assumed a more institutional stamp, his choice of reading material changed to keep pace and gradually shifted from the *Révue Encyclopédique* to the virulently reactionary *Civiltà Cattolica* and the world as he saw it became reduced to two classes: Catholics and atheists.[53]

Still, throughout the period of greatest creativity two themes emerged as constants: tolerance and justice. Of all the possible passages Belli could have copied into the *Zibaldone,* which was to be his son Ciro's intellectual legacy, he chose the writings of Voltaire and Montesquieu which described the evils of intolerance and despotism and the benefits of pluralism to a society. It is within this framework that Belli treats the Jews in his *Sonetti romaneschi.*

E co sto bbèr *ce penzeranno lòro*
Intanto cqui nnun ze po' annà ppiú avanti. . . .
    Sai come va a ffiní? ffinissce poi
Che ssi sti *lòro* nun ce penzeranno,
Un po' ppiú in là cce penzeremo noi.

("Leave it to those in power": that's what these priests always say, by God. But by saying "leave it to them," we can't get anything done. You know what'll happen? If these bigshots don't get moving, before long we'll do it ourselves!)

53. In the outline for a work entitled *La Chiesa* (*The Church*), Belli wrote: "Sophisms, the irony of Voltaire and his followers—Rousseau—The Social Contract—end with *those who are not with me are against me.* But [one day] all heresy will end. Then the world will be reduced to *Catholics* or *atheists.*" (G. G. Belli, *Lettere, Giornali, Zibaldone,* 562.)

The *Sonetti Romaneschi*

Even a cursory reading of the *Zibaldone* will reveal that the Jews were very much on Belli's mind. His curiosity extended beyond the Jewish population of contemporary Rome to Biblical history, the philosophes, Italian and English literature to, simply, things he had heard about Jews on a daily basis. He indexed the Jewish presence in the stories of Boccaccio (*Zib.* III, 1465) and Sacchetti (*Zib.* I, 1262–1282) and the verses of Cesare Caporali.[54] He analyzed Voltaire's approach to the Jews in the *Henriade* (*Zib.* IX, f. 29), Denina's in the *Rivoluzioni d'Italia* (*Italian Revolutions*) (*Zib.* IX, f. 56), and Sir Walter Scott's in his life of Napoleon (*Zib.* IX, f. 239). On a more immediate and less theoretical level, Belli was quite taken with Scott's portrayal of the Jew, Isaac of York, and dedicated several entries to it (*Zib.* VI, 3344–3348, 3381–3382).

All the while he was compiling the *Zibaldone,* Belli was writing dialect poetry and he translated his intellectual interest in Jews into a sizable Jewish presence in the *Sonetti romaneschi.* Here they are referred to mainly in terms of the Judeo-Christian biblical tradition, both Jewish and Christian Testaments, and of their ethnic presence in historical and contemporary Rome.

Of course, this division between Biblical times, ancient, and contemporary Rome reflects the city's history. More importantly, by so dividing the body of the sonnets, Belli reproduces the popular vision of the city's Jews. After all, who were the Jews? For the average Roman, Jews probably fell into three categories: the Hebrews whom they heard about in Sunday sermons, the Jews of ancient Rome who were part of local lore, and the people who shared their city, with whom they may have had frequent encounters, yet who were nonetheless separated from them by ghetto walls.

Belli's technique in populating his sonnets with these Jews is to focus on many stock types, their characters and their trade. He does not give much physical description or list such attributes as "hooked-nose misers," perhaps because the brevity of the sonnet does not encourage it. Rather, he presents a clannish member of God's chosen people, a clever cloth merchant, a rapacious pawnbroker, an able seamstress—all figures of the standard anti-Jewish iconography—and engages them in

54. C. Caporali, *Rime* (Venice: Z. Conzatti, 1673), *Zib.* III, 1464.

generally adversarial dealings with an "average" Christian interlocutor. This allows each character to mirror the other, adding an additional bite to Belli's satire.

"SICU T'ERA TIN PRINCIPIO
NUNCHE E PEGGIO"

("As it was in the beginning only worse")

Although the largest single block of Belli's 2,279 *Sonetti romaneschi* is devoted to satire of the papacy,[55] a sizable number of compositions were inspired by or refer to the Bible. To compile his "Abbibbia" in an atmosphere pervaded with Catholicism and Church tradition, Belli took familiar religious stories and images and presented them as part of a historical continuum projecting them onto contemporary events. The result was a very personal perspective both on Papal Rome and on the community of Roman Jews.

A prime example of this technique of pulling the Bible down to earth and making it pertinent to reality is sonnet 213 *"La bbella Ggiuditta"* ("Beautiful Judith") (14 October 1831). Here Belli takes the Apocryphal story of Judith and Holofernes, translates it into the popular idiom, and in the last strophe uses it as a homily to illustrate a current political situation. In Belli's version of the story, Judith doesn't just cut off the head of Holofernes, she uses a stroke *"da fia de mastro Titta"* ("worthy of [the daughter of] Master Titta") a famous executioner of the time. In the Bible, Judith was able to catch Holofernes unawares when he was drunk and in the midst of sexual passion. In Belli's homily, her bloody deed is justified in the name of religion, *"Se pò scannà la ggente pe la fede"* ("You can slaughter people in the name of religion"), and her prostitution is dedicated to the glory of God: *"E ffà la vacca pe ddà ggrolia a Ddio."* To the politically aware among Belli's contemporaries, this veiled allusion to the sanfedisti, who would lower themselves to any misdeed for the advancement of the Faith, would probably have been evident.

To what extremes might one go for one's faith and how would one weigh the consequences? Belli finds a disconcerting answer in the Jewish Testament account of the wars between Amalechites and Israelites. The Israelites won overwhelmingly and in sonnets 1825 and 1826

55. See in this regard B. Garvin, "La *indiggnità* papale nei sonetti di Belli" in *Tre sondaggi sul Belli*, 49–105.

"Chi ffa, ariscéve I" and "II" ("He Who Does, Gets I" and "II") (29 October 1836) Belli attributes the victory to the fact that they possessed the true religion and hints that at that time, unlike now, God was their friend. The poet based his two sonnets closely on passages from the Bible which he cites in Latin in his notes. In the Scriptures it is written that

> . . .   appena li Sdrelliti
> Terminorno er passaggio der Mar Rosso,
> Scappo ffora un mijjon de Malessciti
> Che ttutti assieme j' appiommorno addosso.
>   Iddio se la seggnò sta bbrutt' azzione,
> Perché allora l' Ebbrei j' ereno amichi
> E aveveno la vera riliggione.
>   Fatti dunque passà cquattroscent' anni,
> Disse a Ssaulle: "Va', e de sti nimmichi
> Nun ce restino ppiù mmanco li panni."

(As soon as the Israelites had crossed the Red Sea, a million Amalechites appeared out of nowhere and attacked them all together. God took note of this crime because at that time He favored the Jews who had the True Faith. Then after four hundred years, God said to Saul: "Go, and let nothing remain of these enemies, not even their clothes.")

God took note of Amalech's surprise attack on the Israelites because He had selected the Jews from among their ancient neighbors to be the repositories of the True Faith. Belli makes this point absolutely clear through his verse structure: in the third strophe of the sonnet the stress in each line falls on the sixth syllable—that is, "seg*gnò*" ("noted"), "Eb-*brei*" ("Jews"), "*vera*" ("true")—thereby reinforcing the natural stress of the words. In his notes Belli quoted a line from the Bible likening the assault on the Hebrews to an attack on God.[56] He then comments on the final strophe by applying a traditional anti-Semitic accusation to the Bible story: "This wonderful passage from Chapter XV of the first book of Kings [Samuel] inasmuch as it probes the inscrutable nature of God's justice, corresponds exactly to Adam's solidarity with all his descendants." For Belli, in this case the "descendants of Adam" are the Jews rather than humankind in general and the stereotype is clannishness, elitism, exclusionism derived from the notion of being the chosen people.

56. ". . . the Lord will have war with Amalek from generation to generation." (Exodus, XVII, 16.)

But Belli also envies the solidarity of the Jews in their ongoing struggle against the plundering Amalechites until the moment of their final victory, as narrated in sonnet 1826 *"Chi ffa, ariscéve II"* ("He Who Does, Gets II"). Here, unfortunately, the picture is clouded by a far less respectable aspect of that victory:

Saulle dunque, in nome der Ziggnore,
Scannò inzino le crape e le vitelle;
Ma, o ffussi pe avarizzia o ppe bbon core,
Prese er re Agaggo e jje sarvò la pelle.
    E ecchete er profeta Samuelle
Che lo chiama idolatro e ttraditore,
E jj' intíma ch'er reggno d'Isdraelle
Passerà a un zu' viscino ppiú mmijjore.
    Poi disce: "Indov' è er Re, cche ttu ssarvassi?"
E 'r poverello je se fesce avanti,
Tremanno peggio de li porchi grassi.
    Allora Samuelle, a ddenti stretti,
je disse: "Mori;" e in faccia a ttutti quanti
Arzò un marraccio e lo tajjò a pezzetti.

(In the name of God, then, Saul butchered even the goats and the calves. But whether for economy's sake or his soft heart, he spared the life of Agag. Then up comes the prophet Samuel who calls him an idolater and a traitor, and intimates that the Kingdom of Israel will be given to a more faithful neighbor. Then he says: "Where is the King whom you saved?" And the poor man came forward, trembling worse than a fattened pig. Then, gritting his teeth, Samuel said to him: "You shall die," and in front of everyone, raised his sword and cut him to pieces.")

Carlo Muscetta comments that "In this [account of war] Belli reveals the fierce realism of the Bible, and translating it, as only he can, imbues it with his horror of Jewish racism and theocratic violence."[57] But this view is too reductive; Belli's message in these two sonnets is far more complex. Here Belli imparts a valuable moral lesson succinctly and with great visual style as he explores the behavior of groups in their struggle for domination. The group in power must defend itself against all comers, especially against neighbors of a different faith which they are constantly seeking to establish as the "true" religion. Therefore one's neighbors must be either subdued totally or totally destroyed "down to the goats and the calves" so that nothing remains, "not even

57. C. Muscetta, cited in G. G. Belli, *I sonetti*, ed. M. T. Lanza (Milan: Feltrinelli, 1965), vol. 4: 1916.

their rags." The ancient Israelites, seemingly unlike Belli's contemporary Roman Jews, enjoyed God's favor. Human fortunes change with the wind, as Belli knew only too well, and the King of Israel fell "to a greater neighbor." The new kingdom was probably better armed and able to impose and defend its own religion, for a while. The racism that Muscetta perceived in these sonnets was not the exclusive property of the Jews. Rather, Belli uses this group to symbolize the eternal struggle for dominance which is the heritage of the theocratic state. The moral of these sonnets, already implicit in the title, is a solemn warning against violence in the name of religion: he who lives by the sword shall be manipulated by others and bring about his own downfall. Similarly those who persist in believing themselves the chosen people, the Jews for example, are merely part of a progression of chosen peoples who enjoy a brief moment of glory only to fall to another group that will itself be eclipsed, and so on.

The question of true religion had been on Belli's mind from his youth and crops up again and again in the *Sonetti romaneschi* well before "*Chi ffa, ariscéve*" in versions that are more down to earth, more clearly satirical, less predicatory. In these sonnets Belli takes his own religion to task along with all the others. In 727 "*La riliggione vera*" ("The One True Religion") (12 January 1833) all but one religion are

> . . .   ·bbuggiarate
> Da nun dajje un cuadrin de callalesse.
>   Tutte ste freggne, com'ha ddetto er frate,
> S'annaveno a ffà fotte da se stesse,
> Cuann'anche Iddio nu l'avessi fregate
> Co 'na radisce che sse chiama Ajjesse.
>   Noi soli semo li credenti veri,
> Perché ccredemo ar Papa, e 'r Papa poi
> Sce spiega tutto chiaro in du' misteri.
>   L'avvanti er Turco, l'avvanti er Giudio
> Un'antra riliggione com'e nnoi,
> Da potesse maggnà Ddomminiddio!

(. . . all lies. I wouldn't give a penny's worth of boiled chestnuts for the lot of 'em. All of this foolishness got screwed, just like the monk said, when God bollixed it up with a new invention called the Virgin Mary. Now we alone are the true believers because we believe in the pope and the pope makes everything clear for us in two mysteries. The Turks claim to have it, the Jews boast about it, [but there isn't] any other religion like ours where you get to eat God!)

No other religion could compete after God created the Virgin Mary. And Catholicism has a real bulwark in the Pope who keeps the faithful as ignorant as possible (hence the oxymoron: "Sce spiega tutto chiaro in du' misteri"—"He makes everything clear for us with two mysteries"). The fewer questions they ask, the greater his power. One of the mysteries that makes their religion greater than any other is the Eucharist. Indeed other religions pale before Catholicism because they worship "five or six Jesus Christs" (306 *Er penurtimo sagramento, e quarch'antra cosa*"—"The Penultimate Sacrament and Some Other Things") (between 12 December 1831 and 5 January 1832).

Finally Belli brushes off the whole question of the true religion as a waste of time and with it his willingness to entertain any debate about the chosen people. "How do I know if the Messiah was born before or after Mohammed or Moses?" he says in 1034 *"Cose antiche"* ("Ancient Matters") (30 November 1833):

> Che ccosa m'ho da intenne io si er Messía
> E' nnato prima o ddoppo de Maometto,
> Oppuro de Mosè? Vvadino in Ghetto
> A ffà ste sciarle: vadino in Turchia.
>   Sò impicci da sbrojjà ddoppo tant'anni?
> L'omo nun pò ssapé cche cquer c' ha vvisto:
> Ma eh? nun dico bbene, sor Giuvanni?
>   Prima o ddoppo, cchi vvòi che jje n'importi?
> Bbasta, o Mmosè, o Mmaometto, o Ggesucristo,
> Quello ch'è ccerto è cche ssò ttutti morti.

(Let 'em go to the Ghetto if they want to talk nonsense. Let 'em go to Turkey. Why bring it up after all these years? A man can only be sure about what he sees. Right, John? Before or after, who cares? OK, that's it: Moses or Mohammed or Jesus Christ, the only thing you can be sure about is that they're all dead.)

Too much blood has been shed in the name of the true religion, too much breath has been wasted defining it and claiming it for one's own. And too much injustice has been done to the powerless who, in turn, exploit those even more expendable than they.

Justice, or rather the plague of injustice, is analyzed repeatedly throughout Belli's "Abbibbia," the Bible being in large part a compendium of episodes of inhumanity toward one's fellows. One of the greatest injustices, according to the Roman poet, is the inflexible system of hierarchy which locks one into a set role, impeding one's progress at every turn, and often forcing one to lead a life of privation and self-denial.

A prime example is the story of Abraham and Isaac which was so important to Belli that he elaborated it over the space of three sonnets. In the first, 757 *"Er zagrifizzio d'Abbramo I"* ("Abraham's Sacrifice I") (16 January 1833), the power relationships are established between God and Abraham, his subject, and between Abraham the patriarch-father and Isaac, his son. Sometime between Noah's Ark and the Ark of the Convenant, God demands a sacrifice of Abraham. When they arrive at the killing ground, in 758 *"Er zagrifizzio d'Abbramo II"* ("Abraham's Sacrifice II") (16 January 1833), Isaac turns to his father to know where the victim is. Abraham has not the heart to tell him the truth and instead tells him to climb the hill. At the top Abraham loses his extraordinary calm and in desperation screams at his son:

> ". . . Isacco, a tté,
> Faccia a tterra: la vittima sei tu."

("Isaac! On the ground! Face down! *You're* the victim!")

The order "faccia a tterra" forces the Bible story into contemporary reality. It echoes the typical command of outlaws to their victims and also functions as a popular judgment on Abraham for violating the sacred bond between father and son. Indeed in the first strophe of 759 *"Er zagrifizzio d'Abbramo III"* ("Abraham's Sacrifice III") (16 January 1833) Belli replaces the patriarch's name with his role of "father" and renders it as a pejorative: "padraccio" and later "cquer boja de padre" ("that executioner of a father"). Another epithet identifies the victim with the Roman masses. This is one of the most common in Belli: "povero cojjone" ("poor bastard"). Even after such a great shock, Isaac is passive, docile, unable to react. He responds to his father with a resigned:

> "Pascenza," disce Isacco ar zu' padraccio,
> Se bbutta s'una pietra inginocchione,
> E cquer boja de padre arza er marraccio
> Tra ccap' e ccollo ar povero cojjone.

("Never mind!" says Isaac to his awful father and he kneels right down on a rock. And that headman of a father poises the butcher knife right between the poor bastard's head and the neck.)

How many times each day does Everyman, the "povero cojjone," have to swallow whatever pride or protest he has left after a life of hardship, hang his head, and mumble "pascenza"?

At this point, lest the sonnet becomes too pathetic, Belli lightens it with *coups-de-scène* from the Bible story. The Angel comes just in time to stop the slaughter and replace the boy with a real sacrificial animal. But though the sheep provides a comic touch with its

Bbee, bbee . . . Cchi è cquest'antro! è un pecorone

(Bah, bah . . . Who's this? It's a sheep!)

it is still a victim to satisfy God. As if Abraham hadn't already understood what the Lord wanted of him, the Angel hammers in the message.

"Dio te vorze provà cco sto setaccio . . ."

("God wanted to test you with this trap . . .")

Here Belli is also criticizing Church hierarchy, which sacrifices (or simply neglects) the flock of common people to get itself out of tight spots. In their unenviable daily lives, the masses have little more dignity than sheep with precious little difference between the sheep's "Bbee, bbee" and their "Pascenza."

So in Belli the popular voice transforms the Bible to its own experience. By retelling Bible stories such as the sacrifice of Isaac, Belli translates Jewish experience in terms that are easily accessible, and in so doing he tends to demystify the Jewish past. In the first sonnet Abraham orders Isaac to collect his things, put on his undershirt, load the donkey, find his father's hat, and kiss his mother goodbye—simple things that any father would ask his son to do before an outing. In addition, Isaac has to carry the butcher knife, that is, the tool of his demise, as Christ did his cross. Thus the pathos of the situation is rendered familiar to the Christian reader.

Furthermore, the essentially Bellian expression "povero cojjone" lifts this group of sonnets from the realm of the popularized Bible to that of allegory of the theocratic state that arbitrarily takes or spares the life of the "povero cojjone," Christian or Jew. In the Abraham sonnets, Belli analyzes the reason behind the sacrifice, that is, the desire (perceived as a necessity) to please God. The power of theocracy looms large in these poems, a force that moved Abraham to sacrifice his firstborn son on whom he doted and for whom he had waited so long. In modern times this authority made it possible for Paul IV to herd Jews into the ghetto and for subsequent popes to keep them there. This is the *raison d'être* of Belli's "Abbibbia," Bible stories used as *exempla* to inform contemporary Roman history.

The Christian Testament occupies a prominent place along with the Jewish one in Belli's version of the Bible, with the Jewish Testament offered in such a way as to bring it closer to the majority of readers and the Christian Testament presented in terms of continuity with the Jewish. One can imagine the surprise of the Roman workingman who goes to church only to discover the truth, which he calls "resia" ("heresy"), about Christ's background in 2065 *"Er predicatore di chiasso"* ("The Popular Preacher") (10 January 1845). The popular preacher

> Disce che Ggesucristo è stat' ebbreo:
> E ppe ffiní de dà in cojjonerie
> Va spaccianno c'Abbramo era un cardeo.

(. . . says that Jesus Christ had been a Jew, and as if that weren't stupid enough he insists that Abraham was Chaldean.)

Or in 2098 *"Er discorzo chiaro-chiaro"* ("The Simple Sermon") (27 March 1846) another preacher asks rhetorically: "After all who was Jesus Christ?" and answers his own question:

> "Era un pover' ebbreo fatto cristiano"

("He was just a poor Jew who became a Christian.")

"Heresy" such as this serves as a bridge between Judaism and Christianity, the Jewish and Christian Testaments.

Even the Nativity is not safe from Belli's mischievous redefinition of Christ's role in the "Abbibbia." Again Christ is just a poor Jew whose sobbing, putative father, Joseph, takes him to the Temple to be circumcised (331 *"La scirconcisione der Ziggnore"*—"The Circumcision of the Lord," 12 January 1832):

> . . .   a fajje fà a l'uscello
> Er tajjo d'un tantin di scinicozzo.

(. . . to have a little of his foreskin cut off.)

"*Scinicozzo*" is Roman slang for "foreskin" and was a term used to annoy the Jews. Belli uses it to disparage the seriousness of Christ's covenant with God, symbolized by his circumcision. It is a matter of principle. Christ lived as the poor Jew he was for thirty years until one day

> fu pe mmanno
> De san Giuvanni bbattezzat' a sguazzo
> In cuer tevere granne der Giordano.

(He was lavishly baptized by Saint John in that big Tiber, the Jordan River.)

No longer content with his lot he betrayed his sacred covenant. True he became a Christian, the first Christian, but in the last line Belli makes it clear that he dislikes fickleness

> Ma le ggirelle io nu le stimo un cazzo.

(But turncoats, they aren't worth a prick.)

with a pun on the slang term for the male member and the meaningless circumcision.

Where, then, are the distinctions between Jesus the Jew and Christ the Christian? How much substantive difference is there between Jews and Christians? Belli's interlocutors have no difficulty in responding, imbued as they are with the dogmas of their faith and stereotyped opinions of the other.

One master Andrea has somehow missed out on learning the truth about the "nazzionaccia ebbrea" ("the foul race of Jews") and is surprised to observe the persecution of the Jews in the *Ghetto de la Rua,* as the ghetto, traversed by Via Rua, was sometimes called. Luckily for him he has an acquaintance less "ignorant" than he who can fill him in on the essential facts, in 1195 *"L'iggnoranza de mastr'Andrea"* ("Master Andrew's Ignorance") (11 April 1834):

> Quanto sete curiale mastr'Andrea!
> Ma pproprio ve dich'io cche mme n'avete.
> Una scittà che cce commanna un Prete
> Pò cconfettà la nazzionaccia ebbrea?
>   Nu lo sapete voi de cos'è rrea?
> [. . .]
>   Nun ve sovviè dd'un certo tar Carvario,
> E dde scert'antri fatti c'aricconteno
> Li quinisci misteri der rosario?

Studiate, mastr'Andrea: fate da omo;
E imparerete che l'Ebbrei mó sconteno
Quello c'aveva d'accadé pp' er pomo.

(How curious you are, master Andrew! I mean you're really dense! Do you honestly think that a city run by a priest is going to do anything to flatter that nasty race of Jews? Don't you know what they're guilty of? . . . Don't you remember about Calvary and those other crimes which you recite with your rosary? Study! master Andrew: be a man! Then you will learn that [still] now the Jews are expiating the sin of the apple.)

Belli utilizes the "ignorance" of his interlocutor, master Andrew, to present a list of accusations against the Jews and to point out the Church's response to the unresolved question of original sin. The Jews continue to expiate (*mò sconteno*) the sin of eating of the forbidden fruit, since they obdurately reject baptism and refuse to come to the True Faith. Their penance, as it were, is the "non-flattering" treatment by the Church, probably a reference to the ghetto and the regulations under which they live. Belli, the devil's advocate, finds such policies obviously in keeping with the crimes committed, at Calvary, for example. But Belli the charitable,[58] the defender of the downtrodden, directs the accusation back at the Church. Persecution he implies, is a product of papal government and accusations against the Jews are perpetuated in prayer.

What if common people were in power in place of the priests? With regard to the Jews there would probably be little change for, as Belli notes in 1508 "*Le scuse de Ghetto*" ("Ghetto Excuses") (6 April 1835), hatred of Jews was the norm, not the exception:

In questo io penzo come penzi tu:
Io l'odio li Ggiudii peggio de te;
Perché nun zò ccattolichi, e pperché
Messeno in crosce er Redentor Gesú.

(In this matter we're of the same opinion. I hate the Jews, too, even worse than you do, because they're not Catholic and because they crucified the Savior.)

In fact, in order to initiate the dialogue, Belli must once again play the devil's advocate, this time not just matching the feelings of the other dialogist but exceeding them ("Io l'odio li Ggiudii peggio de te"—"I

---

58. For the concept of *charitas* in Belli, see G. Vigolo, *Il genio del Belli* (Milan: Il Saggiatore, 1963), vol. 1: 209–215; vol. 2: 333–342.

hate the Jews worse than you do") in order to gain the right footing
to launch his philosophical argument:

> Chi aripescassi poi dar tett'in giú
> Drento a le lègge[59] vecchia de Mosè,
> Disce l' Ebbreo che cquarche ccosa sc'è
> Ppe scusà le su' dodisci tribbú.
>   Ddefatti, disce lui, Cristo partí
> Dda casa sua, e sse ne venne cqua
> Cco l'idea de quer zanto venardí.
>   Ddunque, seguita a ddí Bbaruccabbà,
> Subbito che llui venne pe mmorí,
> Cquarchiduno l'aveva da ammazzà.

(If, looking downward, you fish in the ancient laws of Moses, the Jew says
you'll find that there is something to excuse his twelve tribes. In fact, he
says, Christ left home that day with that holy Friday all planned. Therefore,
Baruccabbà continues, since he came to die, someone had to kill him.)

Belli takes deicide, the most grievous of the accusations against the
Jews, and discusses it with a typical ghetto Jew, Baruccabbà, who de-
fensively attempts to explain it away. The Jew, who has the Scriptures
ready for any eventuality, "fishes" for his "excuses" in the ancient laws
of his people. The specific excuse for the death of Christ is a neat piece
of sophist reasoning: Christ came down to earth (*Partí*/*Dda casa sua*—
He left his home) predestined to die (*Cco l'idea*—With the plan) that
day (*quer zanto venardí*—that holy Friday). It was preordained in heaven,
not decided on earth. *Ddunque* (Therefore)—and Bbaruccabbà bases
his defense on the strength of his conclusion—since he was destined to
die that day, since he came all that way "with that holy Friday all
planned," somebody *had* to kill him. For all anyone knows, it might
have been the Jews themselves who were preordained to do the job. It
is a clever theological argument, but those unwilling to change their
opinion will reply that it's false reasoning, *dar tett'in giú* (looking
downward), with the human intellect, rather than *dar tett'in su* (looking up), for divine inspiration. And so it remains a *scusa*, an unreliable
excuse. As such it will never convince those who know that since the
world began Jews have been guilty for Christ's death.

Original sin at the dawn of time and the death of the savior of
humankind are the two major events that focus the negative Christian

---

59. Here Belli uses the open -*è*- of *lègge* (law) characteristic of Judeo-Roman pronun-
ciation.

view with regard to the Jews. Of course, the Jewish interpretation of the first event is substantially different and the Christian Testament does not enter at all into the Jewish religious vision. Still, the commandments provide a common ground between the two religious groups. The Jews gave the Christians their commandments, and through freewheeling interpretation of these commandments Belli makes his "Abbibbia" a commentary on conditions in contemporary Rome. Among the eight sonnets based on the commandments, the two dealing directly with the relations between Jews and Christians involve the prohibition of sexual commerce between the two groups.

The first sonnet, 848 "*Nono, nun disiderà la donna d'antri*" ("Ninth: Thou Shalt Not Covet Thy Neighbor's Wife") (1 February 1833) is an amused wink at the easy virtue of the women of Rome:

> Forze a Rroma sciamàncheno puttane
> Che vvai scercanno le zzaggnotte in ghetto?
> Vòi fotte? eh, ffotte co le tu' cristiane
> Senza offenne accusí Ddio bbenedetto.
>
> Cqua per oggni duzzina de Romane
> Un otto o un diesci te guarnissce er letto:
> E cche pòi spenne? Un pavolo, un papetto,
> E dd'un testone poi te sciarimane.
>
> Eppuro tu ssei bbattezzato, sei:
> E nnun zai che cquann'uno è bbattezzato
> Nun po' ttoccà le donne de l'ebbrei?
>
> E una vorta c'hai fatto sto peccato,
> Hai tempo d'aspettà lli ggiubbilei:
> Se more, fijjo mio, scummunicato.

(Maybe Rome doesn't have enough whores, so you have to go look for Jewish ones in the ghetto? You want sex? Get it on with your own Christian girls so you don't offend God. Here out of every dozen Roman women, eight or ten will go to bed with you. And, after all, what does it cost? Half a lira, a lira, and you'll still have some change left. Look, you're baptized, aren't you. Don't you know that a baptized Christian can't touch a Jewish woman? And once you've committed this sin, you can wait all you want for absolution; you'll be excommunicated, my son, permanently.)

The ironic title, "Don't Covet Another's Woman," is a paraphrase of the ninth commandment. "Antri," as the sonnet goes on to demonstrate, does not simply mean "others," but in this case specifically, Jews, and is a translation of the "proximi" ("neighbor's") of the commandment. This is the irony, for in Pope Gregory XVI's Rome of 1833, Jews were hardly neighbors of anyone except other Jews. But it's no loss be-

cause all the ghetto has to offer are "zzaggnotte"[60] ("Jewish whores")
whereas there are plenty of Christian prostitutes to go around. The con-
fessor's scruples extend only so far, however, and sin is rather an elastic
concept.

As far as the Church is concerned, the actual mortal sin is sex across
religious barriers. The sixth commandment "thou shalt not commit
adultery" expressly forbids all such contacts outside marriage. From this
one would surmise that any such sex would "offend God," but as Belli
intimates in 2118 *"Sesto, nun formicà"* ("Sixth: Thou Shalt Not Commit
Adultery") (10 April 1846), the category of forbidden flesh is sub-
divided according to gradations of prohibition:

"Ma ssenz'èsse però mmojj' e mmarito
Er fà un omo e una donna quela cosa
Ch'io fo 'ggni notte co mmi' mojje Rosa
Nun è ssempre un peccato provibbito?"—
"Io nun ve dico," repricò er romito,
"Che sta corpa nun zii peccanimosa;
Ma cche la Cchiesa, ch'è mmadr'amorosa,
Sa ddistingue er pancotto e er pan bullito.
Per esempio, si un omo bbattezzato
Vienghi preso in fregnante co un'ebbrea,
E' ssubbito un peccato ariservato.
Ma ppe una donna poi s'arza la mano.
Tutto ne viè ddar fijjo che sse crea:
Ché cquella fa un giudío, questa un cristiano."

("But without being married, if a man and a woman do what I do every
night with my wife Rosa, isn't that always a deadly sin?" And the hermit
replied: "I wouldn't want to tell you that such behavior isn't sinful, but the
Church, our generous Mother, knows how to distinguish six from half-a-
dozen. For example, if a [baptized] Christian is caught in the act [*in flagrante*] with a Jewish woman, it's automatically a sin which stays on his conscience. If, on the other hand, he's caught with a [Christian] woman, we
can look the other way. It's all a matter of the eventual offspring: a Jew bears
a Jew and a Christian, a Christian.")

Sin it is, but if a baptized Christian is caught with an "ebbrea" ("Jew-
ess"), the sin is automatic, serious, and not absolvable. If, however, he
is caught with any other "donna" ("woman"), the Church treats him
with indulgence. This sonnet relies on a series of puns. The first is an

60. Belli uses the Judeo-Roman term, derived from the Hebrew *zonach* (pl. *zonoth*)
to distinguish Jewish prostitutes from their Christian colleagues and then adds "in
ghetto" to reinforce the distinction.

amusing obscene play, "fregnante," on the learned phrase "flagrante" (understood: *delicto*). The second is rather more serious for it opposes *ebbrea/donna* and *giudío/cristiano*. As Belli acknowledged in his notes, "cristiano" in the parlance of the masses signifies "human" ("In Rome the Jews are hardly considered human: in fact, when one wants to talk about humanity, one uses 'cristiano' "). Since a Jew is certainly not a Christian, then following the logic of puns, a Jew is not human and a female Jew is not a woman! And "once one has committed this deadly sin, one is excommunicated for life." The justification is the eventual issue: the first union, Christian man-Jewish woman would produce another Jew; the second, Christian man and woman, Christian off-spring. Once again Belli demonstrates through his "Abbibbia" the direct relationship between Biblical precepts, Catholic dogma, and Church power strategies: the continued strength of the Church lay, in part, in the steady production of Christian children, conceived within the sanctity of the Christian home, or if not, then at least baptized. One troubling doubt still remains: what is the point of the commandment if not to prevent all extramarital relations? By presenting it in this light, is Belli making a value judgment on the commandment, or perhaps on Jews? It might appear that Belli is poking fun at the specific commandment, if it weren't for the identity of the interlocutor: a hermit, the last person whose opinion one would seek on sexual matters. Thus the satire is not directed to the commandment itself and surely not to the Jews, who figure as pawns where the Church is concerned. Sonnets 848 and 2118, written almost thirteen years apart, have little to do with the commandments and even less to do with sex. What Belli is protesting is the Church's continuing attempt to prohibit human contact on even the most elementary level as part of its strategy to isolate and control a recalcitrant minority.

In Belli one almost invariably returns full circle to his reading of the philosophes who pointed out the dangers of a dominant religion to a society. The notions of tolerance, of skepticism toward claims made by various religious groups, the questioning of the Roman church's claim to be the repository of the ultimate truth, all these are ideas that insinuate themselves in Belli's treatment of Jewish characters from the Bible. In his "Abbibbia," Belli attempts to humanize Jewish Biblical figures by transforming the remote, slightly forbidding patriarchs, kings, and "poveri cojjoni" into recognizable characters with a Roman vocabulary and accent. In a similar way he deflates the stern, prohibitive nature of the commandments and uses the whole compendium of ancient traditions to illustrate contemporary events and problems.

"ER GHETTO SANO SANO"

("A Ghettoful of Jews")

In the *Sonetti romaneschi* Jews are, with few exceptions, lower class and indigent. Because they live in a confined space, Belli can focus on them and on their activities as if through a lens. What he sees is a microcosm of poverty, a fascinating reduction of subaltern Rome. The ghetto in Belli is no abstraction; it is as squalid and crowded and deadening to the human spirit as in d'Azeglio's description of it. But for Belli, the ghetto is also a symbol of human destiny, of the tenuous nature of human fortunes.

In its crooked alleys and dark tenements the ghetto Jews depended on their wits to survive. In this they were no different from the rest of the disinherited masses. What set them apart is that whatever their aspirations, their possibilities of success were effectively blocked by the terrible restrictions placed upon them. The roles they were legally permitted to play were limited in number and since these corresponded to stereotypes, the non-Jew saw only stock players whose activities, mentality, and character were predictable and unchanging.

As a known quantity, Jews offered a fixed standard of comparison that one could apply to an ever-evolving social and cultural scene. Belli made use of them in two ways: (1) presenting their nature and activities to serve as metaphors for the conditions and events in the surrounding metropolis; and (2) in confrontational sonnets in which Jew and Christian enter into (generally) commercial or religious arguments or a representative Christian voice offers an opinion on Jewish fortunes, beliefs, and habits.

The inhabitants of the ghetto (in his negative comparisons Belli often uses *giudio/giudii*), then, are symbols of stupidity, incivility, personal dirtiness, dishonesty, even the evil eye. Certain statements are so heretical as to be "worthy of a Jew" ("indeggne d'un giudio") (1337 *"La bestemia reticale"*—"Heretical Blasphemy," 20 October 1834) or, worse yet, words that "not even a Jew would utter" ("potrebbe parlà ppeggio un giudio?") (1162 *"Na resía bbell' e bbona"*—"One Helluva Heresy," 6 April 1834). In terms of personal hygiene, one would have to be

'Na zozza, frittellosa, onta e bbisonta . . .
Che indove tocca sce lassa l'impronta, . . .

(A filthy woman, [all] splattered, greasy and grimy . . . No matter what she touches, she leaves a mark, . . .)

or

Piú ppeggio de la panza d'un giudio

(dirtier than a Jew's belly)

like the shabby woman who tries to hide her repellent appearance behind a large dowry in 1536 "*Trescento ggnocchi sur zinale*"—("Three Hundred *Scudi* on Her Apron," 27 April 1835). And no one but a high churchman is more of a stranger to honesty than a Jew:

Un cardinale è stato bbono tanto?!
Un cardinale ha ccreso tanto in Dio?!
Un cardinale è ddiventato santo?!
    Tu jje dai retta, Ggiuvenale mio?
Si lo disce, eh, ssarà: mma mmó ttratanto
Un cardinale è ppeggio d'un giudio.

(A cardinal was such a good man?! A cardinal believed so much in God?! A cardinal was made a saint? And you listen to him, Juvenal? If he says so maybe it's true. But in my book cardinals are even worse than Jews.) (2091 "*Er paneriggico de san Carlo*"—"St. Charles' Panegyric," 5 January 1846)

In Belli's poetry there seems to be a Jew to fit every category of person. But this variety is more apparent than real, because for the most part the poet is dealing with a limited number of types, not individuals. Belli uses stereotype in order to satirize the underlying prejudice and the mentality of those who reduce reality to these restrictive formulas. One common axiom is that Jews have the evil eye. Therefore if one has just bought a lottery ticket and happens upon a Jew, one would do well to exorcise his malefic influence:

E ssi vvicino a tté passa un abbreo,
Fa' lo scongiuro a la bbarba d'Aronne,
Pe ffà ccrepà cquer maledetto aeo.

(And if a Jew passes nearby, recite a spell to ward off old Aaron's beard and send that damned Jew (*aeo*) to perdition.) (33 "*Devozzione pe vvince ar lotto*"—"Prayer to Win the Lottery," 20 August 1830)

Another truism regarding Jews is that they never give anything away for free, not even when it's someone's rightful due. In sonnet 415 *"Er logotenente"* ("The Lieutenant") (6 November 1832), a police lieutenant, interviewing the wife of an arrested man, gives her a choice of verdict. But if she wants to get her husband out of jail, she'll have to pay for it in the time-honored way:

"Innoscente," dich'io; e llui: "Sciò ggusto";
E ddetto-fatto cuer faccia d'abbreo
Me schiaffa la man-dritta drent'ar busto.

("Innocent," I respond. And he "I'm glad," and without so much as a by-your-leave, that Jew-face shoves his hand right in my blouse.)

When she protests, her husband is declared guilty.

What these stereotyped formulas—"faccia d'abbreo" ("Jew face"), "maledetto aeo" ("damned Jew"), "bbarba d'Aronne" ("Aaron's beard"), and even the "panza d'un giudio" ("Jew's belly")—have in common is the way in which Belli uses them to introduce his characters or define a situation by focusing on some moral, physical, or professional feature of the person or event being presented. This is what the great Belli scholar, Giorgio Vigolo, called *"cosalità,"*[61] that is, the use of energetic metaphors, whereby, with astonishing economy of expression, Belli defined the character or event. In this way stereotype takes on a new aspect: from a totally negative connotation, in Belli it becomes an indispensable tool. Using the shortcut of adapting stereotype to *cosalità* Belli is able to zoom in on a situation or character and in, generally half a line, five or six syllables, mold the reader's approach to the character.

Cosalità inspired by stereotype is very much in evidence as Belli takes the reader on a tour of the ghetto. One of the most common ghetto types, the small merchant usually dealing in cloth, affords an excellent example of Belli's manipulation of stereotype. In the course of the *Sonetti romaneschi* Belli presents two clothiers, one Christian, one Jewish. In 1221 *"La bbona spesa"* ("The Bargain") (21 April 1834) he tells

---

61. G. Vigolo, *Genio*, vol. 1: 105–111; vol. 2: 89–91. A classic example of *"cosalità"* is a letter in *romanesco* to Giovan Battista Mambor (1829) in which Belli invites him out with some friends: "Caterina la guercia, . . . la mojje der froscio, la Cicoriara de ponterotto. . . . Codone, Magnamerda, Panzanera." ("Cross-eyed Catherine . . . the homosexual's wife, the chicory-seller of Ponterotto . . . Big Tail, Shit-eater, Bandit.") (G. G. Belli, *Lettere, Giornali, Zibaldone*, 200–203.)

the usual story of the Jewish shopkeeper who caters mostly to the ignorant masses:

> Ma eh? cche spesa! appena me l'ideo!
> Tre ppiastre[62] un sciallo ch'è una tel-de-raggno!
> [. . .]
> E mme lo confessò ppuro l'ebbreo
> Che llui nun cià un bajocco de guadaggno.
> Pe ffortezza poi . . . disce ch'è fustaggno,
> E cche ppe mmoda se pò ddà al museo.

(Hey, what a bargain! I can't believe it! Fifteen lire for a gossamer shawl! . . . The Jew assured me that he won't make a penny off of this. As for how it'll hold up . . . it's like corduroy, he says, and fashionable? It could go in a museum.)

The credulous masses are the natural victims of unscrupulous Jews who pass gossamer off as corduroy. But if one reads ahead to 1850 *"Er mercante pe Rroma II"* ("The Merchant of Rome II") (6 February 1837) one meets the Jew's Christian colleague, this time not in the ghetto but at large in the city. Christian merchants resented the competition concentrated in the Ghetto de la Rua. This one tries to dissuade a potential customer from shopping in the ghetto:

> Arto sei parmi e un terzo ariquadrato.
> Spiegatelo: nun pare una tovajja?
> Bber fazzoletto! Er ar telaggio nun sbajja.
> Quest' è acciaro, per dio! ferro filato.

(It's six and one-half hands square. Open it: doesn't it look like a tablecloth? What a scarf! Look at the weave. Strong as steel, by God, woven iron.)

So far the sales pitch is the same proclaiming the durability of the cloth and the fairness of the price. Then the haggling starts:

> Una piastra, e lo lasso a bbommercato.
> Che?! A ssei ggiuli[63] sto capo nun ze tajja.
> Costa a mmé ppiú de nove a Ssinigajja
> Da povero cristiano bbattezzato.
> Si vvoi trovate chi vve facci er calo
> Manco d'un ette sott'ar prezzo mio,
> Da quell'omo che ssò vve l'arigalo.
> Chi è cche vve lo dà ppe cquattr'e mmezzo?

62. The *piastra* was worth five lire.
63. The *giulio* was worth half a lira.

Er giudío? Dunque annate dar giudío,
Ma ssarà un scarto: lo condanna er prezzo.

(Five lire and I'm giving you a bargain. What?! I'm not about to cut this
cloth for just three lire. It costs me more than four-and-a-half at Sinigaglia,
poor baptized Christian that I am. If you can find it even a penny lower
than my price I'll *give* it to you. Who's selling it for four-and-a-half? The
Jew? So go to the Jew. But his must be a reject; the price gives it away.)

Here the merchant warns that if the Jew sells for less it is only because
he buys for less; that is, he buys material of inferior quality ("un
scarto"). The man who buys honestly "like a good Christian" has to
hold firm to his price and then try to get out of his rashly made promise
by accusing the Jew of dishonesty. The Jew, however, has no lack of
customers ready to spend absurd sums on inferior merchandise.

There are two assumptions at work here. One is that the Jew pos-
sesses superior business sense so that, in this case, he can buy the same
merchandise at the fair in Sinigaglia for less than the Christian. The
other is that the Jews adhere to the dictum "buy low, sell dear" thereby
cheating their customers at every turn. This makes is possible for the
Christian merchant to persuade his client that the Jew's cloth is defec-
tive: the client is ready to believe the stereotype.[64] What is especially
significant about these two sonnets is that, in Belli's view of commerce,
Jew and Christian speak the same language. Their goals are the same
as are their methods with one important exception: in "*La bbona spesa*"
the Jew has no Christian competition. But in "*Er mercante pe Rroma
II*" the Christian fights the Jew on the level of popular belief reinforced
by the use of *cosalità* in the last strophe, that is, by identifying the Jew
with "prezzo" (money) and "scarto" (inferiority, "a reject at 4.5 lire").

This equation is also applicable to the robbivecchi, the rag-and-bone
men commonly found in the Italian ghettos. Working at the shadowy
margins of commerce, the mobile peddlers were known to receive and
dispose of goods with considerable ease. Besides transporting and dis-
tributing clandestine revolutionary literature, robbivecchi also served as
fences. After the "Jacobins" despoiled a church or a churchman of valuables, or when a churchman died, often the goods would be sold to
or stored with a Jewish robbivecchi as in 2137 "*La vénnita der Cardinale morto*" ("The Dead Cardinal's Sale") (8 May 1846). The Jewish

64. This theme returned to Roman poetry in the compositions of Trilussa. See for
example his poems: "Un macellaro," "Don Michele," "Isacco e Co." of *Tre strozzini* as
well as "L'affare della razza" and "Roba vecchia."

fence had nothing to lose by trafficking in sacred objects as he was bound to go to Hell in any case. The robbivecchi was one of the busiest people in the ghetto, scavenging for useful junk and shouting the characteristic *aéo* to make his presence known. But his most important function was that of moneylender. Belli's *robbivecchi*—also: "moneylender" since Belli does not use the term *usuraio*, usurer—Sor Zalamone disburses thirty *scudi* (one hundred-fifty lire) against a pension passbook worth four hundred lire in sonnet 1979 "*La vennita der brevetto*" ("Pension For Sale") (16 April 1843). As borrower wrangles with lender to get more money for his pawn, Belli adapts theatrical, caricatural Jewish speech to his moneylender.

> E cche ssarieno le vostre protese
> Pe ottanta scudi su la mi' penzione?
> Che me volete dà, ssor Zalamone,
> A rripijjalli a ccinque scudi er mese?—
>   Ve darò vvintidua bbelli piastroni
> Tutti in moneta fina del paese,
> Ve va bbeene? Però ttutte le spese
> A cconto vostro, com'è ddi raggione.—
>   Fregheve, sor giudío, che ggaleotto!—
> Mordivoi, vinticinque, e vve do assai.—
> Ladro!—Bbe', andiamo, saranno vintootto.[65]
>   Tu vvòi pijjamme in gola.—Animo, via,
> Eccone trenta tonni; e, bbadanai,
> Ce state meglio voi per vita mia.

("How much would you charge me to pawn my pension passbook of four hundred lire? What will you give me if I repay you at twenty-five lire a month, Mr. Solomon?" "I'll give you twenty-two big beautiful *piastre* all in this country's currency. OK? But of course you have to bear all the expenses yourself. What's fair is fair." "Screw you, Sir Jew, what a scoundrel!" "*Mordivoi* [for your love] I'll make it twenty-five and I'm giving you a good deal." "Thief!" "Well, all right, twenty-eight." "You want to strangle me." "By my soul, I'll round it off to thirty. And *badanai* [by God] you're coming out ahead, *per vita mia* [I swear on my life].")

At first he offers a paltry twenty-two "bbelli piastroni" ("big, beautiful piastres") "tutti in moneta fina del paese" ("all in this country's currency"). As the client puts pressure on Sor Zalamone, and the Jew begins to give way, the language on both sides becomes more predictable, with the Christian hurling insults such as "rogue," "thief," "Sir Jew," "cutthroat" and the Jew responding with the usual *mordivoi*,

65. Both *-ee-* of *bbeene* (line seven) and the *-oo-* of *vintooto* (line eleven) are Belli's renderings of the sing-song quality of vowels in Judeo-Roman.

bbadanai, and *per vita mia.* In the end the borrower appears to come
out ahead, having wrenched eight additional scudi from the lender,
when in reality the lender has a pension passbook worth almost three
times what he paid for it. Two traditions are at work in "*La vennita
der brevetto*": the giudìata with its farcical haggling, and Renaissance
comedy such as Aretino's *La Cortigiana.* In this play one Rosso taunts
the robbivecchi Romanello Giudeo by pretending to want to buy a
jacket. Romanello discusses the presumed transaction with the stock of
oaths usually ascribed to Jewish characters: "May I never see Messiah,
if this doesn't seem . . . ," "May God not lead me to synagogue Saturday if this doesn't fit you . . ." In Belli's sonnets of a commercial nature,
the Jew lives up to his reputation: no one can get the better of him.[66]

In addition to the shopkeepers and moneylenders grubbing for a
day's earnings, the ghetto boasted artisans of a far more positive fame,
and chief among these were the many seamstresses. There were those
who called Jewish seamstresses the best clothes menders in Rome. Belli
derived two comparisons regarding non-Jewish Roman life from this
popular belief. In the first, sonnet 833 "*E ppoi?*" ("And then . . . ?")
(27 January 1833) the pope, who must listen to everyone's complaints
and attempt to accommodate them, is likened to an expert seamstress:

> . . . Coll'aco, co le forbisce e la stoppa,
> Oggi er Papa è un'ebbrea che ccusce e ttajja,
> E cqua mmette una pezza e llà una toppa.

> (With needle and scissors and thread, today the pope is a Jewess who cuts
> and sews, mending here and patching there.)

Jewish women were known for mending seams and holes so that the
repair would be invisible and last forever, as if they were sewing with
a golden needle:

> . . . Ma mmo sti schertri e li mortacci loro
> Sce vorríano a l'usanza de l'ebbrea
> Ricuscicce la bbocca all'aco d'oro.

> (But now these police thugs, damn their hides!, like Jewish seamstresses
> would sew our mouths shut with a golden needle.) (788 "*Er vecchio*"—"The
> Old Man," 20 January 1833)

This is a sonnet about the theatre and the efforts of the *carabinieri*
(police) to regulate it. The mouth to be sewn shut hermetically and permanently and with such skill as to leave invisible seams belonged to the

66. P. Aretino, *La Cortigiana,* 157.

playwright and, by extension, actors who used the theatre to promote political causes. When it came to protest, the pope, who at other times tried to satisfy everyone by "patching up" their differences, applied a different art in his efforts to silence those who disagreed with him.[67]

Almost as busy as the seamstresses were the clairvoyants. Everyone knew Jews to have supernatural powers at their command, powers beyond any Christian's grasp. In Rome, belief in the supernatural attracted people from varied backgrounds to the many fortune-tellers. The best ones, Belli suggests in 438 *"Le cose perdute"* ("Lost Things") were the Jews. As folklore would have it, Jews could conjure up the answer (in this case a thief's likeness) in a carafe.

Jews were identified with the occult from the Middle Ages onward whether as conjurers, clairvoyants, or witches.[68] Their magical powers were thought to be especially compelling on 24 June, the feast day of St. John the Baptist which in Belli's poetry is celebrated beginning the night before (1095 *"San Giuvan-de-Ggiuggno"*—"St. John's Day in June," 15 March 1834). This is the night when Belli's *popolano* (common man) is especially wary of the witches, warlocks, and sorcerers who worship the devil. During the day one can identify one's enemies, but at night nothing is what it seems. On the eve of San Giuvan-de-Ggiuggno the necromancers of the *Ghetto de la Rua* join their colleagues from the other *rioni* (quarters) of Rome and go to pay homage to St. John their protector as they have for the last *"zeimillanni"* ("six thousand years"). Were one to attempt to spy on them, one would be horror struck to discover that *"Se straformeno in bestie"* ("they are transformed into animals") indeed wild animals ("fiere"):

> . . . e tte dich'io
> C'a la finosomia de quelle fiere,
> Quantunque tutte-quante nere nere
> Ce pòi riffigurà piú dd'un giudio.

(And I tell you that by their beastly faces, all of them black as coal, you can recognize several Jews.)

---

67. See F. Della Seta, "Gli Ebrei nell'opera di Belli," *Rassegna mensile di Israel* 16, fasc. 9–10 (1955): 369–381, 427–437.

68. In his notes to sonnet 1095 Belli explains that "the Jews are known as skillful sorcerers," but Goldoni debunked the fiction of the Jew as magician: "I know that Mirandolano has made use of [the magic] which was once practiced by the ancient Hebrews and which today's Jews claim to have inherited from the cabalism of their forefathers. The only powers they really possess come from superstition, that is, witchcraft and, if I remember correctly, consist mainly of fortune-telling. They make a person's face appear in a mirror or else they divine with a sieve." *Donna di garbo* (Act I, Sc. 12).

Here are the archetypical fears of the supernatural and of the dark. In the popular imagination, this is a situation where Jews fit in perfectly. At best, even in the light of day, Jews lead mysterious lives. Given their renown, as Belli puts it, as "abilissimi maliardi" ("skillful sorcerers") it is just a short step from consulting a clairvoyant out of desperation to imagining that same person transformed into a fearsome and nameless animal. But Belli takes this witches' "sabbath" one step further. In a society in which segregation was the norm, an additional archetypal fear was brought into play when Jews and Christians mingled freely and also by the Jews' ability to alter their appearance at will. The unwary bystander runs the risk of metamorphosis through these devils' henchmen, losing his identity altogether as the poet indicates with the last word of each line: *io* (I) becomes *fiere* (beasts). The beasts are further transformed, become *nere* (black) and, completing the transformation, emerge as *giudio*. Belli's popolano arms himself as he would against vampires: a clove of garlic in the pocket and (in 1857 "*La strega*"—"The Witch") a broom in the window. But what if Jewish sorcerers used this terrible power in their daily lives or as part of their religion?

At the periphery of Belli's world of the occult was the rabbi, a man who read arcane books written in an unintelligible language and was familiar with the *Talmud* and *Kabbala*. Slightly forbidding perhaps because of his learning, the rabbi was the most respected figure in Belli's gallery of ghetto dwellers. As such Belli used him as a standard of comparison for the others.

Rather than call him "rabbi," the poet preferred the Judeo-Roman word for "wise man," *cacamme* from "(c)ha(c)hàm" meaning "wise man."[69] Such wisdom is not the province of just anyone. In sonnet 1250 "*Er rispetto a li supriori*" ("Respect for One's Betters") (28 April 1834) a stable boy exaggerates his own importance:

> . . . L'antro poi che l'inzórfora è un pivetto
> C'un mes' addietro j'amancava er tozzo,

69. Crescenzo del Monte has a caustic comment on the term *(c)ha(c)hàm* and those who adopted it in Belli's Rome: "In those days any pious coreligionist who came from the Holy Land was immediately [called] *(c)ha(c)hàm* (most wise!) and esteemed as a near saint. Often these men were nothing more than spongers who, on the pretext of collecting money for their brothers in the Synagogue of Jerusalem, would stay as long as they pleased, enjoying free room and board, and would leave when they had accumulated a tidy sum." See C. del Monte, *Sonetti giudaico-romaneschi con note esplicative e un discorso preliminare sul dialetto giudaico-romanesco* (Florence: Israel, 1927), vol 1: 79. A similar figure appears in sonnet 462 "*Nun mormorà*" (19 November 1832), but Belli's popolano recognizes him for what he is and sends him on his way.

E mmó cch'è entrato in scuderia pe mmozzo,
Tiè una ruganza da Cacàmme-in-Ghetto.

(And the other one who tends the fire is a boy who just a month ago didn't
even have bread to eat. Now that he got a job as a stable boy, he's as arrogant
as a rabbi in the ghetto.)

Belli often relied on plays on words: here "*Cacàmme*" (from the verb
"caccare," "to defecate") is a scatological pun as well as a learned Hebrew derivation. The stable boy who puts on such airs appears to dominate his surroundings like a rabbi in the ghetto. But on the other hand
his arrogance is worth no more than ordure whether in the ghetto or
in the stalls he cleans.

Since the Cacamme is the Jew par excellence, and convinced, as were
all Belli's clergy, that he professes the True Faith, he is an obvious
target. When used in a comparison, his mention satirizes the other
party, as in sonnet 11 "*Pio ottavo*" ("Pius VIII") (1 April 1829):

Che ffior de Papa creeno! Accidenti!
Co rrispetto de lui pare er Cacamme.

(What a beaut of a Pope they've elected! Damn! With all due respect, he's
the image of the rabbi.)

The hemistich "co rrispetto de lui" ("With all due respect to him") links
the Pope with "er Cacamme" while "lui" ("him"), occupying the crucial sixth position in the hendecasyllable line, acts as a fulcrum balancing
the two figures in ironic ambiguity. On the one hand, Belli appears to
excuse himself for describing the pope in what could be read as scatological terms. On the other hand, "co rrispetto de lui" indicates that
comparison with the rabbi is an insult. But for whom?

Belli's opinion of Pius VIII was none too favorable:

Bbella galanteria da tate e mmamme
Pe ffà bbobo a li fijji impertinenti!.
    Ha un erpeto pe ttutto, nun tiè ddenti,
E' gguercio, je strascineno le gamme,
Spènnola da una parte, e bbuggiaramme
Si arriva a ffà la pacchia a li parenti.
[. . .]
Un gran brutto strucchione de Pontefisce.

(A boon to mommies and aunties to scare [their] children into behaving.
He's got herpes all over, he's lost all his teeth, he's cross-eyed, he drags his

feet, he lists to one side and I'd be surprised if he could even manage to find sinecures for his relatives. . . . A real mess of a Pope.)

At the same time the Cacamme, representing the ghetto, was often the object of scorn, but in Belli such disparagement was mild compared to that reserved for the pope. Indeed, in *"Pio ottavo,"* Pius VIII's infirmities are exaggerated to such a point that he transcends his own person and Pope becomes papacy. Subsumed under the pope's physical deformity is also implied moral decay so that, as Alberto Moravia has pointed out, the figure of Pius VIII symbolizes the "decrepit and anachronistic [system of] temporal power"[70] and given the impossibility of assigning a convincing identity to the *lui* (him) in line two, though Pius VIII is the subject of the poem, the satire also reflects on the Cacamme. The description of the pope, although clearly outrageous, is quite specific, whereas beyond the pun of his nickname, the rabbi remains undelineated. The rabbi is not an individual but a foil. And yet because of the *lui,* he—that is, the office of "rabbi"—is included in Belli's appraisal of the profession of religious leader. If these men are reduced to their function, they assume a metahistorical dimension, symbolizing all popes and rabbis, the papacy and the rabbinate, past, present, and, given Belli's well-known pessimism, future.

Despite his technique of reducing people to categories and then satirizing them on that basis, Belli portrayed the rabbi as the most respected person in the ghetto. And when Belli had a real person in mind, he portrayed him with deference. Such a rabbi was Moisè Sabbato Beer. He was a friend to Popes Leo XII and Gregory XVI and, indeed, his closeness to Gregory XVI earned him the nickname "l'amico del papa" ("friend of the pope") from the Roman people.[71] Beer's friendship developed after the Edict of 1775 forbade such contacts between Christians and Jews. The popes, however, regularly maintained rapports with Jews of high intellectual and financial accomplishment.[72] Beer protested the reenactment of the Edict to Leo XII and asked Gregory XVI to emancipate the Jews and concede them civil rights. Unsuccessful in

70. A. Moravia, "Passeggiate romane" in *L'uomo come fine* (Milan: Bompiani, 1964), 160, cited in Garvin, "La indiggnità," 56.

71. A. Milano, *Ebrei in Italia,* 372.

72. Rabbi Beer was not a "figure of mockery" as Garvin implies was the characterization of all rabbis in the *Sonetti romaneschi* (B. Garvin, "La indiggnità," 57). He was a Cacamme in the philosophical sense of the word, that is, "highly learned" and a "frequent visitor to the Vatican." See A. Milano, *Ghetto,* 115.

both instances[73] he nonetheless continued to consider the popes his friends. Rabbi Beer died on 6 May 1835. Had he lived just a year longer, he would have witnessed two concessions from Gregory XVI granted under pressure from France and Austria. In 1835 Jews were permitted to pawn their belongings alongside the Christian poor at the *Monte di Pietà* and in 1836 to reside in the Roman countryside.

As proof of his regard for Gregory XVI Rabbi Beer wrote a sonnet "in homage, veneration and exaltation for the most glorious election of the new Pope." Belli celebrates this in his own sonnet three days after the death of the Rabbi (1544 *"La morte der Rabbino"*—"The Rabbi's Death," 9 May 1835):

> E' ito in paradiso oggi er Rabbino,
> Che ssaría com'er Vescovo der Ghetto;
> E stasera a *li Scòli* j'hanno detto
> L'uffizzio de li morti e 'r mattutino.
>
> Era amico der Papa: anzi perzino
> Er giorn'istesso ch'er Papa fu eletto
> Pijjò la penna e jje stampò un zonetto
> Scritto mezzo in ebbreo mezzo in latino.
>
> Dunque a la morte sua Nostro Siggnore
> Cià ppianto a ggocce, bbe' cche ssia sovrano,
> E cce s' è inteso portà vvia er core.
>
> Si ccampava un po' ppiú, tte lo dich'io,
> O nnoi vedemio er Rabbino cristiano,
> O er Papa annava a tterminà ggiudio.

(Today the Rabbi, who is sort of the bishop of the ghetto, went to heaven and tonight in the synagogues they recited the prayer for the dead and the morning prayer. He was the Pope's friend; in fact the very day the Pope was elected, he took pen in hand and wrote him a sonnet, half in Hebrew, half in Latin. So when he died the Pope cried huge tears, even though he's the pope, and felt his heart break. I tell you, had the Rabbi lived a little bit longer, either we would have seen him become a Christian, or the Pope would have ended up a Jew.)

73. The visit to Leo XII took place in 1827, to Gregory XVI in February 1831. Gregory is said to have replied: "I would like to do what you ask, but am prevented by the Pontifical Constitutions." See A. Milano, *Ghetto*, 115. Morandi gives a variant: "Apostolic Constitutions." (L. Morandi, ed., *I sonetti romaneschi di G. G. Belli* [Città di Castello, 1889], vol. 4: 199–200.) In December 1831 the Pope expressed his "supreme contentment" that the Roman Jews had stayed out of the insurrections that had recently plagued the Papal State. See M. T. Lanza, *I sonetti*, vol. 3: 1627. In 1832 Gregory XVI obtained the Rothschild loan (see ahead) and under pressure from France and Austria granted some concessions. At the same time he renewed certain restrictions.

On the surface at least, in this sonnet Montesquieu's lesson on religious pluralism seems to have borne fruit. It is as if the two religious traditions have merged in harmony at the highest level: the rabbi is described as the "bishop of the ghetto"; he rejoices in the election of a pope who will later mourn his passing; he is so friendly with Gregory XVI that only death prevents him from becoming a Christian.

But Belli seems to present two divergent opinions on this friendship. If it is possible to separate the enlightened poet from the popular voice he represents in his poetry, then it would appear that although the intellectual hopes that such rapprochement will bring an end to useless acrimony and social injustice, his popular narrator is not at all pleased with the famous friendship. There is a certain air of wishful thinking in the poem expressed in such conciliatory details as calling the rabbi the "bishop of the ghetto" and in describing his sonnet to Gregory as being half in Hebrew, half in Latin, the traditional languages of both religions. In reality the sonnet was written in Hebrew (only the Biblical references were in Latin) with an accompanying Italian translation, lest the pope not understand the poem. Similarly, calling the rabbi the "bishop of the ghetto" has its negative aspect: such is the ignorance about Jews that the rabbi has to be described in Christian terms. Finally, in the last tercet, Belli's popolano pronounces his view of the friendship: had the rabbi lived, one leader would have converted the other. But it would not have been an even exchange. Had the rabbi converted he would have been a "Christian," that is, a Christian and a "human being." Had the pope converted he would have "ended up" or "died" a Jew. He would not, however, have died an "Abbreo" like the Biblical figures, but a "giudio" like all the usurers and petty criminals in the ghetto. Rabbi Beer might have been upstanding, pacificatory, Cacamme, but, for Belli's popolano, the "Rabbino" at the end of line one was no more and no less than, at the end of line fourteen, a "giudio."

"S.P.Q.R."

Occasionally Belli enlarged his field of vision to focus on notable Jews outside the ghetto and events that involved Jews, for better or for worse, in the very fabric of the city of Rome.

Beyond the ghetto walls, dealings between the Church and some Jews were notably different from Rabbi Beer's essentially fruitless experience as a supplicant for Jewish rights. In the relationship between Gregory XVI and Karl Mayer Rothschild the positions were reversed, for in 1832 the pope needed money and Rothschild had it to loan. The Church was overburdened by an enormous deficit caused in part by excessive military and police expenses,[74] to the extent that, to Belli's dismay, the treasury was so empty "there was room for crickets to dance."

> Hai sentito c'ha ddetto oggi er padrone?
> C'avenno inteso er grann'abbreo Roncilli
> C'ar Monte sce bballaveno li grilli
> Ha ddato ar Papa imprestito un mijjone.
> [...]
> Perantro è un gran miracolo de Ddio,
> Che pe sspiggne la Cchiesa a ssarvamento
> Abbi toccato er core d'un giudio.
> Ma er Papa farà espone er Zagramento
> Pe cconvertí a Ggesú bbeniggn' e ppio
> Chi l'ha ajjutato ar zessant'un per cento.

(Did you hear what the boss said today? [He said] that having heard that crickets were dancing in the treasury, the great Jew Rothschild lent the pope a million. . . . Well it's a great miracle that in order to save the Church, God touched the heart of a Jew. But [to get his own back] the Pope will have the Sacrament explained [to Rothschild, hoping] to convert to sweet Jesus the man who helped him out at 61 percent.) (316 *"La sala di Monziggnore Tesoriere"*—"Monsignor Treasurer's Antechamber," 8 January 1832)

The necessity for the loan and the source of the funds raised a public outcry. For this reason *"La sala di monziggnore Tesoriere"* is one of that small number of sonnets which were popular during Belli's lifetime.[75] Although one might expect such potentially scandalous financial deals to have been secret, the title of Belli's poem makes it clear that the condition of the Vatican finances and the measures taken to bolster them were out in the open. The supposed discussion that is the text of the

---

74. L. C. Farini, *Lo Stato Romano dall'anno 1815 al 1850,* 2d ed. (Florence: Le Monnier, 1850), vol. 1: 131, cited in Morandi, ed., *I sonetti romaneschi di G. G. Belli,* vol. 2: 8–9.

75. It was published as part of the sixth chapter of *Le secret de Rome au XIX siècle* (Paris: 1846), in the novel *I misteri di Roma* (Turin: 1835–1855 and 1861–1863) and in *Sonetti umoristici* published by the Roman underground press ("stampati alla macchia") one year after Belli's death in 1864 and consisted of fifty-one of Belli's *Sonetti romaneschi.* For more on Belli and the underground press, see E. Colombi, *Bibliografia di G. G. Belli dal 1813 al 1866* (Rome: Palombi, 1958), 54–55; E. Vergara Caffarelli, ed., "Nota bibliografica," in preface to G. G. Belli, *Li morti di Roma* (Milan: Edizioni Milano-Sera, 1949); "'Palatino,' Miscellanea per il centenario," *Palatino* 7, ser. 3 (1963): 121–124.

sonnet takes place not in the treasurer's chamber, but in the *sala* (ante-chamber) where the servants gather to await orders.

In the last strophe it is evident that Belli's disappointment extends to both parties in the loan, but here it is especially directed at the pope. As Belli saw it, Gregory XVI was taking great risks with a venerable institution, in essence, pawning it to a Jew. If God were willing to perform another miracle, to "touch the [hard] heart of a Jew" a second time, maybe Rothschild could be persuaded to convert. Then the Church would have an important and wealthy convert and the loan would become a bequest. Meanwhile Gregory was willing to gamble what wealth remained to the Church, as Belli subtly implies with the phrase "farà espone." In the context of religious conversion "farà espone" (from *esporre*) means to have something explained, in this case, the Sacrament(s). There is, however, a subtext involving "esporre" in its financial sense, meaning "to obtain credit on the money market" and "to risk." The collateral to be risked is "er Zagramento," with the Sacrament used as synecdoche for the Church. Vigolo gives a variant for the last strophe—a version discarded probably in the name of discretion since the sonnet circulated in public—in which the question of conversion is not mentioned. The absence of conversion means that "espone er Zagramento" is less likely to mean "explain the Sacrament." This limits the choice of meanings to those more directly involved with obtaining the loan:

> Er Papa ha ffatto espone er Zagramento,
> Pe ringrazzià Ggesú bbeniggn'e ppio
> Che ccià ssarvato ar zessantun per cento.[76]

(But [to get his own back] the Pope risked the Sacrament to thank sweet Jesus that the man helped him out at sixty-one percent.)

In this earlier version Belli stated, perhaps rashly, that Gregory XVI had in fact already "*fatto* espone" ("risked") the Sacrament and not, as in the definitive version, been about to do so, "*farà* espone." Finally, in the variant the pope thanks Christ for having saved "us" (*ccià*)—perhaps the papal "we"—thereby demonstrating his primary concern for himself rather than the institution.

The kind of man the pope was dealing with is made immediately clear by Belli's use of the stock phrase "core d'un giudio" ("the [hard] heart of a Jew") and the amount of interest charged. The poet goes on

---

76. G. G. Belli, *I sonetti*, vol. 1: 462, note.

in the same vein in 319 "*Er prestito dell'Abbreo Roncilli*" ("Jew Rothschild's Loan") (9 January 1832):

Ma eh? Gèssummaría! che mmonno tristo!
Fin che sse vedi fà a li ggiacubbini
Va bbe', ma un Papa ha da pijjà cquadrini
Da un omo c'ha ammazzato Ggesucristo!
   Uh rriarzassi la testa papa Sisto
Ch'empí zzeppo Castello de zecchini
Strillerebbe: "Ah ppretacci mmalandrini,
C'era bbisoggno de sto bbell'acquisto? . . ."

(Oh Jesus and Mary! What a sad world! As long as it's only Jacobins who do it, okay, but [to see] a Pope have to take money from someone who killed Jesus Christ! If Pope Sixtus V, who filled Castel St. Angelo with money, ever rose from the dead, he would scream: "Rotten priests, you crooks, did you really need [to get involved in] this imbroglio?")

In both sonnets 316 and 319 the name Rothschild becomes "Roncilli," a Romanization of *ronciglio* (hook). Greed, symbolized by the hook, is an intrinsic component of the anti-Jewish stereotype, hence the distortion of the name and the addition of "Jew": "l'*Abbreo* Roncilli." But the reference to *ronciglio* neatly masks the far bitterer criticism of Gregory XVI begun in sonnet 316. The pope's venality displayed by his desperate act lends force to the Dantean allusion to the *barattieri* (swindlers) in the creation of the name Roncilli.[77] By binding itself to long-term interest payments in order to avert a crisis caused by its own mismanagement of funds, the Church was, in a sense, committing the sin of trafficking in the wealth of the faithful.

By the end of 1832 Belli was still disturbed over indebetedness of the Church to the House of Rothschild and expressed this in two poems. In sonnet 606 "*Er giubbileo III*" ("The Jubilee III") (14 December 1832) he repeats Gregory XVI's desire to be absolved of his debt through the conversion of his creditor and gives that as the premise for declaring the extraordinary holy year. Jubilees were intended, in part, to render Roman Catholicism more attractive to potential converts and to those believers who seemed to waiver in their allegiance. Rothschild, it was clear, was not to be swayed:

77. Belli probably intended to recall Dante's use of the word *ronciglio* to suggest hands with hooked talons instead of fingers, outstretched and ready to grab their prey. In the fifth *bolgia* of Hell (*Inferno* XXI–XXII), home of the swindlers, there are devils armed with hooks who skewer those sinners who venture from under the cover of boiling pitch.

Prima de tutto cuer zu' amico abbreo
Che jje venne un mijjaro pe un mijjone,
Ggira ancora cqua e llà strillanno *aeo*
Senza viení a la santa riliggione.

(First of all that Jewish friend of his, who sold him a thousand while charging a million, still goes around here and there shouting *aeo*, without converting to our holy religion.)

Rothschild might be a great banker, but since "once a Jew, always a Jew," he still goes about shouting *aeo* like his spiritual brothers, the robbivecchi, in the ghetto. Meanwhile the Church has been so taken up with the Rothschild business that it has neglected other duties:

Ma cche stamo a gguardà ll'abbreo Roncilli!
Ve pare che cce siino sott'ar zole
Poc'antri ladri cqui da convertilli?

(But why waste time with Rothschild! Do you think there's any lack of other thieves to be converted?)

The result of the pope's connivance with Jews will be not less than the ruin of the city of Rome as Belli states in the second of the December poems, 622 *"Er motivo de li guai"* ("The Source of Our Troubles") (17 December 1832):

Lo volete sapé? vve lo dich'io
Perché Rroma se trova in tant'affanni:
Ve lo dich'io perché Ddomminiddio
Sce fa ppiove sta frega de malanni.
    E' pperché er Papa s'è ffatto ggiudio
E nnun ha ppiù de Papa che li panni:
E' pperché li ggiudii da papa Pio
Nun porteno piú in testa li ssciamanni.
    Adesso se sperava arfinamente
De védelo sto scànnolo levato,
Ma, gguai pe nnoi, nun ze ne fa ppiú ggnente:
    Perché ppapa Grigorio c'ha pijjato
Tanti cuadrini da un giudio fetente,
J'ha vvennuto, per dio, Roma e lo Stato![78]

78. At the root of Belli's disappointment is a misconception about the rate of interest. The last line of *La sala di Monziggnore Tesoriere* gives the rate at 61 percent whereas Farini's account quotes 65 percent. An observer no less discerning than Stendhal, then consul at Civitavecchia, found the intricacies of the loan difficult to unravel (letter of 26 October 1834, Paris, Archives Affaires étrangers, MD Rome 102, *foglio* 274). The

(You want to know why Rome is in such trouble, why God is trying her so hard with such suffering? I'll tell you. It's because the Pope has become a Jew and all that's left of his papal nature is the vestment. This is because since [the time of] Pius VIII the Jews no longer wear their badge. Now we were finally hoping to see the end of scandal, but nothing's been done. Too bad for us. [And nothing will be done] because, by borrowing so much money from a stinking Jew, Pope Gregory sold him Rome and the Papal State!)

In many ways this sonnet looks ahead to that series of thirty-four poems written between August 1835 and December 1836 and grouped under the collective title *"Er còllera mòribbus"* ("Deadly Cholera") in which the poet explains why the city deserved such a scourge. The traditional contact between the popes and prominent Jews had taken a new and unsettling turn. As long as such relationships stayed at a personal level, as in the case of Rabbi Beer's friendship with Popes Leo XII and Gregory XVI, little harm was likely to come of them. But Gregory XVI had allowed the situation begun in the days of Pius VIII to develop unchecked. Jews circulated with greater freedom than ever before; once they no longer wore the sciamanno, a symbolic but significant barrier fell. Now, when they daily left the Portico d'Ottavia they were truly *out* of the ghetto and, mixing with the general populace, went unrecognized for who they really were. Similarly the pope let down the defenses of the Church itself and allowed a rich Jew *into* the Vatican. Gregory XVI mortgaged the very foundations of the Church on which all Rome depended economically, socially, and spiritually. Acting out of self-interest and venality, he was less like a pope should be and more like a Jew. In the *"Er còllera mòribbus II"* ("Deadly Cholera II") (4 August 1835) series, using the ghetto as synecdoche to conjure up visions of the squalor and decay, Belli warns that one day all Rome, the once-splendid city of the popes, besieged by an epidemic of cholera, could fall into poverty like the ghetto. God would use the stinging whip of disease to chastize the city

---

discount rate of 65 percent on the Vatican 1000-franc bonds was mistaken for the interest rate. For further details, see B. Gille, *Histoire de la Maison Rothschild* (Geneva: Droz, 1965), vol. 1: 227–229. The amount borrowed was also in question: "Apparently in these last days our government has obtained a new loan, which they say was for three million *scudi* at a rate of eighty percent with the usual Rothschild who came up from Naples to Rome." See Agostino Chigi, *Diary,* 10 September 1832, cited in E. Colombi, *Bibliografia,* 54–55.

Pe vvia che Rroma è ddiventata un ghetto
D'iniquità ppiù nere der cappello.

(. . . because Rome has become a ghetto of wickedness blacker than the
blackest hat.)

But already in the Roncilli poems of 1832, Belli senses that Gregory
XVI is dragging his subjects down with him toward a catastrophic punishment such as the cholera epidemic described three years later.[79]

As Belli sometimes dealt with notable Jews outside the ghetto, so
he also described the relationship of the Jews to the Roman monuments
beyond the ghetto walls and to the history they represented. His fascination with the Jews of the past was as intense as his interest in contemporary Jewish life, and his assessment of the history of the Jews in
Rome reveals his disappointed love for his city.

On fictitious visits to Rome's landmarks Belli debunks the cult of
historical monuments and the romanticism of the distant past. The
monuments symbolize a potential for greatness which was not realized.
Belli's knowledge of Roman history only serves to embitter him, for
he senses that the ratio of greatness to corruption is weighted in favor
of corruption. In sonnet 908 *"L'historia romana"* ("Roman History")
(17 February 1833) he laughs at those who are taken in by the canard
"the glory that was Rome."

Bast'a ssapé cc'oggni donna è pputtana,
E ll'ommini una manica de ladri,
Ecco imparata l'istoria romana.

(All you need to know is that the women are all whores and the men a gang
of thieves: there, you've learned Roman history.)

Accordingly, in sonnet 46 *"Campidojjo"* ("Campidoglio") (10 October 1830) Belli recounts not the glories of the site, but the dark side
of its history:

Ecchesce ar Campidojjo, indove Tito
Venné a mmercato tanta ggente abbrea.

(Here we are at the Campidoglio where Titus sold scores of Jews in the
marketplace.)

---

79. On Gregory XVI, see also sonnet 1900 *"Er viatico de l'antra notte"* (21 May
1837) and 2114 *"Er Papa ner Giuveddí ssanto"* (9 April 1846), in which the senility of
Gregory XVI is at once a subject for caricature and compassion.

The poet, and perhaps the Roman Jews of his day, know the reality behind the great monuments. In the "Campo Vaccino" ("Vaccino Square") series of four sonnets, Belli's *cicerone* (tour guide), sor Gregorio, shows a friend the sights. In the last two poems they stop in front of the Arch of Titus. They admire the arch because of its history, or rather because of the vague notion most people have of its history. Modern Jews, however, refuse to approach the arch because for them, who are mostly ghetto dwellers, its inglorious history is all too relevant, as Belli outlines in 40 "*Campo Vaccino III*" ("Vaccino Square III") (10 September 1830):

> A cquer tempo che Ttito imperatore,
> Co ppremissione che jje diede Iddio,
> Mové la guerra ar popolo ggiudio
> Pe ggastigallo che ammazzò er Ziggnore;
>   Lui ridunò la robba de valore,
> Discenno: "Cazzo, quer ch'è dd'oro, è mmio" . . .
>   E poi scrivette a Rroma a un omo dotto,
> Cusí e ccusí che ffrabbicassi un arco
> Co li cudrini der gioco dell'otto.
>   Si cce passònno li Ggiudii! Sammarco!
> Ma adesso, prima de passacce sotto,
> Se faríano ferrà ddar maniscarco.

(At the time when the Emperor Titus made war on the Jews with God's permission as punishment of the people who killed Christ, he gathered together all the valuables exclaiming "What the hell! I'll take the gold for myself:" . . . Then he wrote to a learned man in Rome with the specifications for an arch to be constructed in his honor with money from the lottery. [You want to know] if the Jews were marched under it! By St. Mark you bet they were! But now, rather than pass through that arch they'd have themselves shod by the blacksmith.)

The Arch of Titus symbolizes the Roman conquest of Jerusalem and the destruction of the Second Temple in 70 A.D.[80] Among the bas-reliefs on the inner walls of the arch is a depiction of spoils from the Temple being carried in the triumphal procession as described in 41 "*Campo Vaccino IV*" ("Vaccino Square IV") (10 September 1830),[81]

---

80. The first arch was erected in 80–81 A.D. and is known today only by its inscription, which was copied during the Middle Ages for the original arch no longer exists. The arch known today as the Arch of Titus was built during the reign of Titus's brother, Domitian, with a dedicatory inscription to Titus (*Divo Tito*).

81. See B. Platner, *Topographical Dictionary of Ancient Rome* (London: Oxford University Press, 1929), 45–47.

the most notable among these being a golden *Cannelabbro de Sdraello,* a giant Jewish candelabra or menorah.

Tradition has it that several hundred Jewish captives were forced to march under the Arch of Titus to be shown off along with the other spoils of war and the arch came to symbolize the beginning of the Diaspora. Jewish aversion to the arch was such that to convey it Belli invokes St. Mark: "*Sammarco!*" meaning "absolutely" when referring to something undertaken against one's will.[82] The more popular significance of *Sammarco!* is that St. Mark strove to make a cherry tree bear ripe fruit on his Saint's Day in order to please a pope who was inordinately fond of cherries. In the real world, cherry trees obstinately do not bear fruit in April and the Jews, conquered once, obstinately continue to show their contempt. Jews would allow themselves to be shod like horses before passing once more under the Arch in celebration of imperial, or papal, power.

In more modern times, though able to avoid the humiliation of the Arch of Titus, Jews continued to play a part in public spectacle. The most picturesque of these torments performed in expiation of original sin ("Quello ch'aveva d'accadè pper pomo," "what happened on account of the forbidden apple") and that of deicide ("pperché/Messeno in crosce er Redentor Gesú," "because/they crucified our savior Jesus") was the *palio* or *corso degli ebrei* (the Jews' race) during Carnival. As the guidìata had entertained the crowds for centuries, the palio was the most popular of the Carnival games in Belli's day.[83] The practice of running Jews in this race and its consequences for both Jews and the Roman government so fascinated and disgusted Belli that he returned to the subject repeatedly, dedicating three sonnets to it over the span of fourteen years.

The first composition on the Carnival race is sonnet 722 *"Le curze d'una vorta"* ("Races of Yesteryear") (10 January 1833):

> Antro che rrobbi-vecchi! antro c'aéo!
> Don Diego c'ha studiato l'animali
> Der Muratore, e ha lletto co l'occhiali
> Cuanti libbri stracciati abbi er museo,
>   Disce ch'er Ghetto adesso dà li palj
> Pe vvia c'anticamente era l'ebbreo
> Er barbero de cuelli carnovali

---

82. *Sammarco* here is an abbreviation of the saying "San Marco fa fà le cerase [ciliege] per forza" ("St. Mark forces cherries to bloom").

83. R. Vighi, *Roma del Belli* (Rome: Palombi, 1963), 86.

A Testaccio er ar piazzon der Culiseo.
  Pe ffalli curre, er popolo romano
Je sporverava intanto er giustacore
Tutti co un nerbo o una bbattecca in mano.
  E sta curza, abbellita da sto pisto,
L'inventò un Papa in memoria e in onore
Della fraggellazzion de Ggesucristo.

(Some robbivecchi! some aéo! Don Diego, who has studied Muratore's *Annals* and, wearing his glasses, has read all the old books in the museum, says that now the ghetto gives the money for the palio flags. This is because time was during Carnival when Jews ran instead of horses from Testaccio to the Colosseum. The Roman people used to "dust off" the racers' jackets with whips and sticks to make them run. A pope invented this race and then embellished it with the beatings to commemorate and honor the flagellation of Christ.)

As he so often does, Belli calls on a fictitious character to testify, through some imaginary involvement, to the authenticity of a disturbing historical event. In this case one Don Diego, a bookworm not unlike Belli himself, attests to the popular belief as to the origin and meaning of the tradition. Books such as Muratori's *Annali* ("animali") *d'Italia* (*Annals of Italy*) (1744–1749) told him that the race was accompanied by blows (*pisto* = *pesto*) administered to the passing Jews as retaliation for the flagellation and for hurrying Christ along the Via Crucis, according to some accounts, with blows in a sort of Dantean *contrappasso* ("fitting retribution").

The most important aspect of this tradition as it had evolved in Belli's day is elaborated in the second strophe. In order to avoid the physical and mental anguish of the race, the Jewish community had to pay a yearly tribute. It was commonly believed that the sum went to buy the palio, or prize flag, but actually the *palj* (flags) were never donated directly by the Jews. Rather the amount given was large enough to finance the entire games. Until 1847, the Roman Jewish community was required to disburse numerous annual tributes to the papal exchequer. One of these dating from 1334 amounted to 1130 florins, which allowed the Jews to run the race without riders on their backs.[84] Of the tribute of 1130 florins instituted in 1580, 30 florins were to be allotted annually for a mass to remind the Jews of Judas and the thirty

---

84. F. Vitale, *Storia Diplomatica de' Senatori di Roma dalla decadenza dell'Impero Romano fino ai nostri tempi* (Rome: Salomoni, 1791), 246–247.

pieces of silver.[85] Allowing for the passage of time and the change in the historical situation, the approach of the government toward the Jews was still essentially the same in Belli's Rome as in Titus's day. The Jewish community was still a source of plunder and any number of excuses could be invented to disguise the simple rapacity of the popes.

As part of the payment of tribute, representatives of the Jews were subjected to the ceremony of vassalage described in sonnet 944 *"L'omaccio de l'Ebbrei"* ("The Jews' Homage") (4 May 1833):

> Ve vojjo dí una bbuggera, ve vojjo.
> Er giorno a Rroma ch'entra carnovale,
> Li Ggiudii vanno in d'una delle sale
> De li Conzervatori a Ccampidojjo;
>
> E ppresentato er palio prencipale
> Pe rriscattasse da un antico imbrojjo,
> Er Cacamme j'ordissce un bell'orzojjo
> De chiacchiere tramate de morale.
>
> Sta moral' è cch'er Ghetto sano sano
> Giura ubbidienza a le Legge e mmanate
> Der Zenato e dder Popolo Romano.
>
> De cuelle tre pperucche inciprïate,
> Er peruccone, allora, ch'è ppiú anziano
> Arza una scianca e jj'arisponne: "Andate."

(I want to tell you about a cruel hoax. In Rome on the first day of Carnival, the Jews go to the Capitoline Hill to a room in the Magistrate's Palace and, after presenting the yearly tribute money to get out of an old imbroglio, the rabbi makes a nice speech woven through with moral lessons. The gist of it is that the entire ghettoful of Jews swears allegiance to the laws of the Senate and the Roman people. Then the oldest of the three powdered heads, the "bigwig," raises his leg and [with] a kick answers him: "Get out.")

The tribute money, which the Jewish community could ill afford, was only part of the payment. As if they were spoils of war from the days of imperial Rome, the Jews had to undergo yearly humiliation. Though they no longer had to run a race through the streets, they were still forced to make a spectacle of themselves.[86]

85. The remaining 1100 were to be spent on the Carnival games. When the less expensive Barbery horse race was substituted, the amount of tribute, by then way in excess of actual costs, stayed the same. See F. Morelli, *Delle Finanze del Comune di Roma* (Rome: Tipografia Elzeviriana, 1878), 14.

86. In 1743 the delegation from the ghetto received precise instructions on how to dress for the ceremony and, so attired, had to run a sort of gauntlet of catcalls and other forms of derision from the public gathered to view the proceedings. *Archivio segreto,* Cred.

From the title onward the sonnet consists largely of plays on words to satirize a situation Belli must have found intolerable. *L'omaccio* signifies "homage," which was the official reason for the ceremony. "L'omaccio de l'Ebbrei" then was the Jewish homage. It could also mean "the bad man of the Jews," that is the Cacamme as in the other negative interpretations of that sobriquet. But the poet annotates "omaccio" as an "anfibologia" ("double meaning") referring also to "er peruccone" ("the bigwig"), the chief magistrate, of line thirteen. The "homage" then is the same as the "bad man" who directs the humiliating proceedings. As tradition had it, the chief magistrate put his foot on the rabbi who knelt before him. This was at once a symbolic reduction of the riders and the Jewish "horses" in the old race, as well as a display of supremacy of the peruccone over the Cacamme. In response to the oath of fealty and the tribute money, the rabbi received a kick and a brusque, formulaic: "Andate" ("Get out").[87]

In swearing homage the Jewish community promised to submit to the *Legge e manate* ("laws issued") by the municipal authorities and the people of Rome.[88] This unusual way of writing "laws" is another play

---

6, vol. 100, pp. 402–403, cited in Morandi, ed., *I sonetti romaneschi di G. G. Belli,* vol. 3: 41. In 1746, when they insisted on their usual attire, the Jews were informed that any infraction of the dress code would result in immediate arrest and a fine of 100 *scudi* "if it so please His Holiness," that is, Benedict XIV. See *Archivio segreto,* cred. 7, vol. 40: 116–117, cited in ibid., vol. 3: 41.

87. Massimo d'Azeglio described the ceremony in *I miei ricordi* (1866): "The Senate assembles with the Senator . . . seated on his throne and the Rabbi, with a delegation from the Ghetto, kneels before him. [He reads] an address in which he humbly and repeatedly declares the fealty and devotion of the chosen people to the Roman Senate. After the address is finished, the Senator kicks the Rabbi who recoils, naturally, full of gratitude! During Carnival in the Middle Ages the people mistreated the Jews and sacked the Ghetto. These wretches could appeal to the municipal authorities for help, but they had to back up [their appeals] with money and declare themselves subjects and slaves of the Roman people. The ceremony just described is derived from that, [especially] the declaration of fealty to guarantee safety for themselves and their property. The kick was administered until 1830. A long time ago, in place of the kick, the Senator would put his foot on the Rabbi's neck. And they accuse the Jews of having become bad-natured!" See M. d'Azeglio, *I miei ricordi,* 362. M. Mannucci tells how the oldest magistrate "with a disgusting gesture of the foot" ordered the Rabbi and his delegation to go back to their homes. This corresponds exactly to Belli's "er peruccone, allora, ch'è ppiú anziano/ Arza una scianca e jj'arisponne: 'Andate.'" See M. Mannucci, *Gl'Israeliti in Roma* (Turin: Ferrero e Franco, 1852), 17.

88. In 1770 the Jewish Community was ordered to recite the "traditional" formula: "With a sense of obedience and devotion, we, the delegates and Rabbi of the wretched Jewish Community, come before Your Excellencies' high throne in reverence, to render humbly unto it deference and homage, and to beg you to favor us with your benign

on words, for as Belli indicates in his notes, "legge e mmanate" sounds like "leggi e ceffoni" ("laws and blows"). If read aloud allowing for synaloepha, the eighth syllable of line ten scans as an ellision of the *-ge* of "Legge" and the following *e*. In its written form one notices that the past participle "emanate" ("issued") is divided into the conjuction *e* and the noun *manate* and that, in accordance with the rules for transcribing Roman dialect,[89] the *m* following *e-* is doubled, thus reinforcing the nominative quality of *mmanate* as a separate category meaning "blows." The *Legge e mmanate* were ordered by *Der Zenato e dder Popolo Romano* ("the Senate and the Roman people"). By constructing the second hemistich of line ten and all of line eleven as two parallel phrases dependent on the verb *giura* ("swears"), Belli appears to be recounting hundreds of years of Roman life in the historical present: thus "the entire ghettoful of Jews promises submission to the laws [required] by the Senate and the blows [required] by the Roman people."[90]

The same day he wrote "*L'omaccio de l'Ebbrei*" Belli composed another sonnet in which he examines "der Zenato e dder Popolo Romano" more closely. The result is that in the new sonnet the subtext of line eleven of "*L'omaccio*" is brought neatly to the surface. In 944 "*L'omaccio*" Belli implies broad-based support for the torment of the Jews during Carnival and carries the blame up to the bewigged *Conzervatori* ("Municipal authorities"). In 945 "*S.P.Q.R.*" he replaces the whole traditional apparatus of the "Senatus Populusque Romanus—The Senate and the Roman People" with the government of priests and even alludes to a totalitarian regime: "*Soli preti qui rreggneno*: e ssilenzio" ("Only priests give the orders here, so shut up"). If one takes this in-

---

regard. For our part we shall pray the Lord for continued peace and quiet for the Pope in this happy reign and for the Holy See together with your Excellencies, the glorious Senate and the Roman People." See F. Morelli, *Delle Finanze*, 111–112.

89. See Belli's *Introduzione* to the sonnets in G. G. Belli, *I sonetti*, vol. 1: clxxxv–cxci.

90. In their *Memoria* to Gregory XVI the Jewish community stated that the requirement to pay homage to Rome began in the seventeenth century. Morandi, however, found a chirograph of Clement IX dated 28 January 1668 in which Jews were freed from running the race, but were still required to pay the "usual" homage as they had "since the pontificate of Paul II (1464–1471) or around that time." See Morandi, ed., *I sonetti romaneschi di G. G. Belli*, vol. 3: 44. Though little is known about the origin of the ceremony, its demise is documented. Upon accession, Pius IX received a request from the Jewish community to abolish the ceremony and he obliged. The last homage was paid on 6 February by the Rabbi alone in normal dress. (Instrument of the Capitoline Notary Vitti, 7 February 1847.) In his *motu proprio* of 1 October 1847, Pius IX abolished the obligation.

terpretation of the formula and uses it to inform line eleven of *"L'omac-cio,"* one is then able to trace Belli's view of Roman society up to its logical conclusion at the top of the hierarchy. Er peruccone sat at the head of the government of laymen. Over him sat the priests and at the pinnacle of the ecclesiastical triangle sat the pope. The Carnival tribute was invented by a pope "in memoria e in onore/Della fraggellazzion de Ggesucristo" ("to commemorate and honor the flagellation of Christ") and perpetuated by all the popes who came after him. *"L'omac-cio,"* the nemesis, the personification of the forces of repression and emargination of the Jews, was the pope.

Here then is the *buggera* ("lie" or "hoax"), the traditional and con-sistent and cruel victimization of one marginalized group by the leader of the dominant majority. The buggera, as a revealing metaphor, went well beyond the farcical and pathetic homage the Jews were forced to swear, for it was nothing short of extortion practiced by the established authorities and derived from centuries of popular tradition. Here also is Belli at his most indignant for in this sonnet he indicts all of Roman society from bottom to top. "L'omaccio de l'Ebbrei" is the perfect illustration of Belli's pessimistic view of Roman history and, by ex-tension, contemporary civilization. All one needs to know, he said in *"L'istoria romana"* written just four months earlier, is that from time immemorial the Romans have been a "gang of thieves." Add to this the detrimental effects of absolute power symbolized by the formula S.P.Q.R. and any notion of the "glory that is Rome" becomes untenable.

IN CONCLUSION: "TUTTI L'OMMINI SÒ FFIJJI D'ADAMO"

("All men are Adam's sons")

How did Belli explain Rome's decline from antiquity to his own day? Who suffered and who profited from it? For Belli, the squalid conditions he saw were the result of injustice: injustice derived from and perpetuated by the concentration of wealth and power, first in the person of the emperor and later the pope. In sonnet 1169 *"Li du' ggener' umani"* ("Rich and Poor"), the pope is shown meting out precise and controlled quantities of power through his hierarchy. What trickled down to the parish priest was the charge and the authority to herd the flocks of the faithful into the Church and keep them there. In other words, the orthodoxy of the society had to be maintained if the theocracy that depended on it were to endure and prosper.

Since he held modest employment in that same inherently unjust power structure, Belli had to step back from it in order to see it whole, as if in a laboratory, to form and weigh his impressions of its organization and influence. At certain periods over approximately twenty-seven years[91] he recorded noteworthy situations day by day. Having acquired an intimate understanding of the society, he could comment freely on its extremes—so distant from each other and yet so interdependent. Focusing on the lower classes he sorted out the various groups and subgroups and observed their interaction. The Jews were the one group whose lives were directly regulated from on high at the Vatican, but who were cast down at the very bottom of the heap, both together with and separated from the other subproletarians. Given their special involvement with both poles of society, the Jews enjoyed a privileged position in Belli's meditations on his city.

The Jews, with their "oriental" customs and religion—"Vvadino in Ghetto/A ffà ste sciarle: vvadino in Turchia" ("Let 'em go to the Ghetto if they want to talk nonsense: Let 'em go to Turkey")—added richness and complexity to Roman society. As that society's finest observer, Belli grasped the paradox inherent in the Roman Jews' situation: their actual cultural diversity as an isolated minority among the lower classes compared with their imagined, stereotyped qualities that, in the end, rendered them not all that different from their Christian counterparts. Who, then, could be compared to the pope better than er Cacamme, the rabbi, whose epithet incorporates both positive and negative connotations? This approach required the poet to portray the Jews from the viewpoints of several different elements in Roman society. One particularly effective technique was the conversation between two Christians or, better still, between a Jew and a Christian. The latter was an economical method permitting the poet to explore two points of view and demonstrate the difficulty of meaningful communication between the two groups, as in 1979 "*La vennita der brevetto*" ("Pension for Sale").

91. Though the first sonnet dates from 1820, some editors consider the first sonnet of social criticism to be 11 "*Pio ottavo*" (1 April 1829). Sonnets 1–10 are included in anthologies with the *caveat* that they were "rifiutati" ("disowned") by their author. This is not the case with the Morandi or Vigolo editions, but see M. T. Lanza's preface to her edition, vol. 1: lxxx. In all cases the first ten sonnets contribute to make up the number of 2,279 *Sonetti romaneschi*. Belli ceased writing satirical sonnets in Roman dialect in 1847.

The *Zibaldone* reveals Belli's fascination with Jews and his basic respect for them. In his poetry, however, the voice is almost always uneducated and plebeian and burdened with all the expected centuries-old prejudices and fears occasioned by limited contact. Thus one reads such verses in 1508 "*Le scuse de Ghetto*" ("Ghetto Excuses"), as

> In questo io penzo come penzi tu:
> Io l'odio li Ggiudii peggio de te;
> Perché nun zò ccattolichi, e pperché
> Messeno in crosce er Redentor Gesú.

> (In this matter we're of the same opinion. I hate the Jews, too, even worse than you do, because they're not Catholics and because they crucified the Savior.)

in the same sonnet in which Belli defends the Jews as preordained instruments of God in the crucifixion. Similarly, one finds a considerable difference between the "plebeian" text and the "educated" subtext in the *Roncilli* poems. Although the voice belongs to the treasurer's servant who complains about the pope's taking money from a hardhearted "*giudio fetente*" (stinking Jew) (622 "*Er motivo de li guai*"—"The Source of Our Troubles"; 316 "*La sala di Monziggnore Tesoriere*"—"Monsignor Treasurer's Antechamber"), the hidden meaning expresses Belli's concern for the well-being of the Church.

Where the poetic voice is more clearly that of the enlightened observer is in the sonnets about the Carnival race. Here Belli openly declares his sympathy for the victims of injustice, going so far as to inform his readers that the tale he is about to tell is a "buggera," a cruel hoax on the Jews. At the same time, however, as Belli investigates the injustice done to the Jews—by the various "omacci" ("tyrants") in power, pope or emperor—he satirizes but also perpetuates the same prejudices that occasioned such treatment. What one can glean from this apparent paradox, given Belli's natural inclination toward justice and his intensive reading of the philosophes, is that the poet was predisposed to portray the Jews and others whom he perceived as down-and-out with a certain amount of indulgence and compassion.

Had Belli only presented the Jews in poems such as "*L'omaccio de l'Ebbrei*" ("The Jews' Homage") in which they are portrayed as traditional scapegoats yoked into perpetual submission, he would have become, in a sense, an accomplice of those same "omacci" who conceived of Jews only as victims. He would have betrayed his intention to make "our people speak about themselves . . . about their own customs and their own opinions, however twisted."[92] Any depiction of the Roman lower classes which did not also include the Jews as an active people with lively customs, language, and opinions would have been a travesty of that literary program that Belli maintained intact throughout his poetic career. Instead, in Belli, the Jews, like all other Romans striving to overcome economic hardship, lived by the dictum: "Che sse fa ppe-cora a sto monno/Er lupo se la maggna" ("In this life, those who act like sheep are eaten by wolves"). (1911 *L'abbondanza pe fforza*—"Forced Abundance," 30 May 1837) The only difference between the groups was that Jews had to work harder and exercise their ingenuity more fully. If they were aggressive in business dealings it was not just because this was a typical Jewish trait, but because Jews knew what their Christian colleagues knew: that society offers only two alterna-tives—to eat or be eaten. Hence the similarity between the two clothiers of 1221 *La bbona spesa* ("The Bargain") and 1850 *Er mercante pe Roma II* ("The Merchant of Rome II").

In his letter to Prince Gabrielli regarding the language in which the lower classes present themselves, Belli used the verb "introdurre" (here: "let in") stating that he wished to "let our people in to speak about themselves." Fully cognizant of the novelty of his endeavor, and recall-ing Rousseau's warning that literature that excluded the majority of the population could not aspire to reality much less universality, Belli was saying that he wanted the people to enter Literature as protagonists rather than as supernumeraries. Though in Belli they inhabit an exalted literary sphere (poetry) they still describe themselves as "poveri coj-joni," pawns of authoritarian overlords. They are conscious of the wrongs done them, but are unable to take action to ameliorate their situation. By adopting their language Belli was able to take up the ideals of the Enlightenment, restate them concretely and credibly, and give them a new and popular voice.

The precise transcription of the popular idiom coupled with his dis-tanced vantage point have led some critics to consider Belli a realist of the type that was to find full expression some years later in *verismo*. But Belli's brand of realism was far too personal to admit such a label. Though consistently masked by dialect and sometimes prudently rele-

92. Letter to Prince Placido Gabrielli dated 15 January 1861, thirty years after the *Introduzione* and the program letter to Francesco Spada, in G. G. Belli, *Lettere, Giornali, Zibaldone*, 378.

gated to the subtext, the author's voice maintains a running commentary on the trials of daily life. And the comments often reveal a poet wounded in his personal ideals and his sense of fair play (180 *"Caino"*—"Cain"; 1169 *"Li du' ggener' umani"*—"Rich and Poor"; 40–41 the "Campo Vaccino" ["Vaccino Square"] series). Or else he abandons his cover (though not the dialect) and speaks out (722 *"Le curze d'una vorta"*—"Races of Yesteryear"; 944 *"L'omaccio de l'Ebbrei"*—"The Jews' Homage"). That Belli's is a bitter voice expressing extreme disillusionment with Rome, its history (908 *"L'istoria romana"*—"Roman History") and reality (*"Er còllera mòribbus II"*—"Deadly Cholera II") is nowhere clearer than in the exposition of the fate of the Jews in the city.

The fact that Belli inherited an established folklore on Jews from the stereotyped, anti-Jewish depictions of the Roman satirical tradition—the giudìata and the *Pasquinata*—and the other sources noted in the *Zibaldone*, gave him a tool with which to satirize various aspects of Roman life and poetry. Because he used satire to strike the accuser along with the accused, Jews in Belli's sonnets became agents as well as the objects of satire. But this required considerably more than just a simple observation of Roman Jews.

In order to achieve the colorful, vivid portrait of Jewish life in the *Sonetti romaneschi*, Belli had to familiarize himself with their customs and the peculiarities of their language. The clichés of traditional representation of Jews reveal the novelty of Belli's approach. Bresciani, for instance, stereotypically placed Jews in the upper echelons of international finance while stating dismissively that his character did not correspond to the faceless, ragged masses of Italian ghetto dwellers. Belli, on the other hand, demonstrated considerable knowledge and understanding of the plight of Jews (*"Le curze d'una vorta," "L'omaccio de l'Ebbrei"*) and was able to penetrate layers of prejudice which for many clouded the reality of Jewish life. In Belli's poetry Jews take on a vibrancy denied them in standard portrayals.

Still, we must not assume that Belli's intellectual understanding of Jewish life and his compassion for the victims of injustice meant that he was immune to a stereotypical vision of Jews. Although the voice he uses to impart opinions about Jews, and everyone else, is, yes, a sort of *vox populi*, it is nearly impossible to separate Belli totally from his interlocutors.

When faced with a body of work that focuses so steadily on a specific group, we are tempted to ask where did the author's sentiments really lie? Was Belli anti-Semitic? Because Belli's intellectual background was such a complex one, the question is difficult to answer. On the one hand, given Belli's reading of the Enlightenment philosophers and his passion for social justice—expressed in his sympathy for Cain and the "poveri cojjoni"—one is likely not to condemn him, even if one remembers that his poems employed an acid satirism. One must remember, too, that at the time that Belli composed the *Sonetti romaneschi* (1820–1847), he had not yet turned toward rigid, fundamentalist Catholicism. Nor did the Jews at this time represent the kind of social and political threat that they seemed to pose when the Risorgimento was really underway; indeed, until 1848, the popes had the Jews of the Papal State quite well under control.

What was therefore unique about Belli was—and here he may well have revealed his own unresolved ambivalences—that although he presented a whole array of stereotypical opinions about Jews, his technique of using Jews as literary, satirical foils lessened the impact of their portraits. Because he endowed his Jewish interlocutors with those human foibles that are instantly recognizable in his Christian characters, Belli, to a certain extent, redeemed the Jews from some of the disparaging notions of their ghetto existence.

Still, although he never expressed himself as directly as did the giudìata and the *Pasquinata,* Belli had a treasure in these traditional images of the Jews. This, together with the cultural and physical reality of the ghetto which, in fact, created two Romes; the paradox of frequent Christian-Jewish interaction despite segregation; and the undeniable existence of social barriers that are, ultimately, *not* crossed in the *Sonetti romaneschi,* provide the poet with invaluable material for his trenchant portraits of his world.

1. Von Guise, after Hieronymus Hess: *Die Bekehrung der Juden in Rom* (*The Conversion of the Jews in Rome*, 1823). Conversionist sermons were held on Saturdays in the church of Sant' Angelo in Pescheria near the Roman ghetto. Attendance was obligatory for Jewish men (see page 19). *Courtesy of the Library of the Jewish Theological Seminary of America, New York.*

2. Bartolomeo Pinelli: *Gli ebrei presentano doni irrisòri a Meo Patacca* (*The Jews Present Worthless Gifts to Meo Patacca* from *Il Meo Patacca overo Roma in Feste*, Rome, 1823). The popular character Meo Patacca was pictured as protector of the Roman Jews. The modest nature of their gifts to him bears witness to their impoverished condition and their identification with the old clothes trade. *Courtesy of the Biblioteca Nazionale Centrale, Florence, Italy.*

3. Bartolomeo Pinelli: *Un ebreo messo in una botte e fatto rotolare dalla plebaglia* (*Elderly Jew Put in a Barrel and Rolled by the Rabble* from *Il Meo Patacca overo Roma in Feste*, Rome, 1823). The barrel roll of a Jew down the Testaccio Hill in Rome was a popular part of pre-Lenten festivities (see page 92). *Courtesy of the Biblioteca Nazionale Centrale, Florence, Italy.*

4. Bartolomeo Pinelli: *Tentativo della plebaglia di incendiare il ghetto stornato da Meo Pataca (Meo Pataca Dissuades the Rabble as They Attempt to Set Fire to the Ghetto* from *Il Meo Pataca overo Roma in Feste*, Rome, 1823). Such attacks on the ghetto were not uncommon. In post-emancipation Rome, Jews without the means to move away remained in the ghetto area and were subject to occasional harassment through the 1930s (see page 100). *Courtesy of the Biblioteca Nazionale Centrale, Florence, Italy.*

5. *L'omaggio degli ebrei al Senatore di Roma in Campidoglio (The Jews Swear Homage to the Chief Senator of Rome in the Campidoglio).* This ritual was linked to the Carnival festivities. The kneeling figure in the foreground is the rabbi. Jews were eventually able to avoid this and other humiliations by paying for the Carnival games (see pages 147–150). *Courtesy of the Gabinetto Comunale della Stampe, Rome, Italy.*

6. Bartolomeo Pinelli: *La giostra dei gobbi ebrei al teatro Corea* (*The Race of Jewish Hunchbacks at the Corea Theatre*, 1828). Jews were often required to run races in the place of horses, with or without riders on their backs as part of Carnival festivities in Rome (see pages 145–146). *Courtesy of the Biblioteca Nazionale Centrale, Florence, Italy.*

7. "Avea sulla fronte scolpita la croce, e in cerca dell'ignoto andava proscritto" (Abramo as the Wandering Jew): illustration from A. Liberi, *Il Ghetto* in *Romanziere popolare* (Turin, 1880–1881). The caption reads: "His forehead branded with a cross, he trudged on, an exile in search of the unknown" (see page 196). *Courtesy of the Biblioteca Nazionale Universitaria of Turin, Italy.*

4

The Wolf at the Door

The development of the middle classes and the urban proletariat in the wake of the Risorgimento and subsequent industrialization of the new nation radically altered the nature of Italian literary tastes and literary products. For the first time, the market was characterized by the continual emergence of literary genres in which readers could "recognize" their own concerns and values.[1]

Before unification, aristocratic readers and intellectuals from the new urban professional and merchant classes supplemented their heretofore fairly steady diet of traditional poetry, local histories, and the classics with politically motivated poetry, national histories, biographies, and, the most successful thematic combination of all these genres: the historical novel. The novels of Dumas, for instance, were read along with Guerrazzi and Berchet by Tuscan intellectuals and the politicized nobility because they were imagined to be literary renderings of revolution.[2] Literary development varied throughout the peninsula and was dependent upon the general cultural and political climate of individual regions. Thus, the popularity of the new genres of literature was most notable in Lombardy, Piedmont, and Tuscany; elsewhere, especially in the Papal State and in the south, clerical domination of culture limited the demand for new literary products.

1. See G. Ragone's insightful essay, "La letteratura e il consumo: un profilo dei generi e dei modelli nell'editoria italiana (1845–1925)," in *Letteratura italiana,* ed. A. Asor Rosa (Turin: Einaudi, 1983), vol. 2, *Produzione e consumo,* 687–772.

2. P. Barbera, *Editori ed autori* (Florence: Barbera, 1904), 192, cited in G. Ragone, "La letteratura e il consumo," 704.

After unification, the concept of the historical novel was expanded to include the new forms of fiction: the *romanzo d' appendice* (*feuilleton* or serial novel) and travel-adventure books. Many contemporary situations were also included under the wide umbrella of historical fiction resulting in the large number of *romanzi storico-sociali* (socio-historical novels) in which the reading public "recognized its own presence, passions, and situations in which it had played a part."[3] Since most historical fiction described the past, however, while keeping an eye on the present, it offered a welcome escape from the present together with a reassuring affirmation of the present's ethical values. In its role as "true supplement to historical fact," it gave voice to its own public, albeit indirectly, by recording the moral as well as political and economic conditions of the society and revealing the "inner family—its morality, education, habits, opinions, and prejudices."[4]

The market for this fiction was also shaped by the creation of the Italian state. Unification caused the principal Northern and Central Italian cities to experience considerable population growth through internal migration and movement from the countryside to the city. By 1872, Milan (with its province) had grown to 948,000 inhabitants, Turin to 942,000, Rome to 798,000, Florence to 700,000, and Bologna to 407,000.[5] For many new arrivals, life in the city offered them acculturation into the world of print media. This was especially important for migrants from the south where literacy remained well below 50 percent until after World War I.[6] Even in the north when, later in the century, special editions of popular literary works produced by publishers like Salani circulated in the countryside for a "penny" apiece, readership among the peasantry was nearly nonexistent.[7] But once in the city, there

3. G. Ragone, "La letteratura e il consumo," 704.

4. S. Uzielli, "Del romanzo storico, e di Walter Scott," in *Antologia* 12, no. 39 (1824): 125.

5. These figures were gathered by G. Ottino, *La stampa periodica, il commercio dei libri e la tipografia in Italia* (Milan: Brigola, 1875), cited in G. Ragone, "La letteratura e il consumo," 714. See also, T. Vignoli, *Delle condizioni intellettuali d' Italia* (Milan: Dumolard, 1877).

6. See T. Di Mauro's fundamental *Storia linguistica dell' Italia unita* (Bari: Laterza, 1965), 75–90.

7. "Peasants simply do not read." See Società bibliografica italiana, *I libri più letti dal popolo italiano* (Milan: Società bibliografica italiana, 1906), 11. French peasants, however, we are told, did read popular novels at the time of the Second Empire. See Yves Olivier-Martin, "Sociologia del Romanzo Popolare," in AA.VV., *La paraletteratura* (Naples: Liguori, 1977), 146.

were numerous opportunities for learning to read and these were nourished by publications targeted for a newly literate audience. De Sanctis, for example, writes of Cesare Cantù's efforts to combat illiteracy as early as 1836 with entertaining and instructive literature.[8]

With the significant increase in the number of urban wage earners between the growing middle classes and the burgeoning proletariat,[9] a new literary market was born supplanting, to a sizable degree, publication for the intellectual book buyer of old. Who were the new consumers of literature and what did they read?

A study of the book market done in 1906 gives us a good idea of reading habits in the latter years of the nineteenth century.[10] The study assessed the purchasing habits of men and women, dividing the two groups by social class. Women, it concluded, read more than men, and as women became buyers of literary "merchandise," popular novels were increasingly aimed at them, expressing their desires and reflecting their expectations.[11] Whereas men read largely for self-improvement—with only the lower classes (servants and soldiers) reading strictly for pleasure—women at all levels read mostly for entertainment. Bourgeois women, like their male counterparts, read novels by writers who today are considered classics along with romances, as did the more cultured male members of the class of shopkeepers, civil servants, and clerks. The less-cultured, petty bourgeois men and women read primarily romances and *romanzi d' appendice*.[12] The surprising finding in this survey was that the laboring classes of industrial workers and artisans were enthusiastic consumers of literature.[13] Often auto-didacts, many male laborers[14] read "good" literature and technical works in order to acquire a patina of culture and advance themselves, whereas male servants and soldiers read *romanzi d' appendice* and pornography. Finally, women in the needle trades read romances, *romanzi d' appendice,* and stories in

8. See F. De Sanctis, "Cesare Cantù e la letteratura popolare," in *La letteratura italiana nel secolo XIX* (Bari: Laterza, 1953), vol. 2: 217.

9. See P. Sylos Labini, *Saggio sulle classi sociali* (Bari: Laterza, 1974).

10. Società bibliografica italiana, *I libri più letti.*

11. U. Eco, *Il superuomo di massa* (Milan: Bompiani, 1978), chap. 4, "I *Beati Paoli* e l'ideologia del romanzo 'popolare'," 84.

12. An interesting exception to this finding was that butchers, greengrocers, and coal sellers did not read. See Società bibliografica italiana, *I libri più letti,* 12.

13. See, however, A. Asor Rosa, "La cultura," in *Storia d' Italia,* ed. R. Romano and C. Vivanti (Turin: Einaudi, 1975), vol. 4, bk. 2, *Dall' Unità a oggi,* 1016–1031.

14. Here there are exceptions as well; it seems that carpenters, shoemakers, blacksmiths, and bricklayers did not read. Società bibliografica italiana, *I libri più letti,* 12.

magazines published specifically for them,[15] whereas female servants read stories, horoscopes, and advice columns in periodicals.

The greater the population with even minimal disposable income to spend, the more literature became a consumer good. Unlike the restricted group of friends who had access to Belli's sonnets in Roman dialect or even the mainly religious readers of Bresciani's didactic *Ebreo di Verona,* this explosion in the number of readers formed a powerful commercial force that directly influenced authors and publishers. Those who were illiterate or who could not afford the purchase price would gather in public, at a *cabinet de lecture* or even in the entrance hall of their tenement, for a reading of each installment of their favorite novels. Satisfying the demand for literary entertainment became a highly profitable objective and some publishers—notably Sonzogno and Treves in Milan and Salani in Florence—specialized in supplying their readers with seemingly endless numbers of novels and stories.

For those whose budgets would not permit the purchase of entire volumes, there were weekly and biweekly journals, some of which—like *Il Romanziere illustrato* (*The Illustrated Anthology,* published between 6 May 1865 and 14 May 1868) from Sonzogno at fifteen cents per issue—were made up entirely of fiction. These were novels meant to be consumed rapidly and followed by others like themselves. To assure continuity of market, *Il Romanziere illustrato* and other publications included the first installment of a new novel about every other issue. Literary magazines enjoyed their greatest popularity in the 1870s. In 1872, at least ten were printed in editions of more than ten thousand daily or weekly copies and two of these—*L'emporio pittoresco* (*The Pictorial Marketplace,* a weekly) and *Il secolo* (*The Century,* a daily newspaper with *romanzi d' appendice*), both from Sonzogno—sold more than twenty-four thousand copies.[16] *Romanzi d' appendice* continued to occupy a significant position in the publication of periodicals through the turn of the century. No less an observer than Gabriele D'Annunzio, himself a successful author with his finger firmly on the pulse of the market, remarked on their commercial power:

15. Among the more successful of these were *Monitore delle sarte* and *La ricamatrice moderna,* both published in Milan by Sonzogno.

16. The literary magazines in this sampling are: *L' emporio pittoresco* (24,000 copies weekly); *L' illustrazione popolare* (10,000+ copies weekly); *Il giro del mondo* (10,000+ copies weekly); *Letture cattoliche* (10,000 copies weekly); *Il Romanziere illustrato* (10,000 copies weekly); *La Civiltà Cattolica* (10,000 copies weekly); *Il secolo* (25,000 copies daily); *Gazzetta del Popolo* (15,000 copies daily); *Il Fanfulla* (15,000 copies daily); *Il Pungolo* (10,000 copies daily). See G. Ragone, "La letteratura e il consumo," 715.

Political daily newspapers aimed at the great majority of readers almost always owe their commercial success or failure to the quality of the novels published in their appendices, novels which become longer and more numerous day by day.[17]

With the growing commercial importance of literature aimed squarely at the consuming public at a price much of the public could afford, generally twenty to twenty-five cents, the link between text and social context assumed crucial significance.[18] The public was a narcissistic "beast," complained social critic Edoardo Scarfoglio,

wanting to see itself reflected with all its heartthrobs and vicissitudes as if in a giant mirror. The public, crazy for anatomy, willingly stretches out on the slab so that the novelist can cut it open and thrust his hands into the wound.

The novelist, however, can forget about aesthetic dicta and artful style; to be successful, writers must "walk among the crowd, absorb the sentiments which animate it and glean their material from it."[19]

The context for the convoluted plots common to popular novels was, therefore, no longer only the heroic past of the old-fashioned historical novel but the *attualità* (the current happenings of the day) of the *romanzo storico-sociale*. Up-to-the-minute, a sort of hybrid between novel and newspaper, the ever-increasing pace of current events was translated structurally into the novels' numerous *coups-de-scène* and the seemingly instantaneous incorporation of issues of contemporary importance.

Like the newspaper, these novels changed as values changed, though their authors almost invariably assumed a conservative stance on modern mores. Predictable moral principles were repeated in as many permutations as there were popular novels. Chief among these was the essentially middle-class certainty that innocence and virtue would ultimately triumph over vice. This assumption was rooted in the belief that the society that most closely resembled the reader's way of life—that is, complacently honest and industrious—was the one that would eliminate injustice and provide a happy ending. The denouement, then, was

---

17. Interview with D'Annunzio in January 1895, in U. Ojetti, *Alla scoperta dei letterati* (Milan: Dumolard, 1895), 316.

18. See J. Tortel, "Il Romanzo Popolare," in AA.VV., *La paraletteratura* (Naples: Liguori, 1977), 71–93; U. Eco, "L'industria aristotelica," in *Cent' anni dopo. Almanacco letterario Bompiani* (Milan: Bompiani, 1972), 5–11; R. Barthes, *The Pleasure of the Text* (New York: Farrar, Straus and Giroux, 1975), 14.

19. E. Scarfoglio, *Il libro di Don Chisciotte* (Milan: Dumolard, 1895), 163.

required to reflect nothing less than the "social contract,"[20] that is, to heal any temporary breaks with established morality. This was perhaps the origin of escapist literature and of *letteratura amena* (pleasure reading), the comforting reading experience that would, in turn, assure the novel's commercial success.

Patriot and Jew

Returning to the historical novel of the Risorgimento period written for a prosperous, intellectual, and liberal audience, we find the pervasive theme of nationalism, a literary motif that closely linked historical forces and momentary commercial fortune. Despite its revolutionary aspects, nationalism, the animator of the Risorgimento, found its way into popular literature in a form that was consonant with the conservative nature of the genre. As the century progressed, authors continued to abstract nationalism from the complex political movements before unification and developed it into a major plot element. Thus Risorgimento was represented in popular fiction by the revival of *italianità* (Italianness), which celebrated all elements of life in the peninsula thought to be uniquely Italian and denigrated, at least rhetorically, any foreign influence.

Since Jews comprised the largest distinct ethnic group in nineteenth-century Italy and one that until 1848 (1870 in Rome) lived in Jewish enclaves, the question of their separateness within Italian society was a natural topic for discussion in the historical novel. Popular writers and their readers tended to subscribe to the stereotype of the "nation within the nation," an image constantly reinforced in the demagogic preachings of such as Jabalot. The Jewish people, maintaining its exclusivity by residing in ghettos separate from the general populace and often speaking a strange dialect, was regarded by the average reader as somehow less than Italian; Jews were "foreign" and, therefore, suspect.

There are several such references to Jews in the nationalistic writers of the Risorgimento; even Risorgimento activism, which one might well associate with an enlightened outlook, was no guarantee of tolerance. A case in point is that of the novelist, lawyer, and Mazzinian patriot, Francesco Domenico Guerrazzi, who could not reconcile himself

---

20. See U. Eco, "L'industria aristotelica," 10.

to the presence of Jews in his native Livorno. In his *Note autobiogra-fiche* (*Autobiographical Scribblings*) he discusses the conflict between his "sacred duty" as a liberal to promote the cause of full civil rights for Jews and his inability to abandon the anti-Jewish stereotype that he bore "indelibly etched on his consciousness."[21] Jews, "like cats," appeared to him incapable of responding to friendship or establishing bonds with society outside the ghetto. Indeed, "their affections extended no further than the circumference of a silver coin." To talk of patriotism with such men was a waste of time, for in order to partake fully of nationalist sentiment they would have to change their very essence, and this they were loath to do. They preferred to remain the people whom Moses wrought and live as if in perpetual exile. Unwilling to assimilate, they

travel through the centuries and [float] along in the midst of peoples like oil on water . . . They are the chosen ones; they are the true children of God.[22]

This vision of the Jews of Livorno as fraudulent merchants and avaricious usurers, led the adolescent Guerrazzi, with like-minded friends, to assault the Jewish quarter and, armed with stones, to escalate his attacks on the Jews over a period of time.

These visceral reactions to the Jews inform Guerrazzi's approach to numerous personages in his writings: real ones with whom he had legal disputes, such as the banker Sansone Uzielli, whom Guerrazzi accuses of having no citizenship,[23] or the fictional usurers Anania and Ottolenghi of *Il secolo che muore* (*The Waning Century*) and Zabulone of *I nuovi tartufi* (*New Truffles*). Zabulone boasts of the power of moneylenders to enslave all mankind:

We merchants, we bankers, we smugglers, we captains of coinage, before whom kings bow down and emperors doff their hats, [we on whom] the popes smile—and we're proud of it—we are a slow but constant force, unrelenting,

---

21. F. D. Guerrazzi, *Note autobiografiche* (Florence: Le Monnier, 1899), 87–88.

22. Ibid., 85–86, 92–93, 97.

23. Guerrazzi attempted to moderate his attack saying "I'm not so un-philosophical as to attack a man simply because his religion differs from mine. I declared the Livornese my compatriots and *not* Uzielli because a foolish, despicable coward like him has neither homeland nor compatriots." These remarks were part of a bitter exchange of letters between Uzielli and Guerrazzi, and Guerrazzi and Capponi, about the Geraudino case in 1846. See F. D. Guerrazzi, *Memorie legali e scritti giuridici* (Livorno: Giusti, 1923), 95–118, especially 117.

invincible and at the same time intangible. We raise men up and cast them down as we please.[24]

It has been suggested that Zabulone represents none other than Sansone Uzielli and that the creation of the villain was Guerrazzi's ultimate revenge against Uzielli in particular and Jewish financiers in general.[25] Commerce with the *robevecchi* Nataniele in *Paolo Pelliccioni* also occasions a long diatribe in which, once again, Guerrazzi laments that the Jews will never change, that while protesting their persecution they themselves persecute those who approach them in brotherhood. Livorno is a case in point:

I know of a place where the majority of Jews, having been granted liberty, . . . gnaw at [their fellow citizens] like wood worms.[26]

Good citizenship is unknown to them:

The Jews are to be considered brothers and so they are, but before we accept them into the society of Italian citizens . . . let them cleanse themselves of the leprosy they brought from Palestine and which still taints their blood.[27]

Negative judgments on the unassimilability of contemporary Jews into the Italian society that Risorgimento patriots like Guerrazzi envisioned as an ideal future, were also those of the pre-Risorgimento novelist Carlo Varese, patriot and author of the very popular novel *Sibilla Odaleta* (1827). Varese was a physician at Voghera by profession, but a politician by calling and a spare-time author by inclination. As soon as it was published, *Sibilla Odaleta* was printed "in almost all states, [even the] small ones."[28] It went through twelve Italian editions, was translated twice into French, and was considered the best of the historical novels in the style of Sir Walter Scott.

Varese's story takes place in Tuscany and Naples in 1494 during Charles VIII's sweep through Italy. A Cypriot woman arrives in Naples in search of a Jewish doctor, Abele Malvezzi, who, eleven years earlier, had kidnapped and (the woman believes) murdered her daughter. She is mistaken: the doctor had taken the girl to Naples, changed her name from Sibilla to Lucilla, and raised her as his own. The mother believing

24. F. D. Guerrazzi, *I nuovi tartufi*, in *Scritti di F. D. Guerrazzi* (Florence: Le Monnier, 1847), 131.

25. For identification of Zabulone/Uzielli, see Guerrazzi, *Memorie legali*, 119.

26. F. D. Guerrazzi, *Paolo Pellicioni* (Milan: Guigioni, 1864), vol. 2: 150.

27. Ibid., 151.

28. A. Albertazzi, *Il romanzo* (Milan: Vallardi, 1902), 168.

Lucilla to be Malvezzi's natural daughter, instructs her son, Demetrio, to avenge his sister by killing the girl. Malvezzi and Sibilla/Lucilla live trapped in the Castel dell'Ovo while the fortress is being defended by the chivalrous Ludovico Trivulzio and his son, Annibale. Although she has been raised by Malvezzi without religion, the beautiful girl is chaste and Annibale, equally pure and heroic, falls in love with her. Predictably the novel ends with the downfall of the villain and the marriage of the virtuous couple.

Sibilla Odaleta was the best known of Varese's many novels. It was written in three volumes, in accordance with contemporary tastes, and included the various literary expedients popularized by Scott: subterranean chambers, graveyards, kidnappings, *coups-de-scène,* a generous sprinkling of pithy aphorisms, and turgid speeches in the mouths of humble characters.

Varese's was the first of a substantial line of patriotic novels. Italian youth may well have first become acquainted with Risorgimento rhetoric between the covers of *Sibilla Odaleta,* which preceded D'Azeglio's *Ettore Fieramosca* by six years and Guerrazzi's *L'Assedio di Firenze* (*The Siege of Florence*) by nine years, works usually credited with popularizing the Risorgimento.[29] Carlo Varese was intensely conscious of the importance of having written a patriotic historical novel:

In this way it would be possible to describe the situation of our [beloved] Italy, whose very name we could scarcely utter in safety. So in a few months I set my historical novel *Sibilla Odaleta* [and] that worthless novel was avidly read because it was by an Italian and about Italy and also because it was the first [example] of this sort of literature.[30]

Publishing under the pseudonym "Un Italiano," Varese established an antithesis between the nature and aspirations of Italians and those of Jews early on in the novel. Then, rather than subject his readers to a pointless list of accusations, Varese worked his anti-Semitic observations into a framework of oppositions using the urgency of Risorgimento as a fulcrum. National identity acts both as the starting point and the desired goal in Varese's circular concatenation of arguments, and each Jewish shortcoming is another link in the chain.

Varese has been criticized for plagiarizing liberally from Guicciar-

---

29. Ibid.
30. A. Brofferio, "Carlo Varese al suo amico Angelo Brofferio," in *I miei tempi* (Turin: Botta, 1860), 96–97.

dini's *Storia d' Italia* (*History of Italy*)[31] and using history as a mere device to mask intense patriotism at a time of censorship rather than as an intrinsic plot element. But his portrayal of history goes beyond the mere mechanics of background. As pictured in the novel, each group, "Italians" and Jews, has its distinct history. The plot pits fifteenth-century heroes defending their native soil against usurping foreigners; their defense is the historical example, the glorious heritage that Varese urges nineteenth-century patriots to reenact. But there is also the other group of *semi*-foreigners which acts out its own brand of "history." This is a negative, dangerous history because it is particularistic, intended to benefit only the small group of Jews and not focused on the common good. The history of the Jews, as Varese constructs it, has repeated itself in this manner since time immemorial and, therefore, can only subvert patriotic, "Italian" efforts. The patriots' war, then, must be waged on two fronts: one directed against would-be conquerors and the other intended to expel the villain from their midst. Since in the Romantic age a people's history was the key factor in establishing a sense of national identity, Varese's suggestion in 1827 of an inferior or dangerous history was an unmistakable condemnation.

Sibilla Odaleta is a simplistic mixture of the positive force of Romantic patriotism and the negative force of anti-Semitism, with the former fuelling the latter. The most notable patriotic episode is the appearance of the Tuscan miller, created solely to teach a political lesson with a speech "in defense of our poor Italy."[32] The humble miller is ready to give his life to chase foreigners from the land and restore his country to her former glory. His is a selfless, Romantic vision of duty, motivated solely by altruism. The miller's opposite in this tale of heroes and villains is Abele Malvezzi. Varese bases his portrait of Jews in part on the notion that just as foreign troops could conquer Italy from the outside, Jews worked systematically to destroy society from within. Whereas the miller wants to give his life for the future of Italy, Malvezzi willfully destroys Italy's youth for profit, or so Sibilla's mother thinks.

The woman grieves in a subterranean cavern keeping watch over an urn that she believes to contain the ashes of Sibilla who was, presum-

---

31. See L. Fassò's review of A. Salaroli, "Carlo Varese, il vessilifero del romanzo storico e degli scottiani in Italia," *Giornale Storico della Letteratura Italiana* 96 (1930): 277–304 and specifically the notes to 283–284.

32. C. Varese, *Sibilla Odaleta* (Florence: Veroli, 1831), vol. 1: 23. All further references to the work are incorporated in the text with the indication *SO* followed by the volume and page number.

ably, bled to death by the Jew in order to obtain rejuvenating blood for one of his patients. But this sort of behavior is to be expected from those

damned by heaven, [from] the wicked and cowardly race who betrayed Jesus Christ . . . and who with unmatched cruelty sold the blood of life to the weak for its weight in coin, that silver which is no match in hardness for a Jew's heart. (*SO*, I, 74)

Malvezzi is not only identified with the devil, "damned by Heaven," "a minister of Hell" who reeks of sulphurous fumes (*SO*, I, 68), he is also branded a dealer in human lives who drips the blood vital to Italy's defense against foreign invaders. The destiny of the tribe of Judas is to prey upon the innocent. Varese's Jews harbor no hope of salvation; rather, their dark history will repeat itself throughout the centuries.

Such formulae—"Jew = dealer in human blood" and "Jew = unredeemable villain"—promoted and gave substance to stereotypical certainties lying dormant in the still pond of preconceptions, feelings shared by a large number of readers and, therefore, emphasized in popular fiction. Thus Abele Malvezzi is not portrayed as just any scoundrel, but as *the Jew* and therefore deserving of enduring vengeance.

Accordingly, the mother makes her solemn promise of vendetta:

He has eluded me for eleven years and with a thousand subterfuges, but his destiny is catching up with him . . . every day he comes closer to me, drawn inexorably by fate from which none may escape . . . he wanders the length of Italy changing his dress and altering his appearance along the way lest he be recognized. But in vain! He shan't escape me . . . Yes, we will avenge his insult to humanity. (*SO*, I, 67–75)

In the tradition of the man-of-a-thousand-faces, the Jew is forced by circumstance to disguise his identity, altering both appearance and clothing as he escapes, presumably from the scene of a crime. He is condemned to wander among strangers to avoid recognition. To a provincial people deeply conscious of its origins, rootlessness was threatening and looked upon with suspicion. Thus it is not surprising that wandering figures prominently in folk tradition and literature as a punishment for sin, particularly that of blasphemy.[33] As was the case with Bresciani's

33. On this folk tradition, see particularly Jerszy Kosinski's novel, *The Painted Bird* (Boston: Houghton, Mifflin, 1965). It is significant that the Jews and Gypsies are the wanderers of Europe and share a similar folk image. In Kosinski's tale one never learns whether the protagonist is a Jew or a Gypsy; the popular stereotypes are much the same. See S. Thompson, *Motif-Index of Folk Literature* (Bloomington: Indiana University Press, 1957).

construction of his protagonist, these passages in *Sibilla Odaleta* are oblique references to the Wandering Jew who, if he does not always alter his appearance and clothing, at least adapts his language and behavior in order to blend in with the people he encounters in his ceaseless travel. Yet no matter how he might try to imitate the local inhabitants or how well he might thrive, weed-like, in each alien environment, it is God's will that he must remain separate and, sooner or later, be unmasked as the Jew, agent of the devil, infiltrator corrupting the purity of the community. Then he will have to resume his restless peregrinations.

National identity in the Romantic age was also bound up with religious values. But, predictably, Varese suggests that there is nothing stable in the Jewish character, even though the purity of the faith had always been thought to be a source of pride among its practitioners. Those who equate Jews with pure faith are mistaken, for Jewish identity is anything but spiritual. On learning that Malvezzi has attended Christian, Orthodox, and Jewish worship, Sibilla asks him about his religion. He carefully evades the question, answering that

they were all branches of the same tree, and that to worship God in the form of a Prophet, the Messiah, the Savior, the Golden Calf, an onion, and so on was all one and the same. (*SO*, I, 115–116)

This reference to the many forms of worship is an adaptation of the familiar *Parable of the Three Rings,* a story likely to be known to many if not all of Varese's readers.[34] Just as Varese utilizes history to lend substance to his anti-Jewish arguments, so he adapts captivating stories from literary classics to lend credibility to the lesson he wishes to impart. But whereas the familiar story was used by Lessing and others to foster tolerance, in Varese the story was reworked to evoke the opposite

---

34. Varese's version is closest to that of Lessing's *Nathan the Wise*:
Well then, whose faith are we least like
To doubt? Our people's, surely? Those whose blood
We share? . . .
If each one from his father has his ring,
Then let each one believe his ring to be
The true one.—Possibly, the father wished
To tolerate no longer in his house
The tyranny of just one ring!

J. E. Lessing, *Nathan the Wise,* translated by B. Q. Morgan (New York: Ungar, 1955), Act III, Sc. 7, pp. 78–79.

response. The Jew standing by ready to deride Christians in their religious practices is a stock figure in literary tradition.[35] Varese carries the image one step further: the prideful Jew mocks all religion, even his own. Malvezzi's response to Sibilla's question begins well enough as he declares that all religions are "branches of the same tree." But in the mouth of this Jew, who "abuses" the Old Testament in word and deed, the discourse deteriorates rapidly. In defiance of the Commandments, he goes on to compare worship of God to that of the Golden Calf, so inimical to Malvezzi's own Judaism, or "to an onion or anything at all."

Were Malvezzi to be magnified and projected onto the code of values that, in a sense, defined the national self-image, it would be immediately apparent how, by denigrating his birthright, this Jewish figure is destined to remain at odds with his surroundings. As Italy gained self-identity in Varese's proto-Risorgimental period, it was thought that religion and above all Catholicism would give Italy the strength to free herself and unite.[36] But Abele Malvezzi's presence in this historical novel symbolizes the alien lurking in the midst of a group of gallant patriots and subverting their efforts to defend their way of life. His scorn erodes native religion, the very root that nourishes the struggling country.

Varese reveals Malvezzi's "true Jewish" identity to his readers bit by bit by means of a series of stereotypical devices. So strong is Malvezzi's cupidity, for example, that the doctor cherishes the unshakable conviction that in gold is the ultimate salvation of mankind; it is to contemporary man like the pillar of fire that guided the Israelites across the desert. Gold signifies food, shelter, love, and God: a golden manna, life itself, a reason to live. A general acceptance by the mass of readers of the notion of Jewish avarice seems to underlie both the certainty that "a Jew's heart is smaller than a sparrow's" (*SO*, I, 254), and the metaphor of money as a bulwark against imminent calamity: "The waves

---

35. Beatrice's admonition in the *Divine Comedy* figures early in the tradition:

Be ye then, Christians, slower to be moved,
Not like a feather stirred by every breeze,
And think not every water serves to wash you. . . .
Should wicked avarice suggest aught else,
The Jew among you may not laugh at you; . . .
(*Paradise*, V. 73–81)

D. Alighieri, *The Divine Comedy*, trans. T. G. Bergin (New York: Grossman, 1969).

36. See A. C. Jemolo, "I cattolici e il Risorgimento," in Istituto Luigi Sturzo, Roma, *I cattolici e il Risorgimento* (Rome: Editrice "Studium," 1963), 25–34.

of the Red Sea are banked and ready to break over our heads" (*SO*, II, 136). Greed then is only a natural result of a Jew's conditioning, given

the inborn cowardice of the proscribed race of Israel, [a state of mind] exaggerated by that fear which always magnified the real dangers and created imaginary ones. (*SO*, I, 121)

Upon learning of the arrival of Charles VIII, therefore, Malvezzi fears for his possessions: his money and Sibilla whom he values at ten thousand ducats, the cost of her education.

Sibilla has had the education of a princess: languages, music, dancing, and singing—all in order to increase her commercial value when Malvezzi decides to sell her. By constructing this cultural slur as a shocking "revelation," Varese delivers the reader into the heart of the "tribe of Judas": should a Jew decide to spend money on others, he is not motivated by altruism but only by dreams of profit. This stereotype, though ancient in origin, was perennially reinforced by the presence of the ghetto. It was commonly imagined that vast Jewish fortunes normally remained behind the locked gates of the ghetto, since in their holy literature Jews were instructed to employ their resources for the exclusive benefit of other Jews.

In his insistence throughout *Sibilla Odaleta* on the Jews' attachment to their money, Varese was really saying that Jewish money was wealth that would not circulate to aid in the creation of the new Italy. And this, in turn, reinforced the belief that Jews felt no patriotic commitment to the Risorgimento. Rather, they had a natural aversion to dealing with non-Jews, which meant that they preferred to reside in their own enclaves as "foreigners." Varese expands on this theory, illustrating it with an absurd but telling episode in the third volume when Malvezzi, imprisoned in a tower from which there is only one escape route, notices among the graffiti scrawled on the cell wall a message that provides detailed escape directions in Hebrew!

The existence of a ritual language, which was incomprehensible to most people, added ballast to this record of Jewish misdoings, as if the language itself were a partner in crime. Hebrew was imagined to be a language with practical applications that went beyond religion. It was the antipatriotic tongue of the nation-within-the-nation, part of its dark history. Arcane and exotic, Hebrew was one of the shared secrets among Jews and exemplified the dark magic hidden behind ghetto walls.

Identification of the Jew throughout history with various types of magic is well documented. This includes medicine, for centuries little removed from sorcery in popular representation. Jews had always been physicians in the highest circles;[37] indeed, the period described in *Sibilla Odaleta* was a so-called golden age for Jewish doctors. From the thirteenth century on, Italian medical schools were often the only institutions open to Jews and accepted students from all parts of Europe. During this epoch, popes, cardinals, and nobles preferred Jews as their physicians.[38] Malvezzi is no exception; he is the personal doctor to Ludovico Trivulzio. However, the prestige of Jewish doctors led to a superstitious belief in the "magical arts" of the Jews and developed into fear. Accordingly, Trivulzio begins to distrust the "costly medicines made of pulverized pearls, finest Venetian gold and certain herbs found only on Mount Sinai" (*SO*, I, 113). In a system of fictional logic such as Varese establishes in *Sibilla Odaleta*, only a rich, Jewish doctor would have access to medicines compounded of gold and pearls.[39]

But the most sensational of these traditional accusations against the Jews was the ritual murder libel. Its shock value made it useful material for the novel and the efficiency with which it recalled the age-old stigma, so central to the stereotypical image of the Jew in Europe, made it especially suitable for popular literature. In *Sibilla Odaleta* the blood libel is established early in the first volume, in order to set the pattern for the rejection of Abele Malvezzi. To Varese's credit as a novelist, it is developed in an original way:

A Jew, a scoundrel of a Jew, a minister of Hell, had conceived the insane project to rejuvenate the bodies of the sick by transfusing the blood of strong youths into their feeble veins. So he searched the beaches of the islands of the Archipelago and grabbed any youth whom fate had carried to these shores. Then with unmatched cruelty he sold their blood to the weak for its weight in coin, that metal which is no match in hardness for a Jew's heart. I found out that that abominable [Jew] took my Sibilla to Rome and cruelly murdered her in order to transfuse her blood into the veins of a powerful Greek. (*SO*, I, 74–75)

37. In the Middle Ages Jews held the posts of court physician in both the Moslem and Byzantine courts as well as in Europe. See S. D. Goitein, *Jews and Arabs* (New York: Schocken, 1955).

38. Bonet de Lattes attended both Alexander IV and Leo V. Saladino Ferro d'Ascoli was the greatest pharmacist of his time, and his treatise on pharmacology, one of the many works on medicine printed in Italy in the fifteenth century, remained the basic text until the eighteenth century.

39. In 1581 Pope Gregory XIII forbade Jewish doctors to treat Christian patients and from that time on, only other Jews could take advantage of their coreligionists' medical skills. Special dispensations, however, were granted when popes and cardinals fell ill.

As a Jewish doctor, Malvezzi preyed upon the unfortunate and impoverished, upon defenseless children as well as the bedridden elderly. According to Varese, himself a doctor turned politician, transfusion was an "atrocious means" to prolong life, practiced by "fanatical and ignorant men" and, therefore, a "barbarous stupidity" that violates the norms of common sense, humanity, and religion.[40]

Although it was common for authors who were also doctors to write fiction that hinged on the difficult moral choices their doctor-protagonists had to make, in Abele Malvezzi Varese created a villain whose immorality was assured from the outset. As a physician, Malvezzi is adventurous and imaginative but unorthodox, more a bird of prey than an agent of mercy. In Varese's conservative system, the doctor must curb his desire to save life by any means he can concoct; above all, he must not try to do God's work. But Malvezzi the Jew need not concern himself with the religious implications of his work since he is not subject to the laws of the true God. Malvezzi's God however, allows him not only to attempt to defy death through medicine, but also to take young lives. All of this requires a heart of stone and Varese handily proves this assertion by calling on the biblical example of Abraham's dry-eyed sacrifice of Isaac and stopping his description just short of the Angel's intervention so that the incident stands for the origin of the Jews' thirst for blood.

Varese's use of the familiar Bible story was a common rhetorical technique. A biblical reference, like a historical incident, captures the popular imagination, which reworks it. The event reemerges in folklore, that is in proverbs, cautionary tales, and the like. Even if one may doubt its veracity, nevertheless it becomes entrenched in the unconscious, the repertory of experience. Since much folklore aims at the resolution of universal human problems, the tale may be recalled in case of confrontation with a situation that requires interpretation or action, much in the manner of proverbs. The successful propagandist for the status quo does well to draw from folk stereotypes particularly in an epoch of limited education and social mobility.

If history inspired the patriotic concept of *Sibilla Odaleta*, folktales

40. In his biography of Pope Innocent VIII, Francesco Serdonati recounts that the Pope refused such attempts at rejuvenation: "While he was sick, a Jewish physician offered him the blood of children as a remedy and promised the Pope that it would do him a lot of good. Not only was [this remedy] not accepted, but the Pope even refused it violently saying that he was willing to entrust his life and death only to God." See F. Serdonati, *Vita e fatti d'Innocenzo VIII Papa CCXVI* (Milan: V. Ferrario, 1829), chap. 101: 94–95.

provided Varese with a ready-made plot structure as well as yet another character element for his villain. In addition the familiarity of the tales he imitated (consciously or unconsciously) had the persuasive power of stereotype. Early in volume 1 of the novel, Sibilla's mother recounts the kidnapping of her daughter eleven years earlier as if she were re-telling a folktale, using animal characters instead of people:

There were two roe-bucks playing in a field: hiding behind a thicket a wolf waited until they left their mother's side and stealthily came up behind them. He tried to steal them both, but chance helped the younger one to avoid his claws. The other, though the stronger of the two, was solidly in his clutches and was dragged between the rocks and lost along with the monster, its abduc-tor. (*SO*, I, 66–67)

There is nothing specific in this passage which directly equates the character of the wolf with the Jew, Abele Malvezzi. Instead the animal is presented as a loathsome kidnapper, instantly repellent to the reader. The connection is made when Malvezzi is introduced and Varese ex-plains that the kidnapper is the Jew.

The common folk image of the Jew is that he is dark and hairy, so when Varese characterized the Jew as a wolf who steals young girls, the popular imagination may have recalled the fairy tale, *Little Red Rid-ing Hood*, one of the best-known and most forceful of all the fairy tales. According to Bruno Bettelheim[41] it was safe to assume that much of the public had "encountered" the wolf during childhood, first in the story and then repeatedly in dreams as the embodiment of normal fears associated with the maturation process. Although the wolf is a character in a fairy tale, both his significance and the challenges he represents re-main in one's subconscious, or as Bettelheim put it: "A charming, 'in-nocent' young girl swallowed by a wolf is an image which impresses itself indelibly on the mind."[42]

The plot of *Sibilla Odaleta* follows the fairy-tale format quite closely. Red Riding Hood's wolf is clever and instead of eating the girl in the forest, he awaits a more opportune moment; Malvezzi, screened by the shrubbery, waits until Sibilla has strayed from the right path and left the protection of her mother. The wolf follows Red Riding Hood to a remote spot (Grandmother's house) where an implied seduction of the young girl takes place, after which she is "eaten up"; Malvezzi drags

41. B. Bettelheim, *The Uses of Enchantment: The Meaning and Importance of Fairy Tales* (New York: Knopf, 1976), 166–183.
42. Ibid., 166.

Sibilla beyond the rocks to Naples where he lives with her for eleven years, preparing her for sale. Seduction is not mentioned in the novel, but the possibility cannot be dismissed since a taboo has been broken in that Sibilla is living with a man who is neither her husband nor a kinsman.

By not stating what actually occurs between Malvezzi and Sibilla, Varese allows the reader to imagine the worst after the violation of a strict taboo. The closest the author comes to an allegation is to say of the roe-buck (the animal symbol for Sibilla) that "it *was lost* with the monster, its abductor" ("e *si perdè* col mostro che lo avea involato"). This is a play on words: she was either physically or morally lost, or both. "To be lost" ("*perdersi*") was a common way to express a woman's allowing sex before marriage in nineteenth-century popular literature. In the popular novel, however, it was assumed that despite compelling pressures and overwhelming temptations the Christian heroine would remain pure. In *Sibilla Odaleta,* which focuses almost entirely upon evil, the purity of the beautiful but passive heroine is convincing only insofar as we imagine that Malvezzi considers her merchandise whose commercial value would decrease were he to give in to his natural instincts.

Sibilla's mother promises that though Malvezzi has eluded her for eleven years, she "follows him like the hound chases the hare [undaunted by] the most secret paths through the thick forest." Indeed she is drawing closer day by day and all the disguises in the world cannot save him, for she can always recognize him (*SO*, I, 68). The wolf changes his persona with ease: in the fairy tale he gains access to Grandmother's house by pretending to be Red Riding Hood and then overcomes the girl by dressing in Grandmother's clothing. He succeeds in his disguise for a time, but at last he is unmasked by the forces of Right. Malvezzi, as *the* Jew, also masquerades and with the same result: "He changes his dress and alters his appearance in vain: I have always recognized him."

The young roe-buck, who escaped the wolf's clutches and remained by the side of his good mother, is metamorphosing into a robust lion who will soon be able to vindicate his kidnapped sister and stricken mother. He is the huntsman, who, in the fairy tale, liberates Red Riding Hood and her Grandmother from the belly of the wolf, replacing them with stones and causing the death of the evil-doer. The hunter is a father figure. In *Sibilla Odaleta* three characters assume this role. Sibilla's brother makes contact with Prince Frederick of Aragon, who vows to help the widowed mother recover her daughter, and with Ludovico Trivulzio, who adds a military dimension to the character of the huntsman/father.

In Varese's fable as in the fairy tale itself, the male figures are polarized into good and evil counterparts: the dangerous seducer and destroyer of innocence, that is, the Jew who preys upon others, versus the father figure, righteous hunter, savior, and Christian. The mother in the fairy tale is experienced and knows that her adolescent daughter is not yet ready for sex as an adult and so warns her not to stray from the path. Sibilla's mother is equally prescient and, aided by an arcane map and a black wand, she uses her gifts to plot the wolf's demise. She hunts the wolf almost to the end and then leaves it to the men to do battle with him.

Sibilla, who one assumes was a normal pubescent child frolicking with her brother in the field before her abduction, faithfully mirrors Red Riding Hood up until the moment of the redemption. Whereas the fairy-tale heroine does her share of luring the wolf and Sibilla is too small to resist her kidnapper effectively, both are reduced to helplessness through their encounters with their abductors. Little Red Riding Hood allows herself to be eaten up by him and Sibilla allows her identity to be destroyed. She is renamed Lucilla and wrenched from the religion into which she was born. Although unable to warm to this "father" who disgusts her, she can muster no defense against him and so remains at Malvezzi's side for eleven years:

Inwardly repelled by Old Malvezzi her lips could not pronounce the word "father." She knew him [for what he was]: a consummate criminal, in spite of his attempts to feign an upstanding nature in her presence. Try as he might, he could not conceal his overwhelming passion for gold along with his conviction that any means of procuring it was quite acceptable. Lucilla, who was generous yet faint of heart, blushed every time he mentioned his wealth or his plans for making [more] money. (*SO*, I, 114–115)

As Little Red Riding Hood is trapped in the wolf's belly, Sibilla patiently awaits liberation from the invisible fetters that bind her to her abductor. After Red Riding Hood is freed from the wolf, she is transformed from an immature child into a more knowledgeable adolescent. But Sibilla, despite being abducted, renamed Lucilla, liberated, and finally united with her handsome and virtuous marquis while war and vendetta rage around her, remains tranquil and passive, neither enlightened nor diminished by her adventures. Her passage to a higher plane of existence—the obligatory denouement of the fairy tale—will come about by virtue of her husband's accomplishments. In many ways a conventional female protagonist, Sibilla is not a heroine and as one reads on, it becomes apparent that, in one sense, the novel named for her was a pretext to concoct a tale about "the wolf," a nasty old Jew who carries off a budding young maiden.

Malvezzi is the most interesting character by far. He is the only one that is clearly delineated and whose actions seem the most decisive and meaningful. Why is this, when we know that the wolf/villain is defeated in the end? Malvezzi's portrayal has benefited more than any other character's from the fairy-tale quality of *Sibilla Odaleta*. This is because fairy tales present existential problems—in this case the confrontation with evil—in a direct manner with no superfluous details to cloud the image:

The figures in fairy tales are not ambivalent—not good and bad at the same time as we are in reality. But since polarization dominates the child's mind, it also dominates fairy tales. A person is either good or bad, nothing in between.[43]

Thus, in a novel in which all the "good" characters stand out in only hazy relief from their background of conventional virtue, the reader is directed to focus his attentions upon the "bad" one.

Malvezzi is an egotist, schemer, gold-worshipper, kidnapper, murderer, man-of-a-thousand-faces (none of them honest), the incarnation of evil, "the fiendish Jew" (*SO*, I, 69): a character constructed from a blueprint of commonplaces, whose malevolence compels and fascinates us. In human nature there is an innate attraction to the "wolf" and this is the source of his power over us. Bettelheim concurs, stating that the wolf represents unacceptable tendencies within the hunter:

We all refer on occasion to the animal within us, as a simile for our propensity for acting violently or irresponsibly to attain our goals.[44]

Children are often taught that people are *either* good *or* evil and are not exposed to the duality of good and evil within the single balanced individual, to the fact that a "good" person can anger, be selfish and asocial. The child who recognizes these negative tendencies may seek to shift the burden of evil to a surrogate who then becomes a scapegoat.

43. Ibid., 9.
44. Ibid., 177–178.

In *Sibilla Odaleta,* the wolf, the Jew Malvezzi, is the scapegoat for the hunters, the Christians Don Federico and Ludovico Trivulzio. Malvezzi is cowardly, fearful of the French troops. In opposition to the noble and heroic sentiments expected of a "good" man in a historical novel, his is the "inborn cowardice of the proscribed race of Israel [a state of mind] exaggerated by that fear which always accompanies a guilty conscience" (*SO,* I, 121). The heroes may know only an occasional moment of weakness, but it is certain that the scapegoat can never be strong, despite his attempts to appear brave and resolute:

A Jew cannot bear the presence of a character whose daily habits are the opposite of his own. Similarly his base timidity and greed always come out regardless of the purple robes he likes to wear [to disguise them]. Just like the cat in the old story, who, though transformed into a beautiful maiden, couldn't help pouncing on mice whenever she saw them. (*SO,* III, 401)

Here Varese seals the fate of his scapegoat, declaring him unredeemable. From the particular transgressions of a single villain, the reader is induced to imagine his guilt as metonymically applicable to the whole social, ethnic, or religious group that that character represents. Without ever having to expose himself in a blanket credo, Varese has created a fictional situation in which Jews have extraordinary powers over "normal," ordinary, and familiar people. Thus the author's words transcend their outward function as fiction and become a warning.

To the adult mind, the logic of the fairy tale represents various unassailable truths: the certainties of childhood, or as the poet Schiller argued (somewhat romantically): "Deeper meaning resides in fairy tales told to me in my childhood than in the truth taught by life."[45] One cannot assume that Varese's novel was an attempt to reproduce these "certainties of childhood" as a deliberate anti-Jewish polemic, though at the same time one cannot exclude this intention altogether. It is more likely, however, that Varese recognized that such a Jewish character as Abele Malvezzi was an ingenious fictional device, incorporating as it did the fears of the strange, the magical, the politically subversive along with the ethnic prejudices of his readers as well as the possibility to adapt—albeit unconsciously—the familiar structure of the fairy tale. Whatever his motives, Varese's rendering of the alien, anti-patriotic Jewish abductor/doctor derived considerable persuasive power

45. F. Schiller, *The Piccolomini,* Act III, Sc. 4, cited in Bettelheim, *Uses of Enchantment,* 5.

from the added dimension of the fairy-tale wolf with all that it implied as an archetype of evil.[46]

Mysteries of the Ghetto

The decline in popularity of the historical novel left a gap that was soon filled by the *romanzo d' appendice* (serialized popular novel or the bound novel that imitated serialized novels in content). In the period immediately following the Risorgimento, the aspirations and fears expressed in serial novels were basically those of the preceding decades: on the one hand, xenophobia and apprehension at the imagined breakdown of a homogeneous society, and on the other, the liberal vision of a population in which religious differences would cease to be employed as barriers to real national unity. As one would expect, the former type was far more prevalent than the latter. Several such works had Jewish characters or attempted to describe contemporary Jewish life. Among these were the usurer, Jacob Abraham, in Agostino della Sala Spada's *La vita: romanzo storico sociale* (*Life: A Socio-Historical Novel*) (1872) and the Jewish jeweler, Casnelli, who fences stolen property in Cleto Arrighi's *La Canaglia felice* (*Happy Crooks*) (1885). Only Luigi Onetti's *Madama Reale, ovvero il Bastardo e l' Ebrea* (*Madame Royale, or the Bastard and the Jew*) (1870) presents Jews as undeserving victims of tyranny and bigotry. Yet, even here, the ghetto beauty Deborah is not allowed to win out in the end; in order to disarm her rival for the handsome Giorgio, Madama Reale has her kidnapped, causing her death.[47]

By virtue of the ideas that both unsophisticated and educated readers

46. Guerrazzi reports that the figure of Malvezzi was so disturbing that a group of Livornese Jews demanded that it be changed in subsequent editions. He does not indicate how the protest was made or to whom, but that it extended to the portrayal of Jewish merchants in Rossini's *Gazza Ladra* and to Isaac of York in Scott's *Ivanhoe*. Guerrazzi uses the Jews' reaction to seeing themselves reproduced in literature as part of his anti-Jewish polemic, giving as the cause of their dismay the fact that "[The Jews] have yet to give up their [bad] habits" (*Note autobiografiche*, 83–84).

47. Many popular novels involving Jews are by anonymous or forgotten writers, novels such as *Figlia d'Israele*, which was serialized in *La voce della verità* (Rome) beginning on 2 December 1886 and *La bella israelita* serialized in the *Gazzetta di Torino* beginning on 7 March 1907. Others include Curzio Sparta, *La schiava ebrea. Scene di Roma antica* (Rome, 1875), *La falsa mendicante,* and Vittorio Del Mare, *I nuovi ebrei,* (n.d.). For a listing of several such works, see G. Romano, *Ebrei nella letteratura* (Rome: Carucci, 1979).

had about them, Jews combined in their persons and their environment several important components of the romanzo d' appendice and were ideal characters for popular literature. The novelist created a vivid background of aspects of Jewish life either actually observed or invented. It was then populated by heroes and villains whose exaggerated ethnic characteristics made them larger than life in the popular imagination.

This effect on the imagination is a key element in the success of the popular novel:

The *romanzo d'appendice* both promotes and takes the place of daydreaming in the common man. Indeed it is exactly like dreaming with one's eyes open. . . . In this case one can say that among [common] people daydreaming derives from a (social) "inferiority complex" which resolves itself in lengthy fantasies of revenge, of punishment against those responsible for the wrongs they have suffered . . . [as] a narcotic which deadens the pain.[48]

Readers expected the romanzo d'appendice to have a gripping plot made up of a certain number of shocking episodes of horror and danger, and generally they were not disappointed. They became emotionally involved, the compelling descriptions of the text lending the illusion of actual participation, while they were protected within the walls of their own homes or the site of the public reading. Their enjoyment was derived in part from the security of being able to observe the invented torments of fictional characters as if at the theatre because, as Freud noted, someone else was doing the suffering. This provided the reader (or listener) with a welcome emotional outlet:

In these circumstances nothing stands in the way of the joy of feeling superior. Nothing prohibits us from abandoning ourselves to those emotions which we have [consistently] repressed, such as the need for religious or political, social or sexual freedom. Nothing keeps us from venting these passions in every direction [according to] whatever grandiose scene—which makes up life as it is represented there—is being played out at the moment.[49]

One could therefore pretend to exchange one's conventional world for a more romantic one filled with horrors and pleasures to be explored at one's leisure and in perfect safety.

From the eighteenth-century esthetic of the "beautifully horrible,"

48. A. Gramsci, *Quaderni* notebook 8, reprinted in *Letteratura e vita nazionale* (Turin: Einaudi, 1972), 108.

49. S. Freud, *Psychopathische Personen auf der Bühne*, cited in E. Ghidetti, "Un aspetto della letteratura popolare in Toscana: I misteri," in AA. VV., *Editori a Firenze nel secondo Ottocento* (Florence: Olschki, 1983), 347n.

the popular novel underwent a series of subtle changes, finally developing into the "horribly beautiful,"[50] all the while dosing each volume
with the required scenes of physical and mental anguish. Sadism was a
frequent ingredient of that amalgam of thrills which made this fictional
genre particularly seductive.[51] Long a subject for philosophical discussion, the "sublimity of terror"[52] destined sadism for enduring popularity as a literary motif. The allure of pain and pleasure was described as
"an ineluctable force which swept the unblinking esthete to perilous
heights of sensual experience."[53] Novelists had to construct acceptable
frameworks of plot and setting for their tales-of-terror with locales that
were consonant with the torments described. These stories usually involved at least one sadistic character who asked nothing more than to
be able to inflict or observe the pain of other, preferably innocent,
characters. Sometimes they would have to travel to satisfy their desires:
the *voyeur* became *voyageur*:

I was anxious to see sufferings worse than my own and my curiosity was nearly
insatiable. I've heard of men who undertook long voyages to countries where
one could enjoy the daily spectacle of horrible tortures.[54]

But nineteenth-century Italian popular writers did not need to travel
great distances for inspiration since each major Northern and Central
Italian city and many smaller ones had a Jewish ghetto. The formula
for literary success demanded an exotic site with ample opportunity for
the perpetration of monstrous misdeeds and sufferings from which the
reader could rejoice in the ultimate deliverance of the virtuous. The
ghetto offered this and more. The reality of daily life in the ghetto, so
often sordid and harsh, was, therefore, easily transformed into a novel-

50. M. Praz, *La carne, la morte e il diavolo nella letteratura romantica*, 3d ed. (Florence: Sansoni, 1948), 29.

51. There is a full discussion of this aspect of Romanticism in M. Praz, *Carne, morte,
diavolo*. This fundamental text was translated into English as *The Romantic Agony* (London: Oxford University Press, 1951).

52. E. Burke, *Philosophical Enquiry into the Origin of Our Ideas of the Sublime and the
Beautiful* (1756), cited in M. Praz, *Carne, morte, diavolo*, 22.

53. "Where pure grace ends, the awe of the sublime begins, composed of the influence of pain, of pleasure, of grace, and deformity, playing into each other, that the mind
is unable to determine which to call it, pain or pleasure, or terror: the pinnacle of
beatitude, bordering upon horror, deformity, madness; an eminence from whence the
mind that dares to look further is lost." Anonymous, *Enquiry Concerning the Principles of
Taste* (1785), cited in M. Praz, *La letteratura inglese dai romantici al Novecento* (Florence:
Sansoni, 1968), vol. 2: 11–12.

54. C. R. Maturin, *Melmoth, the Wanderer*, in A. Bianchini, *Il romanzo d'appendice*
(Turin: Edizioni RAI, 1969), 41.

istic fantasy world of brutal murders, sadistic punishments, unlimited power over cowering victims.

Since such atrocities were unthinkable in one's own realistic surroundings, readers had to make a mental leap to isolate this ghetto world, as if dividing humanity into *li du' ggener' umani*, "we" and "they." Having done this, questions of actual proximity became irrelevant; indeed, the idea of such a place was even more stimulating if it was right next door: very near yet very far. If the Jews were foreigners—"In the Ghetto one could hear any number of languages"[55]— their neighborhood was alien, part of the city yet forbidding.

A realistic setting for fictionalized terror was close by in every city and town that had a ghetto. One could have concrete visual confirmation of its poverty, its noisome atmosphere, its dark, fetid alleyways, its dank, subterranean chambers:

He soon felt underfoot the first steps of a dark staircase which seemed to lead right into the bowels of the earth. The crumbling of the steps bespoke their antiquity and the sticky, blackish slime which covered them clung to the soles of his shoes. Two or three times he felt soft, clammy things slink by his feet and he could hear dull sounds of chewing . . . The heavy, gloomy silence was broken only by the scurrying moles and the water which dripped slowly at long intervals from the ceiling . . . Suddenly the beggar thought he saw a human figure creeping along the far wall. (*OG*, I, 64–65)

The novelist had only to fill it with characters and plot their movements to bring it to life. With such a rich humus for fiction so close at hand, it is no wonder that popular novelists frequently chose the ghetto as a site for their stories.

The horrors of ghetto life—both real and imagined—found expression in the very popular *mistero* (mystery), a genre inspired chiefly by Eugène Sue's *The Wandering Jew* and *The Mysteries of Paris*. The mistero was in many ways an exposé through which the author sought to draw attention to social conditions, often with the declared purpose of reforming society by righting age-old wrongs. The second half of the nineteenth century in Tuscany[56] saw three works of this kind which focused on the ghetto. Two of these were misteri: C. Monteverde, *I misteri di Livorno* (*The Mysteries of Livorno*) (1853) and E. Maccanti, *I*

55. C. Invernizio, *L'Orfana del Ghetto* (Milan: Lucchi, 1975), vol. 1: 20. All further citations are from this edition and will be incorporated in the text with the indication *OG*, the volume number and page number.

56. With regard to this aspect of Tuscan literature after 1850, see E. Ghidetti, "I misteri," 341–365.

misteri di Firenze (*The Mysteries of Florence*) (1884); and one was a journalistic pamphlet on the model of the *mistero*, Jarro's *Firenze sotterranea* (*Underground Florence*) (1884).

Monteverde defined the inhabitants of Livorno's Jewish section "poor and revolting rabble"[57] whereas Maccanti concentrated on the effects of the wretched living conditions in the Florentine ghetto. In what he called a "romantic and only semi-serious work" Maccanti expressed genuine concern for those "decent people" who "have a right to call themselves human beings," but are obliged by their poverty to live in the worst of slums. Here, he said, they risk their health in daily contact with filth, dampness, open sewers, and crowds of their neighbors. Maccanti added weight to his already vivid and precise description with a firsthand report of a visit to the ghetto. Because of inadequate light provided by small courtyards and the miasmic air, he saw many people with diseased eyes. His was an undisguised appeal to the municipal authorities that they care for people at least as well as they cared for animals. And lest those same authorities protest that the ghetto dwellers, many of them Jews, should look to their own resources, Maccanti prefaced this section of his *Misteri* with a brief history of the Jews in Florence, ending with the conviction that their contact with Christian society had "civilized them and rendered them extremely moral."[58]

The crusading nature of Maccanti's novel was echoed by Jarro (Giulio Piccini) in his pamphlet *Firenze sotterranea*. By vocation a novelist, Jarro undertook to reveal the moral and physical decay of Florentine slums to the bourgeois readers of the newspaper *La Nazione* (*The Nation*). In Jarro the descriptive powers of the novelist struck a successful balance with the urgency of the investigative reporter. He repeated one point with particular insistence, that is, that though the Jews had always been associated with the ghetto, they should not be considered part of the underworld of thieves and prostitutes. Quite the contrary: the "intelligent, industrious"[59] Jews, "a people of truly splendid qualities," lived there not by choice because it facilitated a life of crime, but instead as a result of segregation, "the most wicked outrage."[60] In spite of scarce means, the Jews had founded houses of worship and study,

57. C. Monteverde, *I misteri di Livorno, romanzo originale dell'avvocato C[esare] M[onteverde] autore dei romanzi* Astorre Manfredi *e* Il duca d'Atene (Volterra: Sborgi, 1853), vol. 1: 16.

58. E. Maccanti, *I misteri di Firenze* (Florence: Salani, 1884), i, 25–27.

59. Jarro (G. Piccini), *Firenze sotterranea* (Florence: Le Monnier, 1885), iv.

60. Ibid., 34.

even a library, cultural institutions that, after the Emancipation, disappeared from the ghetto. With the flight of all but the poorest Jewish families, the ghetto became a "sewer flowing with torrents of vice."[61]

Taking his cue from both the mistero and the tales-of-terror, Ausonio Liberi (pseudonym of G. A. Giustina) set out to expose the ghetto as a social phenomenon, defining it not so much in terms of its appearance as by its effect on the people who lived there. The result was the serial novel *Il Ghetto* (*The Ghetto*) (1881).[62] Calling his novel "socio-historical," he set the story in the Turin of the post-Napoleonic restoration of 1814 and peppered it with quasi-historical figures such as a police commissioner who was the father of Cavour. All of this was little more than window dressing, however, for Liberi's work was really a response to a contemporary problem: the rapid assimilation of Jews into the mainstream of Turin society, to the implied deterioration of the latter.

Up until Unification, Turin had had a fairly homogeneous population, but in the twenty years between its designation as the Italian capital and the appearance of Liberi's novel, the city experienced massive immigration, especially from the South, which altered the nature of the population forever.[63] But the first "alien" group to intermingle with that provincial population, following their emancipation in 1848, were the Jews: a people with a recognizable jargon all their own and with parochial customs that had been consolidated through centuries of ghetto life.[64]

In revealing all the secrets of Jewish life, *Il Ghetto* poses and attempts to answer two rhetorical questions: how can the Jews possibly participate in the values of the dominant majority? and more important still, knowing what all educated Christians know about Jews, would anyone really want them to assimilate? Liberi aims his queries squarely at the Christian reader while at the same time challenging the Jews who were intent on rapid assimilation.[65]

61. Ibid. For an excellent description of the Florentine ghetto and its history, complete with photographs, see also G. Fanelli, *Firenze: Architettura e città* (Florence: Vallecchi, 1973), vol. 2, *Atlante,* 284; G. Conti, *Firenze vecchia. Storia, Cronaca aneddotica, costumi* (1799–1859) (Florence: Bemporad, 1900), 429–435.

62. *Il Ghetto* first appeared in thirty-two installments in the *Romanziere popolare* (Turin: 1880–1881). I am grateful to Andrew M. Canepa for bringing it to my attention.

63. "Torino," *Enciclopedia Italiana* (Rome: Treccani, 1949), vol. 34: 31.

64. For a lively account of the end of ghetto life in Piedmont and the process of assimilation, see G. Artom's family history *I giorni del mondo* (Milan: Longanesi, 1981).

65. On emancipation and assimilation, see A. M. Canepa, "Emancipation and Jewish Response in Mid-Nineteenth-Century Italy," *European History Quarterly* 16 (1986): 403–439.

By way of introduction to the problem, Liberi describes the Jew in his natural ghetto environment which, better than any other, reveals his true nature.

The Jew is a saint within the embrace of his family, but we will observe how contemptible he is in his shop, how greedy and heartless. We'll determine the reason for this and examine its origins. It is probably not entirely his fault. He was a slave and powerless against his oppressors. He was allowed no other activity save for usury. [Once] emancipated and free to enter public life, he reacted.

Yes the Jewish family was holy and good, but Jewish commerce was despicable, as we will demonstrate.[66]

With this passage Liberi establishes the difficulty of really knowing the Jew because of the contradictions between his public and private conduct. Within the family, in private, the Jew is respectable, a "saint," whereas in public, in the shop dealing with Christians, he is wretched, avaricious, and mean. How would he behave if he were to leave the ghetto behind altogether? Liberi proposes to expose the private Jew, in order to prepare his readers for inevitable cohabitation:

History will come to life in this novel, thus instructing and entertaining the reader.

To the best of our ability we will reproduce their customs as they are in real life, along with those habits, weaknesses, vices and virtues which [will] give us a lively portrait of Jewish life. (*G*, 5)

Accordingly, the novel alternates between the "intimate" and "social drama," exposing the two poles of Jewish behavior.

Liberi tells his story through a series of predictable antitheses: good verses evil, Christian verses Jew. But in *Il Ghetto* Christian values are synonymous with middle-class values: the dichotomy between Christian and Jew thus extends beyond religion and urban topography to questions of social class. Unlike the liberated Jewish community that was in a state of flux in the 1880s, Liberi's characters are the Jews of 1814, significantly the year of reghettoization after the first emancipation. If we were to consider that initial period outside the ghetto (1812–1814) as an implied prologue to the novel, it was too short for lasting bourgeois acculturation to take effect. Liberi's Jews were thrust

66. A. Liberi (G. A. Giustina), *Il Ghetto: romanzo storico-sociale* (Turin: Fino, 1881), 5. All further references to *Il Ghetto* follow the pagination of this edition and are incorporated in the text with the indication *G*.

back into the ghetto with their Jewish traditions and mentality intact. There, he demonstrates, the Jews took the values of the majority and replaced them, one by one, with their own, inferior standards.

Nowhere is this stated more plainly than in the author's choice of protagonists; neither Rachele nor her beloved Cosimo are Jews. Rachele stands out among all other ghetto dwellers with her blond hair and her "abnormal" cleanliness extending even down to her underclothing, which, Liberi specifies, is usually worn dirty by the Jews. Though raised in the ghetto she has (miraculously) avoided the ghetto parlance. Her name is Zan-Tedeschi, an adaptation from German, but she is actually Italian, the natural child of a countess. With her noble Christian blood Rachele will be judged fit to marry the hero in the end. She works as a seamstress in her foster father's shop where she falls in love, at first sight, with the dashing Cosimo Sinibaldi. Rachele is all goodness, light, sweetness: the essence of femininity. At the age of fourteen she loves with the maturity of a woman twice her age:

Rachele's love for Cosimo could be likened to a love poem made up of sublime melodies and heroic exploits . . . This love was infinite and all-encompassing and, therefore, eternal. (*G*, 9–10)

Without this love, so chaste and pure and sublime, Cosimo and Rachele could not have lived for even one hour.

Enchanted by this song of songs, Rachele existed only for Cosimo. When he was away, she worried and fervently prayed to God to bless him with all His might. (*G*, 40–41)

She is the perfect picture of Romantic Christian womanhood: self-effacing and dedicated to her man.

Cosimo is the strong, selfless, passionate son of a liberal political exile from Trent and has a glorious life in store for him. He does not realize that Rachele is not a Jew; it is his liberal and generous nature that makes him willing to accept her as he thinks she is. Cosimo represents all that is vigorous, optimistic, and magnanimous in the Risorgimento, and together he and Rachele symbolize the bright future of the new, young nation-in-the-making.

The immediate problem is to liberate Rachele from the ghetto and her sinister foster parents, Abramo and Sara, who are the scum of the Turin underworld. In return for raising Rachele and not revealing her real parents' identity, Abramo and Sara extorted twenty thousand scudi from the Countess, with which they made shady investments. Since Jews were not allowed to own land or real estate, they often employed

Christians as purchasing agents and nominal owners. Such contacts between Jews and Christians were themselves illegal. Abramo and Sara
required the Countess to invest in land for them, all the while continuing to blackmail her. No Christian charity in this home! When they
suspect Rachele of having a lover who might eventually carry her off,
sharply reducing their income, they conspire to marry her to someone
in their control and continue their extortion as before. In this family
the father is a silent partner and the mother's only contact with her captive foster daughter is conflictual, resolving itself in physical, but never
psychological, domination. For instance, when Sara attempts to learn
the identity of Rachele's lover she "engages all her cunning and all her
strength"; she "beats [Rachele] bloody" (G, 18–19), but learns nothing. And when Rachele escapes, Sara enlists the aid of Barabba, a common thief and felonious family retainer, to bring her back.

Barabba is one of the omnipresent monsters of popular literature:

Imagine yourself face-to-face with a giant with thick, kinky black hair cascading
over a low, beetling brow. Imagine a fat, weathered wrinkled face with a hook
nose and, on either side of this proboscis, two eyes like burning coals. [Picture
this] and you will have a portrait of the creature with his bull neck, his protrud-
ing lips and muscular arms. Hairy like a bear, ruddy as molten iron, strong as
steel, but also ragged as a beggar and simple as mush. Such was Barabba, a
half-breed conceived in guilt who lived only to do harm. (G, 27)

An unredeemed product of original sin, a subhuman described with
animal and mineral similes, many of Barabba's characteristics are stereotypical of Jews: the hooked nose, thick lips, and abundant, black
body hair covering a dark complexion.

Capitalizing on the erotic power inherent in the pairing of characters
such as Beauty and the Beast, Liberi sets the scene for a violent encounter between Rachele and Barabba which allows him to juxtapose
blond and swarthy, beautiful and ugly, saintly and sinister. The dark,
hairy brute throws himself upon the lovely, blond Rachele with her fair
skin and delicate hands:

After the murder Barabba emerged from the room with his hands still covered
with blood. Rachele shrieked and swooned.
   Rolling up his sleeves and clenching his fists in bloodthirsty rage, he lunged
at her as she begged the monster for mercy with her hands crossed [on her
breast]. Barabba was unmoved and pressing her to him, hoisted her over his
shoulder like a common piece of furniture. (G, 41)

Later executed for kidnap and murder, Barabba is shown in a gruesome illustration, his head exposed to the public nailed through his monstrous ears to the crossbeam of the gallows. Author and illustrator have avenged the death of Christ: Barabbas has at last been crucified.

The mother-daughter relationship is the best developed in the novel, a device that allows the author ample opportunity to compare his villain with his heroine. Both women are pictured as part of a couple; indeed their world views are limited by the confines of this union. But whereas Rachele is completely passive and reactive, Sara is unusually active and entrepreneurial. So strong is her personality that she has achieved an extraordinary level of influence and autonomy. Because of her homemaking talents and business acumen, she commands the respect not normally accorded to Jewish women.

Religiously speaking, the Jewish woman is respected even less than women in other religions . . . But in Abramo's house, Sara is the queen. . . . She had captivated him to such an extent that he was one of the few Jews who would allow his wife to be the boss. But he wasn't entirely in the wrong since Sara was a good homemaker and kept a sharp eye on the house and the business. (G, 18–19)

But Abramo pays a high price for her intelligence. Unlike Cosimo, instead of the "sublime melodies" of Rachele's "love poem," the hapless Abramo is subjected to frequent tongue-lashings, generally about money.

Having regained her daughter, Sara convinces Abramo to kill her. Always vigilant to the danger around her, Rachele escapes once more, this time to Cosimo. Sara is arrested for conspiracy and killed by Barabba as he awaits execution. Abramo is accused of her death, arrested, and absolved.

As a character in a novel, Rachele may be little more than jejune baggage, but she embodies the solid values in which Liberi's readers were instructed from an early age. She is the ideal Christian martyr, a saint allowing herself to be beaten but never giving in, for she knows instinctively that her steady resolution will succeed in the end. Sara, on the contrary, is in a constant frenzy. Until her murder in prison, she will never know respite from her desperation. With no sense of tradition on which to base the course of her life, she lives by her wits. Her sneering cruelty is powerless against Rachele's streadfast determination to remain unstained by the horrors of ghetto life. And indeed Rachele escapes twice with her honor intact. As a final gesture of unnecessary purification, she disavows her adoptive religion, converts to Christianity taking the name Carmelita, and puts down lasting roots in perfect union with the noble-spirited Cosimo.

In this popular novel inspired by the antagonism between the ruling majority and a willful but dominated minority, Liberi's characters behave in ways that are thought to be emblematic of their respective religious groups; Rachele is a typical Christian, Sara a typical Jew. But if Rachele was raised in the same ghetto atmosphere as was Sara before her, their traditions should be about the same. The fact that the behavior of the two women is diametrically opposed suggests that Liberi is implying that behavioral tendencies are inborn not learned, not just religious but racial in origin. Apart from the physical appearance of his characters, however, until the very end of the book Liberi couches his overt discussion in social rather than racial terms.

Accordingly, the Jews in Liberi's ghetto violate several canons of accepted behavior, all of which Liberi is careful to point out as part of his self-imposed duty to render the Jew "more assimilable" by educating his readers.

Believe me . . . in order to write the intimate history of a people, one must know its rituals, habits, laws and institutions. No people has retained its original, Oriental nationality more than the Jews . . . (G, 57)

Prayer is one of these rites which have been rigidly codified by society. Abramo and Sara—ironically named for the patriarch of Judaism and his wife—are devoted temple-goers. They are the first to enter the sanctuary every day and the last to leave. But their prayers are hollow and their sinning proceeds without pause. Liberi turns to instruct the reader:

Abramo swore to do only good for its own sake. Sara begged forgiveness daily for her sins. But do you put any faith in their words? (G, 30)

He hammers the point home by invoking the proverbial wisdom of past generations:

"He who fasts," said my late lamented grandfather, "but treats no man well, has bread to spare and goes direct to Hell." (G, 32)

The venal Abramo tries to buy God's favor by giving a larger offering than others in the congregation whereas the deceitful Sara prays and prays, reciting long-established formulas that have nothing to do with her real aspirations. After her daily round of vows and supplications she feels the peace that comes from an unburdened conscience. Her relief is totally undeserved, Liberi hastens to admonish, for hers are the prayers that God does not hear. Like those of so many unrepentent sinners in literature, her prayers are empty, thoughtless words. She mumbles about love and charity while plans of kidnap and usury nest in her heart.

Just as fraud subverts the institution of prayer, so immoral desire makes a mockery of the sacrament of marriage. Rachele escapes from the ghetto partly out of disgust at the idea of facing a "traditional communal" Jewish marriage. After a lengthy, pseudoscientific examination of the Jewish woman promiscuously making love, Liberi excuses her experience with the promise of approaching motherhood. But although motherhood is the natural state of the married woman, Jews, he warns, look upon procreation as a political expedient. Communal marriage helps the Jews reproduce as fast as possible for the express purpose of gaining political power through numbers. This in turn allows them to defend their faith and press for civil rights, admirable goals in themselves if it weren't for the danger that the influx of vast numbers of Jews would change the face of society.

Liberi's exposé of the intimate life of Jews and the horrors of the ghetto was in many ways a forum for broad political statements. In his preface the author had declared his intention to examine the dichotomy between the public and private Jew and then, in the same section, inveighed against those who use religion to divide a population on the basis of race, when all Italians

[owe allegiance] to one country, [are of] one mind and [have] one desire, *one faith*, one hope [and] one belief in the future of human progress. (*G*, 6—emphasis mine)

Hidden in the middle of this statement is a clue to Liberi's preoccupation with Jewish assimilation together with its only feasible solution: that the entire population participate in the same faith, or rather, that Jews abandon entirely their religious and cultural identity. Following this line of reasoning, the description, characters, and events in the novel serve as concrete examples of the enormous task that lay ahead of the Jews before they could take their places in society and call themselves Italians. Toward the end of the novel, Liberi reinforces this point in a long excursus in which he reproduces d'Azeglio's pamphlet *Dell'Emancipazione civile degli Israeliti* omitting, characteristically, only the prologue on tolerance in favor of a rhetorical postscript of his own invoking the "sacred principles of Christ: be ye all brothers" and ending with the slogan "Liberty for all men!" (*G*, 129).

The transformation of the ancient Jewish people promises to be a task of herculean proportions as Liberi suggests in the last paragraphs of *Il Ghetto*. The novel ends with the announcement of a sequel, *Abramo,* his adventures as the Wandering Jew. The day he entered prison, Abramo was branded like all Jews in his situation, with a cross on the forehead as a sign of hatred. Actually, the cross burned into the forehead is traditional in many versions of the legend of the Wandering Jew. While in prison Abramo is visited by Geroboamo, a patriarch of the ghetto. Realizing he is to be set free, Abramo begs for forgiveness for his sins. He promises to wander the earth in search of one Rebecca Jacchia, stolen from the ghetto when she was just a baby, and not to return until he has found her. Rather than lengthy, self-imposed punishment (Abramo's wandering) would it not have made more sense to expiate one's sins as Rachele did, by outright conversion?

The purpose of *Abramo*, which was never written, was to illustrate with a familiar legend the near impossibility of assimilation or, as the author queries at the end of *Il Ghetto*:

And the history of the Jewish people? And the diagnosis of that grave illness which is slowly ravaging the Semitic race? Well, why not write about the usurers? And why keep silent about Jewish plutocracy? Why not reveal just how the Jews amassed so much wealth? (*G*, 154)

The nature of that "illness" that steadily "ravages" the Jewish people remains a matter of speculation. Given the breathless, nonanalytical massing of questions at the end of his novel, questions that he would leave unanswered, one suspects that Liberi himself never resolved his own conflicted reactions to the reality of Jewish assimilation.

A lawyer who called himself a liberal, G. A. Giustina[67] (Ausonio Liberi) achieved a certain renown as an anticlerical publicist,[68] a stance corroborated in the preface to *Il Ghetto*. But the denouement of the

---

67. For information on G. A. Giustina see J. Rovito, *Letterati e giornalisti italiani contemporanei,* 2d ed. rev. (Naples: Jovene, 1922), 210; and A. Viriglio, *Torino e i torinesi,* 2d ed. rev. (Turin: Studio ed. libr. piemontese, 1931), vol. 2: 163.

68. Giustina's studies of court cases in the journal that he founded and directed, *Cronaca dei Tribunali,* confirm his reputation.

novel reveals that the author could only conceive of marriage between people of disparate religious origin—a situation that he assumes to be emblematic of the society at large—by elimination not of religious obstacles but of religious differences. The lawyer Giustina, swept up in the anticlerical movement, professed the attitudes of public moment while the private man, the novelist Liberi who only appeared in public disguised in a pseudonym, held more deep-seated, traditional views. Thus with *Il Ghetto* the reader is left with incredible contradictions, such as the juxtaposition of d'Azeglio's treatise on tolerance and the stereotypical usurers Abramo and Sara.

What remains clearly discernible in *Il Ghetto*, in the genre of the mistero and in the novelistic reportage about living conditions in Italian ghettos, is the potent attraction of the ghetto as a *locus* in popular narrative and therefore its place among the formulaic elements that assured market success to fiction writers like Giustina. But quite beyond its role in the recipe for popular literary success, the ghetto did double duty for those authors who situated their plots behind its walls. First, the stories were anchored in the authors' construction of a social setting (their versions of the ghetto) which they portrayed as contemporary reality whereas the behavior of their central characters, both "good" and "bad," reflected the actual moral values of the reading public. Second, since it was depicted as a place without laws, a haven for crime and the most fanciful evil imaginable, the ghetto as literary device afforded an author the freedom to arouse the curiosity of the audience, to shock and titillate and then to recoil from the horror and moralize. The more corrupt the Jewish villains, the more virtuous the Christian hero would appear.

Taking the lead from contemporary mores, authors created seamless worlds in which their ideals could function. But in order for Jewish characters to behave "ideally," that is, according to stereotyped expectations, they had to be projected against an equally improbable backdrop. That setting could only be the ghetto where the reader could savor the Jewish essence full strength, unimpeded by the post-Emancipation realization of developing relations, if sometimes uneasy ones, between Italian Jews and Christians. Accordingly, even though Liberi was personally involved in current political reality in 1880, in his fiction he placed the Jews in a ghetto situation that had already ceased to exist and described them for the good of the society in terms no longer truly relevant to his society.

A Ghetto Orphan

The romanzi d'appendice of Carolina Invernizio were more typical of the genre than Liberi's. With their convoluted plots and myriad secondary characters, often abandoned after just one episode, these works focused largely on the horrors and tribulations that would ultimately lead the heroine to the happily-ever-after of marriage and/or Christian redemption. The numerous subplots held the readers' attention and compelled them to follow each installment. Skip one issue and one might miss a painful demise, a whispered confession, or a crucial recognition on which might hinge a whole new series of conspiracies and murders. The major exponent of the serial novel in Italy, Invernizio wrote well over one hundred novels and was the most popular author of her time. Her work has never ceased to attract readers and has recently enjoyed a new surge of critical attention.[69]

In addition to sensational potboilers, Invernizio wrote articles of a decidedly sociological nature under various pseudonyms. Although she maintained political neutrality in her novels, which were contemporary with the first socialist and feminist movements, her articles gained her the respect of such organizations as the Società operaia di Napoli, a women's labor organization.[70] But with the exception of such novels as *Cuor d'operaio* (*A Laborer's Heart*) and *Il dramma degli emigrati* (*The Emigrants' Tragedy*), she gives sociological reality very little direct fictional treatment. Though Invernizio considered her romanzi storico-sociali effective instruments of mass education,[71] serious social content is either implied rather than declared outright or masked by the complexity of her plots with their constant coups-de-scène.

The social composition of her public and the author's sense of her readers' interests provide a partial explanation of the lack of social real-

---

69. A conference entitled "Homage to Carolina Invernizio" took place at Cuneo in February 1983 and the proceedings, in twenty-seven articles edited by G. Davico Bonino and G. Ioly, were published with the title *Carolina Invernizio: Il romanzo d'appendice* (Turin: Gruppo Editoriale Forma, 1983). Some mention is made of the Jewish villain of *Orfana del Ghetto* in the chapter by P. Valabrega, "L'immagine dell'Ebreo nell'*Orfana del Ghetto*," 73–79. See also A. A. Veronese et al., *Dame, droga e galline: Romanzo popolare e romanzo di consumo tra '800 e 900* (Padua: CLEUP, 1977).

70. Invernizio addressed the group in 1890 with a speech entitled "Le operaie italiane."

71. Speker, "Come si scrive un romanzo popolare. Un'intervista a Carolina Invernizio, *Forum* (1904), cited in G. Davico Bonino–G. Ioly eds., AA. VV., *Carolina Invernizio*, 12.

ity in her narrative. Invernizio's audience comprised many seamstresses, servants, shopgirls, and shut-ins of minimal education who could barely read. Women, then, for the most part, whom the author often addresses directly in the text. But though Invernizio is quoted as having said to Matilde Serao: "You write for the *crème-de-la-crème* and I for all the rest,"[72] her audience spanned the gamut of social classes from the proletariat to the upper middle class, all of which were well-represented in her stories. Delighting in what she called her "merry vendetta" against those critics who snubbed and scorned her stories, she pointed out that her "ardent [female] readers and friends [were] in fact their wives, their sisters."[73] Each number of the *Gazzetta di Torino,* each new offering from Salani in Florence, brought these readers many of the most pressing social problems of the day (e.g., the plight of the urban proletariat in *La figlia del mendicante* (*The Beggar's Daughter*), but drained them of their true pathos in favor of the pathetic and tantalizing "velleities of horror and sin . . . or the ecstacy of sacrifice and suffering," and muffled them in happy endings meant to be "consumed in the silent frustration of bourgeois life."[74] They became the stuff of escapist literature, relief from a stifling atmosphere.

The titles reveal a familiarity with crime as it would have been recorded in the police blotter of any major Italian city, and episodes and characters have their origin in local news and gossip. Indeed, "ninety-nine times out of a hundred" her novels and others like them "are merely a fantastic web of crimes stitched onto a perfectly ordinary canvas."[75] Invernizio often chose the title first before fully working out the plot because she believed "[the title] exerts a certain influence over readers, from the simplest to the most sophisticated, and a good title accounts for half the success of the popular novel."[76] No less an observer than successful publisher Emillio Treves noted: "Our people, which is neither imaginative like the Orientals or mystic like the Scandinavians, is thirsty for sentimentality and not always of the highest quality. Sometimes the choice of a novel is based solely on the word 'love' in the title

72. G. Davico Bonino, introduction to AA. VV., *Carolina Invernizio,* 9.

73. M. Federzoni, "Carolina Invernizio," in U. Eco, M. Federzoni, I. Pezzini, M. P. Pozzato, *Carolina Invernizio, Matilde Serao, Liala* (Florence: La Nuova Italia, 1979), 59; Speker, "Interview," in "Come si scrive," 12.

74. S. Musitelli, preface to C. Invernizio, *Il bacio di una morta* (Milan: Bietti, 1974), 11.

75. E. Ferri, *I delinquenti nell'arte* (Turin: UTET, 1926), 5.

76. Speker, "Come si scrive," 12–13.

or some other work that promises to tug at their heartstrings."[77] Although providing all the transport of make believe, Invernizio's novels were thoroughly researched with regard to locale and offered their readers a rich variety of detailed backgrounds. These were minutely described, following one after the other in rapid-fire crosscutting, carefully designed to induce a desired emotional response.

Invernizio's *L'Orfana del Ghetto* (*The Orphan of the Ghetto*) (1887) is a typical example of the genre. Its title alone was intriguing enough to capture the public imagination a century ago and assure author and publisher a handsome profit. The protagonist is a female, it announces, indicating that the novel conforms to the established (and lucrative) pattern. What's more, the heroine is an orphan, an intriguing characterization that hints at enticing vulnerability and promises tales of sacrifice and, just possibly, scenes of violent death. Her adventures take place in the ghetto with all the exotic squalor that this implies: the nearby/distant place where one can "see sufferings worse than one's own." *L'Orfana del Ghetto*, which went through nine editions and was most recently reprinted in 1975, has remained one of Invernizio's perennially popular works.[78]

The novel stands as a glorification of religious redemption. In the dedication the author remembers that when her family lived in Florence, her mother often went into the ghetto as a sort of missionary dispensing charity and "holy words." She returned home with stories of the terrible human misery she found there. In the dedication Invernizio assures her mother that although the plot is complicated and even audacious, she never lost sight of one guiding principle: respect for the Catholic way of life. Her simple, steadfast and, in the end, unimaginative Christian morality, ever triumphant over her fantasy world of spectres and sinners, earned her Gramsci's double-edged estimation as "*l'onesta gallina* (the honest hen) of popular literature."[79]

L'Orfana del Ghetto is divided into six parts: the prologue, in which the original crimes are committed; part I, "The Mysteries of the Ghetto"; part 2, "Love and Crime"; part 3,"The Spectre of the Past"; part 4, "The Hand of God"; part 5, "A Dead Woman's Vengeance"; part 6, epilogue. Invernizio's novel incorporates several key elements

77. Società bibliografica italiana, *I libri più letti*, 19.

78. *L'Orfana del Ghetto,* first published by Salani in 1887, was reprinted by Salani in 1889, 1891, 1893, 1900, 1903, and 1928. The latest edition, published by Lucchi (Milan: 1975), was used in the preparation of this analysis.

79. A. Gramsci, *Letteratura e vita nazionale*, Q.VIII, p. 107, n. 1.

of the classic *romanzo nero* (Gothic novel), with its accent on suffering in dank dungeons imposed on innocent victims by diabolical sadists who are ultimately vanquished by the combined forces of love and honesty.

The story begins in the prologue on the proverbial dark and stormy night near Piazza Santa Croce in Florence. The noble Renata Ariani has just given birth to the daughter of Fiorenzo Servi, a poor Jew from the ghetto. Fiorenzo wants both mother and child, but realizes that Count Mario Ariani, Renata's father, would forbid him access to them since, for Ariani, a Jew "is worth less than a dog" (*OG*, I, 10).

Paola, an Ariani servant, has been ordered to destroy the infant, but instead baptizes it and, clutching the child, steals out of the palace into the storm. Fiorenzo accosts her and demands his daughter. Seeing a medal around her neck and believing it to be Renata's, he renounces the faith of his fathers declaring Renata's love "his one true God" and vowing to raise their child as a Christian should Renata desire it. With this expedient, the inconvenience of Judaism and its remedy in conversion are suggested early on. At the outset, baptism seemed little more than an attractive alternative, but as the story progresses it becomes a personal necessity and a pivotal element in the plot. Fiorenzo leaves the baby in the ghetto with Susanna and her elderly Babbo Giacobbe, his own adoptive family. The young and beautiful Susanna, ironically named for the "chaste Susanna" of the Bible, has herself just delivered a baby girl whom she rejects since the child is the product of rape by a Christian who had been their guest. Suffering from unrequited love for Fiorenzo, Susanna switches the infants. Fiorenzo takes the child he believes is his and Susanna removes the medal from her new baby and hides it. Fiorenzo's child is thus raised as a Jew and comes to be known as Viola, the Orphan of the Ghetto.

Part I opens with a murder in a lurid flophouse. Taking her cue from the mistero, Invernizio describes the scene of the crime and the verminous inhabitants of the ghetto rookery:

In an inn called The Flood . . . were gathered all the dregs of society: ugly brutes, beggars, thieves, whores. [What looked like] piles of rags covered men and women of every race and color. (*OG*, I, 45)

Similar descriptions of a ghetto dive were available to Invernizio in Maccanti's *I misteri di Firenze* and Jarro's *Firenze sotterranea*, both published just three years earlier. The descriptive formulas are the same although both Maccanti and Jarro attribute their accounts to direct observation. Here, too, people live on top of one another and loathsome piles of rags, thought to be animals, reveal themselves to be women.

> In these wretched little rooms one finds fifteen or twenty filthy straw pallets. For a penny or two, convicts, professional thieves and [their] accomplices can sleep there. Here, too, everyone sleeps together, men and women, one right next to the other, and they dress and undress in full sight of all their neighbors.[80]

With men and women, thieves and whores all sleeping together, the place is an outrage against public decency. The inn is horrifically unsanitary just as Maccanti had described it. Invernizio turns to the reader saying "imagine the fetid air and the noise!" Jarro did the same adding children and flea-bitten dogs to his menagerie and Maccanti in his account provided the concrete detail of stinking sewer gas. Such conditions, they concluded, were "dangerous to public health."[81] Maccanti's *misteri*, in which fiction masqueraded as journalism, and Jarro's investigative reporting, which was colored in its prose style by the *mistero*, established precedents for Invernizio's ghetto inn and lent it an air of veracity. These two accounts along with her mother's impressions of the site provided the author with a foundation on which she could embroider her exotic scenes of conspiracy and punishment. In Invernizio, the sympathetic portrayal by her predecessors, who considered the ghetto first and foremost as the lamentable materialization of human misery, is reworked into a grotesque and provocative vision of Hell.

In a dark, crumbling building close by and similar to the inn lives Viola, an innocent and beautiful blond teenager. Her purity and goodness, like Rachele's, is so out of place in the ghetto as to be regarded as something of a local miracle.

The departure of Fiorenzo immediately after Viola's birth remains one of the unsolved ghetto mysteries. Having sworn vengeance on the most-Christian Arianis, he returns some years later as the Baron Armando Viser with his presumed daughter, Luciana, and enough wealth to carry out his sinister program. A chance meeting between the haughty and selfish Luciana and the simple, generous Viola sets those plans in motion. Using Viola, he exploits Susanna's enduring love for him in a plot against Renata, now the Duchess of Santamaria, her son Raul, and her father.

At the same time Viola meets Count Marcello Delmonte, Luciana's

---

80. Jarro, *Firenze sotterranea*, 33.
81. Ibid., 32; Maccanti, *I misteri di Firenze*, 26.

fiance. Since Viola is the only character who can match Marcello in moral rectitude and selfless dedication to others, after many misadventures the handsome Count will marry the Ghetto Orphan.

Fiorenzo disguises himself as a petty criminal and makes contact with the underworld of the ghetto. Calling himself the "Envoy of Judea" he orders a Jewish criminal who inhabits the subterranean slime to procure him the services of a petty thug, the Christian Toto. Fiorenzo is eager to make any Christian pay dearly for the sordid poverty of his early life as a Jew. Accordingly, he makes Toto his slave and charges him to carry out the vendetta against the one person whose Christianity has hurt him the most. Toto is to kidnap Renata's son.

In part 2 the tentacles of Fiorenzo's vengeance spiral around every character, constricting and sucking them into a vortex of desperation. As crime follows crime in part 3, long-buried wrongs are unearthed. In parts 4 and 5 the guilty are dealt terrible punishments, while the worthy are redeemed through acceptance of the True Faith. In the epilogue Viola and Marcello are united and the Orphan of the Ghetto will presumably never again have to traverse its dark and noisome alleys.

As in the case of Liberi's *Il Ghetto*, *L'Orfana del Ghetto* was inspired by a problem born of Jewish emancipation, that is, the jealousy of the masses and the concern of the wealthy bourgeoisie and the nobility who felt a threat to their social position. Invernizio's response was to exploit the usual anti-Jewish commonplaces, the most prevalent being the identification of Jews with money. Her use of stereotype, however, is quite original: although she applies it across the board to all Jewish characters, the author has thought to modify it according to the distinguishing characteristics of the individual. In *La figlia della portinaia* (*The Concierge's Daughter*), for example, there is mention of a Mr. Levi; because he is thoroughly bourgeois, he is referred to as a stockbroker instead of a usurer and "an excellent person, even though he's a Jew." [82] In *L'Orfana del Ghetto*, however, the author deals at some length with the extremes of the Jewish social scale as reflected in their approach to money. At the upper end of the scale are Fiorenzo and Luciana, the only Jewish characters who utilize and enjoy their wealth openly, in a princely style on a par with the Christians of their class. They have purchased noble titles and are fully cognizant of their power.

As so often happens when dealing with stereotypes, the author exaggerates Jewish resources and influence. To fuel the suspicions of

---

82. C. Invernizio, *La figlia della portinaia* (Florence: Salani, 1920), 80.

those who feared an international conspiracy of Jewish plutocracies after the abolition of the ghetto system, Invernizio puts incendiary propagandistic phrases into the mouth of the beautiful, wealthy, and willful Luciana. An anomalous character in Invernizio's universe, like Liberi's Sara she is unusually liberated for her times. She is convinced that Jews rule the world, so that when Viola chides her for wanting to marry a Christian, Luciana retorts that neither that nor any other impediment will stand in her way:

Now . . . you see . . . *we* own the world. . . . if you had traveled as I have, Viola, . . . if you had frequented [the best] society, you would know that these days money is all that counts. Now then, if Christians have the monopoly on culture and good breeding, we control the wealth. Commerce, industry and gold belong to us and Christians are racing to become our associates. (*OG*, I, 114)

The predictable oppositions are all here. But crass Jewish materialism threatens to change the rules of the society rooted in Christian values and render its "civilization" meaningless. Like the tired refrain to an old song, such fears were later to be repeated nearly unchanged and ad infinitum by the anti-Semitic Fascist press protesting the international conspiracy of the "*demoplutocrazie giudaiche-massoniche*" ("Jewish-Masonic-Demoplutocracies").

The other Jews in the novel are portrayed as common stock types, that is Jews as they "really are": not that different from Fiorenzo/Baron Viser and Luciana, but without the trappings of nobility. Most have two faces, such as the outwardly poor artisan, Babbo Giacobbe, who hoards a secret cache of money and other valuables. He will do anything for money and would rather starve than disturb his golden hoard under the floorboards. His greed is insatiable. For money he harbored the criminal who raped Susanna and fathered Luciana. For money he forgets his devotion to his granddaughter, Viola, and abandons her to pursue the opportunity to amass an even greater fortune, the one thing he truly loves. At the thought of stolen jewelry to fence, his eyes "flash with greed" and "his skinny, claw-like hands can practically feel the jewels" (*OG*, II, 136). As a result, Viola is taken hostage by Renata against the return of her son and Babbo Giacobbe returns to find his strongbox empty. That is more than a Jew can take: he collapses twisting, shrieking, and frothing at the mouth with rage and dies an hour later.

Invernizio never identifies the Christian characters with money, for though they depend upon accumulated wealth for their elegant way of life, their capital is in the form of solid, real property rather than the liquid assets of coins and jewels which are ephemeral, portable, and easily robbed. Part of a logical, ordained hierarchy, they are entrenched atop a solid foundation of landed estates with underlings to work them: an ossified system, though threatened with adulteration by the newly rich. Money, however, is associated with frenetic activity: buying, selling. It is also payment for crime. Money is the instrument for survival and advancement of those like the Jews who are outside the natural order of society.

Fiorenzo Servi is a perfect example: having acquired money of mysterious origin and invested it wisely, he has become ennobled and has rearranged the letters of his name from Servi (which implies the social inferiority of the Jews especially when compared to Ariani, the family he must emulate) to Viser. Armed with his title, Baron Armando Viser contrives to break down the defenses of Christian society and gain respectability, but his inner corruption will ultimately thwart his attempts to ape their way of life. The pressure of accumulated bitterness gives rise to an exaggerated love of power and to the urgency to achieve his revenge by the most draconian means possible, aided by the judicious use of money.

The traditional anti-Semitic accusation of the blood libel, a theme for which authors were continually inventing variations, is intimately associated with Fiorenzo's efforts to make Christian society pay for the torments of his youth. Raul has been warned to fear Jews because they steal Christian children in order to murder them, and sure enough Fiorenzo has him kidnapped and imprisoned in a subterranean vault. Then after a dried human heart is found in a small casket in her home,[83] Susanna is tried for murder. The heart had belonged to the Christian who raped her. In a departure from tradition, no mention is made of actually ingesting blood and both incidents of blood libel are left undeveloped. The second may be merely a pretext to incarcerate Susanna so that Toto can murder her in prison, thereby beginning the process of eliminating the Jewish characters. What is particularly striking, however, is the automatic assumption of ritual murder on the part of Susanna's judges, a conclusion that may have its literary origins in the theme of vampirism so prevalent in the tales-of-terror and early Roman-

83. This is a variation on the popular folktale-motif of the miser who kept his own heart in a strong box: Motif W.153.1. See S. Thompson, *Motif-Index,* vol. 5: 493.

tic fiction.[84] One can only speculate about why Invernizio avoids the explicit mention of vampirism in this regard; these brief allusions to ritual murder leave the reader with the impression that Jewish hands are always covered with blood and that their energies are always channeled toward revenge.

The stereotypes that inform so much of Invernizio's novel, also transcend the social sphere to play a part in the important religious question that, as the author promised her mother, was at the heart of her work. The plot of *L'Orfana del Ghetto* revolves ultimately around the age-old struggle between the Devil and the Angel of the Lord, but the trophy in this version of that ancient rivalry is the Devil himself. Lucifer is incarnated in the persona of the Jews, the tormented Fiorenzo Servi/Baron Armando Viser and the Angel of God is symbolized by the forces of conversion coupled with Christian serenity in the impossibly pure, selfless, and generous Viola.

To create Fiorenzo, Invernizio borrowed a familiar character from the tales-of-terror and adapted it to a Christian framework. On the model of the long-popular Schedoni, the monk in Ann Radcliffe's *The Italian or the Confessional of the Black Penitents* (1797), the handsome, brooding hero is perverted into the Satanic outlaw who lashes out at all who come in contact with him. Invariably of mysterious origin and outwardly refined, the villain is assumed to be of high birth; similarly, Fiorenzo is really the natural son of a wealthy banker. The traditional villain's past is clouded by the hint of some unspeakable misdeed; in Fiorenzo's case this could be the way he amassed his fortune. The hero-turned-villain has a melancholy appearance, bearing traces of spent passions, and unforgettable eyes; Fiorenzo's eyes are compared to glowing coals. The possibility of a criminal past renders Fiorenzo all the more mysterious, especially considering his comfortable presence in high society. With his title and his characteristically Jewish, chameleon-like aptitude for camouflage, he is described as "a perfect gentleman," one who gives of himself "like a brother" (*OG,* II, 93).

This great pretender manipulates the other characters with the agility of a master puppeteer, while remaining backstage pulling the strings. Having discovered their basic weaknesses, Fiorenzo transforms his associates into servants at his beck and call. The miserable Toto, for example, in hiding for a crime he did not commit, literally sells himself to

84. See, for example, M. Shelley, *Frankenstein* (1818); Lord Byron, *A Fragment* (1819); G. Polidori, *The Vampire* (1819); and C. R. Maturin, *Melmoth, the Wanderer* (1820); and others as discussed by M. Praz, *Carne, morte, diavolo,* 80–81.

Fiorenzo for a new identity and future security. At the end, with two murders and a kidnapping to his credit, Toto is back where he began, gone to earth with nowhere to turn. Luciana receives similar treatment. Trained to be cunning and ruthless, she is also naturally beautiful so that men are fatally attracted to her. Gossips attribute her erotic powers to the supernatural: "Jewish women are all witches; they cast spells over men" (*OG*, I, 35). In order to disguise Fiorenzo's crimes and win back Marcello, Luciana uses her charm to frame Viola for the kidnapping and is murdered for her efforts. And Susanna, who for years nurtured Viola and tried to protect her from the realities of the ghetto environment, inexplicably abandons her and, turning to the captive Raul, beats him mercilessly.

References to the devil are woven throughout the novel. Paola baptizes Viola at birth because she firmly believes the storm raging outside to be either the devil's celebration at the birth of his child or heaven's outrage at losing a Christian soul. When Ariani learns of his daughter's union with Fiorenzo, he assumes that the miserable Jew would have had to call on supernatural powers to attract her in the first place (*OG*, I, 13). Believing Renata insane and a succuba of the devil, he fears further contact with her. Giving vent to his inborn cruelty—there was always at least one character like him in every Gothic novel—as soon as Renata gives birth to Viola, he beats her soundly and drags her off to a remote cellar to exorcise her by burying her alive:

This opening revealed an inner courtyard without windows resembling a shaft [covered with] mold in which spiders strung their webs and a large number of moles scurried about.

—From now on this will be the wench's refuge. Let her cry and scream all she wants, no one will hear her. And if Renata doesn't recover her wits and submit to my authority, this will be her tomb. Let there be no pity for the fallen [woman], this rebellious daughter who cast aside [all] natural feelings and the laws of our holy religion, who stained my pure name and tainted the glorious bloodline of the Ariani! (*OG*, I, 40–41)

The persecuted Renata—seduced, impregnated, and abandoned to her fate—was as much a stock character in the romanzo nero as her sadistic father. Her tragic figure extends back beyond Sade and his imitators to medieval hagiographies and the atrocities of martyrdom.[85]

85. G. Davico Bonino, *Introduzione* in AA. VV., *Carolina Invernizio*, 9. On the figure of the persecuted woman in Romantic literature, see M. Praz, *Carne, morte, diavolo*, chap. 3, par. 8 and 9 with respective notes.

Poor Renata was still unconscious on her pallet. But an iron chain had been passed around her waist and linked to another which hung from an iron ring [firmly] embedded in the wall. (*OG,* I, 41)

She has unknowingly tasted the forbidden fruit and fallen from grace and her punishment is long years of madness. In order to convince her that in her liaison with a Jew she had consorted with Satan, Ariani successfully brainwashes Renata by keeping her from the world and allowing her to read only stories similar to her own:

In the end she believed herself possessed like those other girls . . . and she was terrified.
    —Pardon me, Father . . . I have offended you when you were only trying to save me from the Devil's grasp.
    —Are you convinced now that the Jew who possessed you was [nothing more than] a heretic, a demon who would have dragged you down to Hell? (*OG,* I, 189–190)

When she learns that her lover was a Jew and, therefore, that he employed the erotic lure of Satan:

She could still hear his sweet voice which set her blood on fire and made her heart race, [she could still feel] the touch of his lips . . . (*OG,* I, 101)

she attaches herself fervently to her religion with endless prayers and swears vengeance on any Jew unlucky enough to cross her path from that day forward:

He wasn't a man, he was a demon: Holy Virgin, have pity on me! I hate all Jews . . . I hate them! My curse on any Jew I meet from now on! (*OG,* I, 101)

But Renata does meet Fiorenzo again and though his presence causes her an undefinable uneasiness—"Renata could not hear Jews mentioned without giving in to a nervous tremor" (*OG,* I, 94)—she fails to acknowledge their past intimacy. Fiorenzo's jealousy gives way to consummate rage and the devil surfaces within him. Overcome by his innate propensity for evil, the lover becomes an instrument of terror. The Jew's revenge is the devil's revenge and Fiorenzo swears to torment his former beloved with "terror, madness, despair and death" (*OG,* I, 227).

    Fiorenzo's satanic plotting sets in motion the forces of Christian reaction, beginning with Renata. Her father's cruel treatment made her realize the seriousness of her transgression against the traditional values of her rank, her family, her religion:

You gave yourself to a Jew [and] you will die condemned. Pray and weep if you want God to save you! (*OG*, I, xxx)

I have seen the fires of Hell . . . [for] I committed a terrible crime: a Jew who loves a Christian and a Christian who loves a Jew are damned. But I prayed to God, over and over, and he pardoned me. And the Virgin helped me out of Hell and showed me the way to salvation. And now I am the wife of a Christian. I am redeemed! (*OG*, I, 97)

Viola's metamorphosis from ghetto waif to Angel of the Lord also has its origin in terror and hardship. She suffers not so much for herself as for Raul whom she tends during his imprisonment in the depths of the ghetto. One day she discovers his medal of the Madonna and is irresistibly attracted to it. As with Aser in Bresciani's novel, she feels a strange new sense of well-being as she contemplates the image. Raul had been taught to hate Jews, but nonetheless he teaches her a prayer to the Virgin and when she masters it, rewards her with his affection. Later she finds her own medal, which was hidden in Susanna's drawer, and decides to wear it. Marcello is overjoyed. Anxious to remove all obstacles between himself and Viola, as well as to save her soul—"a triumph for the Christian church" (*OG*, II, 82)—he urges her to pray to the Madonna. Predictably, little by little, Viola senses that Judaism is a burden to her, that it keeps her from the life she wants to lead.

When Fiorenzo sees the medal at her throat he recognizes her as his long-lost daughter and, in a rare moment of compassion, reveals that she was baptized on the day of her birth. Nonetheless she converts officially to Catholicism, the religion much more suited to her seraphic nature. Before she can marry Marcello she undergoes a voluntary period of claustration and prayer to wash away the stain of Judaism and the dirt of the ghetto. The convent is a chrysalis from which Viola emerges transformed into Maria, the Countess Delmonte.

As in the case of Sibilla and Rachele, or the heroine of any fairy tale, Viola has had to endure sacrifice and harrowing adventure to be worthy of reaching a higher plane of existence. Through Christianity, the orphan has escaped the gloom, the stench, the thievery, the pall of putrefaction and death that is the ghetto, to begin a new life in the upper echelons of society. In the Jew Viola's conversion to the Christian Maria, the reader has witnessed the complete destruction of an alien identity and its positive reconstruction and assimilation into the mainstream.

In an ordinary crime story the characters are delineated according to their guilt or innocence. Thus in *L'Orfana del Ghetto*, for example, many members of the nobility are outwardly righteous and inwardly decayed. Eventually their crimes against their own families are brought to light after being hidden under years of decorum. Thus Ariani is recognized as a sadist, an adulterer, the natural father of Marcello, and, along with Marcello's mother, the Countess Delmonte, the murderer of her husband. Marcello's mother, who is renowned for her piety, is revealed to be an adulteress, murderess, and supreme hypocrite. Together with Paola, their servant in crime, they take their own lives.

Invernizio's religious purpose is so clear-cut and so loudly proclaimed as to contribute, with *L'Orfana del Ghetto*, an added dimension to this sub-genre of the romanzo nero. After Viola's conversion, Luciana confronts her with the stupidity of that choice. Christianity and Judaism clash face to face:

"Which God? Yours?" interrupted Luciana, her eyes flashing with rage, "I don't know him. He would have us simply put up with any kind of torture and pardon any kind of insult. Well, I don't know how to forgive. When I feel the need for revenge, I get revenge. Your religion isn't for me." (*OG*, III, 35)

Luciana, like all the Jewish characters (with the logical exception of Viola), has been molded by such beliefs. All the Jewish characters are criminals and all except Fiorenzo die in the end.

Ironically religion ultimately saves Fiorenzo from the fate of the other Jewish characters. Because of his diabolical persona, he alone is judged not as a secular archcriminal but along religious lines as Satan himself. In the end, when the devil's work is done and his revenge complete, when Ariani is dead and Renata thoroughly chastized, there is no further need to maintain his demonic state. And, anyway, in this condition Fiorenzo the Devil/Fiorenzo the Jew is disarmed when confronted with the weapons of Christianity, as when Renata manages to hold him at bay by brandishing a large, silver crucifix. But it is not enough to render him powerless: Lucifer must be brought down and humbled, induced to trade his kingdom of Darkness for God's Kingdom of Light, made to rejoin the flock of true believers. It is up to Viola to lead him back to a state of grace.

Viola, who up to this point was weak and unassertive, is able to accomplish this feat by her own humble decision to spend a year in a convent:

". . . because I want to be a Christian, just as you will be, Father."
Fiorenzo bowed his head "[I would have to] renounce my religion!" he murmured.

"But wouldn't you have done as much for my mother? Now you will do it for your daughter. After all, wasn't it the Christian Madonna who reunited us?" (*OG*, III, 254–255)

This simple declaration that he will be Christian is enough to make Fiorenzo swallow his pride, and the renegade Devil bow to the Angel of the Lord. Symbolizing in part those Jews who historically listened to reason to save their souls, the only Jew left alive at the end is at last won over. Fiorenzo denies his Jewish identity altogether and resolves to spend his life in a monastery.

Inspired by "respect for our Catholic Religion" (*OG*, I, 8), like *Sibilla Odaleta* and *Il Ghetto*, *L'Orfana del Ghetto* ends in a positive, optimistic spirit. Invernizio's ideal society, in which all three novels' conflicts are resolved in the epilogue, is life filtered through the kind of Catholicism that teaches one to "despise those methods which men use to enslave others."[86] In the end, Christianity descends like a balsam to soothe the seared, frightful world. Their misdeeds punished, the misfits who treated their fellows in an unchristian manner have been eliminated or metamorphosed to conform to an acceptable pattern of behavior.

In Varese, Liberi, and Invernizio, the redeemed have taken their rightful places in society. From this conclusion it is clear that the three novels have more in common than just their foundation in anti-Jewish prejudice. All three writers understood and satisfied the requirements of their public with similar stories of redemption. What accounts for the mass appeal of this sort of literature?

We analyzed *Sibilla Odaleta* in the light of one fairy tale, *Little Red Riding Hood*. This was possible not only because a specific fairy tale was consciously or unconsciously imitated by the author, but also because the characters were delineated according to well-established stereotypes. In order to assess the persuasive power of such literature, we must expand this line of reasoning to include the other two works.

Although basically paradigmatic in concept, pitting two diametrically opposed elements against each other, such as black/white or Jew/Christian, all three novels rely on a standard, linear plot line to convey meaning. Bearing in mind the basic Straussian[87] paradigms, one

86. A. Manzoni, *Osservazioni sulla Morale Cattolica* (1819–1820)–part 2, Section 3, in *Tutte le opere*, vol. 3: 514.

87. See, for example, C. Lévi-Strauss, "La Geste d'Asdiwal," *L'Annuaire, 1958–59, École pratique des Hautes Études (Section des Sciences religieuses)* (1959): 2–43; "The Structural Study of Myth," *Journal of American Folklore* 68 (1955): 428–444.

can apply Propp's[88] syntagmatic method of analysis, since he bases his schema on specific dramatis personae that function according to a set, chronological sequence of events.

The fairy tale begins with a family situation in which a "lack" is experienced: usually "one member of a family absents himself from home."[89] The family is two-fold, biological and religious, thus implying the concept that the family is the society in microcosm. In the three novels, three little girls are removed from their natural families and raised in a hostile environment: the ghetto, and a Jew's house in an unspecified section of Naples. The hero is introduced: "he who either suffers directly from the action of the villain or who agrees to aid the victim(s)." In these stories they are Sibilla Odaleta and Ludovico and Annibale Trivulzio; Rachele Zan-Tedeschi and Cosimo Sinibaldi; Viola and Marcello Delmonte. The villain is introduced. His role is to disturb the peace of a happy family. He can assume as many masks as there are types of villainy. In *Sibilla Odaleta* he is Abele Malvezzi; in *Il Ghetto,* Sara and Abramo; in *L'Orfana del Ghetto,* Fiorenzo. "The villian makes an attempt at reconaissance" and "receives information about his victim." Malvezzi knows just where to find children of Greek origin in Italy, probably by relying on his magical arts. The other villains employ characters in their control as informers: Abramo and Sara use Barabba to find Rachele, and Fiorenzo commands Toto to gain the confidence of Renata's household so he can kidnap Raul. Next, "the victim submits to deception and thereby unwittingly helps the enemy." Sibilla is docility itself, disliking but never questioning her relationship to Malvezzi. Raul gladly leaves home with Toto, a man he has been taught to trust. Rachele's adventures do not fit the mold in this case only: she attempts to flee the villains, but only because they will not allow her to marry whom she chooses. She never realizes the original deception: that they are not her real parents and that she was not born a Jew. Further, in all three novels, "the villain causes harm or injury to a member of the family." This is the actual mechanism that activates the sequence of events that is the plot. Malvezzi steals Sibilla and prepares her for sale. Sara and Abramo beat Rachele and retrieve her when she escapes. Fiorenzo kidnaps Raul setting in motion the chain of events that result in

88. V. Propp, *The Morphology of the Folktale,* 1920, trans. Laurence Scott, 2d ed. rev. (Austin: Texas University Press, 1968). This is a schematic analysis of the Russian fairy tale.

89. These major plot elements, or "functions," are taken directly from Propp.

six deaths, the revelation of two murders, and immeasurable mental anguish. Propp indicates that abduction of a family member is the most common form of villainly in the fairy tale.

Next, according to Propp, "misfortune or lack is made known; the hero is approached with a request or command; he is allowed to go or he is dispatched." Sibilla's mother enlists her son to find his sister: he makes the "lack" known to Ludovico and Annibale Trivulzio who, while fighting off French invaders, free the girl. Cosimo Sinibaldi gives refuge to Rachele and sets out to get revenge on Abramo and Sara. Marcello Delmonte shelters Viola and helps Renata and her husband, Santamaria, to find Raul. The hero then experiences various adventures that bring him closer to the final decisive meeting: "the hero and the villain join in direct combat;" "the villain is defeated;" "the villain is punished." The Trivulzios, as the Christian hunter/father figures, confront Malvezzi the Jew/wolf and rescue Sibilla. After Sara is murdered in prison, Cosimo sends the police to arrest Abramo who is later released to wander the earth seeking redemption. Marcello learns the truth about his mother's death, a discovery that leads him to unravel the tangled web of crime involving all the major characters. He reveals this knowledge to Fiorenzo who then realizes that he can no longer masquerade as a law-abiding member of the community. Fiorenzo is humbled and attempts to make amends. Instead of the punishment he deserves, he is redeemed in Catholicism. Next, according to Propp, "the initial misfortune or lack is liquidated." Sibilla, Rachele, and Viola are all reunited with family, though for Rachele, "family" refers only to Christian society. And finally: "in the end the hero is married and ascends the throne." Sibilla marries the wealthy Marquis Annibale Trivulzio; Rachele marries Cosimo Sinibaldi; and Viola marries the Count Marcello Delmonte. The ascent of a throne refers to the transformation of the heroine to a higher plane of existence; in these novels, that is translated as belief in Christianity and marriage into a stable, wealthy Christian family.

Although it is unlikely that these authors consciously structured their stories on the model of this popular folktale form, Proppian analysis reveals that in all probability the plots of these novels derive from folktale and, therefore, that in the delineation of the major characters, their creators were reworking archetypal images.

Fairy tales are currently being reevaluated by psychologists because of their nature as an essentially self-contained system reflecting one psychological element through a prescribed sequence of events and a concommitant series of symbolic tableaux. They are sometimes used in analysis because they are believed to be

the purest and simplest expression of collective unconscious psychic processes . . . They represent the archetypes in their simplest, barest and most concise form.[90]

As an aspect of the collective unconscious, each archetype is in a sense a primary reaction, fantasy, or poetic image or even an "elementary impulse toward action"[91] and is directly connected with one's emotional life. Thus the three novels, which are calculated to touch the most basic emotions, are the ideal instruments to reawaken specific, programmed, archetypal images.

The archetypal image is a purely schematic[92] abstract figure exhibiting recognizably programmed reactions. As a villain it is completely negative, as a hero it is completely positive. Underneath the plethora of description, minor characters and coups-de-scène, the design of the popular novel is equally schematic. Basically manichaean in concept, it pits the traditional enemies, good versus evil, hero versus villain, and sometimes, Christian versus Jew, in a primal conflict that is destined to be reproduced as long as there is a public for such stories. The individual characteristics of the dramatis personae are just superficial details to distinguish them from their predecessors and successors. In *Sibilla Odaleta* the mother may grieve, hate, and scheme, but her emotional activity is merely the mechanism that impels the Trivulzios to perform their heroic "function." In *Il Ghetto* and *L'Orfana del Ghetto* (with the exception of the "program" character, Fiorenzo), the characters remain monodimensional and mechanical, neither shedding old attributes nor gaining new insights.

The Jew/villain is the dark emblem of fear, the obstacle that must be surmounted. The Jew represents division from ordered well-being, or in other words, a model of the ego functioning at odds with the all-embracing self (society, the Christian collectivity). His Christian rival is the hero whose purpose it is to unify families, to reconnect people with established spiritual norms in order to renew the basic life principles. The hero can function only in accord with the self, since he

90. M. L. von Franz, *An Introduction to the Psychology of Fairy Tales* (Zurich: Spring Publications, 1973).

91. Ibid., 6.

92. M. Lüthi, *Die Gabe im Märchen und in der Sage* (Bern: Büchler, 1943).

incorporates a divine principle on which the entire welfare—psychic and physical—of the nation depends. In his body lives the totem spirit of the tribe. He,
therefore, has many characteristics that would incline us to look at him as a
symbol of the self, because the self `. . . is the center of a self-regulating system
of the psyche on which the welfare of the individual depends.[93]

The key words here are "nation" and "tribe"—a people that creates
its heroes to incarnate its ideals and which then looks to them to defend
and preserve its values. These values—the "divine principle" of the cita-
tion—are the established norms and customs by which the people, that
is, the totality of its population, defines itself. The heroine symbolizes
purity and virtue, in short, the values and stability of the society. The
villain undermines that way of life; he threatens the welfare of the collectivity by separating the heroine from it. It is up to the hero to repel
danger by eliminating the villain, redeeming the heroine and restoring
her to her proper place. When the hero and heroine are united, order
returns to society along with purity, virtue, and the means to defend it.

The notion of the society refers to certain bourgeois standards of
honor and clean living but also, and for our purposes more importantly,
to its composition, to its homo- or heterogeneity. The danger to society
posed by the villain in the three novels (especially the two written after
Jewish Emancipation, *Il Ghetto* and *L'Orfana del Ghetto*) is assimilation,
which some feared would irrevocably alter the nature of Italian society.
In all three novels, Jews have already ventured out of their enclaves and,
by ruse, gained a foothold in the Christian community. Malvezzi deals
in Christian blood, Abramo and Sara own land, Fiorenzo is a titled aris-
tocrat with an imposing villa in an elegant neighborhood. Overt racism
is not present in these works—"scientific" racism had yet to establish
itself in Italy—although there are some vaguely Lombrosian[94] references to blood and heredity in Invernizio:

It is said that our blood and characters speak [for us]. (*OG,* III, 81)

The voice of blood never lies. (*OG,* III, 263)

Nonetheless in light of the events that would occur fifty years later and
the racial message that would be repeated uninterrupted in popular lit-

93. M. L. von Franz, *Psychology of Fairy Tales,* 37.
94. Cesare Lombroso (1835–1909) pioneered Italian racial studies that were aimed
at explaining certain human aberrations such as delinquency, criminality, and disease, in
works such as *L'uomo delinquente in rapporto all'antropologia, alla giurisprudenza ed alle
discipline economiche* (1876); *L'antisemitismo e le scienze moderne* (1894); *L'uomo bianco e
l'uomo di colore* (1871, 1892).

erature from Invernizio's era into the 1930s, one must not dismiss racial notions as they are expressed here. Liberi, Invernizio, and, to a lesser extent Varese, all make plain their preference for societal homogeneity.

The connection between social stability and homogeneity is most forcefully made in the denouement of the three novels. Conservative resolution of the social problems and relationships that make up the plot is standard fare in popular literature. In the mistero, for example, authors sometimes described their novels as crusades against the injustices that plague their readers in their daily lives. And some popular literature which highlighted economic ills was an effective agent of limited social reform.[95] But, for the most part, after the passions cool, after the heroine is rescued and the villain is eliminated, one finds that the social structures that define the fictional world in the novel remain unchanged. The happy ending is not a social revolution, no matter how modest. Indeed, Umberto Eco concludes, in large measure mass-market literature owes its success to "consolation," that is to the constant repetition of the reader's expectation that, paradoxically,

reform will make those changes in society which will allow everything to settle back into place as it was before. Thus [conservative] ideology and [narrative] structure are perfectly fused. . . . Those characters who convert are actually good in the first place and those who are bad die without repenting. . . . [It is essential that] nothing be resolved so as to upset anyone.[96]

What then happens to the Jewish characters at the end of the three novels? At the end of Varese's, Liberi's, and Invernizio's tales no Jews remain; that is, either the characters themselves or the Jewishness of the characters have been totally eliminated. Malvezzi and Sara are murdered whereas Abramo and Fiorenzo are left alive but rendered harmless by sending them far away. Abramo becomes the Wandering Jew who may never stay in one place for longer than three days. Fiorenzo converts, but even as a Christian he is forced out of society and into a cloistered monastic order. Over the course of his tormented life he has merely traded one ghetto for another. What about the Jewish heroines who convert and are incorporated back into the heart of their societies? At the end of each work we discover that the heroines were never Jews

95. Examples include the founding of prison farms, isolation of prisoners in individual cells, and charitable organizations for ex-convicts, all inspired by Sue's *The Mysteries of Paris*. See U. Eco, "Eugène Sue: il socialismo e la consolazione," in *Superuomo di massa*, 47–48.
96. Ibid., 65–66.

at all but displaced Christians. Their conversions are technically unnecessary but nonetheless de rigeur, like ritual baths or immersion in the river Lethe, to cleanse them of the evil influence of villain and ghetto and render them worthy of their (symbolic) identification with purity. There is no room for Jews of any kind in society as it is portrayed in these works, so in purging that minority the hero frees his people from all danger of corruption.

Purification can occur, however, only in a fictional world in which problems are continually resolved according to a desired pattern. The historical reality regarding the Jews was emancipation followed by massive assimilation, with or without conversion; the process was continuous and inexorable. One antidote or, more precisely, a temporary escape from this situation, was provided by the kind of popular literature we have just analyzed. We remember that a winning strategy to attract readers lay in the choice of title, and that two of the three popular novels feature the ghetto in their titles. Yet by the time that Liberi and Invernizio wrote their novels the institution of the ghetto had ceased to exist in Italy and society was being irrevocably altered by Jewish assimilation. Indeed, with the exception of the most impoverished, Florentine Jews had left the ghetto long before Invernizio began to write. Liberi and Invernizio set about preparing Christian society for the onslaught of Jews from the ghetto despite the fact that Jews had already assimilated and held positions of responsibility as full citizens.

The sub-genre of the romanzo storico-sociale within the genre of the romanzo d'appendice replaced actual history with a sort of "fantahistory," in which fanciful storytelling was combined with carefully researched locales (some streets within the Florentine ghetto) and some characters (Cavour's father in *Il Ghetto*) which were just recognizable enough to impress an undereducated audience. By situating their stories in a vanished ghetto and imagining a society that was still partitioned between Jew and Christian, Liberi and Invernizio were indulging a nostalgic vision of a social condition they may well have desired and which they perceived was desirable to their readers.

Here the reader's wishful thinking enjoyed free rein, for here the wrongs, torments, and tortures that so stimulated the imagination would be resolved in the interests of the common good. A paradoxical world of adventure, intrigue, and even resolution in which the forces of order would always emerge to impart a comfortingly conservative message: in short, a fairy-tale world. Danger narrowly avoided has always been a successful literary topic and the very real phenomenon of Jewish emergence in Italian Christian society provided popular authors with material that in their literary milieu was seen as controversial, material that they could fashion at will to reflect the tastes and satisfy the aspirations of their public.

5

Strangers at Home

*Let us hope that the Jews will be smart enough not to incite
anti-Semitism in the one country where it has never existed.*

Mussolini[1]

Erano due razze in antica tensione.

(They were of two races locked in age-old strife.)

Saba

Introduction

On the occasion of Italy's entry into World War I in
1915, the editor of the influential journal, *Vessillo israelitico,* issued the
following directives on page one:

The hour has come. Our Italy has declared war. We are not searching for the
reasons behind this [since they are] evident. The very fact of war is enough for
us. Italy is at war and we will dedicate ourselves entirely to her. For us any
sacrifice will seem sweet and every privation our duty. We Jews will give all of
ourselves to our country. We will give our sons, our possessions, our lives. Italy
has the right to expect everything from us and everything is what we will give
her. Her honor is at stake and [with it] our honor. Our country must
win, . . . even if we must fall, even if we must die.[2]

1. *Il Popolo d'Italia* (19 September 1920).
2. *Vessillo israelitico* 63, no. 10 (1915): 1.

This is an extraordinary document. It tells us that, despite two thousand years on Italian soil, despite complete integration following unification, many Jews still felt like outsiders or feared that they appeared to be less than fully Italian. It also tells us that some politically aware Jews realized that in wartime, as in any crisis, their loyalties would be tested. Total Jewish dedication to their country's cause was an expected duty. Moreover, it was natural and must appear so to all eyes. What had happened in the history of Jewish life to occasion this concern?

Although throughout the nineteenth century popular literature had depicted Jews largely as ghetto dwellers, after Emancipation (1848–1870) Jews were free to move about as they pleased. At the time of the Risorgimento, the ghettos of some 67 communities, scattered through Northern and Central Italy, housed 37,000 to 40,000 Jews.[3] But many of the communities were very small and once restrictions on Jewish activity were lifted, it was found that these towns offered few opportunities for advancement. When the possibility presented itself, younger and more ambitious Jews left home—just like their non-Jewish compatriots—for the nearest urban centers and, gradually, ventured to major cities.

In the 90-year period 1840–1930, the change in Jewish residency patterns reveals striking developments in Italian Jewish life. In 1840, 25 percent of Italian Jewry lived in towns of 500 people or less, but by 1930 only 10 percent remained.[4] However, Rome, which in 1841 had only 3,705 Jewish inhabitants, by 1931 had grown to 11,000. Milan's Jewish population, only a few dozen in 1841, swelled by 1931 to 6,200 and Turin's went from 1,500 to 3,700.[5] By the time of the so-called "secret" census of 22 August 1938, taken by the Interior Ministry's Office of Demography and Race as part of the Fascist anti-Semitic campaign, their statistics showed that 41,224 Italian Jews and 7,767 Jews of foreign origin lived in provincial capitals and that only 4,137 Italian Jews and 1,975 foreign Jews lived in lesser municipalities.[6]

3. A. Milano, *Storia degli ebrei in Italia* (Turin: Einaudi, 1963), 378; C. Roth, *History of the Jews of Italy* (Philadelphia: Jewish Publication Society, 1946), 501.

4. R. Bachi, "Le migrazioni interne degli ebrei dopo l'emancipazione," in *Rassegna mensile di 'Israel'* 12 (1937–1938): 318–362.

5. A. Milano, *Ebrei in Italia*, 379; L. Livi, *Gli ebrei alla luce della statistica: Evoluzione demografica, economica, sociale* (Florence: Libreria della Voce, 1920), 266–267.

6. One must not take these figures at face value, however, since the census was based largely on Jewish and Jewish-sounding last names. I have reproduced these figures only to demonstrate broad Jewish residency patterns. For an informative account of the intricacies of compiling statistics on Jews in Italy, see R. De Felice, *Storia degli ebrei italiani*

As their populations dwindled, small towns were less able to maintain the standard of Jewish religious and intellectual life which in earlier days had been assured by the immobility of their captive populations. In 1840 there were 108 functioning synagogues in Italy; by 1930 that number was reduced to 38.[7] But even the cities were not immune to this decline in Jewish life; a falling demographic curve was general throughout Italian Jewry.

This was due in part to a drop in the Jewish birth rate[8] and in part to emigration to other commercial centers in the Mediterranean. But the greatest single factor in the drop in Jewish population and, with that, Jewish culture and religious life, was massive assimilation, especially after about 1880.[9] As long as Jews who had known the ghetto and its vibrant traditions were still influential in family life, assimilation was somewhat contained. When they died, they were succeeded by a generation that had no personal experience with an integral Jewish community and scorned an identity that implied separatism. Many Jews contracted mixed marriages with an almost certain result that the offspring would be raised in the dominant religion.

Still, Italian Jewry did not die out, but, indeed, thrived as a largely assimilated community that identified itself as Italian first and whose members took their places in all aspects of Italian life. It is interesting to note, however, that Reform Judaism, a partial index of assimilation in Germany, did not take hold in Italy; Italian Jews attended their synagogues only infrequently, but when they did they wanted to experience the orthodox rite of their forefathers. Given the high rate of intentional assimilation, it is useful to compare "Jewish" and "Italian" society using some statistics from the turn of the century.

At the time of the final emancipation, according to the census of 1872, illiteracy in the general population was 72.96 percent as compared to 5.8 percent among Jews. In 1901, general illiteracy had shrunk to 56 percent and 5.2 percent among Jews.[10] By 1927, general illiteracy ran at 27 percent whereas it was negligible among Jews.[11] Given the

sotto il fascismo (Turin: Einaudi, 1961, 1972), 5–14. See also, E. Nathan, Vent'anni di vita italiana attraverso all'annuario (Rome-Turin: Roux e Viarengo, 1906), 188.

7. C. Roth, Jews of Italy, 502.

8. L. Livi, Ebrei alla luce della statistica, 74–75.

9. See A. Canepa, "Emancipazione, integrazione e antisemitismo liberale in Italia: il caso Pasqualigo," Comunità 29 (1975): nn. 174, 182.

10. For these general illiteracy figures, E. Nathan, Vent'anni, 115; for Jewish illiteracy figures, A. Milano, Ebrei in Italia, 383.

11. For both figures A. Milano, Ebrei in Italia, 383.

low level of illiteracy among Jews, it can be assumed that most Jewish children attended at least elementary school. But in the general population of approximately 30 million in 1900, only about 3,995,000 children attended elementary school and only 91,620 (about 2.8 per 1,000 inhabitants) attended middle school.[12] Although the percentage of Jews among the nearly 4 million elementary school students was negligible due to the small Jewish population in Italy, given the Jewish tendency to gravitate toward commerce and the professions, their percentage among middle school students was disproportionately high.

The census of 10 June 1911 revealed that although 55 percent of the general population derived its income from agriculture, only 8.1 percent of Jews did. However, whereas 30.2 percent of the general population worked in factories, which were usually located in urban centers, not surprisingly, a comparable percentage of Jews (27.2 percent) worked alongside. But though a mere 5.6 percent of non-Jews were engaged in commerce, a full 41.6 percent of Jews were in business. Finally, only 8.7 percent of Italians entered administration or the liberal professions as compared to 23.1 percent of Jews.[13]

Several Jews, representing the full range of professions from which they had been rigorously excluded just decades earlier became prominent in national life. Among these were a mayor of Rome (Ernesto Nathan); a minister of agriculture and the treasury (Luigi Luzzatti); a war minister (General Giuseppe Ottolenghi); and a secretary of state who was of Jewish origin (Sidney Sonnino). Jews also achieved considerable prominence in the justice system, in scientific research, philology, and literature; as well, Jews held major university chairs.

After such intensive assimilation in which Italy appeared on the verge of losing all but the necessary rudiments of Jewish life, why did the editor of *Vessillo israelitico* recognize the need to exhort his readers to demonstrate their Italianness by giving their lives to the war effort? Why, for instance, emphasize an organic union between Jews and Italians by asserting that Italian honor and Jewish honor were one?

The sensation that the eyes of Italy were upon the Jews might well have stemmed in part from the resurgence of Jewish religious and cultural life, between 1890 and 1911, after decades of steady decline. In 1890, Samuel Margulies, the charismatic Galician-born chief rabbi of

12. S. Romano, *Storia d'Italia dal Risorgimento ai nostri giorni* (Milan: Mondadori, 1978), 105.

13. L. Livi, *Ebrei alla luce della statistica,* 120.

Florence, set about to reverse the trend in his adopted city. He revived the near-dormant rabbinical college—Margulies's non-Italian origin is, itself, an indication of the condition of Italian rabbinical studies—and promoted the creation of two journals, *Rivista israelitica* (*Jewish Review*) (1904–1915) and *Israel* (1916–1925).[14] Starting in 1907 and inspired by Margulies, Jewish cultural societies (*Pro Cultura*) were founded in several cities and towns. And in 1911 Florence hosted the first Jewish Youth Congress. That same year, Italian Jewish communities were organized into a Consortium. The Consortium, *Pro Cultura,* and youth groups, and the journals all preached Jewish intellectual and cultural identity and solidarity within the framework of rock-solid Italian allegiance.[15] The numbers of Jews influenced by Margulies and his followers were small, but the Jewish revival combined with the position of prominent Jews in government, business, and the professions disturbed wary nationalists.

The Jewish sentiment that most alarmed ardent nationalists, however, was Zionism. The first Italian Zionist society was established at Ancona as early as 1898 and the institution spread rapidly throughout Northern and Central Italy. In 1901 Modena hosted the first Italian Zionist Congress and in 1903 Rabbi Margulies discussed Zionism with the king. The next year Theodor Herzl, founder of the Zionist movement, had the king's ear and after the war, in 1918, the Italian government endorsed the Balfour Declaration establishing a Jewish homeland in Palestine.

But few Italian Zionists were inspired to emigrate. Rather, they saw themselves as philanthropists, contributing economically to settlement in Palestine, but almost uniquely on behalf of the oppressed eastern Jews from the *shtetls* of Russia and Poland, not for themselves. Acutely aware of the accusation of divided loyalty stemming in part from Zionism and in large measure from the Dreyfus case in France, the official Zionist journal, *L'Idea sionistica* (*The Zionist Idea*), stated unequivocally:

Zionism does not seek to give us a homeland, because we already have one which is noble and beautiful, nor does Zionism promote either political or re-

14. In 1925, *Israel* became *La rassegna mensile di 'Israel'* which is still published today. On the Jewish press, see A. Milano, "Un secolo di stampa periodica in Italia," in *Scritti in memoria di Dante Lattes* (*Rassegna mensile di 'Israel'*) 12 (1938): 96–136.

15. See A. Milano, "Gli enti culturali ebraici in Italia nell'ultimo trentennio (1907–1937)," *Rassegna mensile di 'Israel'*) 12 (1937–1938): 253–269.

ligious goals. It should, therefore, not be considered either a racial or religious challenge [to the established order].[16]

Indeed, the Jewish community demonstrated their Italian heritage repeatedly with their lives. Having won the right after Emancipation to serve in the armed forces, Jews fought in Italy's colonial wars, from Eritrea in 1889, to Adua in 1906, and Tripoli in 1911. Then, in World War I, 261 Jews died, 2 were awarded the gold medal for heroism, 207 the silver, 238 the bronze, and 28 were cited for bravery.[17] Of the three university professors who gave their lives, all were Jews.[18]

Soon after World War I, nationalistic Jews were once again afforded the opportunity to prove their devotion, though in time their allegiance would prove to be ironic at best and in many cases tragic. When in 1919 Benito Mussolini organized the *Fasci di combattimento,* the Fascist movement, he counted six Jews among the "founding fathers" and three Jews were enshrined among the early "martyrs" for the Fascist revolution. Giuseppe Toeplitz of the Banca Commerciale Italiana was one of Mussolini's earliest financial backers, as was Elio Jona who financed Mussolini's newspaper, *Il Popolo d'Italia (The Italian People).*

The Fascists demonstrated their ample and, for most Italians, comforting ability to control crisis situations through their rise to power in the wake of the events of 1922. On 31 July of that year, Italian workers declared a general strike. The Fascist party reacted by threatening to take over those governmental agencies that were incapable of repressing the strikers. The strike failed. From 1 to 4 October, the Socialist party held a congress resulting in its breakup into two factions thereby diminishing its political influence. On 24 October, the Fascist party held a national meeting in Naples and requested governmental power from the king. Unable to wrest power by peaceful means, paramilitary Fascists gathered in Rome, as well as other major cities, intent on occupation: the so-called "March on Rome." Unwilling to declare a state of siege, the king asked Mussolini to form a coalition government, which he did on 31 October 1922. Mussolini finally consolidated his power in 1924 with the assassination of the socialist Giacomo Matteotti, and the subsequent withdrawal from government of social-

16. From *L'Idea sionistica* (Modena, 1901–1911), cited in R. De Felice, *Ebrei sotto fascismo,* 25.

17. See F. Tedeschi, ed., *Gli israeliti italiani nella guerra 1915–1918* (Florence, 1921), cited in R. De Felice, *Ebrei sotto fascismo,* 15.

18. A. Momigliano, *On Pagans, Jews, and Christians* (Middletown: Wesleyan University Press, 1987), 243.

ists and liberals. By 3 January 1925, Mussolini announced the end of representative coalition government and the beginning of the Fascist regime.[19]

Seen from the perspective of hindsight, the early years of fascism display contradictory tendencies regarding the rapport between Jews and the nation in which they lived. Jewish collaboration with the Fascists continued through the hardening of the revolution into a regime. Of the fifteen jurists who drew up the Fascist constitution, three were Jews. Carlo Foà, the dean of Italian physiologists, became editor of the Fascist review, *Gerarchia* (*Hierarchy*). As late as 1932, in a position reminiscent of that of the popes' Jews from earlier centuries, Guido Jung became finance minister. In a truly bizarre move, the jurist Federico Cammeo was appointed an author of the Concordat between Mussolini and the Vatican which, in 1929, established Catholicism as the state religion. Finally, Aldo Finzi, a crack airman, suppressed an anti-Fascist demonstration in Milan and later became Undersecretary of the Interior in Mussolini's government. Ironically, Finzi would later be executed in the massacre at the Fosse Ardeatine, the sandstone quarry outside Rome, in 1944 for having sheltered a group of partisans.

At the same time as Jews were consolidating their positions in government, other Jews were dismissed from important posts. One example for all is Ludovico Mortara, president of the Supreme Court of Appeals—in essence, Chief Justice of Italy—who was rather abruptly fired[20] after a lifetime in the law. And no Jew was honored with membership in the Italian Academy, even though up until the enactment of the Racial Laws of 1938 they occupied the highest ranks of the nation's intellectual life.

Jewish adherence to fascism in its early days is really not surprising. Fascist ideals found resonance among Italians who were intensely nationalistic and antisocialist as was the almost solidly bourgeois Jewish community—despite the fact that the prominent socialists, Giuseppe Emanuele Modigliani and Claudio Treves, were Jews.[21] But although the largely bourgeois nature of Italian Jewry explains in large measure fascism's attraction for the Jews, Jewish class affiliation and its supposed repercussions for society were and continued to be major stumbling

19. S. Romano, *Storia d'Italia*, 181–190, 289–291.

20. C. Roth, *Jews of Italy*, 510.

21. For a numerical history of Jewish membership in the Fascist party, see R. De Felice, *Ebrei sotto fascismo*, 75.

blocks in their acceptance by the early nationalist and, later, Fascist authors, as we shall see.

How did the literary representation of Jews in the twentieth century reflect the changing reality of their lives? By 1900, the ghetto walls and the world of exclusion belonged to a seemingly remote past so that one would naturally expect the image of Jewish fictional protagonists to evolve along with the examples of Jews which were observable in the society at large. Yet when comparing popular narrative of the twentieth century with that of the nineteenth century, one is immediately struck by how stable and unchanging was the model of Jewish iconography. Indeed, allowing for the expansion in the range of social and economic activities brought about by the abolition of the ghetto, Jews seemed to have made little progress toward acceptance. The old stereotypes still functioned as the basis for Jewish portrayal and were openly, even liberally, employed in mass-market fiction. Thus Jews were still portrayed as cowardly, as in the case of Enrico Corradini's rich but cuckolded Beniamino Nicosia who was "clever like a fox" when it came to making plans to cheat his competitor in the junk business and to get his wife back, but "timid as a rabbit" when faced with carrying them out.[22] The Jew's only defenses against "extermination," Giovanni Papini tells us in *Gog,* were cunning, intelligence, and, of course, money.[23] For a Jew, wealth accumulated through usury and avarice was synonymous with "life," and in their communities Jews hoarded

sacks filled with all the currencies of the world . . . gold candelabra, golden goblets, statues made of gold, golden trinkets, gold ingots . . . a mountain of gold. Billions![24]

These possessions were obtained in the usual way, by preying on the weaknesses of others. One Gaspare, "the famous usurer," required only two months to denude the prodigal Arturo of all he had:

Like a vampire he had sucked all of Arturo's blood and spat back coins, one by one, in exchange for the goods he received.[25]

Like "all his kind" he was immune to the

22. E. Corradini, "Beniamino Nicosia," in *Le sette lampade d'oro* (Turin: Streglio, 1904), 279.
23. G. Papini, *Gog* (Florence: Vallecchi, 1931), 103, hereafter in the text as *G.*
24. G. Papini "La leggenda del Gran Rabbino," *Il Frontespizio* 8, no. 9 (1935): 4.
25. C. Corradi, "I prodighi e gli avari," in *Le quattro sorelle* (Milan: Garzanti, 1939), 225.

hatred of the needy people he exploited . . . because for him their loathing was the yardstick by which to measure the profit he made from them.[26]

The mentality of these "enemies of the people and of the poor, [these] starvers" was such that once they accumulated their money, they were maniacally unwilling to part with any of it.[27] Thus, one who had a thriving business lived in a hovel[28] and another with a comfortable nest egg "to adore" liked to think of himself as

extremely poor so as to be forced to devise a way to earn money. . . . He prefers to buy little rolls and make them last for lunch and dinner, tricking himself into feeling full, rather than touch his capital. . . . Therefore, even though from time to time he would stop outside banks to read the stock quotations, he continued to think himself the poorest beggar with an airtight, desperate conviction. (*CD*, 150–151)

These examples are variations on a familiar theme. One might be tempted to treat them as literature begotten by earlier literary models. Yet, for our purposes it is important to assess these works in light of new elements in the representation of Jews brought about by concerns that would find their greatest and most explicit expression in Fascist Italy of the 1930s.

Ideologies

One of the major differences we find in the popular literature of the twentieth century vis-à-vis its Jewish characters, is the subordination of religion to politics as a prime motive for narrative action. In the chapter on Bresciani we saw that a popular literary form was appropriated by the Catholic Right and made to argue a clear-cut political position. The religious aims of Bresciani's novel might seem to be relegated to a secondary position with respect to the political circumstances that inspired *L'Ebreo di Verona*. Yet the spiritual goal of Jewish conversion lent weight to Bresciani's aspirations by providing the newly converted protagonist with a means of salvation through a

26. Ibid, 217.
27. G. P. Callegari, *Il cuore a destra* (Milan: "Quaderni di poesia," 1939), 82, hereafter in the text as *CD*.
28. C. Corradi, "Prodighi e avari," 216.

clean and moral martyrdom at the hands of godless political subversives. In order to render his protagonist acceptable to the devout and
conservative readers of *Civiltà Cattolica,* Bresciani endowed Aser with
those qualities of mind and spirit that, as Bresciani's public knew, normally belonged only to right-thinking Christians. Given Aser's religious
and political orientation, these positive characteristics were pressing for
a chance to surface and guide Aser to the Light. An inevitable internal
struggle consumed the protagonist in nearly each installment culminat-
ing in a formulaic conversion sequence and the liberating religious and
political about-face.

In twentieth-century popular literature, however, conversion was no
longer sufficient to wash away fundamental Jewish corruption. Despite
arch-anti-Semite Roberto Farinacci's assertion that anti-Jewish feeling
among Catholics was the result of careful inculcation—

> We Fascist Catholics . . . take comfort in the fact that, if as Catholics we have
> become anti-Semites, we owe it to the Church's teaching of over twenty
> centuries.[29]

—solutions to the "Jewish question" appeared to reside within the
realm of secular ideology, and the social acceptance of Jews ceased to
be primarily a religious question. As a consequence of this change, literature reflected the exclusionary attitudes about Jews which were repeatedly promoted in the discourse of political theorists and of those
authors who were strongly influenced by the contemporary political
climate.

Beginning with Corradini in 1904 and extending through the
1930s, the decade that produced the most narrative featuring Jewish
characters, religion was replaced by myths of Nation and Race as central motifs in popular literature, concepts that more than any other
would shape the iconography of the Jew. Such literature was the artistic
expression of a system of ideas whose goal was the spiritual and biological unity of the nation.

Since the beginning of the century much of this narrative was in the
hands of ideologues, journalists doubling as novelists, who wrote with
a watchful eye on the marketplace. They wrote for a public raised on
simplistic novels in which the distinctions between good and evil were

---

29. From a review of Salvatore Gotta, in F. Iesi, *Cultura di destra* (Milan: Garzanti,
1979), 129.

rock-solid and inviolable.[30] It is partly for this reason that Gramsci called the authors discussed in this chapter, *inter alia,* "the heirs of Father Bresciani."[31] Gramsci was particularly concerned with the reaction and repression symbolized by Bresciani and its effect on popular culture. He attributed the predominance of Bresciani's brand of literature to the "intellectual situation" under Fascism, that is, to

panic . . . a cosmic fear of demoniacal forces which can only be understood and, therefore, controlled within a climate of universal repression.

The memory of panic endures, he warned; creative spontaneity disappears, and all art becomes "useful propaganda, polemic, implied opposition."[32]

The prolific Enrico Corradini was one such ideologically motivated novelist who argued that the novel's ideological content should follow the same basic rules as its plot construction in order to seize the collective imagination. Corradini and the nationalistic ideologues who helped him found the political party, *Associazione nazionalista italiana* (Italian Nationalist Association) (1910), and who wrote for its journal, *L'Idea nazionale* (*The National Idea*), pictured Italy as a great proletarian collective founded on the bedrock of history, race, and common interests. They imagined that Italy, like all nations from which socialism, democracy, and liberal economy had finally been banished, had substituted corrosive individual egotism with the collective egotism that alone allowed the nation to generate civilization and fulfill its mission in the world. Faced with rising emigration that was draining Italy of some of its best young people, they imagined a nation united by a collective will that would no longer have to rely on emigration. Internal cohesion of their people and common interests coupled with resistance against external forces were the hallmarks of successful nations. Such nations were bound to rise, conquer, and expand.[33]

30. On the Italian reading public, described as having "retrograde" literary tastes, unwilling to improve itself, and seeking only diversion and peace of mind, see B. Corra, "Il fascismo, gli autori e il pubblico," *Quadrivio* 2, fasc. 28 (1934): 1–2. On literary tastes of the period see also G. Cattaneo, *Biblioteca domestica* (Milan: Longanesi, 1983).

31. A. Gramsci, *Quaderni,* notebooks 6 and passim, reprinted in A. Gramsci, *Letteratura e vita nazionale* (Turin: Einaudi, 1972), 145–193.

32. Ibid., 21.

33. E. Corradini, "Principi di nazionalismo," in *Il nazionalismo italiano. Atti del Congresso di Firenze* (Florence: A. Quattrini, 1911), cited in E. Corradini, *Scritti e discorsi (1901–1914),* ed. L. Strappini (Turin: Einaudi, 1980), 163–175.

The mission of *L'Idea nazionale* was to inculcate the idea of the authoritarian State over individual, class, or party deviations from the collective will; combat socialist and Masonic internationalism in favor of irredentist and colonial imperialism; reevoke the "glory that was Rome" as the guiding myth of the people; and reinstate a national religious life by means of State Catholicism. Corradini's watchwords and those of *L'Idea nazionale* were "consolidation," "collective life," "race," "energy," "nature," and "destiny," in short, all components of "Nation." There is little difference between the rhetoric in *L'Idea nazionale* and the later discourse of fascism. Indeed, in November of 1922 Corradini declared himself a Fascist and shortly after published the seminal article "Nazionalismo e fascismo" ("Nationalism and Fascism")[34] in which he argued that the *Associazione nazionalista italiana* should merge with the Fascist movement. The fusion of the two movements in March 1923 resulted in the Italian National Fascist Party, the *Partito nazionale fascista*.

By the time he became a Fascist, Corradini had been a confirmed nationalist for well over two decades. In 1902 he declared himself a follower of "that sincere philosophy which is rooted in nature and has as its goal the triumph of superior individuals and peoples. The empire of these is the highest achievement of civilization."[35] He was at the same time an active novelist and playwright and his literary works are in large measure fictional reworkings of his political and cultural philosophy. Though at times he was criticized for being too literary in his political writings,[36] in his fiction Corradini followed D'Annunzio's example of producing works shot through with abstract and emotional, as well as current, pressing nationalistic themes aimed at the mass market in an attempt to create consensus for his political program.[37]

The technique used by Corradini and other nationalist writers was a simple one. They clothed their political ideas in eternal values expressed in mythic terms (Nation, Race) and emphasized their readers' relationship to them. Thus, an abstract, elusive notion such as the "in-

34. E. Corradini, "Nazionalismo e fascismo," in *L'Idea nazionale* (22 December 1922): 1.

35. E. Corradini in a review of M. Morasso, *L'imperialismo artistico*, in *Marzocco* 43 (26 October 1902), cited in E. Corradini, *Scritti e discorsi*, xvii.

36. G. Prezzolini, "Nel VII anniversario della nascita del *Regno*," in *La Voce* 2: 51, reprinted in D. Frigessi, *La cultura italiana dell '900 attraverso le riviste* (Turin: Einaudi, 1960), chap. 3, "*La Voce* (1908–1914)," 254.

37. See, for instance, M. Morasso, "La politica dei letterati," in *Marzocco* 13 (21 March 1897).

creasingly remote past"[38] was to be understood as the time in which the ethnic and moral composition of the nation was established and intended as a past to be inherited by a specific people. "Nation," then, involved a clearly recognized sense of spiritual community "with those who precede us, in the sense of extending our [own] existence"[39] according to the "divine law in which the life of peoples appears interwoven with [that of past] generations."[40] One fictional protagonist, Ardengo Soffici's Lemmonio Boreo, has a clear sense of continuity as he wanders the Tuscan countryside in search of heroic adventure:

Lemmonio waved back with friendly cordiality. Those three men in their sobriety, with the strength of their nude arms which had been tanned by the sun and with their savage resistance to the pain of their labors, were for him a lesson in solemn virility hardened by work, and they strengthened his own hopes. They were the prototypes of a race, his own race, which had gone on undisturbed for thousands and thousands of years and on which one could always count every time one had to build or destroy.[41]

Similarly, the nation pulses with "vigorous blood,"[42] Corradini wrote, in "a wonderful organ, alive, growing from age to age and forever active."[43]

God decreed that the life of the nation extend from the past into the future as an unbroken chain since the past provides the biological humus for the future. An organic being descended from a common ancestor, the entire nation reacts as one. Corradini relates the exhilarating experience of seeing the pope in St. Peter's along with a "delirious" crowd of people, a micronation of "thousands and thousands of souls become one single soul [in which] twenty centuries of history found expression."[44] The nation reflects its integrity in

38. M. Maccari, *Il Selvaggio* 4 (16 September 1927), cited in A. Asor Rosa, "La cultura," in *Storia d'Italia* (Turin: Einaudi, 1961), vol. 4, "Dall'Unità a oggi," 1506.

39. E. Corradini, "Dell'insegnamento classico in Italia," in *La vita nazionale* (Siena: Lumachi, 1907), 162.

40. E. Corradini, "La vita che non muta," in ibid., 194.

41. A. Soffici, *Lemmonio Boreo* (Florence: Vallecchi, 1921), 22–23. The novel was written in 1911.

42. E. Corradini, "La vita nazionale," in *La vita nazionale,* 9.

43. E. Corradini, "La vita nazionale," in *Discorsi politici (1902–1923)* (Florence: Vallecchi, 1923), 38. The volume *La vita nazionale* (cited earlier) gives a variant of this phrase which differs markedly from the tone of the rest of the paragraph and from other printed versions of Corradini's speech.

44. E. Corradini, "La vita estetica," *Novissima. Albo di arte e lettere* (1903), later in *La vita nazionale,* 200.

common work, common trade . . . ideas and self-interest within a circle of mountains and seas. . . . the people's desire to create its own history, to express its ego, which is like that of the individual yet far more vast and durable.[45]

During the years in which fascism consolidated its grip on the country and the political movement became a regime, such celebrations of Nation and Race were employed to reinforce the Italian identity and to bolster legislative efforts to mold a population of individuals into a people. In 1922 Mussolini spoke of Nation as "our myth" which, in order to become a reality, demanded nothing less than total subordination of one's private concerns.[46] As rhetorical tools, the terms "Nation" and "Race" enjoyed great emotional appeal. They were collectivizing concepts that at the same time triggered powerful and very personal sentiments—more than others able to shape the iconography of the Jew.

Of the two, "Nation" lent itself more easily to definition than did "Race." Even though Corradini and Oriani used the word "race" as early as 1904, a strict, pseudobiological definition of an Italian race was not codified until 1938.[47] Still the Italian people was trumpeted by writers like Alfredo Oriani, who seized on phrases such as "the profundity of its race" and "its popular genius." The Italian race was "a people of rulers," a notion of superiority that held out the promise of glorious future conquests.[48] In this social, nonbiological sense, race was invoked throughout the first thirty-eight years of the century as a standard of participation and, what is more, worthiness for participation in Italian society. When measured against this image of society, the Jewish push toward assimilation was perceived as disruption, or in the works of especially zealous nationalists, as defilement.

With the exception of extremists like Giovanni Preziosi, editor of the fiercely anti-Semitic *La vita italiana* (*Italian Life*) and translator of the bogus *Protocols of the Wise Men of Zion*, most writers, publicists, and politicians, including Mussolini, used a rather loosely defined notion

45. E. Corradini, "La vita nazionale," in *La vita nazionale,* 5–6.

46. B. Biancini, *Dizionario mussoliniano* (Milan: Hoepli, 1940), 145–146, hereafter in the text as *DM.*

47. See, for instance, the delineation of the Italian race together with the documentation of the 1938 racial provisions in R. De Felice, *Storia degli ebrei italiani sotto il fascismo* (Turin: Einaudi, 1972), 604–609; also L. Preti, *Impero fascista, africani e ebrei* (Milan: Mursia, 1968), 24–32; also M. Michaelis, *Mussolini and the Jews* (Oxford: The Clarendon Press, 1978), 171–173 and passim.

48. A. Oriani, *La rivolta ideale* (Bologna: Cappelli, 1924), 139, cited in A. Asor Rosa, "La cultura," 1077.

of race. The end result was that even after hundreds of pages were filled and speeches made on the subject, until the publication of specific laws in 1938, the exact nature of the racial campaign was not clear. On one occasion Mussolini called race "the material out of which we intend to build history" and cited the "racial question" as a source of major concern for Fascists.[49] But at the same time Mussolini attempted to disassociate his notion of race from the "scientific" concept that was taking hold in Germany. Unlike Germany, he said, Italy needed no scapegoat to atone for the debacle of World War I and her "national pride" had no use for the "delirium of race." Furthermore, he declared, "anti-Semitism does not exist in Italy" because "Italian Jews have always been good citizens and as soldiers they have fought bravely."[50] In the same year, 1932, he went even further in denying racist foundations to fascism in his *Treatise on Fascist Doctrine:*

Fascism . . . is the simplest form of democracy when the people is defined as it should be, that is qualitatively and not quantitatively. . . . Neither a race nor a specific geographical region, but a stock which perpetuates itself throughout history, a multitude united by an idea. (*OO*, XXXIV, 20)

Given what we know about the climate of nationalistic affirmation in Italy, it is easy to assess the utility of such a loosely defined concept of race to orators and publicists and to see why its ambiguity was so potentially dangerous. Mussolini's denials aside, the seemingly neutral equation "race equals the 'material' with which to build 'history'" contains a blueprint for Italy in which "history" means tradition traced from a collective past and projected into the future and "the material" suggests the genetic continuity of a preferred racial type. Yet we are told that this "stock which perpetuates itself throughout history" is not a race and that in any case racism is "95 percent sentiment" and "delirium," sentiment gone awry.[51]

If we compare the *Italian Encyclopedia (Treccani)* article "Racism" with the *Treatise on Fascist Doctrine* we note an almost complete consonance between Mussolini's approach and the standard, established definition of racism. The *Treccani* defines racism as the "recognition of the existence of races which are by nature superior or inferior and the repercussions of this fact on political, social, cultural, religious and in-

49. B. Mussolini, *Opera omnia,* ed E. and D. Susmel (Florence: La Fenice, 1959), vol. 17: 219, hereafter in the text as *OO.*
50. E. Ludwig, *Colloqui con Mussolini* (Milan: Mondadori, 1950), 72.
51. Ibid.

tellectual history."[52] It is crucial, therefore, that the select group of eth-
nically determined superior beings form a discrete society that shares a
common history. As Mussolini envisaged ethnic Italian society it was
united by an "idea." The notion of the "idea," however, eludes satisfactory definition and must be accepted as one of those words that in the
Fascist "kingdom of words" became facts.[53] Thus reified, this "idea"
could be applied to as many situations as events warranted. Here we
have a clue to the dangers alluded to earlier: "idea," "stock/race," "history" are multivalent words that refer to hidden and, therefore, irrefut-
able traits.

The *Treccani* article goes on to say that no Italian *race* exists, only
an Italian *people* and an Italian *nation*. Similarly no Jewish *race* or *nation*
exists, only a Jewish *people*.[54] But the fundamental building block of
both *nation* and *people* is *race*, so we are back where we started. Terms
such as "national pride," "the people," "history," "the idea," and even
"race" to some extent, are referents whose foremost appeal is emotional,
not intellectual, and whose ultimate effect is one of obfuscation rather
than clarification.

Enthusiastic response to Mussolini's oratory about race is a perfect
example of the emotional acceptance of rhetoric which could not stand
up to intellectual scrutiny. Mussolini boasted of having introduced
racism, "a major conquest," into Italian history, of having spoken of
the Aryan race as early as 1921 and of having kept the racial question
in the forefront ever since. He continued discussing race throughout
the 1930s and in the end left a rich body of texts on the subject. In
1938, after the Interior Ministry's Office of Demography and Race was
created and *La difesa della razza* (*The Defense of the Race*) was founded
to fuel the racial campaign, and especially after the "Racist Scientists"
declared that "the concept of race is [to be understood] only in biological terms" (14 July 1938),[55] Mussolini would occasionally express him-

52. *Enciclopedia italiana* (1938–1948), appendix II, 669.

53. F. Venturi, "Il regime fascista," in AA.VV. *Trent'anni di storia italiana (1915–
1945)* (Turin: Einaudi, 1961), 186–187, cited in M. Isnenghi, *Intellettuali militanti ed
intellettuali funzionari: Appunti sulla cultura fascista* (Turin: Einaudi, 1979), 29. Mussolini acknowledged this tendency toward reification on 24 May 1924 saying that "At certain times words can be facts"; cited in E. Leso, "Aspetti della lingua del fascismo. Prime
linee di una ricerca," in AA.VV. *Storia linguistica dell'Italia del Novecento*, Atti del
V congresso internazionale di studi (Rome: 1971) (Rome: Bulzoni, 1973), 148.

54. *Enciclopedia italiana* (1949, photographic reproduction of 1935 edition), vol. 28:
911.

55. The complete *Manifesto degli scienziati razzisti* is reprinted in De Felice, *Ebrei sotto
fascismo*, 541–542.

self "quantitatively." By misusing technical language, he disposed his
listener to think in terms of concrete analysis; by adapting language to
his political purpose, he created ambivalence in everyday words and
used them in ways that their actual meaning would normally not permit. Mussolini and the publication that imitated him found it opportune to choose words that appeared technical and convincing, but
which were actually noninformative and served to impede analysis. One
of the most frequent of these terms was "blood"; in the first issue of
La difesa della razza one could read that blood was the symbol of those
"concrete values of race, biological and ethnic values, . . . and genius."[56]
Mussolini's "allocutions," however, were in large measure not intended
to transmit information so much as to be "a means of contact between
my soul and yours, between my heart and your hearts," an attempt to
establish an intuitive, "pre-logical" rapport with his audience.[57] Thus,
with regard to racial differentiation, Mussolini preferred to speak of its
more abstract, "spiritual" aspects using "cultural" rather than scientific
terms.[58] His language was, therefore, more suited to the vast public
than that of many organs of propaganda; it was more allusive, more
akin to that of fiction.[59] In addition, given his position at the end of a
long line of nationalist thinkers, he enjoyed such a privileged status as
political and cultural arbiter that his pronouncements could be considered as a synecdoche for fascism itself. It is for this reason that an
analysis here of some of his speeches pertaining to race will yield concepts useful to understanding the literature of the period.

The speech "*Scoperta!*" ("Eureka!") given on 26 July 1938 affirmed
the Aryan origins of the Italian people as outlined in the *Manifesto of
Racist Scientists,* an ancestry still visible in the bodies of the people. But
the importance of history, of traceable origins, transcended mere physical appearance:

Ladies and gentlemen, we are talking about race. Italian women and men . . .
have never had any connection to the Semitic or other extra-European races.
Those who wish to observe these types in all their classical purity and nobility

56. *La difesa della razza* 1, no. 1 (1938), 3, cited in M. A. Cortelazzo, "Il lessico del
razzismo fascista," *Movimento operaio e socialista* 7, no. 1 (new series) (1984): 64.

57. See E. Leso, "Aspetti della lingua del fascismo," especially 148–149.

58. M. A. Cortelazzo, "Il lessico," 63. Cortelazzo compares Mussolini's lexicon on
racial matters to that of *La difesa della razza* and reports on the various interpretations
of the word *razza.*

59. For an insightful look into language that is absorbed by reader and listener rather
than logically *understood* and processed, see F. Iesi, *Cultura di destra,* pt. 2, "Il linguaggio
delle idee senza parole," especially 102–119.

of line are urged to examine the high reliefs of the *Ara pacis*. To call oneself Aryan means to declare that one belongs to a historically determined group of races: to the Indo-European group and specifically to those groups which have created world civilization.[60]

Here Mussolini has established clear criteria for belonging to Italian society in the opposition Indo versus "extra"-European. The notion of *in* versus *out* is easily visualized as, for instance, a circle or enclosure labeled "in" or "Aryan," "Italy" or "we," surrounded by non-European races, "Semites" or "they." The speaker then reinforces the *in* with a specific, familiar visual image. The altar with its classically pure, noble figures is a clever mnemonic device, easily pictured in the mind at a time when such symbols were widely used. Mussolini's description of the altar employs the abstract term "purity" and immediately supplies the listener/reader with concrete ways to apply the term, both personally and to the surrounding world. This purity is the result of another: the purity of origins and the history of the Italian people. Purity has been steadfastly preserved—within the imaginary circle—from what Mussolini called "foreign contributions (hybridism) through naturalization." Of inestimable value, this purity of Indo-European peoples is responsible for the creation of world civilization. In Mussolini's picture of the world, all this—purity, Aryanness, civilization, *Ara pacis,* Italy, Indo-European peoples—lies within a zone that is surrounded and constantly menaced by potential contamination and corruption. Chief among threats to Fascist perfection were Bolshevism, which seventeen years earlier Mussolini had called "a tragic madness,"[61] and the Jews who were thought to practice it.

Just as he had celebrated the origins and unique qualities of the Italian people in *"Scoperta!,"* in a later speech, *"Anche nella questione di razza noi tireremo dritto!"* ("We'll Hold Firm Even on the Racial Question!"), Mussolini boasted of the originality of Italian racism. Italian Fascism had never "imitated anyone or anything."[62] This equivalence of national-racial origins with the beginnings of racial consciousness effectively elevated racism to the status enjoyed by history thus assuring it a place in the official—if somewhat artificially created—national ethos. From its position in the pantheon of Fascist initiatives, rac-

60. B. Mussolini, "Scoperta!," *Il Popolo d'Italia* 25 (26 July 1938): 207; *OO,* XXIX, 125–126.

61. B. Mussolini, "Discorso di Bologna," *Il Popolo d'Italia* 7 (1921): 1, 81.

62. B. Mussolini, "Anche nella questione di razza noi tireremo dritto!," *Il Popolo d'Italia* 25 (31 July 1938), 212; *OO,* XXIX, 126.

ism contributed invaluable prestige to the nation by endowing it with an unmistakable aura of superiority. This prestige was what enabled nations to hold onto empires. The subjugating mechanism of prestige could not function without a "clear, severe racial consciousness."[63] Mussolini envisioned the racially superior inhabitants of that imaginary inner circle reaching out into the surrounding unorganized, "nonhistorical," barbaric zone, "conquering it by force of arms and ruling it with prestige." Ruling meant civilizing: the empire then would inhabit a sort of gray, semicivilized zone around the inner circle with exchange between the two areas but never a melding of the two because of the racial superiority of the inner circle.

How did the Jewish question complicate this vision? The Jewish problem was but one aspect of this same phenomenon, but one that required continual vigilance since

for sixteen years, despite our policies, world Judaism has been an implacable enemy of Fascism. In Italy our policies have generated what can only be called a strong impetus among the Semitic elements to assault us. (*OO*, XXIX, 146)

This threat was two-fold: from international Jewry, as Fascist writers and spokesmen had warned all along, and from those whom Mussolini perceived were its Italian Aryan defenders, whom he called the "unexpected friends of Jews." Thus before the racial legislation, Jews had overstepped what racists considered unmarked boundaries by co-opting Aryans to their defense. In so doing, it appeared that Jews were attempting to redivide the Italian people, which fascism had finally united through race. The old notion of two Italies (one from the Po valley, the other southern) had been replaced: *all Italians,* Mussolini explained,

are neither Hamitic nor Semitic nor Mongols. So if we are none of these races, we are obviously Aryan and we descended [into Italy] from the Alps, from the North. We are, therefore, Aryans of the Mediterranean type [and racially] pure. (*OO*, XXIX, 190)

Possessing racial superiority and a higher form of civilization, the Italians disarmed, civilized, and absorbed would-be conquerors such as the Lombards. Why, then, have the Jews remained intact and "racially pure" for "ten centuries" within Italian borders? Like the pamphleteers of the late-eighteenth and early-nineteenth centuries, Mussolini marvels at the durability of these people. Although it is unlikely that he was

63. B. Mussolini, "Discorso di Trieste," *Il Popolo d'Italia* 25 (16–18 September 1938): 259–261; *OO*, XXIX, 146.

familiar with specific texts in this tradition (Jabalot, Lammenais),[64] the references to the "marvelous," almost supernatural endurance of the Jewish people and to their presumed but fallacious racial purity had become a standard element in the cultural undercurrent regarding Jews.

The Jews, Mussolini argued, were the most "racial" people in the world and unassimilable given their large number. The Jewish population, he warned, was seventy thousand and not forty-three thousand as the Jews wanted people to believe,[65] and a large percentage of that group was solidly anti-Fascist. Like the notion of racial purity, this exaggeration of population figures is traceable throughout the literature about Italian Jews.[66] When he mentioned the numerical threat posed by Jews to the National Council of the Fascist party, it is reported that Mussolini drew prolonged applause. The National Council considered itself the reliable interpreter of the sentiment of the Italian people and of Fascist political rhetoric. Thus, in accepting Mussolini's account of a Jewish peril, the council appeared to endorse the notion that there were no points of contact between Jews and non-Jews.

Mussolini further emphasized the lack of commonality between the two peoples who had inhabited the same soil but completely different spheres for nearly two millenia. Despite the number of Jews who had intermarried or who no longer identified themselves as Jews, Mussolini assured his listeners that the impossibility of assimilation was the opinion of the Jews themselves, a situation arising from and justified by Jewish self-image. This idea was suggested in part by the history of Jewish protest against assimilation beginning in the later-nineteenth century in the Jewish press. In current popular literature as well, Jewish authors were not above negative depiction of Jews in "mainstream" business and social relations. One of these was Alfredo Segre, whose *Agenzia Abram Lewis* (1934)[67] reinforces the stereotype of Jew as usurer. An extreme view of assimilation, which was really a strident expression of Jewish

64. Roberto Mazzetti's books *L'antiebraismo nella cultura italiana dal 1700 al 1900* (Modena: Società tipografica, 1938); *Orientamenti antiebraici della vita e della cultura italiana* (Modena: Società tipografica, 1939); and *La questione ebraica in un secolo di cultura italiana dal 1800 al 1915* (Modena: Società tipografica, 1938), with their reprints of seminal treatises in the history of the Jewish question, would not be published until 1938–1939.

65. On the divergence between these figures, see R. De Felice, *Ebrei sotto fascismo*, 6–11.

66. According to De Felice, the 1931 census counted 39,112 Italian Jews and the 1938 census recorded a total population of 47,252. See De Felice, *Ebrei sotto fascismo*, 6.

67. A. Segre, *Agenzia Abram Lewis* (Milan: Mondadori, 1934).

self-hatred, came from Pitigrilli (Dino Segre), author and Fascist de-lator,[68] whose quasi-pornographic novels were publicly disdained but widely read. In his fiction he pictured Jews as seizing any opportunity to erase their identity. The heroine of *Mosè e il Cavalier Levi* declares with a mixture of wistfulness and disgust:

If it were possible to turn a switch and cease being a Jew, cease ever having been a Jew, cease having a Jewish name . . . and a nasal voice . . . on condition that no one would know you had turned the switch . . . there wouldn't be one Jew left on the face of the earth.[69]

In his "Discorso segreto," one of Mussolini's most important speeches concerning the Jews, the Fascist leader recounted a list of Jew-ish cultural attributes which he set in direct opposition to the supposed "Aryan" way of life. Choosing the order of characteristics with care, Mussolini presumed to retell the cultural history of the two races. As proof of his allegations he assured his audience that he was merely quot-ing from a typical—and anonymous—Jewish book:

Jews are the people of the sand, Aryans the people of the rock; we Jews are the people of the tent and you Aryans the people of the city; you are the people of the State whereas we don't even have a word to express the concept State in our language. We have remained a tribe. (*OO, XXIX*, 191)

The construction of this discourse is telling, for here Mussolini ably intimates that the two peoples who occupy the same political borders are set on two irrevocably separate courses that are moving in opposite directions from each other. Thus whereas Aryan civilization progressed from the primeval rock to the complex organization of the State, the Jews remained in a primitive condition of tribalism, weak and disrup-tive. The lists of attributes in opposition to each other cause the listener to compile a mental scorecard whereas the spare, crisp style and rhetor-ical structure suggest a passage of time that affected both factions, but allowed only one of them to develop. Once again Italian-Jewish rela-tions were rendered as a *we-they* rivalry in which Aryans used to or-der and progressive civilization inhabited the imaginary inner circle, whereas Jews were content with the outer reaches where all progress was impeded by chaos and barbarism.

68. For a gripping account of Pitigrilli's connivance with Fascist authorities to the detriment of Turinese Jews, see A. Stille, *Benevolence and Betrayal: Five Italian Jewish Families under Fascism* (New York: Summit Books, 1991).

69. Pitigrilli (Dino Segre), *Mosè e il Cavalier Levi,* cited in A. Stille, *Benevolence and Betrayal,* chapter 2.

Mussolini's notion of spheres of influence occupied by specific groups (Jews, non-Jews) within precise political borders or even within abstract concepts such as Italian civilization or culture was the culmination of a long history of nationalist sentiment. As a corollary to their general discussion of Nation and Race, early nationalists and later Fascist propagandists added the concept of Class in the form of rhetoric aimed at revealing the "sins of the bourgeoisie" by which they meant the values of the upper middle class. Their disdain was reflected in the portrayal of Jews' inherent middle-class nature as a divisive influence on the nation and a corrosive element eating at the heart of the race. Thus Corradini imagined the bourgeoisie solidly arrayed against the nation and implacable in its attempt to keep Italy from fulfilling its glorious destiny. The core of the national organism had been co-opted by "cunning lawyers . . . cynical *arrivistes* . . . the part of the country that is weak and sick," who were plunging Italy into mediocrity.[70] The bourgeoisie had twisted the whole concept of government, turning the parliament into a "bazaar" and observing its natural relationship with the people: "Between parliament and the nation there are no points of contact! All the bridges are down."[71] Having taken government away from its natural constituency and commercialized it, the bourgeoisie was in a better position to follow its habitual inclination: to seize political power and use it to embroil its fellow man.

The gulf between government and the people matched the economic and, especially, moral abyss between the bourgeoisie and the laboring classes which Corradini, Oriani, Prezzolini, and the novelists of the 1930s mentioned often in their writings. The bourgeoisie had an outstanding debt to society. The masses—"which are the material of history,"[72] "the best, the strongest and the most generous of all our brothers,"[73] the repositories of national virtue—looked to the middle classes for something to believe in: country and personal sacrifice. But the bourgeoisie had nothing to offer them. Morally bankrupt, these "broken-down masons, Jews, and anti-Fascist xenophiles" (*DM*, 4) had systematically eroded the myths by which these people lived without replacing them. The masses worked while the bourgeoisie in their cities

70. E. Corradini, "Le elezioni," *Il Regno* 1 (1904): 48, cited in D. Frigessi, *Cultura attraverso riviste,* vol. 1: 519.

71. A. Campodonico, "La fine di un sogno mediocre," *Il Regno* 3, no. 7 (1906), cited in D. Frigessi, *Cultura attraverso riviste,* vol 1: 546.

72. E. Corradini, *La guerra lontana* (Milan: Treves, 1911), 211.

73. E. Corradini, *La patria lontana* (Milan: Treves, 1910), 193–194.

talked about work. The bourgeoisie was synonymous with the city, which, "creates nothing, but consumes . . . like a pyre which gives light by burning what was created far from itself. . . . All cities are sterile."[74] The city was an unnatural environment in which people preyed on each other. Bourgeois opportunism was a corrupting force that sapped the strength of the nation and was even responsible for Italy's diminished international influence ("Italietta").[75]

Despite Mussolini's assertion that Jews lived outside the "Aryan" sphere of organized life, the nationalists insisted on the link between Jewish and bourgeois culture. Indeed, the Jews were inextricably identified with the bourgeoisie in their intense urbanism and parasitic tendencies; they devoured everything the nation had to offer, but, versed only in trade and other infertile arts, gave nothing in return.[76] These people who had been traditionally ostracized from Nation and national life had, upon emancipation, sought and found their spiritual home in the ethos and activities of the bourgeoisie. Used to the ghetto that, it was imagined, meant living by their own rules and entirely for their own benefit, they swelled the ranks of the middle class, alienating it still further from the moral directions of the nation. Thus Soffici's Lemmonio Boreo is discouraged to find vast regions of Italy "afflicted with commercialism" and "Judaism," which Soffici defined elsewhere as hypocrisy.[77]

Building upon the views expressed by the early nationalists, Fascist propagandists added that commercialism, parasitism, and hypocrisy had rendered the Jews unfit to fight the domestic and imperial "battles" of Fascist life and unable to muster the moral and physical courage to "vivere pericolosamente e romanamente" ("live dangerously while reproducing the virtues of the ancient Romans") as fascism demanded. The *Treccani* attributed all the Fascist virtues to the superior races— "valor in war, ability to command, creativity, inventiveness"—and to the inferior races the imputations normally associated with Jews—"a

74. G. Papini, in *Fiera Letteraria* (1928), cited in A. Asor Rosa, "La cultura," 1502– 1503n.

75. G. Prezzolini, "Le due Italie," *Il Regno* 1, no. 26 (1904), cited in D. Frigessi, *Cultura attraverso riviste*, vol 1: 502. With the expression *Italietta* Prezzolini alluded to Italy's defeat at Adua in 1896.

76. A. Oriani, "I deicidi," *L'Attualità* (21 January 1904), reprinted in *Fuochi di bivacco* (Bari: Laterza, 1918), 191–195.

77. A. Soffici, *Lemmonio Boreo*, 53. The definition of Judaism appears as a parable in Soffici's *Giornale di Bordo* under the entry for 14 February. (Florence: Vallecchi, 1921), 343.

subaltern ability to carry out orders" but coupled with "disruptive, criticizing and licentious tendencies which should be held in check."[78] Echoing what Corradini, Oriani, Prezzolini, Campodonico, and Papini had written years earlier, Mussolini outlined the ways in which Jews were ill-suited to life in the New Italy. Quite beyond their racial unsuitability, their bourgeois mentality was "clearly refractory to the Fascist mentality." They were socially divisive, pitting worker against peasant. Xenophilic in outlook they favored Britain and France whereas true Fascists loved only Italy. They were cursed with "timid pessimism which blanched before difficulties" whereas the Fascists' "virile pessimism" gave them the courage to confront any obstacle. Jews held courage, sport, war, and almost all physical activity in contempt. In their condition of nonvirility, Jews and the rest of the bourgeoisie were naturally disposed to take moral "beatings" from the Fascists who, in their virility, were morally obligated to establish order in society, in Mussolini's words, to "administer heavy punches to the belly."[79]

The democratic bourgeoisie was a group difficult to identify and for this reason its vulnerability was limited to political rhetoric. Its status was primarily that of a polemical target. By aligning himself with his listeners in a common "battle" against these defeatists and subversives who sought to upset Fascist order and reverse Fascist progress—Jews, intellectuals, and other nonconformists—Mussolini was able to infuse his audience with the emotional "elementary passions" that are the underpinnings of political discourse in general and Mussolini's in particular.[80]

The desire for conformity was one of these "elementary passions": the inherent image that each member had of the surrounding society, of personal space, and its contiguity with public space. Since contiguousness implied a metaphysical extension or reflection of oneself in others, this sense of space with its accompanying notion of boundaries was easily manipulated by Fascist propaganda and channeled into concerns about racial purity and ethnic homogeneity. The grip of the Fascist ethic was strengthened even further because spiritual uniformity was also projected onto these two elements of Nation. Mussolini cele-

78. *Enciclopedia italiana* (1938–1948), appendix II, 669.

79. B. Mussolini, "Discorso segreto" to the National Council of the Fascist Party, 25 October 1938 in *OO*, XXIX, 185–196.

80. G. Folena, preface to *Retorica e politica, Atti del II convegno Italo-tedesco* (Bressanone, 1974) (Padua: Liviana, 1977), par. 1552 #1, p. xv.

brated religious conformity as a valuable accomplishment of the New Italy and warned against heresy:

Religious unity is one of the greatest strengths of a people. Compromising it or attempting to undermine it in any way is a crime against the nation (*lesa nazione*).[81]

Such ironclad identification of religion and Nation allowed little room for interpretation, though "compromise" and "undermine" are generalizations and left undefined in the speech. They are, however, less compelling rhetorically than the emphatic "in any way" which qualifies them. The inflexible tone of this expression strengthens "compromise" and "undermine" in their role as heretical crimes against the nation and weakens the paradoxical nature of the imprecise terms that constitute the unequivocable declaration.

Mussolini's speeches were dutifully reproduced by *Il Popolo d'Italia*, which reached a broader cross-section of the populace than the *Italian Encyclopedia*. Although intended as an instrument of popular instruction, in reality the *Treccani* appealed mainly to a readership with some intellectual preparation. Similarly, Mussolini's statement on the non-existence of anti-Semitism in Italy was taken from private conversations that, when published in 1932, reached only about twenty-five thousand readers.[82]

But the readers of the popular press could not expect to find a straight, linear approach to the Jewish question in their daily paper; as late as the autumn of 1938, Mussolini divided Italian Jewry into the categories of bad and not-so-bad. Those who had earned military or civil honors could expect "comprehension and justice" from the regime; the others would be subject to a "policy of separation" (*OO*, XXIX, 146). Given Mussolini's vacillating approach toward the Jews and the media's deliberately ambiguous language during the *ventennio* ("twenty-year" period of fascism), fascism sometimes appeared to embrace even the Jews, at least the large numbers of them who continued to see themselves as loyal Fascists.

In trying to imagine the impact of such messages on the masses

81. B. Mussolini, "Sintesi del regime," *Il Popolo d'Italia* 21, no. 67 (20 March 1934): 1, cited in R. Carbonelli, "Dolicocefalo biondo," *Il Frontespizio* 9, no. 2 (1937): 135; *OO*, XXVI, 190.

82. A Mondadori, "Cronistoria dei *Colloqui*," introduction to E. Ludwig, *Colloqui con Mussolini*, xxv.

before anti-Semitic legislation, indeed when such legislation was still considered a thing of the past, we would have to overlook those hints of future excesses which we of today immediately recognize in the speeches and articles of that period. We can, however, realize how confusing they must have appeared.

Looking back on the period, another source of confusion is the fact that cultural life during fascism was complex and not monolithic, for, despite the regime's attempt to fashion all aspects of culture according to its vision of a perfect society and to hermetically exclude those elements that did not conform to this vision, fascism was unable to construct an impenetrable legislative wall. There *was* opposition to the Fascist control of culture, even some limited protest, for example, about the growing exclusion of Jews from "official" cultural life. A quiet voice of dissent was raised from some of the many small literary journals that flourished briefly during the late 1920s and 1930s. The Florentine literary review *Solaria* was criticized for its so-called "Jewish outlook" by writers who identified with the nativist and ruralist *Strapaese* movement and who wrote for the antimodernist *Il selvaggio* (*The Savage*) and *Il Bargello* and the militantly Catholic *Il Frontespizio* (*Frontispiece*) because *Solaria* published Jewish writers. *Solaria* collaborator, the novelist Elio Vittorini, recalled: "They called us dirty Jews because we used to publish Jewish writers and because of all the good things we had to say about Kafka or Joyce."[83]

Solaria used the "cosmopolitanism" and "internationalism" of the Jewish writers like the Triestine Italo Svevo as a means of breaking the near stranglehold that the provincialists appeared to have on Italian culture.[84] The writers for such staunchly anti-Semitic journals as *Il Frontespizio* clearly identified Jews with "cosmopolitanism" and the attendant ills of modern urban civilization. And "internationalism," it will be remembered, was traditionally considered one of the serious shortcomings of Jewish populations in countries around the world. Significantly, however, despite *Solaria*'s intent to open culture to a variety of influences, Jewish stereotype was so solidified that even *Solaria,* a jour-

83. E. Vittorini, *Diario in pubblico* (Milan: Bompiani, 1957), 174, cited in E. Tannenbaum, *The Fascist Experience: Italian Society and Culture, 1922–1945* (New York: Basic Books, 1972), 295.

84. See, for instance, critic G. Debenedetti's letter to Alberto Carocci, editor of *Solaria,* about Svevo's Jewish personality in *Solaria* 3–4 (1929), cited in E. Tannenbaum, *The Fascist Experience,* 295.

nal as far to the left as one could find in the early years of the regime, was not immune to the use of stereotypes such as "internationalism."

The 1930s also saw a measure of protest among a limited number of writers. The Florentine reviews *Letteratura* (*Literature*) directed by Alessandro Bonsanti and *Campo di Marte* (*Drill-Ground*) directed by Vasco Pratolini and Alfonso Gatto were both open to writers critical of the regime such as Carlo Emilio Gadda and half-Jew Alberto Moravia, whose respective novels, *Cognizione del dolore* (*Acquainted with Grief*) and *L'Epidemia* (*The Epidemic*), were excerpted in *Letteratura*. *Campo di Marte* was even more openly critical of the cultural policies of the regime and lasted for only one year (August 1938–August 1939). In its pages Pratolini lamented the regime's awarding of the Biella prize to the thinly disguised propaganda of Gian Paolo Callegari's novel *La terra e il sangue* (*Blood and Sand*). Even Giuseppe Bottai, the minister of education, published a small review, *Primato* (*Supremacy*) (1940–1943), which was occasionally critical of the propaganda offered as art by the regime. But like the articles of the *Treccani,* these were relatively small publications created for the intellectual elite and, as such, without much real influence. Such open but, ultimately, ineffectual criticism of the regime would be allowed to continue for a brief time after which the journals would, like *Solaria* and *Campo di Marte,* be closed down.

But one of the major contradictions about Jews stems from the fact that, as was suggested earlier this chapter, in some ways the discourse on Jews had changed little since the nineteenth century, despite the history of their assimilation.[85] Visible, tangible assimilation had made it possible for Jews to hold positions of national responsibility[86] and had created a climate of concord between Jews and Christians in the early years of the century, which had prompted Croce to write his statement on the lack of anti-Semitism in Italy. Yet, as the Jews of Europe were to discover, even extensive assimilation was no guarantee against the tragic effects of anti-Semitism. The Jewish experience in Italy after 1938 bears this out.[87]

Ample clues revealing the level and nature of feeling about the place of Jews in Italian society abounded in various aspects of popular cul-

85. See A. M. Canepa, "Cattolici ed ebrei nell'Italia liberale (1870–1913)," *Comunità* 32, no. 179 (1978): 43–109.

86. One example for all is the prime ministry of Luigi Luzzati.

87. A. M. Canepa, "Cattolici ed ebrei," 44; "Reflections on Antisemitism in Liberal Italy," *The Wiener Library Bulletin* 30 (1978): 105.

ture. Evidence that deep-seated convictions about Jews had not been erased in the years since Emancipation was available in literature that enjoyed wide circulation. Without a systematic study of these works, however, the connection between such disparate novels and stories might not be apparent and anti-Jewish sentiment encountered there might simply be dismissed as bad taste, to be expected of Bresciani's spiritual "heirs."

Fascism's Fiction

The political discourse outlined in the first section re-acquaints us with the rhetoric about Jews, the old familiar stereotypes of the preceding century, refashioned to serve a new master. There were, however, important differences between the former model and its Fascist incarnation. In the nineteenth century the moral example of a second chance at life through conversion was a stock element of religio-political oratory and reflected in popular literature whenever Jews of redeemable moral fiber were concerned. Under fascism, however, the introduction of racial concerns into politics and literature caused the demise of the optimistic notion that Jews could rise above their well-known limitations.[88]

Jews in the popular literature of the 1930s lost any potentially positive traits and in so doing abrogated any claims nineteenth-century authors had given them to repentance and a happy denouement of their story. An integral part of that former notion and, therefore, destroyed with it was the common plot device by which it would be revealed that a "good" Jew was really a misplaced Christian who had never really been Jewish at all. For Jews who had come late to mainstream Italian culture, who were perceived by the most implacable of antiurban, antibourgeois theorists as allied with modernist forces that sought to "sway, corrupt and especially destroy that treasure of our race . . . that great friend and protectress of the people: tradition,"[89] and who, in any case had existed for centuries only at the fringes of Italian life, there was no longer a way out. The problem was no longer that Jews were not willing to convert, as it had appeared in the nineteenth century

88. One notable exception was Mario Puccini's novel, *Ebrei* (Milan: Ceschina, 1931), but this was a special case and not without its own difficulties.

89. M. Maccari, *Il Selvaggio* 4, no. 2 (30 January 1927), cited in A. Asor Rosa, "La cultura," 1505.

especially before Emancipation. The problem, as it was expounded in literary and political discourse, was that conversion would not make Jews any more acceptable since the values they offended were so powerful and at the same time so intangible as to be beyond their grasp, socially as well as racially. The predominant literary and political models of the 1930s, then, with their hypernationalistic emphasis on the collective were stridently integrative when depicting non-Jews and equally xenophobic in their treatment of Jews, who were to remain strangers in their own land.

As we have seen, the political discourse of the first decades of the century emphasized unity in all its imaginable forms. First and foremost, one of the greatest achievements that fascism was to ascribe to itself was to have succeeded in finally uniting the Italian people. In 1921 Mussolini had stated categorically:

> Fascism must require that within its borders there will be no longer Venetians and *Romagnoli*, Tuscans, Sicilians and Sardinians, but Italians all and only Italians. (*OO*, XVII, 218)

As time went on Mussolini and others would speak of having eliminated entrenched regional rivalries and created Italy.[90] Thus in all the organs of propaganda one could read articles such as this one stressing the fundamental unity of the Italian people:

> . . . of the country and of the city from whom we will never again be separated. And we want the whole population to work together, to suffer and rejoice together. And let us never be divided again.[91]

The new Italy of Fascist rhetoric was the realization of Corradini's dreams, and those of Oriani, Soffici, and the other nationalists: a land of ethnic and spiritual unity. What remained was for Italy to find a way to express its uniqueness.

One would have expected to see the early development of a peculiarly Fascist style that would exert a formative influence on literature and the visual arts. But beyond continuation of the vision of nationalists such as Corradini and D'Annunzio, that did not occur.[92] Still, Corradini's insistence on the subordination of the individual to the collective

90. In this regard, see M. Isnenghi, *L'educazione dell'Italiano: il fascismo e l'organizzazione della cultura* (Bologna: Cappelli, 1979).

91 G. Puccio, "Per la formazione dell'italiano nuovo," *La Vita Italiana* 37, no. 1 (1931), 63.

92. See E. Montale, "Il fascismo e la letteratura," in *Auto-da-fé* (Milan: Il Saggiatore, 1972), 20–25.

through which it finds realization and expression[93]—the "thousands and thousands of souls become one"—was echoed throughout the period. Just as it was imagined that the collective spoke with the voice of the individual, so under the Fascist regime, in the absence of a standardized Fascist aesthetic, the individual authorial voice had the duty to anchor crucial cultural myths in the public memory.

In this way literature became, in a sense, a controlled substance that, through the prestige of the printed page, was called upon to legitimate and propagandize the present. Authors took the common reader's "personal" virtues of dogged honesty, of a natural tendency toward hard work, unswerving loyalty, and entrepreneurial energy and magnified them until they acquired exaggerated moral value. These morally charged narrative elements were then centered onto the reigning Fascist cultural myth and publicized as the keys to victory in domestic "battles." Through literature as one medium of propaganda, the regime attempted to lull the public into believing that it was protagonist of its own history for the first time. This impression was reinforced in novels modeled on the *romanzo d'appendice,* promoting, for instance, Italian autarchy by featuring the inspiring stories of self-made industrialists. Publishers ground out many rags-to-riches stories, such as the one in which by living the Fascist ethic, working day and night, a humble young worker became manager of the Biellese Dye Works and partner in the firm alongside the son of his former boss.[94] The people, then, became the "heroes of daily life" because in abandoning the notion of merely personal gain, the individual acted in the interest of the collective. The collective, however, was said to exist in order to contribute to the State, which, in the person of its leader, was the incarnation of the will of the individual. In 1929 Mussolini described the Nation's dependence on individual sacrifice: "Nation can only exist inasmuch as it is a people. A people progresses only inasmuch as it is numerous, industrious and orderly. Power is the result of [the union of] this fundamental trinomial" (*DM,* 170). Or as Leonardo Sinisgalli, *Littore* (Lictor) of 1934, put it: "[there is an] intimate harmony between the Fascist ethic and the will of the best [of us]."[95] The State, in turn, was said to

93. See G. Deleuze, paper delivered and reprinted in "Psicanalisi e politica," Atti del convegno, May 1973 (Milan: Feltrinelli, 1977), 10, cited in M. Isnenghi, *Intellettuali militanti,* 31.

94. See M. Isnenghi, *L'educazione dell'italiano,* 18–22, regarding this (for which Isnenghi provides no title) and other examples.

95. L. Sinisgalli, "Rapporto di un littore dell'Anno XII," in *Eia, eia, eia, alalà! La stampa italiana sotto il fascismo 1919–1943,* ed. O. del Buono (Milan: Feltrinelli, 1971), 277. See also R. Dombrowski, *L'esistenza ubbidiente* (Naples: Guida, 1984), chap. 1.

provide the public with a spiritual world that was new and healthy, or rather which people perceived as such.[96]

This vision of national life presupposed unity of purpose among all the people. But there was one group in the country who, it was imagined, would not engage in these domestic battles and whose goals were not perceived as consonant with the will of the majority. Just as Jews were regularly singled out by political orators and journalists for their presumed rejection of Nation, so the novelists, particularly in the 1930s regularly attributed the unpardonable crime against the nation to their Jewish characters.

"Nation" could mean the physical country and it could mean the race living within its borders. It could also refer to its direct opposite, Bolshevism and internationalism, as in the case of Salvator Gotta's German Jews who corrupt an honest, impressionable Italian in *Lilith*.[97] Hans and Else Wolf are well-known socialists in touch with Trotsky and other revolutionaries. Else initiates a sexual relationship with Andrea and tries to lead him beyond his parochial intellectual upbringing to freedom of thought. But Andrea and Else separate and he goes on to serve his country by producing five children and becoming an engineer. In the sequel, *Il Paradiso Terrestre (Earthly Paradise)*[98] Andrea is widowed and finds Else again. This time diversity of race, "something in their blood which divided them," ends the relationship definitively. Life with Else would have meant exile to an alien spiritual realm. Else had long feared the inevitable moment when Andrea would realize it,

when your [race] might stir in you. So much so that I felt as I do now and as you will think of me from now on—an outsider who speaks a language which is incomprehensible to you.[99]

Gotta bridged the short distance between the concept of boundaries—Corradini's "circle of mountains and seas"—and the racial question by creating basic existential dilemmas that coincided with Fascist dogma. He accentuated them by constructing his plot to hinge upon them.

Virgilio Brocchi, author of extraordinary popularity, addressed simi-

96. Anonymous, transcription of Dino Alfieri's report to the Senate on popular culture (21 May 1937), *Il Popolo d'Italia* 24, no. 14 (22 May 1937): 1. See also P. Murialdi, "La stampa quotidiana del regime fascista: Dal Minculpop al crollo del regime—Alla ricerca della cultura popolare" in V. Castelnuovo and N. Tranfaglia, *La stampa italiana nell'età fascista* (Bari: Laterza, 1980), 192.

97. S. Gotta, *Lilith* (Milan: Baldini-Castoldi, 1934).

98. S. Gotta, *Il Paradiso Terrestre* (Milan: Baldini-Castodi, 1935).

99. Ibid., 210.

lar problems in his *Volo nuziale (Nuptial Flight)*.[100] He fashioned his discourse using the unassuming language of the middle class, a familiar, homey kind of expression best suited to evoke recognition of familiar social questions. At first his statements regarding relations between "Italians" and Jews appear to portray the two groups as equals, but instead we find that for Brocchi Jews did not quite live up to middle-class standards:

> The Meyers were perfectly Italian despite their name. They were Italians and Jews and, like many Jews, . . . even though they were not observant, they were . . . always ready to demonstrate their brotherhood with charity to the most Catholic Institute for the Blind. (*VN*, 123)

Thus we read three positive statements about Jews which are immediately partially contradicted by qualifiers: "*despite* their name"; "*even though* they were not observant"; "*demonstrate* their brotherhood." Ignoring the reality that most Italian Jews had either fully Italian or at least Italian-sounding names (often resulting from conscious Italianization, such as Morpurgo for Marburg and Sacerdote for Cohen), Brocchi perpetuated the stereotype of the Jew as foreigner by giving the family the German name Meyer and then setting up an opposition between "perfectly Italian" and "*despite* their name." The Meyers are "good" Jews, but not really since they don't practice their religion. "Like many Jews" they are willing to cross entrenched barriers and "*demonstrate* their brotherhood," that is, make an artificial gesture of human solidarity. "Like *many* Jews," but, therefore, unlike all the other Jews who, Brocchi implied, perhaps realize the artificiality of politically motivated contribution to a "most Catholic charity" or do not feel or are not willing to *demonstrate* "their brotherhood." To come full circle, those who withhold their charity to Catholic institutions are not "perfect Italians."

But Brocchi was by no means advocating close relations between Jews and "Italians." When Jewishness threatens to invade the very lives of his characters through intermarriage, deep-rooted emotions rise to the surface:

> [When I pass someone] on the street, it makes no difference to me whether they're Christian or Jewish. But I must confess that I can't stand the idea of being the grandmother of little Jews. . . . Baptize them, at least, as they come along. (*VN*, 131)

100. V. Brocchi, *Il volo nuziale* (Milan: Mondadori, 1932), hereafter in the text as *VN*.

The technique here is the same: Jews create no discomfiture in Christians *from afar*, but *within* one's own family heterogeneity is not acceptable. Baptism is the least a Christian mother can do to facilitate natural family relations. The family was a special target of Fascist social policy; it was expected that women would bear many children and see to it that they conformed to standards of behavior and of expectation.[101] Uniformity of religious instruction was one way to bring this about.

In Brocchi as in Gotta, the prolific and widely read "protagonists in the creation of bourgeois light reading (*letteratura amena*) of the early-twentieth century,"[102] modesty of expression seemed to camouflage the seriousness of their attachment to the social barriers they examined in their fiction. What inspired Brocchi, Gotta, and many popular authors like them were the same concerns regarding Nation and Race that inspired political propagandists such as Guido Landra. Landra had been hired in 1937 to head the office on race studies by the Ministero della Cultura Popolare (*Minculpop*) (Ministry of Popular Culture), the agency created to "promote popular culture by increasing the participation of the people in national culture."[103] Telesio Interlandi, editor of the racist newspaper *Il Tevere* (*The Tiber*), labored at the forefront of anti-Semitic propagandizing as did Professor Edoardo Zavattari, who outlined the "bio-psychic characteristic of the Italian race" and railed against the dangers of miscegenation.[104] And the more insurmountable the barrier—specifically race, a stain that could not be washed away by baptism—the more rhetorically inflated the representation of that barrier would become.

It is important to remember that literary discussion of Jewish racial unsuitability together with lack of national loyalties and bourgeois parasitism did not suddenly appear in 1938 as the expression of the racial campaign nor did the absolutist tone that characterized some literary portrayals of Jews earlier in the 1930s. The latter months of 1938

101. See for instance the several short excerpts from articles in the Fascist press on the duties of women in *Eia, eia, eia, alalà!*, 64, 328–329, 371 and passim. A feminist perspective is provided by M. A. Macciocchi, *La donna nera: Consenso femminile e fascismo* (Milan: Feltrinelli, 1976), as well as M. Mafai, *Pane nero: Donne e vita quotidiana nella seconda guerra mondiale* (Milan: Mondadori, 1987), especially 17–72, 99–113.

102. U. Rena and P. Operti, *Dizionario storico della letteratura italiana* (Turin: Paravia, 1959), 568.

103. P. Murialdi, "La stampa quotidiana" in *La stampa italiana nell'età fascista*, ed. V. Castronuovo and N. Tranfaglia, 192.

104. Prof. Zavattari, director of the Institute of Zoology of the University of Rome, published "Ambiente naturale e caratteri bio-psichici della razza italiana," *Difesa della razza* (5 August 1935), cited in *Eia, eia, eia, alalà!*, 347–348.

did see the subject of race pervade every possible medium of communication, but the motif of the desire to maintain a comfortable distance from the Jews had never disappeared entirely from popular literature. The stumbling block was identified by Callegari in 1938–1939.

Even after he converts he'll still be a Jew. It's a matter of race: they know who they are, they're different, and they live only for themselves. (*CD*, 273)

It is the very one described by E. A. Butti in *Nel paese della fortuna* (*Fortune's Country*) in 1911. Butti's character, Eckstein, hobnobs with aristocrats, but draws their hatred when the usurer in him surfaces and he lends them money to cover their gambling debts to him. Similarly, in Ugo Ojetti's short story, "*Il primo amore di Memmè Kohn*" ("Memmè Kohn's First Love") (1912), Kohn blurts out his conviction that money and breeding are equivalent and that aristocracy is only a title to be bought. The fundamental differences between Jews and non-Jews continued to concern writers such as Alfredo Panzini in his *Viaggio con la giovane ebrea* (*Travels with a Jewish Girl*) (1935). In the absence of physical barriers, cultural distance could be expressed through stereotypical labeling of Jewish characters. Thus there were still the robbivecchi of old, but in Michele Saponaro's *Bionda Maria* (Blond Maria) (1936), Corradi's *I prodighi e gli avari* (*Prodigals and Misers*), and Corradini's *Beniamino Nicosia* they were promoted to "antique dealers."

Three Jewish characters in novels from the 1930s—Papini's *Gog* (1931), Carli's *L'Italiano di Mussolini* (*Mussolini's Italian*) (1930), and Callegari's *Il cuore a destra* (*The Heart on the Right*) (1938)—are a cut above those mentioned so far. All three hold positions of influence in sectors of intrinsic importance: philosophy, finance, and nationalized industry.

Giovanni Papini's *Gog* is a satire on modern life written by a man who considered himself a militant organizer of culture. A best-selling author and ardent promoter of Futurism, Fascism, and Catholicism within an active career spanning the years 1903–1956, Papini founded *Il Leonardo, Lacerba, La Rinascita* (*Rebirth*), collaborated on *La Voce* (*The Voice*), *Il Regno* (*The Kingdom*), *Il Frontespizio,* taught in universities, founded and directed cultural institutes, and left collected works in ten volumes. Thus, Papini was often at the center of cultural debates though his world view was notably cynical and detached. In *Gog* Papini is primarily concerned with the ways in which philosophical certainties can be called into question and even overturned by people and populations whom he imagines are in some way beyond the reach of standard social control.

The first of these people is Gog himself, a "bourgeois superman"[105] and symbol for all that is foreign to a closed, provincial society. Gog is a Hawaiian half-caste descendent of cannibals, monstrous to look at, barbaric, and incredibly rich. Having amassed his fortune, "the most fearsome instrument of creation and destruction in the modern world" (*G*, 7), this savage is intent on acquiring an education by being "introduced to the most refined delights of a decaying society." This, he hopes, will help him break through social barriers despite his background and appearance. Following his "perverse ability to sniff out the most extreme ideologies" (*G*, 8) he travels throughout the world, giving Papini the opportunity to exhibit him in varied intellectual and moral situations "as a symbol of the false and bestial in cosmopolitan civilization . . . the spiritual ills from which today's civilization is suffering" (*G*, 11–12).

Having learned about literature and visited Gandhi and Henry Ford (he would later visit Marx, Freud, Einstein, Lenin), Gog advertises for a secretary. Out of the sixty-three candidates for the job, forty-seven are Jews. Benrubi, a university professor of philosophy and philology, gets the job. He is "typical of his race": short with curved shoulders, hollow cheeks, deep-set eyes, and an olive complexion "like mud in a swamp" (*G*, 98). During the interview Gog asks him "Why are the Jews usually so intelligent and so timid?" (*G*, 98). Benrubi's answer, which forms the body of the chapter "Le idee di Benrubi" ("Benrubi's Ideas"), is a tour-de-force of philosophical and Jewish history.

After the Diaspora, Benrubi recounts, "stateless, ungoverned, defenseless Jews were scattered here and there in the midst of the multitudes who hated them." In self-defense they invented two weapons: money and intelligence. Do Jews love money? No, but it is their alternative to armaments that were prohibited them. All in all they chose the better weapon for "men destroy each other with iron, but they buy one another with gold. . . . Florins became the Jews' lances . . . dollars their machine-guns" (*G*, 99). Jewish capitalism is likewise a "legitimate defense"; if through capitalism Jews are "among the rulers of the earth," Europe can blame its own "moral and religious decadence" (*G*, 99). The "will of their enemies had forced the wretched of the Bible, the cap-

105. See the pages devoted to *Gog* in M. Isnenghi, *Papini* (Florence: La Nuova Italia, 1972), 124–131, especially 126.

tives of the ghetto, to rule over poor and rich alike [with their money]"
(*G*, 99). This incredible power was forced on the Jews "against their
nature, against their will" (*G*, 99); for this reason they have suffered
ever since.

To put an end to this torment the Jews unleashed a second weapon:
their formidable intelligence. Unable and unwilling to launch a decisive
war on Western civilization, they have seen fit to mount a subtle, almost
invisible attack against the intellectual foundations of Christendom,

to pull down, humiliate, unmask and dissolve the ideals of the *Goyim* . . . to
undermine and dirty your most cherished beliefs, the pillars which supported
the logic on which your thought is based. Since the time Jews have been allowed to write what they wish, all of your spiritual constructs are in danger of
falling. (*G*, 99)

When Jews were legislated out of the academies, when titles and degrees were denied them, when they were forbidden to acquire the
knowledge that Gog seeks to emulate, Western philosophy was safe, a
bastion of social control. But once the Jews were freed in the name of
that same philosophy and allowed to take their place in society, they
assimilated this once-foreign culture and began to manipulate it. Philosophy affects the whole society in the form of laws, business, and religion; the Jewish onslaught produced nothing short of a revolution.
Marx weighed the spiritual superiority of humankind and reduced it to
a question of economics; Lombroso debunked genius and Freud destroyed our notions of morality; Reinach called the covenant between
God and man a relic of unstable taboos; and Einstein rid our universe
of its orderly firmaments leaving us perpetually relative time and space,
uncertain and unfathomable. Papini goes on to list many other Jewish philosophers and their revolutionary doctrines and observes that
Europe is under the spell of these great Jews.

This "age-old method of administering corrosive poisons," Benrubi
reminds Gog, "is the greatest Jewish vendetta [first] against the Greek
world, then the Latin and the Christian" (*G*, 103). The attack continues
to go well: Jewish capitalists dominate world commercial markets and
Jewish thinkers dominate world intellectual markets. Despotic in material things and anarchic in spiritual matters, Jews are the incarnations
of the two extremes Christians fear most. Christians have become the
Jews' servants and their intellectual victims. Now the people who killed
God and destroyed the idols of Christian philosophy command their
subjects to kneel before the only idol they left intact, Money, and the

Jews rejoice in their freedom and their power. While remaining separate, "the pariah among peoples can finally celebrate the sweetness of a double victory!" (*G*, 103–104).

Unlike many literary accounts of Jews in which authors repeat a familiar litany of stereotypes, Papini's portrayal of Benrubi was highly personal. Indeed the Benrubi episode is, in many ways a *catalogue raisonné* of those philosophers whom Papini the philosopher considered especially influential on Western thought, minds he held in awe. Yet, the terminology used to introduce the Jewish cultural vendetta: "pull down," "humiliate," "unmask," "dissolve the ideals of the *Goyim*," as well as "undermine and dirty your most cherished beliefs," suggests Papini's own identification with the target of Jewish revenge. "Humiliate" may also be a useful clue to Papini's deeper feelings; perhaps in the treatment of philosophical history "Le idee di Benrubi" is Papini's oblique admission of his own failure as a philosopher.

There are, however, indications in Papini's earlier writings that his approach to the Jews was always troubled. Jews were present in Papini's cultural universe well before *Gog*. In his *Dizionario dell'Omo Salvatico* (*Dictionary of the Savage Man*), a satirical exposé of the ills of modern society, Papini includes a "warning" for the Jews ("Agli ebrei"—"To the Jews"). After begging their "humble pardon" as the chosen people for the long history of "offenses" against them, he remarks that they bring it on themselves by reminding people as they do of Cain, Judas, and Barabbas. What stands between Jews and Christians is Jews' "love of power, of money, of quantity."[106] Thus, in Papini's intellectual system, a banker is "always a Jew (even if by a fluke he's a Christian) . . . " meaning that significant economic and political prerogatives that exclude social justice from among their goals and leave everyday citizens feeling powerless are synonymous with his definition of a Jew:

Wars, peace, revolutions, ministries, abundance, famines—all are in his hands. The only things he cannot do are stop the sun, make rain, love a poor man or avoid damnation. . . . And he attunes his soul to the current stock quotations . . .[107]

As their "vanity and avarice"[108] separate Jews from the common man, so do they bar Jews from their fellow man's religion. The Catholic

106. G. Papini and D. Giuliotti, *Dizionario dell'Omo Salvatico* (Florence: Vallecchi, 1923), "Antisemitismo," 190.

107. Ibid., "Banchiere," 319.

108. Ibid., "Aronne," 228.

Papini expressed his desire for Jewish conversion, but the *Dizionario* makes it clear that conversion involves far more than repentance and baptism. Were the "assassins of Christ" to convert, they would be welcomed as the greatest Christians of all. Unfortunately, because of their inability to humble themselves and renounce wealth and power, "the hills of Golgotha will rise between you and me like a wall of impassable mountains."[109]

Papini's pessimistic 1923 approach to conversion remained unaltered in 1935 when he imagined the Jews as more than willing to shed their burden of religious diversity. The Jews in "*La Leggenda del Gran Rabbino*" ("The Legend of the Chief Rabbi") were pictured as exasperated: tired of being different, tired of being

despised and segregated, hated and persecuted, blamed for everything and exiled. After all these hundreds of years of feeling like lepers in a foreign land, like the descendents of Cain or like Judas' hirelings, we, too, feel the need to shake friendly hands, to see the smile of hospitality, to be invited to your table, to feel the kiss of pardon. [If this is possible] crowds of Jews will rush here from ghettos and synagogues all over the world, wherever Jews have been decimated, robbed and banished.[110]

But "*La leggenda del Gran Rabbino*" is a cautionary tale in which Papini seeks to demonstrate that even in matters as solemn as conversion, Jews have inborn tendencies that leave them spiritually impoverished. The Gran Rabbino tries to buy religious and cultural acceptance for Jews in return for huge sums of money and mass conversion. But the pope fears that having killed Christ once, were they to inundate the Christian world, they would do so again, and as the Gran Rabbino takes his leave of Pope Celestino VI, the pontiff weeps for the "perfidious Jews."

Papini's depiction of the death of civilization and the impossibility of a religious solution to cultural conflict was sure to catch the imagination of anti-Semites such as Preziosi. In his review of *Gog*, Preziosi agreed with Papini that Jews intended to destroy national cultures and cited Germany's concern that its culture not fall prey to non-Germans. One way to preserve national culture was to withhold positions of social and political responsibility from all those foreigners and Jews who were not "recognized participants in the common . . . culture and destiny." Preziosi specified that he was "not speaking of race so much as of national culture."[111]

109. Ibid., "Agli ebrei," 17. See also "Barabba," 324.
110. G. Papini, "La leggenda del Gran Rabbino," 3–5.
111. G. Preziosi, "Il segretario di Gog," *La Vita Italiana* 37, no. 1 (1931): 1–7.

Given Papini's tendency to assume diverse cultural identities during his lengthy intellectual odyssey, serious criticism of his work was by no means consistently positive or negative. In many ways he defied definition. He could be a "pragmatist or a modernist, nihilist superman or apologist for Church and fatherland, heretic or dogmatist."[112] Croce and Russo criticized his irrationality,[113] but Gramsci saw through all the *personae* and the criticism they aroused. Gramsci recognized early on that in spite of all of Papini's whims and inconsistencies, despite his bizarre genius, Papini was "not much different from the average bourgeois Italian," that is, "his opinions were forerunners of those of the general bourgeoisie."[114] To this we must add that in 1931, when he wrote *Gog,* Papini was an editor of *Il Frontespizio,* the anti-Semitic journal directed squarely at the educated Catholic bourgeoisie, and was militant in his Catholicism, which Isenghi describes as "provincial in scope and suffocating."[115] Despite his original literary expression in "Le idee di Benrubi"—for example, the use of graphic images such as portraying Christian civilization as a shaky scaffolding—and for all his deliberate complexity, Papini subscribed to a well-established pattern of representing Jews. The references to economic servitude to the international Jewish conspiracy coming from the mouth of a Semitic anti-Semite are the "banal verbal padding" Gramsci mentioned and standard fare in literature inspired by Fascist political discourse.[116] Papini's vision resembles that of many others: a society in which power no longer resides with the population that is both more numerous and religiously and intellectually—others would say racially—homogeneous. Instead, for the first time "Western" Christian civilization is being challenged by Jewish "hatred of the multitudes" and the multitudes are in danger of seeing their ideals toppled and crushed. The originality of Papini's contribution to the tradition of Jewish portrayal lies in having expressed the Jewish threat in intellectual terms that were, therefore, on a somewhat higher plain than Carli's or Callegari's treatment of the material or the rest of Fascist literature regarding Jews.

112. M. Isenghi, *Papini,* 7–8; see also G. Papini, "Anch'io sono borghese," *Lacerba* 2, no. 8 (15 April 1914): 113–115.

113. See M. Isenghi, *Papini,* 8.

114. A. Gramsci, from *Grido del Popolo* (March 1918) in *Scritti giovanili 1914–1918* (Turin: Einaudi, 1958), 185, cited in M. Isenghi, *Papini,* 9.

115. M. Isenghi, *Papini,* 131.

116. On the figure of the Semitic anti-Semite, see S. Gilman, *Jewish Self-Hatred: Anti-Semitism and the Hidden Language of the Jews* (Baltimore: Johns Hopkins Press, 1986).

Mario Carli's[117] Jew, the Triestine Massimiliano Lind, represents the hidden enemy in the midst of the population, the economic enslaver of the people. His selfishness and mistaken confidence in his superiority make him the antithesis of Mussolini's ideal Italian. A financial wizard, his business dealings are intended to subvert the Fascist drive toward autarchy; indeed whatever sacrifices he makes are strictly for his own profit. As founder and head of the Banca Latina del Commercio, an organization that, despite its name, is an agent of the mythical *alta banca internazionale ebraica* ("high-level international Jewish banking"), Lind is one of the three or four top financiers in Europe and in a position to destroy Italy. Having founded his bank just before the Italian intervention in World War I, Lind lent money to the nation and after Caporetto provided arms at favorable rates, which represented great personal financial risk. His gamble paid off and he acquired the reputation as a "true and loyal believer" in the nation and a "praiseworthy patriot," which allowed him to become the "absolute arbiter of Italian finances."[118]

What is particularly interesting about Lind is that Carli probably modeled him on the historical figure Joseph Toeplitz, and Lind's Banca Latina del Commercio on Toeplitz's Banca Commerciale Italiana. Toeplitz was a Pole who took Italian citizenship in 1912 after having worked at the bank since 1894; he became its director in 1904. Toeplitz risked a large percentage of the bank's capital, though the amounts involved were not revealed until late in 1930 after Carli had completed his novel. Even without this information, by November 1929 when Carli started writing there was already a well-established tradition of opposition to Toeplitz in the press. In 1914–1917 Preziosi had railed at Italy's "enslavement" to the "German" Toeplitz.[119] Only a few years later the "German" Toeplitz became known as the "Jew" Toeplitz.[120]

Indeed, despite Toeplitz's merits as one of the first and major financial backers of the Fascist movement, the early Fascist anti-Semites at-

---

117. Journalist and Fascist publicist, together with his fellow futurist, Emilio Settimelli, Carli collaborated on *L'Italia futurista* and founded *L'Impero* in 1923. Later he wrote several novels and published a well-known anthology of Fascist writers.

118. M. Carli, *L'italiano di Mussolini* (Milan: Mondadori, 1930), 123–124, hereafter in the text as *IM*.

119. See the long series of articles under the general heading "La Germania alla conquista dell'Italia" (1914–1917), especially those regarding the Banca Commerciale Italiana, by Giovanni Preziosi in *La Vita Italiana*.

120. R. De Felice, *Ebrei sotto fascismo*, 55.

tacked him regularly.[121] Among these one of the most vociferous was Filippo Tempera, director of the nationalist Roman periodical *Don Chisciotte* (*Don Quixote*). For Tempera, Italy's problems were rooted in the machinations of the Jewish financial monopoly.[122] In the pages of *Don Chisciotte* Tempera invited Mussolini to liberate Italy from the various Jewish "Holoferneses" and from Toeplitz in particular. The international Jewish banking monopoly controlled the finances of the Right and Left, Tempera argued, so as to be always on the winning side. Jews also controlled society's regulatory agencies—diplomacy and the law— as well as all the outlets for information—the press and education—the better to swindle their fellow citizens with impunity. Jews had no concept of loyalty so as not to be held accountable by any nation or special interest. Their wide-eyed Italianness was a ruse; in reality, like snakes-in-the-grass, they were just waiting for the right moment to poison the Fascist revolution.[123]

The same discourse, with or without reference to Toeplitz, could be found throughout *La Vita Italiana* and later *Il Tevere*. Armed with this vision, which had become commonplace during the first decade of fascism, Carli works it bit by bit into his novel. First he focuses on Lind/ Toeplitz's foreign birth complicated by his Jewishness. He invents faceless characters to voice the opinions of the man-in-the-street: "'Wait and see if he doesn't double cross us when the time is right,' somebody prophesied." "'When you're Austrian until age thirty you can't just become an Italian all of a sudden,' declared someone else." But others know better than to debate the national loyalties of a Jew: "A Jew is neither Austrian nor Italian. He goes wherever opportunity beckons" (*IM*, 123). This last surmise is spoken by the voice of reason: to accuse a Jew of being a foreign agent of a "nation within the nation"—historically probably the most common anti-Semitic accusation—is to forget their trademark individuality. The truth Carli demonstrates is that Jews

121. As Andrea Mortara noted in 1938, contrary to what Mussolini had said in the "Discorso di Trieste" (18 September 1938), Italian Jews were anything but anti-Fascist. They had helped the movement in the early days by financing the March on Rome (Toeplitz) and "even today there are Italian industrialists of Jewish origin among the major backers of the 'regime.' . . . all of which proves that the attempt to justify anti-Semitism with the pretext of anti-Fascism is absolutely ridiculous." In A. Mortara, *Ebrei italiani di fronte al "Razzismo"* (Tunis: 1938), cited in R. De Felice, *Ebrei sotto fascismo*, 425.

122. See F. Tempera, *La guerra e la pace d'Italia insidiata dalla Banca Commerciale di Joseph Toeplitz* (Rome: Società tipografica italiana, 1921).

123. F. Tempera, *Don Chisciotte*, 16 January 1923, cited in R. De Felice, *Ebrei sotto fascismo*, 78n.

have no nation outside of their money. As Papini indicated in his *Dizionario,* the identification of "Jew" with "bank" was so widespread that at times Carli uses "Lind" metonymically to indicate the bank.

Lind's financial maneuvers are the sort of conspiracies that a reader familiar with more than a decade of Preziosi's and Tempera's accusations would have come to expect from the *alta banca internazionale ebraica.* Contrary to Mussolini's directives to free Italy from dependence on foreign products, the Banca Latina has the monopoly on all importation and distribution of raw materials: petroleum, coal, iron, grain. While Italy was mustering all her technological strength to find fuel under native soil, the Banca Latina,

insensitive to the titanic efforts of the nation which longed for economic independence, continued in secret to invest its capital in import firms while it did its utmost to sabotage [Italy's] quest for liberation. (*IM,* 126–127)

Carli's hyperbolic language in describing Mussolini's "passionate propaganda" in favor of autarchy reproduces the rhetoric employed in so many speeches: Italy's efforts are *titanic,* the product of intense *longing* for economic *liberation.* Such language reappears programmatically each time a character mentions Italy or invokes the nation.

Carli owed his emphatic approach to political themes in part to the D'Annunzian influence that he and other authors like him never quite overcame, but principally to his occupation, which demanded an immediate and inflated style. Thus in the novel we find Carli the publicist's paeans to the *Duce:* "Mussolini alone is, in every deed, the *new Italian.* We are but pale shadows of what we would like to be and the best thing we know how and are ready to do for him at any time is to die for him" (emphasis the author's) (*IM,* 246). Likewise Carli's protagonist and Lind's implacable enemy, Falco D'Aquilonia, is ever-prepared to translate his leader's rhetoric into action. A prime example here is the "battle" for land reclamation; Carli describes Falco's own land as a "tragic desert . . . a parched malarial land, desolate as the steppes . . . a land in agony" (*IM,* 15–16) which was waiting for a savior who would bring it back into the orbit of productivity. As his *Duce* exhorted him to do, Falco would strive to attract the laborer back to the fields, to foster an "inseparable bond between the *colono* [farmer] and the earth just like the one created by God between the branch and the leaf, between weight and the center of gravity, between faith and the divine idea" (*IM,* 251). This ponderous catalogue of elements which increase in pomposity as they become more abstract recalls the technique of verbal accumulation which Mussolini used to great advantage, for example, "I urge them to go out and seek more liberty, more air, more light, more humanity, more socialism."[124]

Lind's yearnings for more and more money and infinite power are expressed in equally charged language: he *burns* with desire for wealth, he is *crazed* with the *febrile* need to dominate all humankind (*IM,* 124–125). Building these inflated emotions into his plot Carli has his Jewish villian overreach his grasp in his efforts to thwart Falco so that not even the prestige of the bank can provide him a shield. As a result of the banker's fight against autarchy, Falco D'Aquilonia, "Mussolini's most devoted Italian," denounces Lind in parliament and moves to have him declared a *nemico della patria* (traitor), but his father, Uberto D'Aquilonia, prevents the move in the Senate.[125]

Uberto, "the most convinced anti-Semite in Italy" and at the same time the best friend of that "thoroughgoing Jew" will allow his friendship with Lind to blind him to the banker's subversive activities. Unaware of Lind's viperous worship of money—"All it takes is money, my good man, to conquer the world" (*IM,* 129)—Uberto commits the grave error of telling him about Falco's secret device to find petroleum. Events spiral into a whirlwind of spying, sex, betrayal, and suicide as Falco falls for Lind's mistress, Cora, and then realizing she has stolen his machine renounces her as a traitor,

a docile puppet in the hands of the Jew who pays you . . . that foreigner Lind, Lind the enemy of the nation, that foul Masonic Jew, Lind! (*IM,* 215–216)

As Mussolini described it, the Fascist mentality is distinguished by its "virile pessimism," which obliges real men to strive to maintain order and prevent harmful aberrations in society. Falco subscribes wholeheartedly to this notion of healthful violence calling it "sacred and necessary when employed in the service of an enlightened mind, but damnable if used for its own sake" (*IM,* 45). Lind's abuses of his

124. E. Leso, "Aspetti della lingua del fascismo: Prime linee di una ricerca," in *Storia linguistica dell'Italia nel Novecento,* Atti del quinto convegno internazionale di studi (Rome: 1971) (Rome: Bulzoni, 1973), 146, cited in I. Paccagnella and M. Cortelazzo, "La lingua politica in Italia: Linee di ricerca," *Beiträge zur Romanischen Philologie* 20, no. 2 (1981): 235–244.

125. This incident also has a historical precedent. Toeplitz was likewise denounced in Parliament on 14 June 1918 by Hon. Colajanni for his association with the Genoese Electrical Works which Colajanni called a "den of traitors." Colajanni attempted to have Toeplitz declared "not a gentleman and therefore unfit to direct the Banca Commerciale Italiana," but was unsuccessful. See F. Tempera, *Don Chisciotte,* 26–28.

position of trust and responsibility to the nation add up to violence of the latter sort and Falco resolves to fight violence with violence. Catching Lind off guard Falco administers "blue-ribbon punches," a taste of the future for the "traitor to Nation and Religion" (*IM*, 313) in Mussolini's Italy. What awaits Lind and those of his kind who, through disloyalty or even simple religious diversity, would weaken the fabric of the nation, is an end to tolerance, an end to the material and social progress generously provided by their host country:

> Now Lind was really down; now the bold plutocrat was no more than a pile of rags trampled under the Fascist heel, crushed without pity as if that imitation of a man whom [Falco] had knocked out were the incarnation of every anti-Fascist: [one] of the subtle, secret, treacherous pestilence of bandits whom we have tolerated for too long, finally identified and punished. (*IM*, 230)

Responding much like Bresciani to the menace of the secret societies and using similar language to describe their insidious nature, Carli has in Falco a version of the great Hero (read: Mussolini) who one day will rid the land of the "infamous Jew who betrays us and brings us to the brink of ruin" (*IM*, 243).

The "infamous Jew" (*infame giudeo*, *IM*, 243)[126] Lind had broken through the social barriers around the "inner circle" and insinuated himself into the good graces of high society. Having gained the trust of counts and marquises he penetrated to the center of power and appropriated a most sensitive position for himself. He works tirelessly but not for the benefit of the "inner circle," not for the nation. Rather, like the stereotypical usurers, he bleeds it dry by channeling its capital (blood) outside "the organism of the State" (*DM*, 88) to the rapacious foreigners of the *alta banca internazionale ebraica*. Falco must unseat the criminal and either kill him or drive him away from the center of power to a situation of absolute marginalization. Falco sends the police to arrest Lind, while Cora leaves evidence condemning the banker before she commits suicide for her shameful part in his "betrayal of the Nation" and for her love of Falco (*IM*, 314). Thus cleansed of the

126. Carli's connotative renderings of "Jew" become more derogatory as his story unfolds. At first he uses the terms *israelita* (p. 123) and *ebreo* (p. 123). *Ebreo* then becomes *ebreo di razza* (p. 128), an expression implying familiar stereotypes. After the theft, Falco uses *giudío*, which is ghetto terminology and the unusual *semita* (p. 215), which probably derives from the more familiar *antisemita*, and finally *giudeo* (p. 243). This is the traditional progression in reverse, as *La difesa della razza* described it: ". . . from the vulgar epithet *giudeo* given to the poor, we pass to the less vulgar *ebreo* for the middle class and to the rich *giudei* we say: *israeliti*." (II, 2 [1939], 40, cited in M. A. Cortelazzo, "Lessico del regime fascista," 63.)

threat from the outside, the "inner circle" must be strengthened to resist future attack. Falco will accomplish this by reclaiming the land and having a son who, as Mussolini's new Italian in this Fascist fairy tale, will lead his nation to new conquests.

Lind is vanquished because even though he could mimic the life of the inner circle, being unwilling to accept the personal sacrifice it required, he could not conform to it. But what else, in Carli's view distinguished this quintessential Jew from "Mussolini's Ideal Italian"? Although Lind is tall, straight, and elegant, quite the opposite of the stereotypical ghetto Jew, his smile is stylized and reveals him to be untrustworthy, a "bird of prey with hooked beak and rapacious eyes" (*IM*, 124). He is cold, putting money before everything, corrupting with calculation the passion that comes from Latin virility (*IM*, 147):

He refused to separate his struggle for supreme plutocracy from his loves and hates; [rather] he would entangle them in the web of his financial concerns and so much so that one no longer knew whether he was fighting for his heart or his wallet. (*IM*, 243)

In Carli's vision the Jew's love of money dominates all the other human emotions. This misdirection of passion away from the heroic and generative values—land and selfless virility—toward the sterile, selfish, and ephemeral values represented by the desire for wealth which was at the core of the Jewish personality made it impossible for the Jew to be other than dangerous to fascism.

Gian Paolo Callegari's[127] Jews consider themselves to be the implacable enemies of Fascist society and reject the whole concept of Nation. Callegari's portrayal of Gabriele Gold, protagonist of *Il cuore a destra*, and of his associate, Budrio, therefore, originates in the author's sense of nationalism betrayed. Like Lind, Gold is a foreigner, a Hungarian, who infiltrated an economically sensitive area, the Consorzi Tessili Italiani, the firm responsible for supplying the nation's cloth, and very cleverly maneuvered the directorship away from its rightful owner. Also like Lind, Gold assumed this post not out of a sense of duty to Fascist Italy, but because it was the fastest way to become a millionaire. As the title *Il cuore a destra* suggests, Gold's heart is unnaturally on the right, the same side as his wallet. Using the implications of this contrivance—the heart beating under the wallet—as a fixed point of reference necessary for cohesiveness of plot, Callegari raises the question of

---

127. Callegari collaborated on *Illustrazione italiana* and *La Tribuna* and two of his novels won Fascist literary prizes.

loyalty—to nation, to religion, to family, to friends—on a much more extensive scale than Carli.

Although less programmatically encomiastic than Carli, Callegari also draws his arguments, some of his metaphors, and his doctrinaire method of presenting them from Fascist political rhetoric. The characters around Gold for example, complain repeatedly that he is

a foreigner, out of place in our way of life, [a man] of a different race who always has one foot out the door . . . who always carries a passport valid for every country in Europe. (CD, 36)

Like all of his kind in Italy, he is "a guest who, in spite of his [Italian] citizenship, is always anticipating wherever comes next" (CD, 259). But, Gold reasons, any kind of nationalistic sentiment is inopportune for Jews; since Gentiles are always in the majority and Jews are the chosen race, "we . . . should not mix with Gentiles, but rather float along above them like oil [on water]" (CD, 68). We have already encountered the propagandistic technique of putting anti-Semitic and unpatriotic statements in the mouths of Jews. Mussolini did it in the "*Discorso segreto*" and so did the periodical *Popolo di Roma* (*The Roman People*) ten years earlier with a "quotation" allegedly from Rabbi Margulies of Florence:

Italian Christians will perhaps be a little surprised and disturbed to learn that there is another people in Italy which declared itself completely separate [*completamente estraneo*] not only from our religious faith but also from our nation, from our people, from our history and our ideas. A guest people, that is, which stays amid us like oil amid water, together but not really mixed [*insieme ma senza confondersi*], to use the expression of the late Rabbi of Florence, Margulies.[128]

For Gold, country is "just a simple matter of residence" (CD, 81) and indeed he owes his presence in Italy to chance rather than choice. Callegari's protagonist was forced to flee his native Hungary after swindling his firm and poisoning his countrymen with, ironically, rotten pork. He met some Hungarian Jews in Vienna who enlisted his aid in a plot to capture the world's financial centers. These criminals recognized his inability to form sentimental ties, his self-absorption, and his draconian nature, and hired him as their man in Rome. Once in Rome, Gold looked up an Italian soldier from the war and discovered that his marriageable sister was the only daughter of Massara, the elderly

128. M. Michaelis, *Mussolini and the Jews*, 31.

founder of the Consorzi Tessili Italiani. Since there was no room for a Jew in the Massara family, in order to penetrate the world of Italian capitalism for the benefit of his coreligionists, Gold became Catholic. Here there was no moving inner turmoil, no inspiring account of a hard-won conversion. There are some in the family who recognize the deception, but like most ambitious Jews Gold simply takes on whatever coloration the circumstances warrant. He runs the firm "with no talent, just a lack of ethics" (*CD*, 276) and, in the end, is in a position to cheat all of the Massaras out of their stock in the company that once was theirs and to send his wife to prison on a trumped-up charge.

Although the lives of those around him are circumscribed by well-defined and predictable levels of sentiment and by prescribed codes of behavior, Gold operates as a completely free agent. He structures his life according to whim and opportunity; he is responsible only to himself and able to deceive whenever his behavior is called into question. He need only pretend to be a citizen above suspicion who avoids politics, pays his taxes, and obeys the law in order to infiltrate an important industry and seize control. No ties restrain him or make him question his actions; rather he sees himself as part of the faceless crowd, "a world unto himself, outside the jurisdiction of society" (*CD*, 74).

Gold's complete refusal of the concept of loyalty also implies denial of any roots. Rootlessness, a condition of perpetual diaspora, is perhaps the key to a large measure of anti-Jewish feeling. Stereotype pictures Jews as cowardly and disloyal, ready to flee at the first sign of danger, and therefore, requiring wealth that is mobile and easy to transport: money or jewels. Land, the source of wealth for non-Jews, is out of the question for Jews within the parameters of the stereotype.

Under the influence of extreme nationalism, as during fascism, rootlessness assumed a racial dimension. The Fascists held that "land and race are indivisible: from the land comes the history of the race and the race dominates, develops and enriches the land" (*DM*, 214). The land is fertile and gives life, but for Gabriele Gold the only fertility rests in a gold coin from his father which he is warned to guard as his "seed." Without it Gold feels "without seed, without roots in the earth, without tomorrow" (*CD*, 61) or as Callegari paraphrases the famous proverb, for a Jew "while there's gold, there's seed" (*CD*, 85).

Money does not represent the sum total of Gold's experience with "seed." At the beginning of his adventures he abandoned his mother in Hungary and by the end of the novel is about to relinquish his only child. References to Gold's unnatural conduct during his marriage are

the occasion, throughout the book, for statements about the unassimilable nature of the two seeds: not all bloods can mix. "Our blood united
with theirs can only bring unhappiness" (CD 277–278), the Massaras
complain. Even though the races do mix in his daughter, Gold keeps
his distance from her, from his wife, and his in-laws so that nothing
will interrupt the making of money. Callegari, therefore, is telling us
that to a non-Jew "seed" is fertility, land, roots, family, the past, and
the future—the premise for a fruitful life—whereas to a Jew "seed" is
artificial, metallic, hard, and infertile, but also ephemeral, with no past
and an uncertain future.

The instability of monetary wealth combined with the Jews' natural
tendency to hold onto money causes Gold to hoard his "seed" in a
drawer, opting to starve rather than spend. At first glance, Gold's approach appeared to coincide with the Fascist rhetoric about money.
Mussolini declared, "Our currency is the intangible flag of the Nation"
(DM, 142), "the sign of our wealth, the fruit of our labors, . . . of our
sacrifices, of our tears, of our blood" (DM, 17). Money was tantamount
to "the blood which circulates in the organism of the State," but, Mussolini warned, "wherever blood does not circulate, the Senate becomes
anemic or dies" (DM, 88). Money imprisoned in Jewish hands was
blood that did not circulate, infertile seed that brought no new life to
the State. Jewish control of finance—the logical extrapolation of Gold's
preferring to hoard his "seed" and starve—was nothing less than a
stranglehold on the State and a direct attack against Nation.

The monumental struggle between the two concepts of "seed," as
between those who do and do not respond to nationalism, is about to
be resolved on a nationwide scale, Callegari fears, in favor of the fearsome power of money. Indeed world Jewry, symbolized by Gold and
his accomplice Budrio, is plotting nothing less than the downfall of the
world economy. It should not take long because, Budrio reminds Gold,
Jews like themselves are at the financial helm of every major state:

All that is required is a revolution of world proportions . . . then all we need
to do is infiltrate all economic centers and pull in the Jews along with us. Once
we seize power, everything will fall into place. . . . But we can not be openly
Bolshevik; rather we must pretend to embrace the goals of Fascism and favor
stability, law and order. Then once we get to Geneva, . . . (CD, 176–177)

Then out of the cataclysm, with the help of the Society of Nations,
would come the realization of their goal: the creation of a Jewish state

in Palestine.[129] Budrio's entire function in *Il cuore a destra* is to predict disaster. It is clear from several of his speeches that if the bad seed, money, and the race that commands it is allowed to triumph over nation then an entire way of life will change. Jews are international and cannot be contained within national boundaries. They owe their allegiance to supernational forces whose identity and activities only they understand, to the so-called *demoplutocrazie-massoniche-giudaiche* (Jewish-Masonic-Demoplutocracies).[130] The logical effect of an international Jewish revolution on Fascist Italy would be the end of autarchy and without autarchy the concept of national boundaries would lose much of its meaning. Daily life all over the world would be dedicated solely to making money, signaling the immediate death of spiritual life. Without Mussolini's "divine idea" as a guide, national identities would become irrevocably confused, cultures would flow into one another, and empty into the great stream of money.

To be true to its own ideology Fascist society was morally bound to prevent these catastrophes. Ranking high in the regime's scale of values was domestic war: "the cleansing of those corners where our chameleon-like [enemies] have taken refuge" (*DM*, 4). Foreign war was a logical consequence of success in the domestic war of cleansing, that is, of racial-national superiority: "Only war channels human energies to the peak of tension and confers the seal of nobility on those peoples who are capable of undertaking it" (*DM*, 108). In Callegari's novel it is the "chameleon-like enemies" who are at war against a peace-loving Italy. While assuming the guise of patriotic businessmen dedicated to autarchy, Gold and his henchmen are secretly subverting their host society:

Bisogna conquistare le posizioni. Noi siamo gente in perpetua lotta anche se sembriamo dei tranquilli commercianti: siamo una scolta assediata da duemila anni nel campo nemico. Si sorride, si stringe la mano, si applaude e si fischia: ma la guerra nostra è guerra.

(We must conquer our positions in society. We are a people in perpetual struggle even if we seem to be quiet merchants. We are like a sentry under siege for two thousand years in the midst of enemy territory. We smile, we shake hands, we applaud, we whistle. But [have no doubt] our struggle is war.) (*CD*, 187)

129. For a detailed account of the Fascist approach to Zionism, see M. Michaelis, *Mussolini and the Jews*, passim.

130. Several Fascist publications such as *Il Tevere* and *La difesa della razza* identified the international Jewish enemy with this meaningless catch-all phrase along the lines of *alta banca internazionale ebraica*.

In Callegari's approach to his Jewish characters there are no euphemisms. He uses a starkly bellicose vocabulary to outline the Jewish menace, as we see from the Italian version: *conquistare, perpetua lotta, scolta, assediata, campo nemico,* and *guerra.* We remember that Carli was no less direct in describing the pernicious Lind as

incarnata tutta la gente antifascista, tutta la sottile, segreta, perfida lue dei troppi tollerati insidiatori.

(the incarnation of every anti-Fascist, [one] of the subtle, secret, treacherous pestilence of bandits whom we have tolerated for too long.) (*IM,* 230)

Carli's depiction of Lind gains its strength from nonsemantic as well as lexical elements: alliteration of *s* and *t* which gives the impression that this definition of the Jew was spat in disgust.

Both Callegari's and Carli's portrayals of the Jews in their midst go way beyond mere description or plot expedients. Lind and Gold are complete villains who betray, one by one, all aspects of life that Fascist culture holds sacred. Using these novels, the authors are sounding an alarm, alerting their readers to present dangers. *L'italiano di Mussolini* is typical of the popular genre; though the protagonist loses his life in the service of his country, the novel ends happily with the triumph of fascism and the downfall of the Jewish criminals. *Il cuore a destra,* however, is unusual within the popular genre in that there is no real denouement. Though the plot covers the years 1920 to 1930, it was completed in December 1938, just after the publication of the racial laws. Its ominous ending suggesting the triumph of the villain serves both as a warning and as an apology for those laws designed to isolate the Jews and, thus, protect the government and its citizens from the Jewish peril.

In their fictional accounts of the Jewish mentality, Papini, Carli, and Callegari tell their stories largely in terms of Christian response to Jews: reactions that made of the Jewish *presence* a Jewish *problem.* All three picture Jews as having destroyed the traditional social limits that were described by Otto Weininger in *Sex and Character*:

The Jew, par excellence, is the breaker-down of . . . limits. He is at the opposite pole from aristocrats, with whom the preservation of the limits between individuals is the leading idea. The Jew is an inborn communist. The Jew's careless manners in society and his want of social tact turn on this quality, for the reserves of social intercourse are simply barriers to protect individuality.[131]

131. O. Weininger, *Sex and Character* (New York: G. P. Putnam's Sons, 1907), 311, translated from the German *Geschlecht und Charakter* (Vienna: 1903). The Italian version was published as *Sesso e carattere* (Turin: Bocca, 1912), 296. For an account of the ac-

The Jewish threat was largely a matter of this sensation of rightful boundaries overstepped, of protective walls tumbling down, of physical contiguity but cultural incommunicability, a situation that was magnified to the point of racism, reified in Fascist political propaganda and reflected in popular literature. This threat to the defining and protective limits of traditional society was central to the inspiration of the authors who wrote about Jews throughout the 1930s.[132]

There is, however, one important exception to the preceding statement. Faced with essentially the same subject matter, Mario Puccini attempted to reverse the traditional point of view, that is, to consider the destruction of the barriers in terms of the Jews' sense of themselves and of their place in Italian society.

Novelist and critic Mario Puccini was born in Senigallia and grew up in Ancona—two important centers of Jewish life—and from an early age lived in close contact with their Jewish populations. The physical proximity between Christians and Jews in Ancona contrasted with their ethnic differences continued to fascinate this keen observer of human nature well into middle age until in 1931 he decided to explore these two worlds in his novel *Ebrei* (*Jews*). Given the political climate of 1931 Puccini wrote a companion piece to justify his choice of topic: "*Perchè ho scritto, io cattolico, un romanzo filosemita*" ("Why I, a Catholic, Have Written a Philo-Semitic Novel").[133] Although the title of his article is both openly polemical and defensive, his explanations are couched in the nostalgic language of childhood memories.

Puccini begins by expressing his debt to the Jewish people for "stimulating his imagination," this people that

lived in a way that was so different from ours: surrounded by an aura of fabled traditions.

Despite his intention to show Jews in a positive light, in an era in which the notion of Jewish separateness was already being openly promoted, Puccini is also drawn to observe Jews as exotica:

---

ceptance of Weininger's theories in Italy, see A. Cavaglion, *Otto Weininger in Italia* (Rome: Carucci, 1983).

132. Alberto Cavaglion errs, therefore, when he limits the incorporation of Weininger's ideas to the "second half of the 1930s," in his *Otto Weininger in Italia*, 159. As Cavaglion himself notes (p. 158) Weininger is discussed among Papini's revolutionary philosophers in *Gog*. For more on Papini's use of Weininger see Cavaglion, *Otto Weininger in Italia*, 58–62.

133. M. Puccini, "Perchè ho scritto, io cattolico, un romanzo filosemita," *Rassegna mensile di Israel* 5, no. 12 (2d series) (1931): 627–628.

Our life was out in the open for whomever wanted to look in, but the Jews, even though they were schoolmates, they must have led a very different life in the bosom of their families. And I was sure that their life was a hundred times more poetic than ours.

His adolescent, romantic idealization of the Jews changed little as the author matured. He was pleased to find that Jews "too had aspirations, and profound ones" and that they were "no longer satisfied with a life that is merely commercial."

This realization, he tells us, inspired him to write two short stories in 1921, "Polemizzare con la verità" ("Arguing with Truth")[134] and "Digiuno" ("Fasting").[135] "La Verità" pits a modern, assimilationist educated son, Gianfranco Mantova, against his traditional father, Mosè, a cloth merchant. "Tradition" in this case means caricatural greed and avarice that rubs off on the son and turns him into a "perfect Jew."[136] Gianfranco travels on business to find the truth about himself and discovers that he cannot assimilate enough to feel Italian cultural traditions as his own. In the end he abandons his books together with his self-respect and opens a textile shop in direct competition with his father.

The autobiographical "Digiuno" proposes no solution to overcome this barrier between the two ways of life as Puccini ponders the religious origin of the differences between Jews and Christians. As a boy he is struck by the differences between himself and his Jewish classmates and is both attracted and repelled by the mysterious quality of the ghetto with its "dark passages" and the "black maws" of its courtyards. He accepts invitations from the timid Jewish boys even though he suspects they are not sincere, so great is his desire to penetrate this other world and uncover its secrets. Sensing the austerity of Judaism he concludes that whereas his religion is concrete, iconographic, and understandable, Judaism is abstract and mysterious, even frightening. This fundamental difference also conditions nonreligious aspects of Jewish lives. Thus Christians are open and friendly and choose homes on broad, sunny streets whereas Jews are timid (Puccini uses the stereotypical *guardinga*, which traditionally means "overly cautious" in the sense of "cowardly") and courteous but insincere, and their timidity and unfriendliness is reflected in their dark ghetto. All in all, the accessible

134. Published as "La verità," in *Essere o non essere* (Rome: Mondadori, 1921).
135. M. Puccini, "Digiuno," in *Avventure e ritratti primaverili* (Florence: La Voce, 1921).
136. M. Puccini, "La verità," 283.

Christian community represents brotherhood whereas the inaccessible Jewish community stands for separatism.

In "Digiuno" Puccini the boy concludes that despite their differences one should not harm the Jews like his friends did; later in *Ebrei*, a mature Puccini attempts to demonstrate that where there is a Jewish problem it is due "more to circumstances than to race . . . when one denies the Jew the respect he deserves as a man, a citizen and a soul." [137] He wrote his novel

with the firm desire to state an unequivocal truth . . . that Jews pose no danger to the societies in which they live, but if anything they improve them. . . . I wish my novel to be a great fresco in which one can observe the human and historic strength of this immortal race. [138]

It remains for us to gauge to what extent Puccini achieved his goal given the political and literary-rhetorical climate of the 1930s.

Ebrei begins and ends with a debate on the place of the old, particularistic religious values in the modern world and Puccini's characters line up either on the side of tradition or of assimilation. During the course of the novel only one will develop and change his point of view. It won't be old Carlo Manasse, who opts for the protection afforded by the status of "nation within the nation" which he takes to mean avoidance of any Christian influence ranging from elementary school to political involvement. The young protagonist Carlo Moscato, on the other hand, rejoices in the hard-won possibility of "leaping over the [ghetto] gate because now we are strong enough to conquer the real world." [139] Moscato realizes that unassimilated Jews, "unable to see beyond the ghetto" (*EBR,* 12) and unorganized among themselves are nothing more than "one tasty mouthful" for the superior peoples who will inevitably conquer them. It upsets Moscato to hear Manasse speaking in the weak and defeatist terms of the past:

Nostalgia, longing, waiting, hope: that's the entire history of our people. (*EBR,* 5)

However, he is relieved to find at least "one Jew who talks about something besides money and business" (*EBR,* 9). But in this novel money and business are Jewish traditions just as much as are religious practices.

137. M. Puccini, "Perchè ho scritto," 628.
138. Ibid.
139. M. Puccini, *Ebrei,* 70, hereafter in the text as *EBR*.

In both cases, warns Manasse, Jews should stick close to their roots, avoiding the slippery slope of assimilation which desires nothing more than to "incorporate and thereby destroy" the Jewish people.

On one level this novel outlines the risks Jews take when they try to expand their horizons. Carlo and Susanna Moscato "leap over the gate" and abandon their Jewish matrix by moving to the country, cultivating the land and becoming cloth *manufacturers* instead of cloth *merchants,* imitating Christians while believing themselves still Jews. But the country is the undisputed realm of Don Quirino, a good-hearted but astute priest on the lookout for converts. He intuits the childless Susanna's desire for motherhood and through the orphans in his care leads her closer and closer to conversion. Susanna runs to Carlo at the military High Command for advice but, unable to find him, she leaves him a book on conversion. The rest of the story is devoted to Carlo's anxiety about his wife, her eventual pregnancy, which terminates her desire to convert, and Carlo's soul-searching and return to the faith and the "city within the city" of his fathers.

Puccini makes it clear that with this choice Carlo and Susanna are returning to a stereotypical world dominated by the ghetto mentality of their parents. If it weren't for their middle-class stature, Samuele Moscato and his wife would appear to have stepped out of the pages of Invernizio and Giustina. Samuele is a cloth merchant whose imagination is stimulated only by money. He is convinced that the Christian tenant who lives above his store is out to rob him, whereas Carlo's mother prefers to deprive herself of the pleasure of wearing her jewelry so as not to advertise her wealth to potential thieves. Susanna's parents, Davidino and Sara Sacerdoti, still live in the old ghetto. He is a petty merchant and she a famous baker known as La Tòmbola. La Tòmbola makes most of her money on Saturdays by cheating impoverished shop-girls out of their hard-earned wages with her private numbers game. In her tiny shop in a dark, narrow street she serves as a parody of the classic Jew, wreaking her petty vengeance on Christianity. Carlo ponders the significance of this mentality in modern times:

Perhaps this is our real *forma mentis*: we feel we have to fight to the last drop of blood against our adversary who is (always) stronger than we and who can only be defeated through astute deceptions, through careful calculation. Perhaps it's wrong to believe that this kind of cleverness will disappear with the last tenant of the old, closed ghetto, of that former persecuted Jewry. Perhaps it's wrong to think that this mentality is a throwback rather than our fundamental nature. (*EBR,* 137–138)

These one-dimensional characters are balanced in part by the more realistic Levi Naim. A war hero, Naim demonstrates that modern Jews

no longer look like victims: their shoulders are no longer curved and their mien is no longer servile. They are no longer there to be stepped on, but to tread [fearlessly] themselves; they will not receive blows but give them. (*EBR,* 131)

Naim is completely assimilated, an officer for whom no patriotic sacrifice is too much. But Naim dies in World War I: a Jewish martyr for Italy who, in the 1930s, provides Puccini with a useful moral *exemplum,*

a symbol of the Jewish race, representing its original, inborn virtues and the changes wrought upon it by modern life. He is certainly my most beloved character.[140]

Naim's death leaves the novel without decisive, forward-thinking Jews. At the outset Carlo Moscato argues passionately that assimilation was the only viable alternative for the twentieth century. Later on when faced with Susanna's religious crisis he questions the wisdom of that position, allows that it is tantamount to abandoning his people, and gradually relinquishes his independence from the past.

Carlo's surrender to his past is in its own way a kind of death, a symbolic death that provides Puccini with another moral exemplum, though a more subtle one. Throughout most of the story Carlo continually passed judgment on his parents and in-laws and the image that emerged was largely negative; any positive assessment was oblique and unconvincing. Thus his family is timorous, apprehensive, suspicious, calculating, dishonest (La Tòmbola), and essentially blind to the reality all around them. What saves these characters is Carlo's affectionate but *detached* view of them at the beginning. By the end of his spiritual journey, however, Carlo's gaze is still affectionate but resigned. Manasse, who represented an extreme example of religious and cultural motivations, has finally won.

Puccini has also essentially surrendered his "good intentions" and repeated the viewpoints of *his* cultural matrix. He tells the reader that yes, the overwhelming majority of Jews do conform to their reputations, to the vision molded by popular and, to a lesser extent, serious literature and by religious and political forces. We have seen how Puccini's characters fit the literary stereotypes; the author also reproduces 1930s political ethos and rhetoric as a vehicle for his portrayal. For instance,

140. M. Puccini, "Perchè ho scritto," 628.

while proposing assimilation as the salvation of "this small people scattered to the winds," Carlo Moscato says that if instead of dispersing, this people

invece se esso si è infiltrato, come già si è infiltrato e potentemente, nell'ossatura vitale della nazione di cui è ospite, vengan pure dei venti devastatori, travolgenti; ma polarizzato ormai in ogni fibra della società moderna, ed elevato a posti di commando, esso resisterà e vivrà. Non solo; ma in ore critiche, torbide, chissà non possa anche salire al rango di protagonista, guida e testa della vita di domani.

(insinuates itself, if it penetrates as it already has done, [but] in force, into the vital framework of those nations which are [currently] its hosts, then let the devastating winds of revolution blow. But then [the Jewish people] will have reached the heart of every sinew of modern society and it will even have taken command: thus it will endure and thrive. Indeed, come critical and troubled times, it may well attain the rank of protagonist, of guide and leader for the future.) (*EBR,* 13)

At first glance this speech appears to reinforce Puccini's stated goal: to demonstrate that Jews are capable of succeeding in the non-Jewish world, that they have the necessary strength and leadership qualities to make a contribution to modern society. But if we examine its language we note the paradox between the message and the familiar phraseology of anti-Semitic rhetoric that we encountered in Fascist orators and publicists and in the essayists and pamphleteers of the eighteenth and nineteenth centuries. The most obvious examples are *infiltrato, nazione,* and *ospite,* buzzwords with centuries-old histories.[141] Read in this way, it is as if Puccini were really saying: Jews do not take their place in society openly and directly; rather they insinuate themselves (*si è infiltrato*) and once in they don't stop until they reach its most vulnerable spot (*l'ossatura vitale*). Theirs is a parasitic relationship to society for they take over the host "organism" (*l'ossatura vitale della nazione di cui è ospite*) and once anchored in the heart of society (*in ogni fibra della società*) they cannot be dislodged. The typically misplaced biological terminology repeatedly employed in Fascist political rhetoric effectively highlights the Jewish threat: there is a vast difference between "taking one's place in society" and "penetrating to the heart of society's every sinew," for all the mixing of corporal metaphors. Once inside, the parasites will endure and thrive, biding their time until a crisis (*ore critiche*) will al-

141. One example for all is F. F. Jabalot, "Degli ebrei nel suo rapporto colle nazioni cristiane," in Mazzetti, *L'antiebraismo nella cultura italiana,* 123–142.

low them to take the lead (*posti di commando*), to rise to the top (in D'Annunzian terms, *salire al rango di protagonista*) and dictate the future (D'Annunzio again: *guida e testa della vita di domani*).

Elements of such discourse are already present in Jabalot, as we have said, as well as in Bresciani—the secret societies that wait like coiled snakes for the precise moment to strike, an image later borrowed by Tempera in *Don Chisciotte* when he describes the Jewish banking monopoly as "poisonous serpents." The deadly secretive nature of Jewish machinations finds expression in Papini as well, when Benrubi describes Jewish intellectual vengeance as a subtle attack on Christendom, and in Callegari when Budrio outlines his plan to subjugate the world by "infiltrating all economic centers and pulling in other Jews along with him." Puccini's version is phrased more elegantly, but the similarity with Callegari is striking:

Callegari: Occorre infiltrarsi nei centri economici e tirarci su l'uno con l'altro dentro . . . (*CD*, 177)

Puccini: . . . già si è infiltrato e potentemente, nell'ossatura vitale della nazione . . . (*EBR*, 13)

Callegari: . . . quando si è padroni occorre ben poco a disporre di tutto. (*CD*, 177)

Puccini: . . . elevato anche a posti di commando, esso [può] anche salire al rango di . . . testa e guida della vita di domani. (*EBR*, 13)

Carli's Massimiliano Lind followed just this tactic of infiltration, of cold calculation, to end up as "the absolute arbiter of Italian finance" (*IM*, 124). Thus, in spite of itself, Puccini's philo-Semitism finds itself in strange company.

Puccini repeatedly demonstrates his debt to contemporary popular literary and political rhetoric which he applies to his concept of Jewish self-image. One example for all is his tendency to divide the world into active and passive, those who tread and those who are trodden upon, those who give blows and those who receive them. All this recalls the violence of Futurist literature as well as the realization of Fascist virile pessimism that administers moral "beatings" to the effete bourgeoisie, together with Carli's most Fascist hero, Falco, who showers the cowering Lind with "blue-ribbon punches."

In the end, the influence of popular literature within this rhetorical context confounds Puccini's stated goals in writing his novel, so that his insistence that Jews have made progress and are more like the rest of the population is disproved by his own plot. Despite his intention to display Jews in a completely new light and orient his reader toward a positive appreciation of them, his portrayal serves mainly to reify the representational differences between the Jewish and Christian worlds. For instance, the plot hinges on an initial movement out of the all-enveloping cultural and religious Jewish enclave and the subsequent return to the "ghetto." Having tried to assimilate, having done his patriotic duty to the nation, Carlo finally realizes that he cannot live both as a Jew and as an integrated Italian. If forced to choose between his religion and his country, he tells Don Quirino,

Why should we Jews care about Italy if we are of different blood and born here by mistake, even perhaps to our detriment.

I wouldn't hesitate for a second to dump my country into the sea to save my religion. (*EBR*, 86–87)

Massimiliano Lind and Gabriele Gold made that choice in favor of religion. What Puccini imagines as the Jewish credo—that Jews must not meld with the surrounding culture but remain a world unto themselves—is a perfect example of the "nation within the nation." Carlo takes giant steps back to the ghetto—a backward world as we saw it through his eyes—and he does so willingly. The condition of life in the ghetto is life at the margins of society with people who will never reach the "inner circle," who will never play an active role in the wider world. He renounces the "rank of protagonist" to go back to where his people lives as it always has: a "contemplative people . . . nothing more than [that]" (*EBR*, 658), a "tasty mouthful" for the people of the "inner circle" who will one day expand and conquer. The logical outcome of this is that Jewish shoulders will curve once more, ready to receive the blows of the superior nations. However, Carlo realizes that it is impossible to live as a Jew without reverting to the old ways. The moral of *Ebrei,* then, is that to be a Jew is to be in an inferior position, at the mercy of others, to lead a passive life far removed from the vital center of social and political life.

This vision clearly contradicts the interpretive key that is Puccini's apologetic article. Why in a book described as "[a novel of] constant meditation, of persistent controversy. . . . Perhaps the only novel of ideas generated from the problems of daily life . . . in our recent literature"[142] did an author as experienced and respected as Mario Puccini

142. S. Battaglia, "Struttura e tecnica narrativa di M. Puccini," in *Novecento* (Milan: Marzorati, 1982), vol. 3: 2811.

not fully accomplish his objective? Angelo Orvieto intuited part of the problem with the book in 1931, shortly after its publication. In an article published three months before Puccini's article, Orvieto notes that the protagonist is too traditional and not at all representative of Italian Jewry. "No one," he says "is nostalgic for the ghetto and no one hopes it will return."[143] Orvieto alludes to Puccini's obsessive fascination with a people whose otherness appeared so at odds with the homogeneous society. His constant references to mystery in comportment and ritual in "Digiuno" and "Perchè ho scritto . . ." lead one to question his professed closeness with Jews. Did he ever really hear Jews quoting the Talmud as Carlo does or isn't he rather seizing on a piece of exotica that has historically been a target of Christian misunderstanding and attempting to put it in a positive light? Beyond his early experience in two centers of Jewish life, one suspects that Puccini was not close enough to Jews to avoid the pitfalls of traditional representation when writing about them.

The overriding current in portraying Jews was the pervasive descriptive tradition that gave an iconographic dimension to common anti-Semitic notions. Puccini described his novel as philo-Semitic whereas Carli's, Callegari's, and, to an extent, Papini's novel are anti-Semitic. In comparison to our sampling of the literary climate of the 1930s then, Puccini has consciously endeavored to swim against the tide. Yet though the slant of his novel reflects his stated intentions, the iconographic tradition, like an undertow, moved him to use language and express a vision of Jews that, in the end, differed little from those of authors whose point of departure was so different from his. A common thread links novelists as varied as Puccini and Papini with Carli and Callegari and these in turn with Mussolini and the other authors of militant political discourse. All of them drew their inspiration from the same well, the same cultural undercurrent in their reflections on Italian society and the Jewish place in it.

143. A. Orvieto, "Ebrei in un romanzo italiano," *Rassegna mensile di Israel* 5, no. 9 (2d series), (1931): 487.

Conclusion

In this study we have examined the representation of Jews in the literature written by non-Jews, believing popular literature to be the best source material for our attempt to assess the nature and recent history of underlying opinions about Jews in Italian mass culture between roughly 1800 and 1938. Close readings of these texts have revealed a disconcerting similarity of attributes applied both to specific Jewish fictional characters and to Jews in general. Several words and phrases used in connection with Jews appeared over and over again with little or no modification throughout the period in question.

The most common of these refer to the Jewish attitude toward money and to Jewish financial dealings. Accordingly, we have seen Jews repeatedly called "usurers," "unscrupulous bankers," "perfidious plutocrats who live only to amass wealth." The perceived Jewish propensity for accumulation stemmed from being born "greedy," "hook-nosed misers," and from obeying the teachings of the Talmud, long misunderstood as a primarily anti-Christian tract.

The profound differences between Jews and Christians were not just a matter of holy writ, however. As "deicides," it was imagined that Jews had heavy sins to atone for. They rejected Christ partly because they were "in league with the devil" in order to corrupt Christian society. Taking their cue from Judas, Jews were "hypocrites," "criminals," "traitors" with "shifty eyes," "men-and-women-of-a-thousand-faces." Bereft of the inner peace and moral fortitude enjoyed by Christians, Jews were also pictured as "cowardly."

279

Sins against the Catholic faith as outlined in nineteenth-century literature were very similar to the sins against the nation under fascism. In the 1930s, but also well before, religious unity was a central component of nationalism. Thus, Jews were described as "outsiders," "foreigners," "guests" (mostly unwelcome), who formed a "nation-within-the-nation." Even after they had left the ghetto far behind, they carried their alienness, their racial and cultural differences with them. This was the unshakable "stench of the ghetto," though that phrase had other possible applications as well.

Jews preferred not to mix with their fellow citizens, but instead to live separate but among them "like oil on water." Jews could wander the world and always be at home. Their inability to bond with Christian society made them "corrosive elements" within the nation. Jews were always trying to "insinuate themselves into vital economic centers" in order to appropriate them. Similarly, as "members of secret societies," Jews worked to subvert the organized State.

This seemingly descriptive language applied to Jews was a reduction of standard literary models of characterization to an easy-to-use system of stereotype. But the actual ability of these set phrases to describe is merely an illusion because, as with all stereotypes, they are fallacious shortcuts to understanding which in the end are not at all informative. Rather, they are labels, tools used to categorize Jews. The iconographical opposition of we versus they, of the racially and politically superior "inner circle" versus the inferior outer margins of society, which derived in large measure from the example of nearly three hundred years of enforced Jewish separation in ghettos, made it difficult for many writers to imagine Jews as individuals instead of objectifiable categories.

Stereotypes about Jews, especially as used in popular literature, took the place of actual inquiry into Jewish reality for the mass of undereducated non-Jews. And yet, when strung together as above, these labels reveal not so much about the Jews as about the majority population, its expectations of those who lived in its midst, and its codes of behavior. Labels identifying the Jews with "corrosive elements" inexorably eating through society's defenses to take over the vital economic nerve centers of the nation suggest a feeling of vulnerability in the authors who made use of them. An insecurity as unfounded as the phrases themselves, vulnerability in the face of a tiny minority, less than one-tenth of one percent of the total population, with two thousand years of history on Italian soil.

Anti-Semitism, it has been said, is "protean." Anti-Semites attack from any direction; any attempt to refute their claims elicits instant modification and is, therefore, futile.[1] The fact, then, that stereotype— in this case the image of the Jew in Italian popular literature—is not based on realistic observation, is its strength rather than its weakness. Since these false descriptions of Jews were not verifiable in everyday experience, they had to be taken on faith. By the same token, however, since the Jews were not distinguishable in the population, especially after the end of the ghetto period, and since there were so few of them to observe, anti-Jewish commonplaces were difficult to disprove. What is more, their usage was institutionalized by years of continual application and their meaning was understood and subconsciously assimilated by generations of readers.

From Emancipation through the turn of the century, it was easy to see that Jews were making their mark on Italian society by occupying posts of prestige and influence in politics, the military, commerce. One would expect the depiction of Jews in literature to reflect this new age in Italian Jewish history. And yet, despite Jewish religious and cultural assimilation and progress, or perhaps because of them, in Jewish literary representation pervasive tradition allowed for little change. The template of words and phrases applied to Jews remained the same in 1930 as it had been in 1830, constituting a rhetorical tradition that emphasized the alienness and particularism of the Jews.

But longevity is perhaps the major attribute of stereotypes about Jews. It should come as no surprise, therefore, that, despite over sixty years of achieved status since unification, Jewish characters in literature had not made major strides toward a more realistic portrayal. To be sure, in the 1930s most Jews were no longer pictured in ghettos. They were, however, still defined largely in terms of money—although they and their financial dealings had graduated from the pawnshops to the banks, major corporations, the stock exchange. Thus, though the arena for Jewish misdeeds had grown in status to national importance, the mentality that writers imagined was the driving force behind their financial intrigues was that of a century earlier behind ghetto walls. Where Jews had once been the implacable enemies of Christianity, now, readers were told, they dedicated their expertise to undermining the state. They turned their financial wizardry to the benefit of Jews in other countries, to the Bolsheviks, to Fascist Italy's sworn enemies.

1. P. Johnson, "The Oldest Poison: Anti-Semitism from Antiquity to Hitler," *Times Literary Supplement* 4594 (19 April 1991): 5; see also the book Johnson reviewed, R. Wistrich, *Antisemitism: The Longest Hatred* (London: Methuen, 1991).

Once powerless outsiders, they now nested in the heart of the regime from which they were poised to force the downfall of the Italian nation.

Since many Jews were stunned by the mounting evidence of Italian racism in 1937–1938, one may wonder about the pervasiveness and the influence of the literature we have examined in this study. For one thing, the existence of such literature is by no means a uniquely Italian phenomenon. A glance at English, French, and German literature of the period covered in this study, circa 1800–1930s, reveals similar portrayal of Jewish characters, activities, and aspirations. All three national literatures manifest many instances of uneasy relations, reflecting at times a low tolerance for diversity coupled with ingrained distrust.[2] Clearly, as with other national literatures, not all Italian authors confronted Jews and Judaism as alien, a case in point being Manzoni's use of Jewish religious themes in his *Inni Sacri* and his firm belief that Jewish spirituality would eventually save Christianity.[3] Indeed, it would be futile to attempt to establish an absolute causal link between literature that was not expressly propaganda and attacks on or legislation against Jews over the roughly century-and-a-half covered here. But we must remember that writers of *popular* literature were guided by the tastes and opinions of their readers. They gave consumers what those same consumers wanted. That writers of "high" literature such as G. G. Belli and writers of "middle-brow" literature such as Mario Puccini reproduced these same stereotypes, in many cases using the language of popular expression, demonstrates just how pervasive, how accepted, traditional Jewish iconography was at various levels of Italian culture. Memoirs of Jews who grew up in this period suggest that anti-Semitism was rarely overt during their youth.[4] Rather, their perceptions suggest that this complex mixture of racial and religious feeling was unconscious. Yet, these sentiments were unchanging, floating along just below the surface in a constantly flowing cultural undercurrent of abiding opinion about Jews. And each new literary example, each new sermon in the days when the Church was actively fanning the flames of anti-Jewish sentiment, and, later, each newspaper article

2. For a compact but informative account of the representation of Jewish characters and themes in these national literatures, see *Encyclopedia Judaica*, vols. 6 (English), 7 (French and German).

3. See F. Ruffini, *La vita religiosa di Alessandro Manzoni* (Bari: Laterza, 1931), vol. 2.

4. See, for instance, Vittorio Segre, *Storia di un ebreo fortunato* (Milan: Bompiani, 1935).

against Jews under fascism, added another drop that, over time, swelled the stream.

In November of 1938 the alarm was sounded. The old descriptions, the traditional certainties about Jews were called forth and manipulated by those who had a stake in isolating Jews once more from their fellow Italians. These descriptions served orators, propagandists, and political rhetoricians in that domain in which, as R. *decreto legge* #1728 has shown us, words in a certain sense did become facts. They were pressed into service not only as art and entertainment to influence the mind but also as political tools to decide the fate of thousands of people. That destiny was a brutal one, yet little or no protest was heard from intellectuals, journalists, or other arbiters of culture.

Once the violence of Nazi occupation touched the lives of non-Jews, that is after 8 September 1943, many people quietly rallied to the support of Jews. Their often heroic achievements are now being documented.[5] But we are concerned here with the years before war and occupation loosened the regime's grip over its subjects. Ours is the period when consensus with its myths of unity and stability still guided the nation. In November of 1938 the social fabric was torn apart just as surely as if ghettos had been reconstructed across the land.

From the end of World War II until about 1980, Italian interest in its Jewish community grew quietly but steadily, as evidenced by the gradual increase of books about Jews and the growing popularity of Jewish writers such as Primo Levi and Giorgio Bassani. From about 1980 onward, however, Jews have become the object of intense concern to Italian intellectuals. As Italians have discovered and been forced to confront disturbing racist attitudes toward people of color who continue to flood its shores in search of work, so has it begun to reassess its attitudes, both historical and contemporary, toward the Jews. Media polls bluntly asking "Are we racist?" have targeted various levels of the population, particularly after the bombing of the Rome synagogue in 1982 and the more recent attacks on African workers in Florence. Many newspaper articles have been devoted to anti-Semitism in Italy[6] and even articles on the Jewish situation in Austria and Poland inevitably

5. In addition to Zuccotti, *The Italians and the Holocaust: Persecution, Rescue, Survival* (New York: Basic Books, 1987), see L. Picciotto Fargion, *Il libro della memoria: gli Ebrei deportati dall' Italia (1943–1945)* (Milan: Mursia, 1991), for an inevitably partial but well-deserved listing of those who helped.

6. See, for example among many others, G. Spadolini, "Italiani d'Israele: Radici culturali mai troncate," *La Stampa* 119, no. 14 (17 January 1985): 3; D. Del Rio, "Il Vaticano ha riabilitato gli ebrei: 'Restano il popolo prescelto da Dio'," *La Repubblica* 10,

refer back, implicitly or explicitly, to Italy.[7] Furio Colombo ascribes the strong anti-Israeli sentiment expressed during the recent Gulf War to the "political and religious diseducation" that has followed in a continuum from the lack of protest to the racial laws fifty years earlier on the part of cultural and religious figures.[8] And the silence, in a sense, continues. How come, Colombo wonders, a country given to commemorating its dead by renaming streets and piazzas, has not so honored its Jewish victims of the Holocaust as it has, for example, members of the Resistance? His point is an intriguing one. Have these victims of the events of those years been considered more Italian and, therefore, more worthy of commemoration than the Jewish victims of Fascist persecution? It is difficult to imagine a time in which Jewish relations with majority national populations will not be a subject of intense, emotional debate. And as long as the debate persists, it is not far-fetched to imagine that the stream of preconceptions will continue to flow, albeit uneasily, just below the surface.

Meanwhile, the question has been asked whether the Holocaust in Italy began in 1943 or with the Racial Laws in 1938.[9] We can begin to answer it by recognizing that although Fascist racial legislation was dictated by the highest power in the regime, it took root in a fertile terrain: the hearts and minds of the mass of Italians. Long before there was a Fascist regime or even a Fascist party, commonly held notions about Jews were manifested in and in turn bolstered by literature written for the popular market. It is perhaps here, in the quiet and enduring reaches below the surface of events, that we may find our answers.

---

no. 135 (25 June 1985): 11; E. Scalfari, "I due destini di Giobbe e Davide," *La Repubblica* 11, no. 4, 5 (January, 1986): 1; S. Malatesta, "'Io, ebreo italiano' Un coro di testimonianze sofferte racconta una condizione difficile: Pregiudizi, ostilità, diffidenze reciproche. Siamo un paese antisemita?" *La Repubblica* 11, no. 5 (7 January 1986): 5; G. Moltedo, "Comunione e Liberazione: Il Sabato anti-ebraico," *Il Manifesto* 18, no. 12 (15 January 1988): 3; S. Quinzio, "L'antisemitismo dietro le scuse: Dove nasce l'odio per gli ebrei" *La Stampa* 124, no. 125 (5 June 1990), section 2, 2; L. Paolozzi, "Alle origini dell'odio," *L'Unità* 67, no. 153 (1 July 1990): 13; C. Paterno, "Gli etnei e il modernismo, un itinerario pericoloso" *L'Unità* 67, no. 153 (1 July 1990): 13; E. Scalfari, "Scalfari risponde. Le ragioni oscure di chi odia gli ebrei," *Il Venerdì di Repubblica* (7 November 1990): 11–12; F. Colombo, "Il silenzio della cultura genera mostri antisemiti," *La Stampa* 125, no. 118 (1 June 1991): 18.

7. See, for example, B. Spinelli, "Varsavia: antisemitismo nuovo fantasma," *La Stampa* 124, no. 149 (29 June 1990): 15; A. Spinosa, "Ebreicidio: Mayer: come Hitler arrivò alla 'soluzione finale'," *Tuttolibri, La Stampa* 124, no. 157 (7 July 1990): 6; E. Scalfari, "Le ragioni oscure di chi odia gli ebrei."

8. F. Colombo, "Il silenzio della cultura genera mostri antisemiti."

9. Zuccotti, *The Italians and the Holocaust*, 286.

Index